ASP.NET Core 5 for Beginners

Kick-start your ASP.NET web development journey with the help of step-by-step tutorials and examples

Andreas Helland

Vincent Maverick Durano

Jeffrey Chilberto

Ed Price

BIRMINGHAM—MUMBAI

ASP.NET Core 5 for Beginners

Commissioning Editor: Richa Tripathi

Acquisition Editor: Denim Pinto

Senior Editor: Rohit Singh

Content Development Editor: Kinnari Chohan

Technical Editor: Gaurav Gala

Copy Editor: Safis Editing

Project Coordinator: Francy Puthiry

Proofreader: Safis Editing

Indexer: Pratik Shirodkar

Production Designer: Alishon Mendonca

First published: December 2020

Production reference: 2040221

Published by Packt Publishing Ltd.

Livery Place

35 Livery Street

Birmingham

B3 2PB, UK.

ISBN 978-1-80056-718-4

www.packt.com

Packt.com

Subscribe to our online digital library for full access to over 7,000 books and videos, as well as industry leading tools to help you plan your personal development and advance your career. For more information, please visit our website.

Why subscribe?

- Spend less time learning and more time coding with practical eBooks and Videos from over 4,000 industry professionals

- Improve your learning with Skill Plans built especially for you

- Get a free eBook or video every month

- Fully searchable for easy access to vital information

- Copy and paste, print, and bookmark content

Did you know that Packt offers eBook versions of every book published, with PDF and ePub files available? You can upgrade to the eBook version at packt.com and as a print book customer, you are entitled to a discount on the eBook copy. Get in touch with us at customercare@packtpub.com for more details.

At www.packt.com, you can also read a collection of free technical articles, sign up for a range of free newsletters, and receive exclusive discounts and offers on Packt books and eBooks.

Contributors

About the authors

Andreas Helland has a degree in software engineering and 20 years of experience in building products and services. He has worked both with the development side and the infrastructure side and holds a number of Microsoft certifications across both skill sets. This background led him to become an early adopter of Azure and the cloud.

After building up his knowledge working in the telecommunications industry, he switched to consulting, and he currently works as an architect for Capgemini, where he assists customers with utilizing the cloud in the best ways possible. He specializes in Azure Active Directory and works closely with the Identity teams at Microsoft, both in testing new services and providing feedback based on learnings from the field.

I want to thank Ed for roping me in on this project – of course there's time available to write a book! Thanks to Vince and Jeffrey for bringing in their content and perspectives – it would have been a thin (and less exciting) book if it was only me doing the writing. I enjoyed working with you! Thanks to Packt for making sure there's been plenty to do when we have to spend most of our time at home – books are the perfect companion activity for that.

Vincent Maverick Durano works as a software engineer/architect at an R&D company based in Minnesota. His jobs include designing software, building products and services that impact the lives of people. He's passionate about learning new technologies, tackling challenges, and sharing his expertise through writing articles and answering forums. He has authored several books and has over 15 years of software engineering experience. He has contributed to OSS projects and founded AutoWrapper and ApiBoilerPlate. He is a 10-time Microsoft MVP, 5-time C# Corner MVP, 3-time CodeProject MVP, and a contributor to various online technical communities. He's from the Philippines and married to Michelle and has three wonderful children – Vianne, Vynn, and Vjor.

I want to thank Ed for bringing me on board to be part of this book and to my other co-authors: Andreas and Jeff – you guys are awesome! It was fun and a great experience working with you. To Kinnari, Francy, and the Packt team – thank you!

Jeffrey Chilberto is a software consultant specializing in the Microsoft technical stack, including Azure, BizTalk, ASP.NET, MVC, WCF, and SQL Server, with experience in a wide range of industries, including banking, telecommunications, and healthcare in the United States, Europe, Australia, and New Zealand.

Special thanks to Kinnari, Francy, and the Packt Team for the drive and support; Andreas for his leadership and vision; Vince for his dedication and measured advice; and Ed for bringing the authors together, his wit, and his contributions to the ASP.NET community.

Ed Price is a senior program manager in engineering at Microsoft, with an MBA in technology management. He has run Microsoft customer feedback programs for Azure development, Service Fabric, IoT, and Visual Studio. He was also a technical writer at Microsoft for 6 years, helped lead TechNet Wiki, and now leads efforts to publish Microsoft's Reference Architectures on the Azure Architecture Center (focusing on web development scenarios). He is the co-author of four books, including *Learn to Program with Small Basic* and *Hands-On Microservices with C# and .NET Core 3, Third Edition* (from Packt).

What do you do when the world is quarantined in 2020 from COVID-19? You write a book! I want to thank the ASP.NET community and my amazing partners on this book: Andreas for being our technical leader, Vince for joining us last (only to show us up by providing the most content), and Jeffrey for being our rock and anchor (and for writing amazing run-on sentences in his biography).

About the reviewers

Adwait Ullal is a technology consultant based in Silicon Valley. He works with Fortune 500 companies to provide cloud and enterprise architecture guidance. Adwait's prior experience includes application and solutions architecture, specializing in Microsoft technologies. Adwait has presented on cloud and enterprise architecture topics at local code camps and meetups.

Francis Emefile is a software developer from Nigeria. It has always fascinated him how collaboration coupled with technology is capable of achieving great results. While at university studying electrical/electronic engineering, he gravitated towards computer programming out of curiosity and necessity. With the idea of building a hub where students could get information around campus, he soon discovered that his technical skill was not enough to bring his idea to life, so he taught himself programming. After graduation, he got a job as a software developer and has been building impactful and exciting products ever since. He is presently working with a bank, where he crafts code with an amazing team to build solutions for the bank's huge customer base.

Packt is searching for authors like you

If you're interested in becoming an author for Packt, please visit `authors. packtpub.com` and apply today. We have worked with thousands of developers and tech professionals, just like you, to help them share their insight with the global tech community. You can make a general application, apply for a specific hot topic that we are recruiting an author for, or submit your own idea.

Table of Contents

3

Dependency Injection

4

Razor View Engine

5

Getting Started with Blazor

Section 2 – Walking

6

Exploring the Blazor Web Framework

7

APIs and Data Access

8

Working with Identity in ASP.NET

9
Getting Started with Containers

Section 3 – Running

10
Deploying to AWS and Azure

11
Browser and Visual Studio Debugging

12
Integrating with CI/CD

13
Developing Cloud-Native Apps

Assessments

Other Books You May Enjoy

Index

Preface

ASP.NET Core is a powerful and effective framework that's open source and cross-platform. It helps you build cloud-ready, modern applications, such as web apps and services. Complete with hands-on tutorials, projects, and self-assessment questions, *ASP.NET Core 5 for Beginners* is an easy-to-follow guide that will teach you how to develop using the ASP.NET Core 5 framework. You'll learn about the framework using C# 8, Visual Studio 2019, Visual Studio Code, Razor Pages, Blazor, Kestrel, IIS, HTTP.sys, Apache, Docker, AWS, and Azure.

You'll learn how to write applications, build websites, and deploy your web apps to AWS and Microsoft Azure. You will thoroughly explore your coding environment and recommended best practices, and we'll provide code samples to systematically cover the top scenarios that you'll face in the industry today. By the end of this book, you'll be able to leverage ASP.NET Core 5 to build and deploy web applications and services in a variety of real-world scenarios.

Who this book is for

This book is for developers who want to learn how to develop web-based applications using the ASP.NET Core framework. Familiarity with the C# language and a basic understanding of HTML and CSS is required to get the most out of this book.

What this book covers

Chapter 1, Introduction to ASP.NET Core 5, provides a short history lesson, going from .NET 1.0 via different paths to "one .NET to rule them all" with .NET Core, and how ASP .NET Core fits on top of that. There are a lot of terms that we'll cover and explain. There are also several tools that will be valuable for you as you move throughout this book, so we'll introduce a couple of these here.

Chapter 2, Cross-Platform Setup, explains how, given that .NET Core is not limited to running on Windows, developing on Linux and Mac is not an obstacle to building .NET apps. For Linux, the latest Windows 10 feature update provides an excellent developer companion with Windows Subsystem for Linux 2, which enables you to run natively on Linux and to debug from Windows. There are a couple of things that you'll need to be aware of when going cross-platform, and these details will be pointed out in this chapter.

Chapter 3, Dependency Injection, explains the dependency injection (DI) software design pattern and demonstrates how to use it to achieve inversion of control (IoC) between classes and their dependent classes. We'll cover the framework services, and we'll explain the service lifetimes and registration methods. Finally, you'll learn how to design services for DI.

Chapter 4, Razor View Engine, explains the concept whereby coding a page could become easier and more productive than ever before and you'll learn how Razor powers the different ASP.NET Core web frameworks to generate HTML markup (by using a unified markup syntax). To get a feel for the different web frameworks, you'll build a simple To-Do list application using Model View Controller (MVC) and Razor Pages to create a dynamic web app. In addition, you'll learn the pros and cons of each web framework.

Chapter 5, Getting Started with Blazor, explains how it's time to get familiar with a framework that enables you to build an interactive web UI with .NET. You can write with C# with JavaScript (and instead of JavaScript). You can share your server-side and client-side app logic that's written in .NET, and you can render your UI as HTML and CSS (which is great for mobile browsers). We'll kick things off by understanding the different Blazor hosting models for building powerful web applications and weigh their pros and cons. We'll then take a look at the high-level objective to achieve the goal of using cutting-edge technologies to build a real-world application. In this chapter, you'll be using Blazor to create a Tourist Spot application with real-time capabilities. You'll start building the backend side of the application using an ASP.NET Core Web API in concert with Entity Framework Core, and finally you'll set up real-time updates using SignalR.

Chapter 6, Exploring Blazor Web Frameworks, puts together the remaining pieces to complete the goal highlighted in *chapter 5 , Getting Started with Blazor*. In this chapter, you'll be creating two different web applications using the different Blazor hosting models: Blazor Server and Blazor Web Assembly. This chapter is the heart of the book, where you experience what it's like to build different applications, using various technologies that connect to one another. The step-by-step code examples and visual illustrations make this chapter fun, exciting, and easy to follow.

Chapter 7, APIs and Data Access, takes you on a tour, as we explore how APIs and data access work together to achieve two main goals: serving and taking data. We'll take you on a whirlwind tour of Entity Framework, REST APIs, **Database Management Systems (DBMSes)**, SQL, LINQ, and Postman. We'll start by understanding the different approaches when working with real databases in Entity Framework Core (EF Core). We will then look at how to use EF Core with an existing database, and we'll implement APIs that talk to a real database using EF Core's code-first approach. You will build an ASP.NET Core Web API application in concert with Entity Framework Core to perform basic data operations in a SQL Server database. You will also implement the most commonly used HTTP methods (verbs) for exposing some API endpoints and we'll perform some basic testing.

Chapter 8, Identity, aims to teach the basics of the concept of identity in an application, both from the frontend (how a user authenticates) and how the backend validates this identity. It will explain different methods, such as basic auth and claims-based auth, as well as introducing a modern identity suite (Azure AD). The major OAuth 2 and OpenID Connect flows will be explained to give an understanding of which to use in your applications.

Chapter 9, Containers, introduces the concept of breaking up monoliths and we'll provide a basic understanding of why everybody seems to be talking about containers today.

Chapter 10, Deploying to AWS and Azure, explains what is meant when we say that ASP.NET was born to be deployed to the cloud, and then we'll explore a few platforms, including Amazon Web Services (AWS) and Microsoft Azure (and we'll explain why we're focusing on these two platforms). Then, we'll delve in and show you how to get your project deployed (in a quick and basic way) on both AWS and Azure!

Chapter 11, Browser and Visual Studio Debugging, covers some of the great features available in modern browsers for detecting the cause of errors and how to troubleshoot issues. We'll also look at Visual Studio's support for debugging, and how the IDE can make you a better programmer.

Chapter 12, Integrating with CI/CD, goes into the tools and practices that programmers should be familiar with in the modern DevOps world.

Chapter 13, Cloud Native, explains how, given that a lot of job descriptions these days include the word *cloud*, and while not all code produced will be run in a public cloud, it is necessary to understand both what *cloud native* means, as well as which steps are involved in designing applications to take advantage of cloud capabilities. This could be cloud storage versus local disk, scaling up versus scaling out, and how some tasks previously handled by Ops are now the developer's responsibility. By the end of this chapter, you should understand why performing the *lift and shift* of an existing app is a lot different than starting out in the cloud.

To get the most out of this book

You are assumed to have basic working knowledge of the C# language. All code has been tested on Windows 10, where exceptions are noted. The main software used in this book is Visual Studio Code and Visual Studio 2019, both of which can be downloaded for free from Microsoft. The specific instructions can be found in the chapters:

Software/hardware covered in the book	OS requirements
Visual Studio Code	Windows, macOS X, and Linux (any)
Visual Studio 2019	Windows, macOS X

If you are using the digital version of this book, we advise you to type the code yourself or access the code via the GitHub repository (link available in the next section). Doing so will help you avoid any potential errors related to the copying and pasting of code.

Download the example code files

You can download the example code files for this book from GitHub at `https://github.com/PacktPublishing/ASP.NET-Core-5-for-Beginners`. In case there's an update to the code, it will be updated on the existing GitHub repository.

We also have other code bundles from our rich catalog of books and videos available at `https://github.com/PacktPublishing/`. Check them out!

Code in Action

Code in Action videos for this book can be viewed at `http://bit.ly/3qDiqYY`.

Download the color images

We also provide a PDF file that has color images of the screenshots/diagrams used in this book. You can download it here:

```
https://static.packt-cdn.com/downloads/9781800567184_
ColorImages.pdf
```

Conventions used

There are a number of text conventions used throughout this book.

`Code in text`: Indicates code words in text, database table names, folder names, filenames, file extensions, pathnames, dummy URLs, user input, and Twitter handles. Here is an example: "The preceding code renders the `App.razor` component with `ServerPrerendered` as the default rendering mode."

A block of code is set as follows:

```
<body>
    <app>
        <component type="typeof(App)"
            render-mode="ServerPrerendered" />
    </app>
    @*Removed other code for brevity*@
</body>
```

When we wish to draw your attention to a particular part of a code block, the relevant lines or items are set in bold:

```
    <script src="_framework/blazor.webassembly.js"></script>
    <script src="storageHandling.js"></script>
</body>)
```

Any command-line input or output is written as follows:

```
dotnet run
Base64 encoded: YW5kcmVhczpwYXNzd29yZA==
Response: Hello Andreas
```

Bold: Indicates a new term, an important word, or words that you see on screen. For example, words in menus or dialog boxes appear in the text like this. Here is an example: "Select the **ASP.NET Core Web Application** template and click on **Next**."

> **Tips or important notes**
> Appear like this.

Get in touch

Feedback from our readers is always welcome.

General feedback: If you have questions about any aspect of this book, mention the book title in the subject of your message and email us at customercare@packtpub.com.

Errata: Although we have taken every care to ensure the accuracy of our content, mistakes do happen. If you have found a mistake in this book, we would be grateful if you would report this to us. Please visit www.packtpub.com/support/errata, selecting your book, clicking on the Errata Submission Form link, and entering the details.

Piracy: If you come across any illegal copies of our works in any form on the internet, we would be grateful if you would provide us with the location address or website name. Please contact us at copyright@packt.com with a link to the material.

If you are interested in becoming an author: If there is a topic that you have expertise in, and you are interested in either writing or contributing to a book, please visit authors.packtpub.com.

Reviews

Please leave a review. Once you have read and used this book, why not leave a review on the site that you purchased it from? Potential readers can then see and use your unbiased opinion to make purchase decisions, we at Packt can understand what you think about our products, and our authors can see your feedback on their book. Thank you!

For more information about Packt, please visit packt.com.

Section 1 – Crawling

In this section, you will learn the basics of .NET Core 5, including an overview, goals/values, new features, and its history. We'll also help you refresh your C# skills, and we'll cover setting up your cross-platform environment, as well as building apps and pages with CSHTML, MVC, Razor Pages, and Blazor (by using a unified markup engine—Razor). Finally, we'll explain the dependency injection software design pattern.

This section includes the following chapters:

- *Chapter 1, Introduction to ASP.NET Core 5*
- *Chapter 2, Cross-Platform Setup*
- *Chapter 3, Dependency Injection*
- *Chapter 4, Razor View Engine*
- *Chapter 5, Getting Started with Blazor*

1
Introduction to ASP.NET Core 5

.NET 5 is the latest and greatest in the .NET platform. .NET 5 is the successor of .NET Core 3.1 This chapter takes a short tour through the history of the .NET Framework before diving into what this version brings to the table. The chapter wraps up with a look at utilities and tools you will want to have before proceeding with exploring the details in the chapters that follow. We will cover a broad range of topics, including cross-platform usage of .NET, different methods for creating the visual layer, backend components such as identity and data access, as well as cloud technologies.

We will cover the following topics in this chapter:

- Explaining ASP.NET Core
- Refreshing your C# knowledge
- Learning what's new with .NET 5 and C# 9
- Understanding websites and web servers
- Exploring Visual Studio Code
- Leveraging Windows Terminal

Technical requirements

This chapter includes short code snippets to demonstrate the concepts that are explained. The following software is required:

- Visual Studio 2019: Visual Studio can be downloaded from `https://visualstudio.microsoft.com/vs/community/`. The Community edition is free and will work for the purposes of this book.

- Visual Studio Code: Visual Studio Code can be downloaded from `https://code.visualstudio.com/Download`.

- .NET Core 5: The .NET Core framework can be downloaded from `https://dotnet.microsoft.com/download/dotnet/5.0`.

Make sure you download the SDK, and not just the runtime. You can verify the installation by opening Command Prompt and running the `dotnet --info` cmd as shown:

```
C:\Users\andreas>dotnet --info
.NET SDK (reflecting any global.json):
 Version:   5.0.100-preview.5.20279.10
 Commit:    8139f1b74e

Runtime Environment:
 OS Name:     Windows
 OS Version:  10.0.20150
 OS Platform: Windows
 RID:         win10-x64
 Base Path:   C:\Program Files\dotnet\sdk\5.0.100-preview.5.20279.10\

Host (useful for support):
  Version: 5.0.0-preview.5.20278.1
  Commit:  4ae4e2fe08
```

Figure 1.1 – Verifying the installation of .NET

Please visit the following link to check the CiA videos: `https://bit.ly/3qDiqYY`

Check out the source code for this chapter at `https://github.com/PacktPublishing/ASP.NET-Core-5-for-Beginners/tree/master/Chapter%2001/Chapter_01_HelloWeb`.

Explaining ASP.NET Core

The first version of .NET was released in 2002, so it doesn't sound impressive that we're getting at version 5 since it's been 18 years. However, it is slightly more complicated than that, both with the numbering system and due to various sidetracks. A complete history could possibly be a book on its own, but to understand where we are now, we will take you on a short walk down memory lane.

When .NET came on the scene, there were a couple of options available to you for choosing a programming language depending on your scenario. Visual Basic was popular for introductory type programming since it was, as the name implies, visually oriented and easy to get started with. However, VB wasn't great for writing complex applications at scale with high performance. Windows itself was mostly written in C and C++ and was the preferred route for professional-grade software. While these languages were (and still are) highly capable, they were notorious for allowing the programmer to shoot themselves in the foot due to things such as making the coder responsible for memory management and other low-level operations that were hard to debug and troubleshoot.

In parallel with the language implementations offered directly from Microsoft, Sun Microsystems released Java as a solution to these challenges. Instead of producing native code, the tooling produced managed code that abstracted memory management and made things easier. The syntax of the language was in the C++ style, so transitioning from C++ was easy for developers looking to make the switch to Java. It was also a stated goal that the code written should be portable to multiple platforms. This was enabled by a **Java Virtual Machine (JVM)**, which was installed to execute on a given system.

Managed versus unmanaged code

Programming languages have evolved over the years. Where the first computers were programmed by physically turning switches and levers, you can now write instructions where even non-programmers are able to figure out what some of the commands mean.

One often refers to the relative closeness to the computer's native language (zeros and ones) by referring a language as low-level (close) or high-level (abstract). At the lowest level, you have languages like assembler language, which theoretically have the least overhead (provided you can find highly talented programmers), but in addition to being complex, an assembler language is not portable across different CPU architectures. C# leans more towards the other end of the spectrum, with more natural language and many of the "hard things" are hidden from the programmer. And there are also languages that are even more high-level, such as Scratch (a block-based language), targeted at kids wanting to get into programming. (There is no formal definition of low versus high.)

One of the mechanisms C# uses to achieve this is by having an intermediate layer (for .NET this is the Common Language Runtime) that translates your code in real time to the underlying machine code understood by your computer. This means that the programmer does not need to handle allocating and releasing memory, does not interfere with other program's processes, and so on, and generally does a lot of the grunt work. To cater to the developers and enable them to create applications with a minimal re-learning experience, .NET was in demand for these platforms, but .NET was not built to run without the desktop components available.

The concept is not new to or unique for C#, and it is also the concept used in Java. Originally, it was conceived back in the IBM mainframe era. On personal computers, it was initially challenging since managed code will always have an overhead due to the translation that occurs, and on resource-constrained computers (when .NET 1.0 was released), it can run slow. Newer computers handle this much more efficiently, and .NET has been optimized over the years, so for most applications, it is not much of an issue any longer if the code is managed or not.

Introducing the .NET platform

Microsoft took inspiration from Java, as well as their learnings from the ecosystem they provided, and came up with .NET. The structure of the platform is displayed in *Figure 1.2*.

.NET was also based on managed code and required a **Common Language Runtime (CLR)** to be installed to execute. The C# language was released in the same time frame, but .NET also supported Visual Basic and J#, highlighting that it was a more generic framework. Other programming languages that required extra software to be installed for running applications had the challenge of getting end users to install it themselves. Microsoft, on the other hand, had the advantage of supplying the operating system, thus giving them the option of including .NET as a pre-installed binary.

.NET – A unified platform

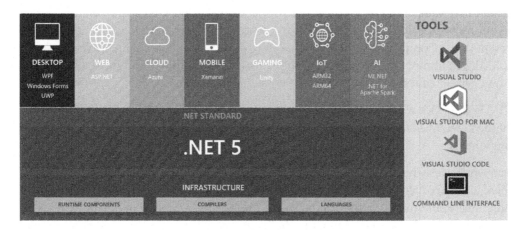

Figure 1.2 – The .NET platform

.NET Framework was, as the second part of the name implies, intended to be more complete than dictating that a certain language must be used and can only be used for specific types of applications, so it was modular by nature. If you wanted to create an application running as a Windows service, you needed other libraries than an application with a graphical user interface, but you could do it using the same programming language.

The original design of .NET Framework did not technically exclude running on other operating systems than Windows, but not seeing the incentive to provide it for Linux and Apple products, it quickly took dependencies on components only available on desktop Windows.

While Windows ran nicely on x86-based PCs, it did not run on constrained devices. This led Microsoft to develop other versions of Windows such as Windows Mobile for smartphones, Windows CE for things such as ATMs and cash registers, and so on. To cater to the developers and enable them to create applications with a minimal re-learning experience, .NET was in demand for these platforms, but .NET was not built to run without the desktop components available. The result was .NET being split into multiple paths where you had .NET Compact Framework for smartphones and tablets and .NET Micro Framework for Arduino-like devices.

Essentially, if you were proficient in C#, you could target millions of devices in multiple form factors. Unfortunately, it was not always that easy in the real world.

The libraries were different. If you wrote your code on the desktop and wanted to port it to your mobile device, you had to find out how to implement functionality that was not present in the Compact version of .NET. You could also run into confusing things such as an XML generator being present on both platforms; even though they looked similar, the output generated was not.

.NET Framework was released along with Windows operating systems, but often this was not the newest version, so you still had to install updates for it to work or install additional components.

Even worse was when you had to run multiple versions of .NET on the same machine, where it was frequently the case that these would not play nicely with each other and you had to make sure that your application called into the right version of the libraries. While originating with C++ on Windows, the challenge carried over to .NET and you may have heard this being referred to as "DLL Hell."

This book uses the term **ASP** in the title as well (ASP.NET). ASP has a track of its own in this history lesson. In the olden days of Windows NT, rendering web pages was not a core component for a server but could be installed through an add-on called **Active Server Pages** (**ASP** for short) on top of Internet Information Server. When .NET was released, this was carried over as ASP.NET. Much like the base components of .NET, this has also seen multiple iterations in various forms over the years. Initially, you had ASP.NET Web Forms, where you wrote code and scripts that the engine rendered as HTML for the output. In 2009, the highly influential ASP.NET MVC was released, implementing the Model-View-Controller pattern, which still lives on.

Patterns

A pattern is a way to solve a common problem in software. For instance, if you have an application for ordering products in an online store, there is a common set of objects and actions involved. You have products, orders, and so on commonly stored in a database. You need methods for working with these objects – decrease the stock when a customer orders a product, applying a discount due to the customer having a purchase history. You need something visible on the web page where the customer can view the store and its products and perform actions.

This is commonly implemented in what is called the **Model-View-Controller** (**MVC**) pattern.

The products and orders are described as Models. The actions performed, such as decreasing the number, retrieving pricing info, and so on are implemented in Controllers. The rendering of output visible to the end user, as well as accepting input from end users, is implemented in Views. We will see this demonstrated in code later in this book.

Patterns cover a range of problems and are often generic and independent of the programming language they are implemented in.

This book will touch upon patterns applicable to ASP.NET Core applications, but will not cover patterns in general.

Confusingly, there were other web-based initiatives launched separately, for instance, Silverlight, which ran as a plugin in the browser. The thinking was that since a browser restricted code to a sandbox, this could act as a bridge to accessing features usually only available outside a browser. It didn't become a hit, so although you can still make it run it is considered deprecated.

With Windows 8's app model, you could write apps installable on the device using HTML for the UI that were not directly compatible with an actual web app. Relying on the Windows Store for distribution, it was hampered by the fact that not all users upgrade immediately to new Windows versions, and developers mostly preferred reaching the largest audience instead.

At the same time as Windows 8 and .NET 4.5 were launched, Microsoft came up with **.NET Standard**. This is a set of APIs that are in the Base Class Library for any .NET stack. This meant that certain pieces of code would work equally well in a desktop Windows application as a mobile app intended for Windows Phone. This did not prohibit the use of platform-specific additions on top, but it was easier to achieve a basic level of portability for your code. This did not mean you achieved *write once run everywhere* use cases but was the start of the cross-platform ecosystem we are seeing now.

Microsoft was mainly concerned with growing the Windows ecosystem, but outside the company, the Mono project worked on creating an open source version of .NET that could run applications on Linux. The Linux effort did not initially take off, but when the creator, Miguel de Icaza, started the company Xamarin, focusing on using this work to make .NET run on iOS and Android devices, it gained traction. Much like the reduced versions of .NET, it was similar to what you had on the desktop, but not identical.

Outside the .NET sphere, technology has changed over the years. In 2020, you can get a mobile device more powerful than a 2002 desktop. Apple devices are everywhere in 2020 whereas in 2002 it was still a couple of years before the iPhone and iPad would be launched. Another significant thing was that in 2002, code written by Microsoft would primarily be read and updated by their employees. Open source was not a thing coming out of Redmond.

These trends were tackled in different ways. Microsoft started open sourcing pieces of .NET back in 2008, though it was not the complete package, and there were complaints around the chosen license, which some felt was only semi-open source.

Fast forward to 2016 when .Net Core was announced. .NET was on version 4.6.2 at the time and .NET Core started with 1.0. From that point in time, the original .NET has been referred to as "Classic" .NET.

The mobile platform issue partly resolved itself by Windows Mobile/Windows Phone failing in the market. Xamarin was acquired, also in 2016, which meant that mobile meant the operating systems were from Google and Apple.

Microsoft had by this time committed fully to open source and even started accepting outside contributions to .NET. The design of the language is still stewarded by Microsoft, but the strategy is out in the open and non-Microsoft developers make considerable contributions.

Microsoft learned from the past and recognized that there would not be a big bang shift towards using .NET Core instead of .NET Classic. Regardless of whether developers would agree the new version was better or not, it was simply not possible for everyone to rewrite their existing code in a short matter of time, especially since there were APIs not available in the initial version of .NET Core.

The .NET Standard message was re-iterated. You could write code in .NET 4.6 targeting .NET Standard 1.3 and this would be usable in .NET Core 1.0 as well. The intent was that this could be used for a migration strategy where you moved code piece by piece into a project compatible with .NET Standard and left the non-compatible code behind while writing new code to work with .NET Core.

Unfortunately, it was hard for people to keep track of all the terms – .NET, .NET Classic, .NET Core, .NET Standard, and all the corresponding version numbers, but it is still a viable strategy mixing these to this day.

.NET Core was, as stated, introduced with a version number of 1.0. Since then it has increased the numbers, reaching 3.1. At first glance, this means that it does not sound logical that the next version would be called .NET Core 5. There are three main reasons why this numbering was abandoned:

- .NET Core 4.x could easily be mixed up with .NET 4.x.

- Since there is a .NET 4.x (non-Core), the next major number of this would be 5.

- To illustrate how the two paths "merge," they meet up at version 5. To help avoid confusion, "Core" was dropped from the version name.

.NET Classic has reached the end of its life when it comes to new versions, so going forward, (after .NET 5), the naming will be .NET 6, .NET 7, and so on with .NET Core as the foundational framework.

.NET Classic will not be unsupported or deprecated soon, so existing code will continue to work, but new functionality and investments will not be made.

Supportability strategy

Traditional .NET Classic versions have enjoyed long supportability although not with a fixed lifetime, instead depending on service pack releases and the operating system it was released with.

With .NET Core 2.1, Microsoft switched to a model common in the Linux ecosystem with versions that are dubbed **LTS (Long-Term Support)** and non-LTS. An LTS release will have 3 years of support, where non-LTS only has one year. Minor versions are expected to be released during the support window, but the end date is set when the major version is released.

Figure 1.3 shows the .NET release timeline, focusing on its supportability schedule.

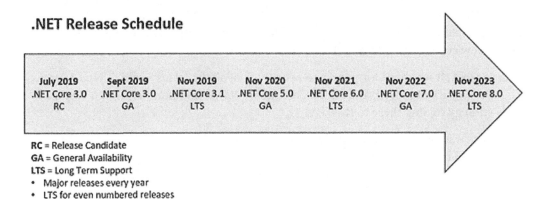

Figure 1.3 – .NET supportability schedule

Obviously, we can't guarantee a new release will be deployed every year, but that's the current plan. From .NET Core 3.1, the planned cycle is a new version in November of every year, and LTS every other year. .NET 5 was released in November 2020 as a non-LTS release. .NET 6 is targeted as an LTS release in November 2021.

This does not mean that code written in an unsupported version breaks or stops working, but security patches will not be issued, and libraries will not be maintained for older runtimes, so plan for upgrades accordingly. (Microsoft has a track record of providing guidance for how to update code to newer versions.)

It has at times felt like a bumpy ride, but unless you must deal with legacy systems, the current state of affairs is more concise than it has been in a long time.

This section was mostly a history lesson on how we got to where we are now. In the next section, we will do a friendly walk-through of a basic web application based on C# code.

Refreshing your C# knowledge

The C# language is extensive enough to have dedicated books, and there are indeed books that cover everything from having never seen programming before to advanced design patterns and optimizations. This book is not intended to cover either the very basic things or esoteric concepts only applicable to senior developers. The target audience being beginners, we will take a short tour through a `Hello World` type example to set the stage and make sure things work on your machine.

If you feel comfortable with how the Visual Studio web app template works and want to dive into the new bits, feel free to skip this section.

We will start with the following steps:

1. Start Visual Studio and select **Create a new project**.

2. Select **ASP.NET Core Web Application** and hit **Next**.

3. Name the solution `Chapter_01_HelloWeb` and select a suitable location for this book's exercises (such as `C:\Code\Book\Chapter_01`) and click on **Create**.

4. On the next screen, make sure **ASP.NET Core 5** is selected and choose **Empty** in the middle section. It is not necessary to check **Docker Support** or configure **Authentication**.

5. Once the code is loaded and ready, you should verify your installation is working by pressing *F5* to run the web application in debug mode. It might take a little while the first time, but hopefully, there are no errors and you are presented with this in your browser:

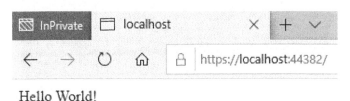

Hello World!

Figure 1.4 – Running the default web app template

Nothing fancy, but it means you are good to go for doing more complicated things in later chapters. If there are problems getting it to run, this is the time to fix it before proceeding.

Let's look at some of the components and code that make this up.

Move your mouse to the right-hand side in Visual Studio, click on **Solution**, and you will see a drop down of files appearing as shown in the following screenshot:

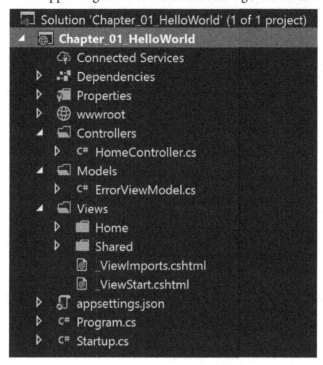

Figure 1.5 – The file structure of the web app in Visual Studio 2019

This structure is specific to the empty web application template. You are more likely to use an MVC or Blazor template to build more advanced stuff, unless you want to write everything from scratch.

Let's look at the contents of `Program.cs`:

```
using Microsoft.AspNetCore.Hosting;
using Microsoft.Extensions.Hosting;
namespace Chapter_01_HelloWeb
{
  public class Program
  {
    public static void Main(string[] args)
    {
      CreateHostBuilder(args).Build().Run();
    }
```

```
    public static IHostBuilder CreateHostBuilder(string[] args)
=>
        Host.CreateDefaultBuilder(args)
          .ConfigureWebHostDefaults(webBuilder =>
          {
              webBuilder.UseStartup<Startup>();
          });
  }
}
```

We see a `Main` method, which in this file has the single purpose of starting a process for handling web requests and processes. You can have different types of host processes running, so the recommended pattern is that you run a generic host process, and then further customize it to specify that it is a web hosting process. Since this is the first chapter of the book, you have not been introduced to other types of hosts yet, but in *Chapter 2, Cross-Platform Setup*, we will get into an example for spinning up a different host type.

In this case, we used the `Empty` web template, but this is boilerplate code that will be similar in the other web-based templates as well.

There is a reference to `Startup` in the previous code snippet and this refers to the contents of `Startup.cs`:

```
using Microsoft.AspNetCore.Builder;
using Microsoft.AspNetCore.Hosting;
using Microsoft.AspNetCore.Http;
using Microsoft.Extensions.DependencyInjection;
using Microsoft.Extensions.Hosting;
namespace Chapter_01_HelloWeb
{
  public class Startup
  {
      // This method gets called by the runtime. Use this method
      // to add services to the container.
      public void ConfigureServices(IServiceCollection services)
      {
      }
      // This method gets called by the runtime. Use this method
      // to configure the HTTP request pipeline.
```

```csharp
public void Configure(IApplicationBuilder app,
    IWebHostEnvironment env)
{
    if (env.IsDevelopment())
    {
        app.UseDeveloperExceptionPage();
    }
    app.UseRouting();
    app.UseEndpoints(endpoints =>
    {
        endpoints.MapGet("/", async context =>
        {
            await context.Response.WriteAsync("Hello World!");
        });
    });
}
}
```

If you have not written web apps in C# recently, this might be something you are unfamiliar with. In .NET Classic, the ceremony of setting up the configuration for your web app was spread across multiple config files, and the syntax could be slightly different between configuration types. A particularly heinous issue to figure out was when you had a "hidden" web.config file overriding what you thought was the file that would apply. It was also very much a one-size-fits-all setup where you would include lines of XML that were simply not relevant for your application.

In .NET Core, this is centralized to one file with a larger degree of modularity. In more complex applications, it is possible that you'll need to use additional files, but the starting template does not require that. The pattern to observe here is that it is in the form app. UseFeature. For instance, if you add app.UseHttpsRedirection, that means that if the user types in http://localhost, they will automatically be redirected to https://localhost. (It is highly recommended to use https for all websites.) While there is not a lot of logic added in this sample, you should also notice the if statement checking if the environment is a development environment. It is possible to create more advanced per-environment settings, but for a simple thing like deciding whether the detailed exceptions should be displayed in the browser, this is a useful option for doing so.

It is not apparent from the code itself, but these features that are brought in are called **middlewares**.

Middlewares are more powerful than the impression you get from here; this will be covered in greater detail in later chapters.

The `Configure` method runs as a sequence loading features dynamically into the startup for the web hosting process. This means that the order of the statements matters, and it's easy to mix this up if you're not paying attention. If `app.UseB` relies on `app.UseA` loading first, make sure that's what it looks like in the code as well.

It should be noted that this approach is not specific to web-based apps but will be applicable to other host-based apps as well.

The lines that generate the visible output here are the following:

```
app.UseEndpoints(endpoints =>
{
    endpoints.MapGet("/", async context =>
    {
        await context.Response.WriteAsync("Hello World!");
    });
});
```

Let's change this to the following:

```
app.UseEndpoints(endpoints =>
{
    endpoints.MapGet("/", async context =>
    {
        await context.Response.WriteAsync("<h2>The time is now:
            </h2>" + DateTime.UtcNow.ToString());
    });
});
```

This code means that we tell the .NET runtime to wire up an endpoint listening at the URL and write a response directly to the HTTP conversation. To demonstrate that we can go further than the original "Hello World!" string, we're outputting HTML as part of it in addition to using a variable that generates a dynamic value. (Note: the browser decides whether HTML should be rendered or not in this example, therefore, you might see the tags without the formatting on your computer.)

If you run the application again, you should see the current time being printed:

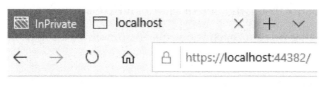

The time is now:

8/24/2020 8:14:16 PM

Figure 1.6 – Hello World with the current time printed

If you have worked on more frontend-centric tasks, you might notice that while the previous snippet uses HTML, it seems to be missing something. Usually, you would apply styling to a web page using Cascading Style Sheets (CSS files), but this approach is a more stripped-down version of CSS where we don't touch that. Later chapters will show you more impressive styling approaches than what we see here.

If you have ever dabbled with anything web before, you have probably learned, either the hard way or by being told so, that you should not mix code and UI. This example seems to violate that rule pretty well.

In general, it is indeed not encouraged to implement a web app this way as one of the basic software engineering principles is to separate concerns. You could, for instance, have a frontend expert create the user interface with very little knowledge of the things going on behind the scenes in the code, and a backend developer handling the business logic only caring about inputs and outputs to the "engine" of the application.

The approach above is not entirely useless though. It is not uncommon for web apps to have a "health endpoint." This is an endpoint that can be called into by either monitoring solutions or by container orchestration solutions when you're dealing with microservices. These are usually only looking for a static response that the web app is alive so we don't need to build user interfaces and complex logic for this. To implement this, you could add the following in `Startup.cs` while still doing a "proper" web app in parallel:

```
endpoints.MapGet("/health", async context =>
{
    await context.Response.WriteAsync("OK");
});
```

If you have worked with early versions of Visual Studio (pre 2017), you may have experienced the annoyance of working with the project and solution file for your code. If you added or edited files outside Visual Studio and then tried going back for the compilation and running of the code, it was common to get complaints in the **integrated development environment (IDE)** about something not being right.

This has been resolved and you can now work with files in other applications and other folders just by saving the resulting file in the correct place in the project's structure.

The project file (`.csproj`) for a .NET Classic web app starts at 200+ lines of code. For comparison, the web app we just created contains 7 lines (and that includes 2 whitespace lines):

```
<Project Sdk="Microsoft.NET.Sdk.Web">
    <PropertyGroup>
        <TargetFramework>net5.0</TargetFramework>
    </PropertyGroup>
</Project>
```

To view this in Visual Studio, you have to right-click the project name and choose **Unload Project** before choosing **Edit .csproj**. When you finish editing the file, you need to reload the project to work with it again.

At this point, we recommend that you play around with the code, make edits, and see how it turns out before proceeding.

In this walk-through, we relied on Visual Studio 2019 to provide us with a set of templates and a graphical user interface to click through. .NET does not force the use of Visual Studio, so it is possible to replicate this from the command line if you want to work with a different editor. Run the `dotnet new` command to see the available options with some hints to go along with it:

```
C:\Users\andreas>dotnet new
Getting ready...
Templates                                       Short Name            Language       Tags
--------------------------------                ----------------      ----------     ----------------
Console Application                             console               [C#], F#, VB   Common/Console
Class library                                   classlib              [C#], F#, VB   Common/Library
WPF Application                                 wpf                   [C#], VB       Common/WPF
WPF Class library                               wpflib                [C#], VB       Common/WPF
WPF Custom Control Library                      wpfcustomcontrollib   [C#], VB       Common/WPF
WPF User Control Library                        wpfusercontrollib     [C#], VB       Common/WPF
Windows Forms (WinForms) Application            winforms              [C#], VB       Common/WinForms
Windows Forms (WinForms) Class library          winformslib           [C#], VB       Common/WinForms
Worker Service                                  worker                [C#]           Common/Worker/Web
Unit Test Project                               mstest                [C#], F#, VB   Test/MSTest
NUnit 3 Test Project                            nunit                 [C#], F#, VB   Test/NUnit
NUnit 3 Test Item                               nunit-test            [C#], F#, VB   Test/NUnit
xUnit Test Project                              xunit                 [C#], F#, VB   Test/xUnit
Razor Component                                 razorcomponent        [C#]           Web/ASP.NET
Razor Page                                      page                  [C#]           Web/ASP.NET
MVC ViewImports                                 viewimports           [C#]           Web/ASP.NET
MVC ViewStart                                   viewstart             [C#]           Web/ASP.NET
Blazor Server App                               blazorserver          [C#]           Web/Blazor
Blazor WebAssembly App                          blazorwasm            [C#]           Web/Blazor/WebAssembly
ASP.NET Core Empty                              web                   [C#], F#       Web/Empty
ASP.NET Core Web App (Model-View-Controller)    mvc                   [C#], F#       Web/MVC
ASP.NET Core Web App                            webapp                [C#]           Web/MVC/Razor Pages
ASP.NET Core with Angular                       angular               [C#]           Web/MVC/SPA
ASP.NET Core with React.js                      react                 [C#]           Web/MVC/SPA
ASP.NET Core with React.js and Redux            reactredux            [C#]           Web/MVC/SPA
Razor Class Library                             razorclasslib         [C#]           Web/Razor/Library
ASP.NET Core Web API                            webapi                [C#], F#       Web/WebAPI
ASP.NET Core gRPC Service                       grpc                  [C#]           Web/gRPC
dotnet gitignore file                           gitignore                            Config
global.json file                                globaljson                           Config
NuGet Config                                    nugetconfig                          Config
Dotnet local tool manifest file                 tool-manifest                        Config
Web Config                                      webconfig                            Config
Solution File                                   sln                                  Solution
Protocol Buffer File                            proto                                Web/gRPC
```

Figure 1.7 – Listing the available templates in .NET

To replicate what we did in Visual Studio, you would type `dotnet new web`. The default project name will be the same as the folder you are located in, so make sure you name your folder and change it accordingly.

This should put you in a place where you have some example code to test out and verify that things work on your system. There is, however, more to the C# language, and next, we will take a look at what the newest version of C# brings.

Learning what's new in .NET 5 and C# 9

The general rule of thumb is that new versions of .NET, C#, and Visual Studio are released in the same time frame. This is certainly the easiest way to handle it as well – grab the latest Visual Studio and the other two components follow automatically during installation.

The tooling is not always tightly coupled, so if for some reason you are not able to use the latest versions, you can look into whether there are ways to make it work with previous versions of Visual Studio. (This can usually be found in the requirements documentation from Microsoft.)

A common misconception is that .NET and C# have to be at the same version level and that upgrading one implies upgrading the other. However, the versions of .NET and C# are not directly coupled. This is further illustrated by the fact that C# has reached version 9 whereas .NET is at 5. .NET is not tied to using C# as a language either. (In the past, you had Visual Basic and currently, you also have F#.) If you want to stay at a specific C# version (without upgrading to the latest version of C#), then after you upgrade .NET, that combination will usually still work.

Things that are defined by the C# language are usually backward compatible, but patterns might not be.

As an example, the `var` keyword was introduced in C# 3. This means that the following declarations are valid:

```
var i = 10; // Implicitly typed.
int i = 10; // Explicitly typed.
```

Both variants are okay, and .NET Core 5 will not force either style.

As an example of .NET moving along, there were changes going from .NET Core 1.x to .NET Core 2.x where the syntax of C# did not change, but the way .NET expected authentication to be set up in code meant that your code would fail to work even if the C# code was entirely valid. Make sure you understand where a certain style is enforced by .NET and where C# is the culprit.

You can specify which C# version to use by editing the file for the project (.csproj) and adding the LangVersion attribute:

```
<Project Sdk="Microsoft.NET.Sdk">
  <PropertyGroup>
    <OutputType>Exe</OutputType>
    <TargetFramework>net5.0</TargetFramework>
  </PropertyGroup>
  <PropertyGroup>
    <LangVersion>9.0</LangVersion>
  </PropertyGroup>
</Project>
```

It can be hard to keep track of what can be changed and optimized in the code. With the .NET Compiler Platform released in 2014, nicknamed Roslyn, this improved greatly with the introduction of real-time analysis of your code. Where you previously had to compile your code for the IDE to present errors and warnings, these are now displayed as you are writing your code. It doesn't confine itself to calling out issues preventing your code from running, but will also suggest improvements to be made.

For instance, consider the following:

```
Console.WriteLine("Hello " + name);
```

Roslyn will suggest String interpolation as an option:

```
Console.WriteLine($"Hello {name}");
```

In a nutshell, this is illustrated in the following figure:

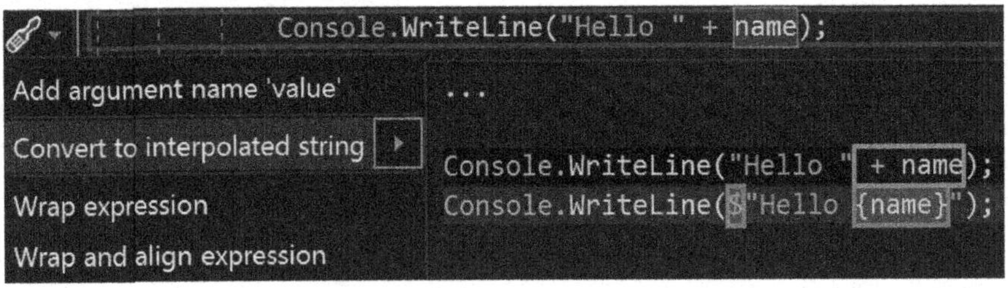

Figure 1.8 – Code improvement suggestions

For a trivial example like this, it may not look like much of an improvement, but it often makes longer strings more readable. Either way, it is a suggestion, not something that is forced upon you.

This means that when the topic is "what's new," that can be broken into two sections – .NET and C#. What's new in .NET will mainly be covered in other chapters. What's new in C# gets a walk-through here and will be used in code samples in subsequent chapters. Note that not all of the code in the book will use C# 9 syntax everywhere, and as long as the new syntax is mainly stylistic, you are advised to choose your own style if you are not part of a larger development team forcing a set of standards.

What's new in .NET 5?

A good deal of improvements is under the hood, making things run more smoothly and better all round. There are, however, a couple of more noticeable improvements too. This chapter will only provide a couple of highlights as the details will come later in the book.

Closing the gap with .NET Classic

With .NET Core 1.0, it was impossible for many projects to be ported from .NET 4.x because there simply were no corresponding libraries for some of the features. .NET Core 3.1 removed this barrier for most practical purposes and with .NET Core 5, the framework is considered feature complete on the API and library side.

Some technologies have been deprecated and have thus not been carried over (see the *Removed/changed features* section later in this chapter for that). A few such technologies are listed here:

- **Unified .NET with Single Base Class Library**: Previously, Xamarin apps (mobile apps) were based on the Mono BCL, but this has now moved into .NET 5 with improved compatibility as an outcome.

- **Multi-Platform Native apps**: A single project will be able to target multiple platforms. If you use a UI element, .NET will handle this appearing as a control native to the platform.

- **Cloud Native**: Current .NET Code will certainly run in the cloud, but further steps will be taken towards labeling .NET a cloud-native framework. This includes a reduced footprint for easier use in containers and single file executables, so you don't need the .NET runtime to be installed, and aligning the cloud story and the local developer experience so they are at feature parity.

- **Blazor WebAssembly**: .NET Core 3.1 introduced Blazor apps that were rendered server-side. With .NET 5, they can also be rendered client-side, enabling offline and standalone apps.

  The goal is that the code is close to identical, so it will be easy to switch from one hosting model to the other.

- **Multi-Platform Web apps**: Blazor apps was originally conceived as a vehicle for web apps and works great in a browser. The goal is that this will work equally great for a mobile device, or a native desktop application.

- **Continuous improvements**: Faster algorithms in the BCL, container support in the runtime, support for HTTP3, and other tweaks.

Having discussed what's new in .NET 5, let's move on to C# 9.

What's new in C# 9?

The overarching goal of C# 9 is simplification. The language is mature enough that you can do most things you want in some way, so instead of adding more features, it is about making the features more available. In this section, we will cover new ways to structure your code and explain some of the new code you can create.

Top-level programs

A good example of simplification is top-level programs. With C# 8, the Visual Studio template created this code as the starting point for a console app:

```
using System;
namespace ConsoleApp2
{
  class Program
  {
    static void Main(string[] args)
    {
      Console.WriteLine("Hello World");
    }
  }
}
```

There is a reason why there are so many lines of code to do so little, but for a beginner, it is a lot of ceremony to get going. The preceding snippet can now be written like this:

```
Using System;
Console.WriteLine("Hello World");
```

This does not support omitting classes and methods in general throughout the program. This is about simplifying the `Main` method, which often does little more than bootstrapping the application, and which you can only have one of in a given application.

Init-only properties

When working with objects, you usually define and create them like this:

```
static void Main(string[] args)
{
  InfoMessage foo = new InfoMessage
  {
    Id = 1,
    Message = "Hello World"
  };
}
public class InfoMessage
{
  public int Id { get; set; }
  public string Message { get; set; }
}
```

In this code, the properties are mutable, so if you later want to change the ID, that is okay (when the accessor is public). To cover the times when you want a public property to be immutable, a new type of property is introduced with init-only properties:

```
public class InfoMessage
{
  public int Id { get; init; }
  public string Message { get; init; }
}
```

This makes the properties immutable so once you have defined them, they cannot change.

Init accessors and read-only fields

Init accessors are only meant to be used during initialization, but this doesn't conflict with read-only fields and you can use both if you have needs that require a constructor:

```
public class City
{
  private readonly int ZipCode;
  private readonly string Name;
  public int ZipCode
```

```
    {
        get => ZipCode;
        init => ZipCode = (value ?? throw new
            ArgumentNullException(nameof(ZipCode)));
    }
    public string Name
    {
        get => Name;
        init => Name = (value ?? throw new
            ArgumentNullException(nameof(Name)));
    }
}
```

Records

Init works for individual properties, but if you want to make it apply to all properties in a class, you can define the class as a record by using the record keyword:

```
public record class City
{
    public int ZipCode {get; init;}
    public string Name {get; init;}
    public City(int zip, string name) => (ZipCode, Name) =
        (zip,name);
}
```

When you declare the object as a record, this brings you the value of other new features.

With expressions

Since the object has values that cannot be changed, you have to create a new object for the values to change. You could, for instance, have the following:

```
City Redmond = new City("98052","Redmond");
//The US runs out of zip codes so every existing code is
// assigned
//a 0 as a suffix
City newRedmond = new City("980520","Redmond");
```

Using the `with` expression enables you to copy existing properties and just redefine the changed values:

```
var newRedmond = Redmond with {ZipCode = "980520"};
```

Value-based equality

A trap for new programmers is the concept of equality. Given the following code, what would the output be?

```
City Redmond_01 = new City { Name = "Redmond", ZipCode = 98052
};
City Redmond_02 = new City { Name = "Redmond", ZipCode = 98052
};
if (Redmond_01 == Redmond_02)
  Console.WriteLine("Equals!");
else
  Console.WriteLine("Not equals!");
```

The output would be `Not equals` because they are not the same object even if the values are the same. To achieve what we call equal in non-programming parlance, you would have to override the `Equals` method and compare the individual properties:

```
class Program
{
  static void Main(string[] args)
  {
    City Redmond_01 = new City{ Name = "Redmond", ZipCode =
      98052 };
    City Redmond_02 = new City{ Name = "Redmond", ZipCode =
      98052 };
    if (Redmond_01.Equals(Redmond_02))
      Console.WriteLine("City Equals!");
    else
      Console.WriteLine("City Not equals!");
  }
}
public class City
{
  public int ZipCode{get; set;}
```

```
public string Name{get; set;}
public override bool Equals(object obj)
{
    //Check for null and compare run-time types.
    if ((obj == null) || !this.GetType().Equals(obj.GetType()))
    {
        return false;
    }
    else
    {
        City c = (City)obj;
        return (ZipCode == c.ZipCode) && (Name == c.Name);
    }
}
...
}
```

This would render the output that the two cities are equal.

In Records, this behavior is implied by default and you do not have to write your own Equals method to achieve a value-based comparison. Having if (Redmond_01.Equals(Redmond_02)) in the code should work just like the previous code snippet without the extra public override bool Equals(object obj) part.

You can still override Equals if you have a need for it, but for cases where you want a basic equality check, it's easier to use the built-in functionality.

Data members

With records, you often want the properties to be public, and the intent is that init-only value-setting will be preferred. This is taken as an assumption by C# 9 as well, so you can simplify things further.

Consider the following code:

```
public data class City
{
    public int ZipCode {get; init;}
    public string Name {get; init;}
}
```

It can be written like this:

```
public data class City {int ZipCode; string Name;}
```

You can still make the data members private by adding the modifier explicitly.

Positional records

The following line of code sets the properties explicitly:

```
City Redmond = new City{ Name = "Redmond", ZipCode = 98052 };
```

Having knowledge of the order the properties are defined in, you can simplify it to the following:

```
City Redmond = new City(98052, "Redmond");
```

There are still valid use cases for having extra code to make it clearer what the intent of the code is so use with caution.

Inheritance and records

Inheritance can be tricky when doing equality checks, so C# has a bit of magic happening in the background. Let's add a new class:

```
public data class City {int ZipCode; string Name;}
public data class CityState : City {string State;}
```

Due to a hidden virtual method handling the cloning of objects, the following would be valid code:

```
City Redmond_01 = new CityState{Name = "Redmond", ZipCode =
98052, State = "Washington" };
City Redmond_02 = Redmond_01 with {State = "WA"};
```

What if you want to compare the two objects for value-based equality?

```
City Redmond_01 = new City { Name = "Redmond", ZipCode = 98052
};
City Redmond_02 = new CityState { Name = "Redmond", ZipCode =
98052, State = "WA" };
```

Are these equal? Redmond_02 has all the properties of Redmond_01, but Redmond_01 lacks a property, so it would depend on the perspective you take.

There is a virtual protected property called `EqualityContract` that is overridden in derived records. To be equal, two objects must have the same `EqualityContract` property.

Improved target typing

The term target typing is used when it is possible to get the type of an expression from the context it is used in.

For instance, you can use the `var` keyword when the compiler has enough info to infer the right type:

```
var foo = 1 //Same as int foo = 1
var bar = "1" //Same as string bar = "1"
```

Target-typed new expressions

When instantiating new objects with `new`, you had to specify the type. You can now leave this out if it is clear (to the compiler) which type is being assigned to:

```
//Old
City Redmond = new City(98052,"Redmond");
//New
City Redmond = new (98052, "Redmond");
//Not valid
var Redmond = new (98052,"Redmond");
```

Parameter null-checking

It is a common pattern for a method to check if a parameter has a null value if that will cause an error. You can either check if the value is null before performing an operation, or you can throw an error. With null-checking, you make this part of the method signature:

```
//Old - nothing happens if name is null
void Greeter(string name)
{
   if (name != null)
      Console.WriteLine($"Hello {name}");
}
//Old - exception thrown if name is null
void Greeter(string name)
```

```
{
    if (name is null)
        throw new ArgumentNullException(nameof(name));
    else
        Console.WriteLine($"Hello {name}");
}
//New
void Greeter(string name!)
{
    Console.WriteLine($"Hello {name}");
}
```

For methods accepting multiple parameters, this should be a welcome improvement.

Pattern matching

C# 7 introduced a feature called pattern matching. This feature is used to get around the fact that you do not necessarily control all the data structures you use internally in your own code. You could be bringing in external libraries that don't adhere to your object hierarchy and re-arranging your hierarchy to align with this would just bring in other issues.

To achieve this, you use a switch expression, which is similar to a switch statement, but the switch is done based on type pattern instead of value.

C# 9 brings improvements to this with more patterns you can use for matching.

Removed/changed features

It is always interesting to start trying out new features, but there are also features and technologies that have been removed from .NET.

It is common to do house cleaning when bringing out new major versions, and there are many minor changes. Microsoft maintains a list of breaking changes (in .NET 5) at https://docs.microsoft.com/en-us/dotnet/core/compatibility/3.1-5.0.

As stated previously in this chapter, .NET Core 1.0 was not feature complete compared to .NET Classic. NET Core 2 added a lot of APIs, and .NET Core 3 added more of the .NET Frameworks. The transition is now completed, so if you rely on a feature of .NET Classic that is not found in .NET 5, it will not be added later.

Windows Communication Framework

Web services have been around for many years now, and one of the early .NET frameworks for this was **Windows Communication Framework (WCF)**. WCF could be challenging to work with at times but provided contracts for data exchange and a handy code generation utility in Visual Studio. This was deprecated in .NET Core 3, so if you have any of these services that you want to keep, they cannot be ported to .NET 5. This applies both to the server and client side.

It is possible to create a client implementation manually in .NET Core, but it is not trivial and is not recommended. The recommended alternative is moving to a different framework called gRPC. This is an open source remote procedure call (RPC) system. gRPC was developed by Google with support for more modern protocols, such as HTTP/2 for the transport layer, as well as contracts through a format called ProtoBuf.

Web Forms

Windows Forms was the framework for creating "classic" Windows desktop apps (Classic being the pre-Windows 8 design language). This was ported over with .NET Core 3.0.

The web version of this was called Web Forms. That is, technically, there were differences in the code, but the model, with a so-called "code-behind" approach, was similar between the two. It was recommended to move to MVC and Razor style syntax in newer versions of .NET Classic as well, but Web Forms was still supported. This has not been brought over to .NET Core, and you need to look into either MVC or Blazor as alternatives.

Having covered both what's new and what's no more, we will now look more closely at the components that present your web apps to the world at large.

Understanding websites and web servers

Web servers are an important part of ASP.NET apps since they, by definition, require one to be present to run. It is also the major contributor to the "it works on my machine" challenge for web apps (where it works on your machine, but it doesn't work for your customers).

The history of .NET has been closely linked to the web server being **Internet Information Services (IIS)**. IIS was released several years before .NET, but support for .NET was added in a later version. For a web application to work, there are external parts that need to be in place that are not handled by the code the developer writes. This includes the mapping of a domain name, certificates for encrypting data in traffic, and a range of other things. IIS handles all of these things and more. Unfortunately, this also means that creating an optimal configuration might require more knowledge of server and networking topics than the average .NET developer would have.

IIS is designed to run on a server operating system, and since Visual Studio can be installed on Windows Server, it is entirely possible to set up a production-grade development environment. Microsoft also ships a reduced version called IIS Express as part of Visual Studio that enables you to test ASP.NET apps without installing a server operating system.

IIS Express can do most of the things the developer needs to test ASP.NET apps, with the most important difference being that it is designed for handling local traffic only. If you need to test your web app from a different device than the one you are developing on, IIS Express is not designed to enable that for you.

We will present a couple of configuration components you should be aware of as well as utilities and methods for troubleshooting web-based applications.

Web server configuration

While this book targets developers, there are some things regarding web servers that are valuable to understand in case you need to have a conversation with the people responsible for your infrastructure.

When developing web apps, it is necessary to be able to read the traffic, and it is common that one of the things one does to make this easier is running the app over plain HTTP, allowing you to inspect traffic "over the wire." You should never run this in production. You should acquire TLS/SSL certificates and enable HTTPS for production, and ideally set up your local development environment to also use HTTPS to make the two environments comparable. Visual Studio enables the automatic generation of a trusted certificate that you need to approve once for the initial setup so this should be fairly easy to configure.

Certificate trust

Certificates are issued from a **Public Key Infrastructure (PKI)** that is built in a hierarchical manner, typically with a minimum of three tiers. For a certificate to be valid, the client device needs to be able to validate this chain. This is done on multiple levels:

- Is the root **Certificate Authority (CA)** trusted? This must be installed on the device. Typically, this is part of the operating system with common CAs pre-provisioned.

- Is the certificate issued to the domain you host your site on? If you have a certificate for `northwind.com`, this will not work if your site runs at `contoso.com`.

- Certificates expire so if your certificate expires in 2020, it will fail to validate in 2021.

There is no easy way for you as a developer to make sure that users accessing your site have the clock configured correctly on their device, but at least make sure the server is set up as it should be.

Session stickiness

Web apps can be stateful or stateless. If they are stateful, it means there is a sort of dialogue going on between the client and the server, where the next piece of communication depends on a previous request or response. If they are stateless, the server will answer every request like it is the first time the two parties are communicating. (You can embed IDs in the request to maintain state across stateless sessions.)

In general, you should strive to make sessions stateless, but sometimes you cannot avoid this. Say you have the following record class:

```
public data class City {int ZipCode; string Name;}
```

You have also taken the time to create a list of the top 10 (by population) cities in every state and expose this through an API. The API supports looking up the individual zip code or name, but it also has a method for retrieving all records. This is not a large dataset, but you do some calculations and figure out that you should only send 100 records at a time to not go over any limits for HTTP packet size limitations.

There are multiple ways to solve this. You could write in the docs that the client should append a start and end record (with the end assumed to be start +99 if omitted):

```
https://contoso.com/Cities?start=x&end=y
```

You could also make it more advanced by calculating a `nextCollectionId` parameter that is returned to the client, so they could loop through multiple calls without recalculating start and end:

```
https://contoso.com/Cities?nextCollectionId=x
```

There is however a potential issue here occurring on the server level you need to be aware of.

Since your API is popular, you need to add a second web server to handle the load and provide redundancy. (This is often called a web farm and can scale to a large number of servers if you need to.) To distribute the traffic between the two, you put a load balancer in front of them. What happens if the load balancer directs the first request to the first web server and the second request to the second server?

If you don't have any logic to make the `nextCollectionId` available to both servers, it will probably fail. For a complex API serving millions of requests, you should probably invest time in implementing a solution that will let the web servers access a common cache. For simple apps, what you are looking for might be *session stickiness*. This is a common setting on load balancers that will make a specific client's requests stick to a specific web server instance, and it is also common that you need to ask the person responsible for the infrastructure to enable it. That way, the second request will go to the same web server as the first request and things will work as expected.

Troubleshooting communication with web servers

You will eventually run into scenarios where you ask yourself why things are not working and what actually goes on with the traffic. There are also use cases where you are implementing the server and need a quick way to test the client side without implementing a client app. A useful tool in this regard is Fiddler from Telerik, which you can find at `https://www.telerik.com/fiddler`.

This will most likely be useful in subsequent chapters, so you should go ahead and install it now. By default, it will only capture HTTP traffic, so you need to go to **Tools | Options | HTTPS** and enable the checkmark for **Capture HTTPS CONNECTs** and **Decrypt HTTPS traffic** as shown:

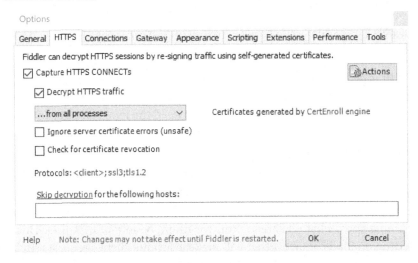

Figure 1.9 – Fiddler HTTPS capture settings

A certificate will be generated that you need to accept installing and then you should be able to listen in on encrypted communication as well.

This method is technically what is known as a man-in-the-middle attack, which can also be used with malicious intent. For use during your own development, this is not an issue, but for production troubleshooting, you should use other mechanisms to capture the info you need. The web application will be able to intercept the valid traffic it receives (that it has the certificate for decoding), but with a tool capturing at the network level, you'll potentially collect extra info you should not have.

Fiddler can also be used for crafting HTTP requests manually, so it is a useful utility even if you're not chasing down bugs:

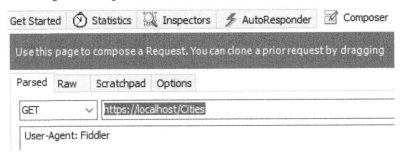

Figure 1.10 – Fiddler HTTP request constructor

If it is an error you are able to reproduce yourself by clicking through the website, Visual Studio is your friend. You have the **Output** window, which will provide process-level information:

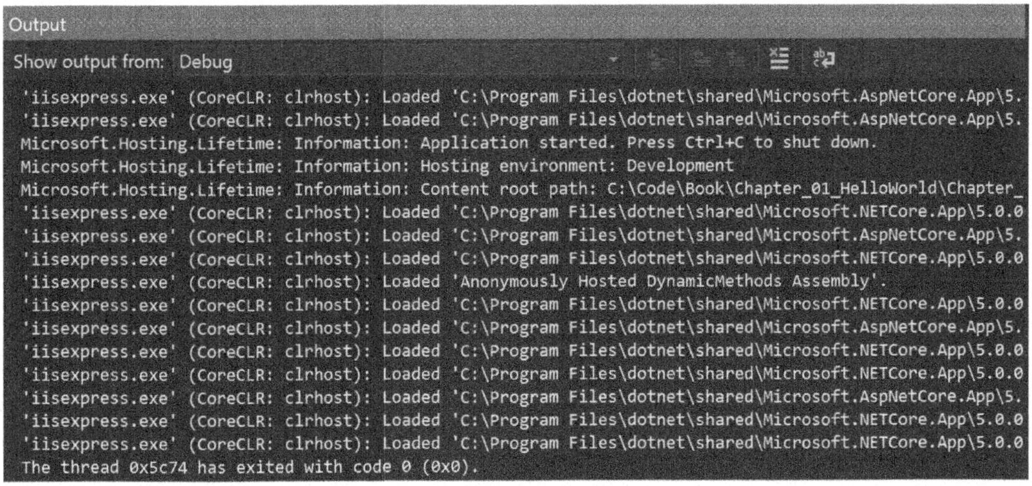

```
Output
Show output from:  Debug                                          ⊼≡  ᵃᵇ↵
'iisexpress.exe' (CoreCLR: clrhost): Loaded 'C:\Program Files\dotnet\shared\Microsoft.AspNetCore.App\5.
'iisexpress.exe' (CoreCLR: clrhost): Loaded 'C:\Program Files\dotnet\shared\Microsoft.AspNetCore.App\5.
Microsoft.Hosting.Lifetime: Information: Application started. Press Ctrl+C to shut down.
Microsoft.Hosting.Lifetime: Information: Hosting environment: Development
Microsoft.Hosting.Lifetime: Information: Content root path: C:\Code\Book\Chapter_01_HelloWorld\Chapter_
'iisexpress.exe' (CoreCLR: clrhost): Loaded 'C:\Program Files\dotnet\shared\Microsoft.NETCore.App\5.0.0
'iisexpress.exe' (CoreCLR: clrhost): Loaded 'C:\Program Files\dotnet\shared\Microsoft.AspNetCore.App\5.
'iisexpress.exe' (CoreCLR: clrhost): Loaded 'C:\Program Files\dotnet\shared\Microsoft.NETCore.App\5.0.0
'iisexpress.exe' (CoreCLR: clrhost): Loaded 'Anonymously Hosted DynamicMethods Assembly'.
'iisexpress.exe' (CoreCLR: clrhost): Loaded 'C:\Program Files\dotnet\shared\Microsoft.NETCore.App\5.0.0
'iisexpress.exe' (CoreCLR: clrhost): Loaded 'C:\Program Files\dotnet\shared\Microsoft.AspNetCore.App\5.
'iisexpress.exe' (CoreCLR: clrhost): Loaded 'C:\Program Files\dotnet\shared\Microsoft.NETCore.App\5.0.0
'iisexpress.exe' (CoreCLR: clrhost): Loaded 'C:\Program Files\dotnet\shared\Microsoft.NETCore.App\5.0.0
'iisexpress.exe' (CoreCLR: clrhost): Loaded 'C:\Program Files\dotnet\shared\Microsoft.AspNetCore.App\5.
'iisexpress.exe' (CoreCLR: clrhost): Loaded 'C:\Program Files\dotnet\shared\Microsoft.NETCore.App\5.0.0
'iisexpress.exe' (CoreCLR: clrhost): Loaded 'C:\Program Files\dotnet\shared\Microsoft.NETCore.App\5.0.0
The thread 0x5c74 has exited with code 0 (0x0).
```

Figure 1.11 – Visual Studio output window

Troubleshooting is often complicated and rarely fun but looking directly at the protocol level is a useful skill to have when dealing with web applications, and these tools should help you along the way to resolving your issues.

Choosing a web server option

As noted, IIS Express is included by default in Visual Studio 2019, and if the code you are developing is intended to run on a windows server with the full version of IIS, it is a good choice. However, there are some drawbacks to IIS Express as well:

- While requiring less overhead than the full IIS, it is "heavy," and if you find yourself running debugging cycles where you constantly start and stop the web server, it can be a slow process.

- IIS Express is a Windows-only thing. If your code runs on Linux (which is a real scenario with the cross-platform support in .NET Core), it is not available as an option.

- If you are writing code for containers/microservices, the full IIS adds up to a lot of overhead when you have multiple instances each running their own web server. (With microservices, you usually don't co-locate multiple websites on a web server, which is what IIS is designed for.)

To support more scenarios, .NET Core includes a slimmed-down and optimized web server called Kestrel. Going back to the `Hello World` web app we created earlier in the chapter, you can open a command line to the root folder and execute the command `dotnet run`:

```
C:\Code\Book\Chapter_01_HelloWorld\Chapter_01_HelloWorld>dotnet run
info: Microsoft.Hosting.Lifetime[0]
      Now listening on: https://localhost:5001
info: Microsoft.Hosting.Lifetime[0]
      Now listening on: http://localhost:5000
info: Microsoft.Hosting.Lifetime[0]
      Application started. Press Ctrl+C to shut down.
info: Microsoft.Hosting.Lifetime[0]
      Hosting environment: Development
info: Microsoft.Hosting.Lifetime[0]
      Content root path: C:\Code\Book\Chapter_01_HelloWorld\Chapter_01_HelloWorld
```

Figure 1.12 – Output of dotnet run

If you open the browser to `https://localhost:5001`, it should be the same as launching IIS Express from Visual Studio.

You don't have to step into the command line to use Kestrel. You can have multiple profiles defined in Visual Studio – both are added by default. By installing a Visual Studio extension called **.NET Core Debugging with WSL2**, you can also deploy directly to a Linux installation. (Linux configuration will be covered in *Chapter 2, Cross-Platform Setup*.) You can edit the settings manually by opening `launchSettings.json`:

```
{
  "iisSettings": {
    "windowsAuthentication": false,
    "anonymousAuthentication": true,
    "iisExpress": {
      "applicationUrl": "http://localhost:65476",
      "sslPort": 44372
    }
  },
  "profiles": {
    "IIS Express": {
      "commandName": "IISExpress",
      "launchBrowser": true,
      "environmentVariables": {
        "ASPNETCORE_ENVIRONMENT": "Development"
      }
```

```json
        },
        "Chapter_01_HelloWorld": {
          "commandName": "Project",
          "launchBrowser": true,
          "applicationUrl": "https://localhost:5001;
                http://localhost:5000",
          "environmentVariables": {
            "ASPNETCORE_ENVIRONMENT": "Development"
          },
          "WSL 2": {
          "commandName": "WSL2",
          "launchBrowser": true,
          "launchUrl": "https://localhost:5001",
          "environmentVariables": {
            "ASPNETCORE_URLS":
            "https://localhost:5001;http://localhost:5000",
            "ASPNETCORE_ENVIRONMENT": "Development"
          }
        }
      }
    }
}
```

This file is only used for development purposes on your machine and is not the configuration used for production.

For production use, Kestrel and IIS are the main options. Which one to use depends on where and what you are deploying to. For on-premises scenarios where you have Windows servers, it is still a viable option to deploy to IIS. It comes with useful features out of the box – if you, for instance, want to restrict the app to users that have logged in to Active Directory, you can enable this in IIS without modifying your code. (For fine-grained access control, you will probably want some mechanisms in the code as well.)

If you deploy to containers, Kestrel is an easier path. However, you should not deploy to Kestrel without an ecosystem surrounding it. Kestrel "lives with the code" – there is no administration interface that you can configure when the code is not running. This means that activities such as managing certificates are not covered out of the box. If you deploy to a cloud environment, that usually means you will bring in other components to cover what Kestrel itself does not. Certificate handling is provided either by the container host or a separate service you place in front of the web server.

Now that we have understood the importance of websites and web servers in ASP.NET apps, let's move on and dive into Visual Studio Code.

Exploring Visual Studio Code

Development in .NET has always been associated with Visual Studio, and the pattern has been that with new versions of Visual Studio comes new versions of .NET. Visual Studio is still a good companion to developers since it has been optimized over the years to provide you with everything needed, from writing code, improving upon it, and getting it into a production environment.

As a pure text editor, it doesn't shine equally strongly. In 2015, Microsoft decided to make this better by releasing **Visual Studio (VS)** Code. VS Code provides syntax highlighting, the side-by-side comparison of files, and other features a good editor should have. An integrated terminal is provided, so if you are writing a script, you do not need to switch applications to execute it. In addition, it supports extensions that enable you or other developers to extend the built-in functionality. For instance, you have probably opened a JSON file only to find it slightly off with line breaks and indentation – there is an extension called **Prettify JSON** that fixes that.

VS Code is not limited to editing various text-based files. It has built-in Git support, it can be configured with a debugger and connected to utilities for building your code, and a lot more. It's not limited to the .NET ecosystem either – it can be used for programming in JavaScript, Go, and a range of other languages. In fact, it is, at the time of writing, the most popular development tool on Stack Overflow across languages and platforms.

Navigating through VS Code is mostly done on the left-hand side of windows:

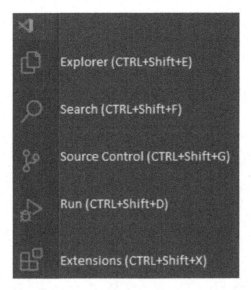

Figure 1.13 – Visual Studio Code navigation menu

As you install extensions, more icons may appear in the list. (Not all extensions have an icon.)

In the lower-left corner, you will also find the option to add accounts (for instance, an Azure account if you are using extensions leveraging Azure). See Figure 1.14, for the Visual Studio accounts icon.

Figure 1.14 – Visual Studio accounts

In the mid to right lower pane, you can enable some console windows:

Figure 1.15 – Visual Studio output tabs

Note that you may have to enable these through the menu (**View | OUTPUT/DEBUG CONSOLE/TERMINAL/PROBLEMS**) the first time. These give you easy access to the running output of the application, a terminal for running command-line operations, and so on. The relevance of these depends on what type of files you are editing – for something like a JSON file, the **DEBUG CONSOLE** tab will not bring any features.

For the context of this book, you will want to install the C# extension:

Figure 1.16 – C# extension for Visual Studio Code

This is an extension provided by Microsoft that enables VS Code to understand both C# code and related artifacts such as .NET project files.

If you work with Git repositories, you should also check out the third-party extension called GitLens, which has features useful for tracking changes in your code.

In this section, you've explored IDE environments and got familiar with the VS Code. Let's now learn how you can leverage the Windows terminal.

Leveraging Windows Terminal

In the MS-DOS days of computing, everything revolved around the command line, and to this day, most advanced users have to open up a cmd window every now and then. The problem is that it has not always been a great experience so far in Windows. During Build 2020, Microsoft released their 1.0 version of **Windows Terminal**. While you can do most of your programming entirely without this, we recommended that you install it, because there are many advantages that we'll show you later in this book.

Windows Terminal supports multiple tabs, and not only the "classic" cmd, but also PowerShell, Azure Cloud Shell, and **Windows Subsystem for Linux (WSL)**:

Figure 1.17 – Windows Terminal

Azure Cloud Shell delivers an instance of the command-line interface for Azure, the Azure CLI, hosted in Azure. This means that instead of installing the Azure CLI locally and keeping it up to date, you will always have the latest version ready to go. You need an Azure subscription for this to work, but it has no cost other than a few cents for the storage that acts as the local disk for the container containing the executables.

WSL will be covered in greater detail in the next chapter, but the short version of this is that it gives you Linux in Windows. This is the Linux Shell (not a graphical UI), so this also fits into the Windows Terminal experience.

Regardless of which of these types of Terminal you run, they have many options you can configure, which makes them extra helpful for programmers. You can choose fonts that are more suited for programming than Word documents. You can install so-called glyphs, and, for instance, display directly on the prompt information about which Git branch you are on. This book will not require you to be using Git as that is aimed at managing and keeping track of your code, but it is easy to get started with even without knowing the commands in detail, so it comes highly recommended to experiment with it. In most development environments these days, it is the de facto source code management technology. Microsoft provides support for Git both in Azure DevOps and GitHub, but there are other providers out there as well and it is not specific to Microsoft development or .NET.

The end result might look like the following:

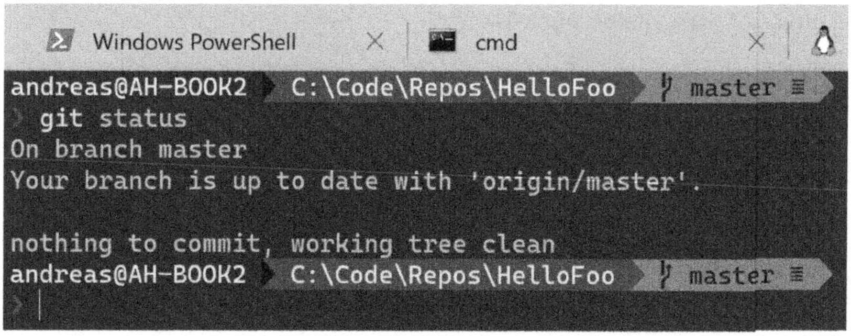

Figure 1.18 – Windows Terminal with Git support enabled

It is downloadable from the Windows Store as well as directly from GitHub, but the Store is better if you want automatic updates.

The extended Git info requires a few extra steps, which you can find at `https://docs.microsoft.com/en-us/windows/terminal/tutorials/powerline-setup`.

Summary

We started with a history lesson to enable you to understand where .NET Core came from, enabling you to share context with seasoned .NET developers, and have a common understanding of the .NET landscape. It has been a long ride, with the occasional sidetrack and the odd confusing naming here and there. The closing of this part showed how things have been simplified, and how Microsoft is still working to make the .NET story more comprehensible for developers – juniors and seniors alike.

We also went through a basic web app to refresh your C# skills. The focus was mainly on showing the different components that make up an MVC-patterned web app and did not go extensively into generic programming skills. If you struggled with this part, you might want to go through a tutorial on the C# language before returning to this book.

We introduced a range of new things while learning what's new in the .NET Core framework and version 9 of C#. This was a high-level view and introduced the features that will be covered in greater detail in later chapters.

Since this book is about creating web applications, we covered some web server-specific details to give background that will be useful both later in the book and in real life.

The chapter was wrapped up by showing off some tools and utilities that are recommended for your programming tool belt. Remember, the more tools in your belt, the more opportunities you'll have in your career!

In the next chapter, we will cover the cross-platform story for .NET 5. This includes getting started with .NET both on Linux and macOS as well as explaining some of the concepts around cross-platform support.

Questions

1. Why was .NET Core introduced?

2. What is the supportability strategy for .NET Core?

3. Can you explain the MVC pattern?

4. What are init-only properties?

5. Can you consume WCF services in .NET 5?

Further reading

- *Hands-On Design Patterns with C# and .NET Core* by Gaurav Aroraa and Jeffrey Chilberto, from Packt Publishing, available at `https://www.packtpub.com/application-development/hands-design-patterns-c-and-net-core`

- *Programming in C#: Exam 70-483 (MCSD) Guide* by Simaranjit Singh Bhalla, Srinivas Madhav Gorthi, from Packt Publishing, available at `https://www.packtpub.com/application-development/programming-c-exam-70-483-mcsd-guide`

2
Cross-Platform Setup

One of the major improvements Microsoft talked about when launching .NET Core was the possibility of running .NET code on platforms other than Windows. With each iteration, the cross-platform story has been improved upon, and in addition to making sure the code can run on other operating systems, great improvements have been made in enabling Linux to run on Windows as well. In the context of running web applications, Linux is a great host operating system for doing so, and in this chapter, we will go through how you can get started with .NET across platforms. You will learn how to leverage the .NET framework and how to get set up and started on a Windows computer, as well as on Linux and macOS. We'll also see how to troubleshoot various Linux on Windows scenarios, including Windows Subsystem for Linux version 2 (WSL2). By the end of the chapter, you'll have your system ready for cross-platform development.

We will cover the following topics:

- Leveraging the .NET framework
- Getting started on Windows, Linux, and macOS
- Debugging Linux on Windows with Visual Studio 2019

Technical requirements

This chapter is about running code on different operating systems, so if you want to test all the options, you will need several devices:

- The code for Windows and Linux will work on a Windows computer.
- The code for macOS requires a Mac system.
- The code for Windows can run on a Mac if you use Fusion/Parallels or Bootcamp.

In addition to the devices, you will also need the following:

- Visual Studio Code, which is available for Windows, Linux, and macOS
- Visual Studio 2019, which is available for Windows and macOS

Please visit the following link to check the CiA videos: `https://bit.ly/3qDiqYY`

Check out the source code for this chapter at: `https://github.com/PacktPublishing/ASP.NET-Core-5-for-Beginners/tree/master/Chapter%2002`

Leveraging the .NET framework

Starting with a bit of trivia, there was a time when Microsoft played very well with other operating systems. When Windows 3.0 was developed, Microsoft collaborated with IBM in developing an operating system called OS/2. Windows ran on top of MS-DOS, so it was not technically an operating system like it is today. In contrast, OS/2 was a complete operating system, without requiring you to go through DOS first. The nifty thing about OS/2 was that it included binaries from Windows, so it was able to run Windows applications on a non-MS operating system. Not only that, but since OS/2 had a different model of operating and more advanced (at the time) memory management, it was able to run Windows apps better than Windows itself. Instead of the entire computer locking up when an application crashed, you just terminated the app before you continued what you were doing.

The partnership was not without its problems, both culturally and technologically. The two companies had their differences, so it did not last. Microsoft moved on to build the Windows NT platform for the professional market and Windows 95 for the consumer market, and OS/2 died out on its own. From that point in time, Microsoft was not a name you used in the same sentence as the term cross-platform, and every bit of effort went into building the Windows ecosystem.

.NET was not present from the beginning of Windows, and it had its own growing pains over the years, which we covered in the previous chapter.

Fast forward to modern times, and Microsoft will be more than happy to tell you how great Linux runs on their cloud computing platform and will provide you with everything you need in order to make .NET code run on the Linux operating system. It took 20 years to turn the ship around, but it certainly is a different path being taken these days. Let's first see why we should go cross-platform and when we shouldn't go cross-platform.

Why cross-platform?

When we use the term *cross-platform*, we may actually be referring to different things.

You have the .NET 5 SDK that you need to develop .NET applications. The fact that this works on macOS means that developers do not need a Windows computer to develop software for Windows, and since Macbooks are popular in the tech community, this broadens the potential developer audience for .NET.

You also have the .NET runtime that is required for running .NET applications. The fact that this works on Linux means that you are not forced to run your applications on Windows, and for servers this is a big thing. With a classic Windows Server with a UI running Internet Information Services, the operating system alone takes up multiple gigabytes of space. A trimmed down Linux installation, with a command line, could be as little as 50 megabytes. If you want to run cloud-native apps, this is a major win.

Why not cross-platform?

OS/2 was an interesting experiment, but even if the partnership had remained amiable, it would probably have been complicated in the long run to enable this type of cross-platform solution. We explained in the first chapter how there are differences between managed and native code, and the approach IBM used was basically bringing in Windows to provide native capabilities. .NET was not invented at the time, and other frameworks also did not necessarily have great cross-platform features. Over time, this would not be a sustainable approach. Imagine keeping up with patches—a security flaw in Windows would require IBM to update their operating system and maintain compatibility through extensive testing and validation.

The short version of this explanation: if you rely on native/unmanaged code, cross-platform can be painful.

Native and unmanaged code is still required for some applications, and then cross-platform might not be the best option for those situations. For instance, in the early days of iPhones, there was no flashlight app, but some clever people figured out that they could interact with the camera and use the flash as a flashlight. This was before Xamarin was a viable option, but it is likely this would have been outside the scope of .NET managed code to implement it.

If you want to squeeze every last CPU cycle out of the device the code runs on, then collected memory objects (that are garbage) might throw you off, because you cannot reliably predict them. If you can handle the overhead of managing memory yourself, you may want to go with a lower-level language for full optimization. A traditional example of this is games where early 3D titles had critical sections written in assembly code, as well as algorithmic tweaks to math operations that you simply cannot control when using a library. On the flip side, this didn't just affect cross-platform; the developer also had to account for which generation of CPU your machine ran, for certain instructions in the code.

Combining cross-platform and single-platform code

You might think that it sounds hard to write an entire game if you had to keep track of the actual hardware and not rely on libraries. That is correct. It was hard, and most developers used a combination of languages to create their games, since less critical parts certainly could be implemented in more developer-friendly languages.

This leads to the question of whether this can be done with .NET as well. The answer is that yes, it is possible through a feature called **Platform Invocation Services**, or **P/ Invoke** for short. This is a mechanism for escaping the managed .NET runtime. You call into APIs and services that are exposed through interfaces that are native to the platform, or components implemented in languages other than the .NET family. For instance, you could call into a driver written for a specific piece of hardware that's not supported by .NET.

While Microsoft can make sure the .NET runtime works across platforms, it isn't possible to guarantee this when you step outside the .NET ecosystem. So, you might have a .NET application that's a mix between a cross-platform and single-platform. It is possible to develop strategies for handling this, but this level of cross-platform implementation is outside the scope of this book. We will, however, explore a similar concept in the coverage of Blazor, where you can perform a so-called JavaScript interop to step outside what .NET provides.

.NET cross-platform availability

So, when we say cross-platform, do we mean *every* platform out there? No, not really, but there are quite a range of options:

- Windows x86/x64/ARM: ARM is not widely available from OEMS, but Microsoft has the Surface Pro X device that runs Windows on ARM. Note that not all the regular Windows apps are available on this platform, so even though there are emulation options, your mileage may vary.

- macOS

- Linux

- iOS (through Xamarin)

- Android (through Xamarin)

Note that while macOS is suitable for developing .NET web applications, it is not really an option for running the apps for other environments, even though there is technically nothing stopping you. Web applications are, by nature, implied to have a server that runs the backend code. Apple does not provide hardware for server use cases—their devices are designed to be clients.

ARM-based macs

Apple has announced that they will transition to using CPUs that they designed, instead of CPUs from Intel. This architecture is not compatible with the current build of .NET for macOS. .NET does not require Intel CPUs or a specific CPU architecture (as evidenced by Windows for the ARM architecture), but the runtimes would still need to be updated.

At the time of writing this book, it is not known what Apple is planning for future devices, and it is not known what steps Microsoft will take to ensure that .NET runs on these devices. For the purposes of this book, we have used Intel-based Mac devices, and we cannot speculate as to what will happen in the future at this time.

What cross-platform does not do for you

The fact that .NET supports cross-platform does not mean you have to implement an application that will work on all the operating systems. If you want to use Windows to develop an application that will only work on Linux, that is OK. However, you should be aware that cross-platform support does not guarantee that all the code you write will work across all the platforms.

For instance, if your application saves text to the filesystem, you might attempt to write a text file to `c:\WebApp\HelloWorld.txt`. This type of reference to a file is a Windows operating system artifact. There will be no warning when writing this code and .NET will not prevent its compilation either. As long as the app runs on Windows, everything should be good.

If the app is running on Linux, however, you will get a runtime exception, because Linux does not understand that type of filesystem. Linux would want you to reference the file as `/mnt/c/webapp/HelloWorld.txt`. (Different distributions have different conventions for the actual file hierarchy.) If you have good exception handling, the app might get around this gracefully, but if not, it will simply stop running and leave you with a bad cross-platform experience.

We will revisit how these challenges can be tackled later in this chapter, after we have covered the basics of getting things running on multi-platform.

Getting started on Windows, Linux, and macOS

The first step toward the cross-platform journey is to get the basics working across the platforms we've mentioned—Windows, Linux, and macOS. We will walk through this in the following sections, to make sure you are on track with this part of the multiplatform story.

Windows

We touched upon getting started with .NET 5 on Windows in the previous chapter, so you should already have a functioning setup for this platform if you followed that guide. Hence, we will not repeat those instructions here.

Linux

Linux is a popular operating system for server workloads, and it powers a large number of the virtual machines that run in Azure. It is not as popular as Windows for the average end user on their desktop, but for a developer, there are a number of benefits to using Linux.

When developing microservices that run in containers, Linux is a good choice since, in many cases, you will be able to run trimmed-down images. Containers is not a topic for this chapter—you can look forward to *Chapter 8*, *Containers*, for that, but Linux is a part of the cross-platform story for .NET, even without containers.

You can install Linux directly on your computer, and you can install everything you need for .NET development, but here we will show you how to develop on Linux, using Windows, through Windows Subsystem for Linux.

Windows Subsystem for Linux (WSL)

Linux is great for development, because many of the tools needed for a programmer are part of the operating system. However, for general office use that involves applications, such as Outlook and Word, Windows is generally a better choice for most people. The natural follow-up to this is that it would be great if you could have both Linux and Windows at the same time.

Windows has supported virtualization in different forms for a long time, and because Linux runs on the same hardware as Windows (as well as being available for free in many cases), it has been a common option to run a virtual machine with Linux, if you need it. However, the point of virtual machines is having something separate from the host machine. Thus, even minor things, such as getting files into and out of the Linux virtual machine, has been a less than smooth experience.

In 2016, Microsoft brought the Linux operating system closer to being a part of Windows by introducing **Windows Subsystem for Linux** (WSL), where you could install special builds of selected distributions into Windows 10. This was further improved with WSL2, which was introduced with Windows 10 2004, where Linux can be made an integrated part of Windows. (The current release of Windows 10 is named 20204 to signify that the release was first released in the year 2020 and the fourth month, April.)

Let's install WSL2 before we proceed with running code on Linux.

Note that this is the install procedure as of the May 2020 version of Windows 10. Things may change in future versions.

Your computer will need to be capable of running Hyper-V and Windows 10 2004 (or later). Most modern computers will be able to run Hyper-V, but if your developer machine is virtualized, then there may be issues enabling WSL2.

To install WSL2, perform the following steps:

1. Open Command Prompt as an admin.

2. Run the following command to install WSL:

```
dism.exe /online /enable-feature /featurename:Microsoft-
Windows-Subsystem-Linux /all /norestart
```

3. Enable Virtual Machine Platform by using the following command:

```
dism.exe /online /enable-feature /
featurename:VirtualMachinePlatform /all /norestart
```

4. Reboot your computer.

5. Download the latest WSL2 kernel from https://wslstorestorage.blob.
    core.windows.net/wslblob/wsl_update_x64.msi.

6. Run the installer, as shown in *Figure 2.1*:

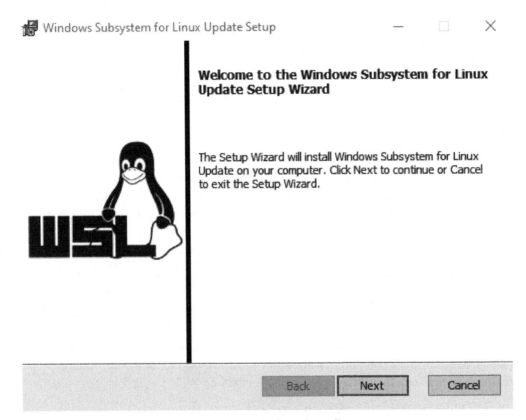

Figure 2.1 – WSL2 kernel installer

7. Make WSL2 your default version by using the following command:

```
wsl --set-default-version 2
```

8. Download a Linux distribution from the Microsoft Store. For this book, we have
    used Ubuntu 20.04 LTS (see *Figure 2.2*):

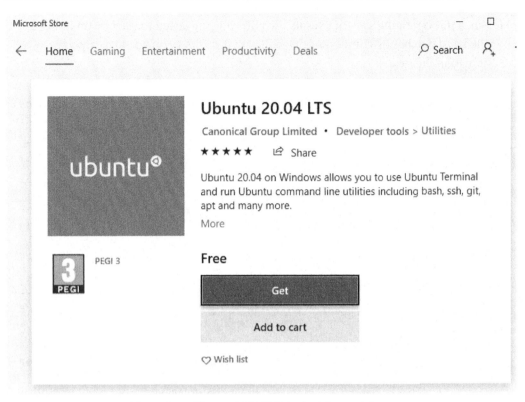

Figure 2.2 – Ubuntu 20.04 LTS in the Microsoft Store

9. Click Launch to start Linux for the first time:

Figure 2.3 – Setting the username and password for Linux

10. Define a username and password for your Linux installation (see *Figure 2.3*). (This
    is not related to your Windows credentials and can be something different.) You
    should now find yourself in a regular Linux shell.

11. Since this operating system lives its own life, it is suggested to start by updating to the latest patches by running `sudo apt update && sudo apt upgrade`, as shown in *Figure 2.4*:

```
andreas@AH-BOOK2: ~                                                          —    □    ✕
Get:39 http://security.ubuntu.com/ubuntu focal-security/universe Translation-en [18.2 kB]
Get:40 http://security.ubuntu.com/ubuntu focal-security/universe amd64 c-n-f Metadata [1628 B]
Get:41 http://security.ubuntu.com/ubuntu focal-security/multiverse amd64 Packages [1172 B]
Get:42 http://security.ubuntu.com/ubuntu focal-security/multiverse Translation-en [540 B]
Get:43 http://security.ubuntu.com/ubuntu focal-security/multiverse amd64 c-n-f Metadata [116 B]
Fetched 17.1 MB in 4s (4743 kB/s)
Reading package lists... Done
Building dependency tree
Reading state information... Done
79 packages can be upgraded. Run 'apt list --upgradable' to see them.
Reading package lists... Done
Building dependency tree
Reading state information... Done
Calculating upgrade... Done
The following packages will be upgraded:
  accountsservice alsa-ucm-conf apparmor apport apt apt-utils bind9-dnsutils bind9-host bind9-libs busybox-initramfs
  busybox-static ca-certificates curl dbus dbus-user-session dbus-x11 distro-info-data fwupd fwupd-signed
  gir1.2-glib-2.0 glib-networking glib-networking-common glib-networking-services initramfs-tools initramfs-tools-bin
  initramfs-tools-core landscape-common libaccountsservice0 libapparmor1 libapt-pkg6.0 libcurl3-gnutls libcurl4
  libdbus-1-3 libfwupd2 libfwupdplugin1 libgirepository-1.0-1 libgnutls30 libjson-c4 libldap-2.4-2 libldap-common
  libnetplan0 libnss-systemd libpam-systemd libproxy1v5 libpulse0 libpulsedsp libpython3.8 libpython3.8-minimal
  libpython3.8-stdlib libseccomp2 libsqlite3-0 libsystemd0 libudev1 netplan.io open-iscsi openssh-client
  openssh-server openssh-sftp-server pulseaudio-utils python3-apport python3-distupgrade python3-problem-report
  python3-requests python3-update-manager python3.8 python3.8-minimal sosreport strace systemd systemd-sysv
  systemd-timesyncd tzdata ubuntu-minimal ubuntu-release-upgrader-core ubuntu-server ubuntu-standard ubuntu-wsl udev
  update-manager-core
79 upgraded, 0 newly installed, 0 to remove and 0 not upgraded.
Need to get 26.1 MB of archives.
After this operation, 135 kB of additional disk space will be used.
Do you want to continue? [Y/n]
```

Figure 2.4 – Updating your Linux distribution

12. Press *Y* to continue, and you should be good to go.

Windows should also have automatically configured integration with your non-Linux hard drive partition. So, if you open Windows Explorer, you should find Tux (the Linux mascot) there:

Figure 2.5 – Linux integration in Windows Explorer

You can also browse the Linux filesystem from Windows and copy files to and from your Linux partition (see *Figure 2.6*):

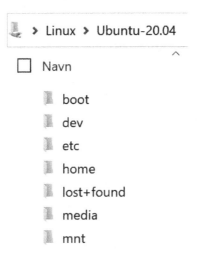

Figure 2.6 – Linux filesystem in Windows Explorer

Note that, under the hood, the Linux filesystem is treated differently to the Windows filesystem, so only place files that you intend to run inside Linux in these folders, and vice versa. If you have applications that run inside Linux, these should not be placed in the Windows partition. It will not cause corruption to do so, but the performance might be degraded.

The Ubuntu installer automatically started up a command line, but if you followed the instructions in the previous chapter for setting up Windows Terminal, Ubuntu 20.04 should have been added automatically. This book uses Windows Terminal going forward in this chapter, but both options should work.

Installing .NET on Linux

We recommend you install .NET on Ubuntu by using APT:

1. Run the following commands to add Microsoft's repositories:

```
wget https://packages.microsoft.com/config/ubuntu/20.04/
packages-microsoft-prod.deb -O packages-microsoft-prod.deb
sudo dpkg -i packages-microsoft-prod.deb
```

2. Install the SDK:

```
sudo apt-get update; \
sudo apt-get install -y apt-transport-https && \
sudo apt-get update && \
sudo apt-get install -y dotnet-sdk-5.0
```

> **Note**
>
> There are a couple of different ways to install .NET on Linux, and things may change over time. If you experience issues while installing .NET, check the instructions online at `https://docs.microsoft.com/en-us/dotnet/core/install/linux-ubuntu`.

Everything should now be in place for creating and running a .NET application. It is time to test the theory in practice:

1. Create a new directory and change into it:

```
mkdir LinuxHelloWorld && cd LinuxHelloWorld
```

2. Linux running in WSL2 does not support a graphical UI yet, so we need to do the editing via non-graphical utilities:

```
sudo vi View/Home/Index.cshtml
```

3. Vi is not exactly intuitive, but press *Insert* and edit the code to look like this:

```
@{
    ViewData["Title"] = "LinuxHelloWorld";
}
<div class="text-center">
    <h1 class="display-4">Running on @Environment.
        OSVersion</h1>
</div>
```

4. To save and exit, press *Esc* followed by *:wq*, and then hit *Enter*.

5. Test the app with `sudo dotnet run`. You should see the output indicate that it is running. See *Figure 2.7*:

```
warn: Microsoft.AspNetCore.DataProtection.KeyManagement.XmlKey
      No XML encryptor configured. Key {93bbb3ea-ece7-448c-b40
info: Microsoft.Hosting.Lifetime[0]
      Now listening on: https://localhost:5001
info: Microsoft.Hosting.Lifetime[0]
      Now listening on: http://localhost:5000
info: Microsoft.Hosting.Lifetime[0]
      Application started. Press Ctrl+C to shut down.
info: Microsoft.Hosting.Lifetime[0]
      Hosting environment: Development
info: Microsoft.Hosting.Lifetime[0]
      Content root path: /mnt/c/Users/andreas/LinuxHelloWorld
```

Figure 2.7 – Using dotnet run on Linux

6. You can test this with some more cross-platform magic. You do not have a browser running on this Ubuntu. You most likely do have one in Windows 10, so you can open that and browse to `https://locahost:5001`. See *Figure 2.8* for an example of browsing a web app that's running on Linux:

LinuxHelloWorld   Home Privacy

Running on Unix 4.19.104.0

Figure 2.8 – Browsing a web app that's running on Linux

7. Return to the Linux shell and terminate the running app with *Ctrl+C*.

We saw that the `vi` utility was sufficient for the minor edits that we made to the code, but not everyone will want to go all-in on Vi as an editor for writing C# code.

Vi "exit strategy"

If you are new to Vi, it can be confusing, because it works differently to most text editors that you might be used to in the Windows world. You might end up being unsure about what you have actually edited, or how to correct it. The exit strategy (if you feel like a mistake was made) is to quit Vi without saving the changes. This is done by pressing the *Esc* key, pressing : (the colon) (you should see it appear in the lower-left corner), and then typing *q!* (include the exclamation mark), followed by *Enter*. You can then re-attempt editing with a clean slate.

Fortunately, there is another option here as well. In the previous chapter, we showed you how useful Visual Studio Code is, so if you haven't already installed it, please do so. We will step through how to use Visual Studio Code (VS Code) as the editor for your code on Linux:

1. Open Visual Studio Code (in Windows 10).

2. Install the **Remote – WSL** extension from within VS Code. See *Figure 2.9*:

Figure 2.9 – Visual Studio Code Remote WSL extension

3. Go back to your Linux shell in WSL and type `code` . (including the punctuation mark).

4. After an initial bit of setup work, Visual Studio Code will load in Windows 10. You will observe that there's an indicator in the lower-left corner referring to WSL. See *Figure 2.10*:

Figure 2.10 – Visual Studio Code connected to WSL

5. If you have the **C# Extension** installed in VS Code, you can go to the debug pane (at the bottom). See *Figure 2.11*:

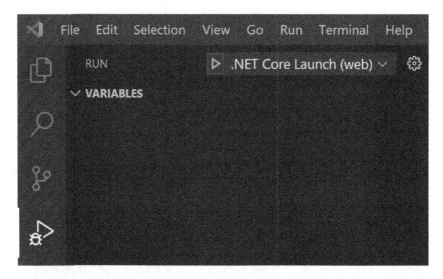

Figure 2.11 – .NET Debug tab for Linux

6. Click the little green arrow to start the debugger. When things have finished building, you should see the same output as before with the `LinuxHelloWorld` app running in the browser. (VS Code launches the browser for you.) If you take a look in the Terminal window, you will see the application starting in WSL. See *Figure 2.12*:

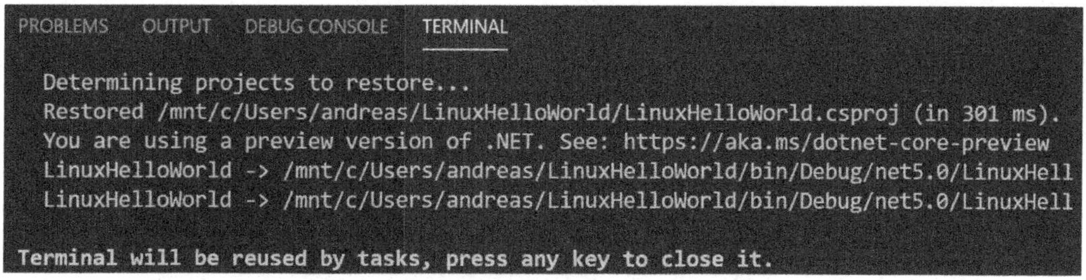

```
PROBLEMS   OUTPUT   DEBUG CONSOLE   TERMINAL

Determining projects to restore...
Restored /mnt/c/Users/andreas/LinuxHelloWorld/LinuxHelloWorld.csproj (in 301 ms).
You are using a preview version of .NET. See: https://aka.ms/dotnet-core-preview
LinuxHelloWorld -> /mnt/c/Users/andreas/LinuxHelloWorld/bin/Debug/net5.0/LinuxHell
LinuxHelloWorld -> /mnt/c/Users/andreas/LinuxHelloWorld/bin/Debug/net5.0/LinuxHell

Terminal will be reused by tasks, press any key to close it.
```

Figure 2.12 – Visual Studio Code terminal output

This session is separate to the one you are running in the Windows Terminal shell, so you can work in parallel there if you like.

Now you can develop code in Windows, which executes on Linux running on Windows. This can take a little while to digest, but the takeaway from this section is that the cross-platform story for Linux is powerful.

If you have an Apple device (that's running macOS) available, then you can bring that out now. Next, we take a look at the mac story for .NET.

macOS

There are two main tools you can use for developing a .NET application on a Mac. You can either use Visual Studio for Mac or Visual Studio Code. We will take a look at using Visual Studio Code (VS Code) first. You can download it from `https://code.visualstudio.com/`.

After installing Visual Studio Code, we recommend that you make it accessible from the shell, so that you can start it from the Terminal.

To make VS Code accessible, perform the following steps:

1. Launch Visual Studio Code.

2. Open the command palette (*Shift+cmd+P*) and type `shell command`, as shown in *Figure 2.13*:

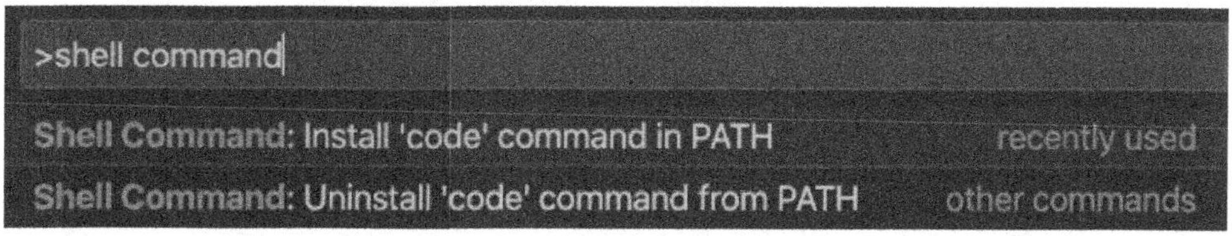

```
>shell command

Shell Command: Install 'code' command in PATH        recently used
Shell Command: Uninstall 'code' command from PATH     other commands
```

Figure 2.13 – The shell command installer

3. You will also want to make sure the C# extension is installed for VS Code. See *Figure 2.14*:

Figure 2.14 – Visual Studio C# extension

Once this is done, you can install .NET by going to `https://dotnet.microsoft.com/download?initial-os=macos`.

4. Open the installer, and you will be greeted with a wizard for installing .NET. See *Figure 2.15*:

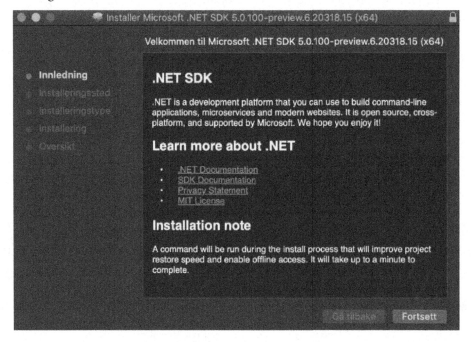

Figure 2.15 – The .NET installer for macOS

Unless you want to modify where the installation is stored, you can click through it by choosing the **Next** option.

5. To verify the .NET version on macOS, open the Terminal and run `dotnet --version`. See *Figure 2.16*:

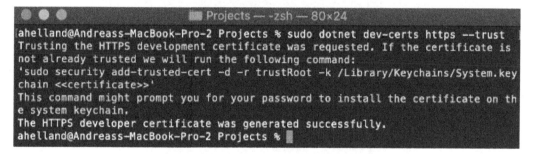

Figure 2.16 – Verifying the .NET version on macOS

6. You also need to generate certificates to run with HTTPS. This is done with the `sudo dotnet dev-certs https --trust` command, as shown in *Figure 2.17*:

```
[ahelland@Andreass-MacBook-Pro-2 Projects % sudo dotnet dev-certs https --trust
Trusting the HTTPS development certificate was requested. If the certificate is
not already trusted we will run the following command:
'sudo security add-trusted-cert -d -r trustRoot -k /Library/Keychains/System.key
chain <<certificate>>'
This command might prompt you for your password to install the certificate on th
e system keychain.
The HTTPS developer certificate was generated successfully.
ahelland@Andreass-MacBook-Pro-2 Projects %
```

Figure 2.17 – Generating and installing developer certificates on macOS

7. Create a folder (`mkdir webapp`) and change into it (`cd webapp`).

8. Run `dotnet new mvc` to generate a simple web app. Then, run `code .` to open it in Visual Studio Code.

9. You might see a notification in the lower-right corner about missing assets. See *Figure 2.18*:

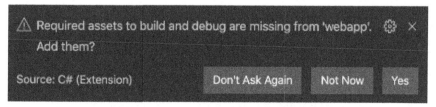

Figure 2.18 – Missing assets in Visual Studio Code

You should click **Yes** to add the assets.

10. VS Code shows the file structure on the left-hand side of the UI. See *Figure 2.19*:

Figure 2.19 – The file structure in Visual Studio Code for Mac

11. Open `Index.cshtml` and make a minor edit to the contents:

```
@{
    ViewData["Title"] = "LinuxHelloWorld";
}
<div class="text-center">
    <h1 class="display-4">Running on @Environment.
        OSVersion</h1>
</div>
```

12. To set a breakpoint, click next to the line number (6).

13. There is a separate debug section:

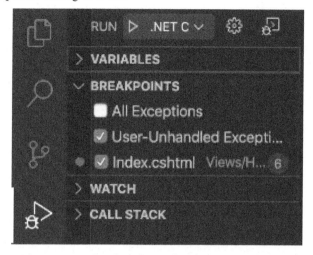

Figure 2.20 – Visual Studio Code debug pane on macOS

14. Click the little green arrow to start your program. It should start up your browser, which should look like the following figure:

Figure 2.21 – Browsing a web app that's running on macOS

You will notice that it does not say Mac or Apple, but for starters, the main concern you solved was that you managed to get .NET working. That completes your installation of VS Code on a Mac.

As mentioned, you can install a more complete version of Visual Studio on macOS as well.

Visual Studio 2019 for Mac

Visual Studio Code is not a bad experience. However, Visual Studio 2019 is available on macOS, so you might prefer that.

In general, there is a more "Mac-ish" feel over it. (The look, feel, and interactions have been built to feel similar to the overall Mac experience.) The file hierarchy is in the left pane, as shown in *Figure 2.22*:

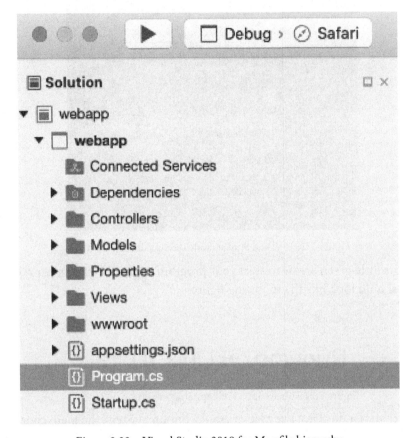

Figure 2.22 – Visual Studio 2019 for Mac file hierarchy

In the middle of Visual Studio, the main pane has a slightly different look to its Windows counterpart (see *Figure 2.23*):

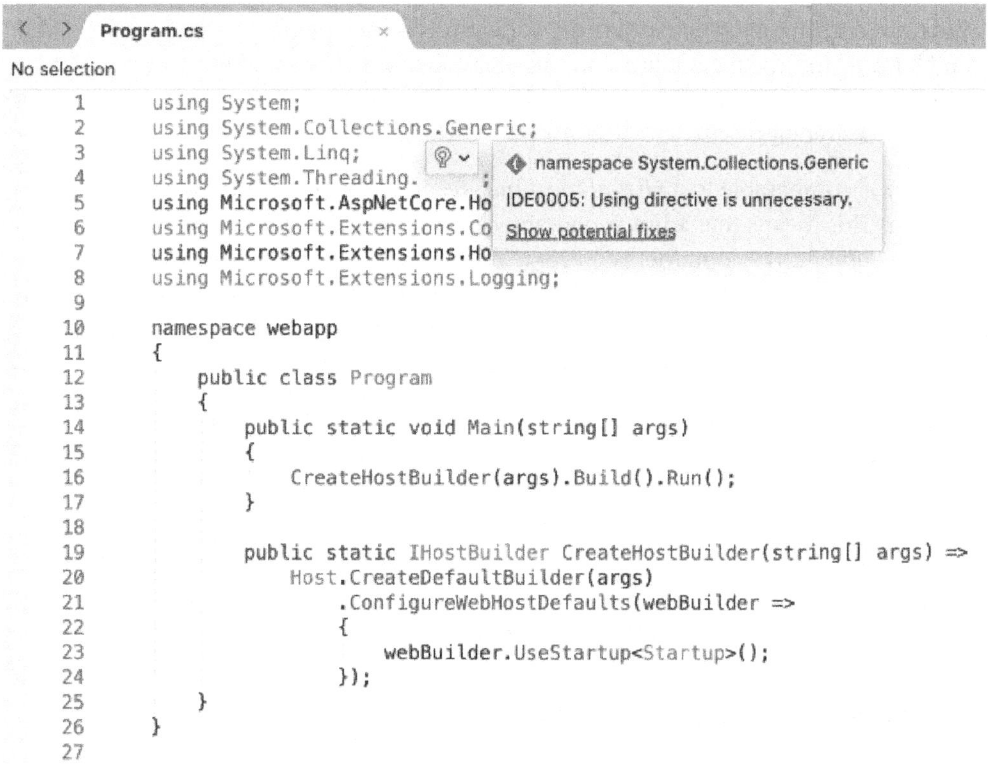

```
‹  ›  Program.cs                        ×

No selection
     1      using System;
     2      using System.Collections.Generic;
     3      using System.Linq;              💡 ⌄    ◆ namespace System.Collections.Generic
     4      using System.Threading.         ;    IDE0005: Using directive is unnecessary.
     5      using Microsoft.AspNetCore.Ho        Show potential fixes
     6      using Microsoft.Extensions.Co
     7      using Microsoft.Extensions.Ho
     8      using Microsoft.Extensions.Logging;
     9
    10      namespace webapp
    11      {
    12          public class Program
    13          {
    14              public static void Main(string[] args)
    15              {
    16                  CreateHostBuilder(args).Build().Run();
    17              }
    18
    19              public static IHostBuilder CreateHostBuilder(string[] args) =>
    20                  Host.CreateDefaultBuilder(args)
    21                      .ConfigureWebHostDefaults(webBuilder =>
    22                      {
    23                          webBuilder.UseStartup<Startup>();
    24                      });
    25          }
    26      }
    27
```

Figure 2.23 – Visual Studio 2019 for Mac main pane

As with the Windows experience, there are more options in Visual Studio 2019 (VS 2019) than Visual Studio Code. Thus, for web app development, it is mostly a matter of which tool you prefer, with some more knobs and dials in VS 2019 than VS Code, while the basic functionality is present in both. For VS 2019, Visual Studio Community for Mac is the free version.

Visual Studio for Mac was originally based on Xamarin Studio for Mac. If you are into mobile development for Apple's platforms, it might be a better choice to use the full version of Visual Studio rather than Visual Studio Code. We will revisit this topic later in this chapter, in the *Cross-platform for mobile devices* section.

A word on cross-platform and containers

Containers is a hot topic these days, and they will be covered in detail in *Chapter 9, Containers*. However, we should explain the relationship between containers and cross-platform.

The previous sections showed us running code directly on a platform. The Linux version ran on Ubuntu, and the macOS version ran on a Macbook. For more advanced use cases, you might want to containerize your code, but this does not mean you can freely mix and match the technologies.

A container is comparable to a *virtual machine lite*, and it depends on the host it is running on. This means that a Linux container needs to run on a Linux host. Running a Windows Server 2019 container requires a Windows Server 2019 host. This extends across Windows Server versions as well—a Windows Server 2016 host will run Windows Server 2016 containers and will not support Windows Server 2019 containers. A Linux container on Windows 10 is not covered by cross-platform compatibility.

However, WSL2 can function as a Linux host. Thus, you can run a Linux container on top of WSL and achieve a cross-platform container development story. We'll expand on this in *Chapter 9, Containers*.

With the right hardware, you can use Windows with Hyper-V and have a Linux virtual machine as a Linux host for running Linux-based containers on top.

It's no wonder you might get confused with all the layers of virtualization involved in this.

Making your code cross-platform

When beginning to build a cross-platform solution, you need to make sure that the Hello World web app runs on more than Windows. However, there is more to enjoying the benefits of these platforms. Let's look both at how Microsoft supplies built-in mechanisms and what you can do yourself.

Background worker services

In an ASP.NET web app, a lot of the things happening in the user interface are event-driven. For instance, in the previous chapter, we showed you some of the new features in C# 9, including an example class for US cities, which consists of a name and a zip code. Thus, if you extended that to an ASP.NET application, you might build a web page that includes a textbox for entering a zip code and a button for looking up the corresponding city name.

Zip codes are fairly static and not something that change every week. However, you might still want to make sure that your database is up to date, and so you could choose to perform a synchronization with the US Postal Service's master database (for example). This would not be driven by an end user clicking in the UI, but it would happen by itself in the background.

.NET has a template that would be suitable for this *worker*, which generates a console app that you can extend with such functionality. The default behavior is printing the current datetime, which is sufficient for our purposes, but you can make it more advanced on your own.

In order to do this, you first need to open up the command line, create a new directory, and change into this directory. Once you're done, perform the following steps to create a new solution:

1. Run `dotnet new worker`.

2. Run `dotnet add package Microsoft.Extensions.Hosting.WindowsServices`.

3. Run `dotnet add package Microsoft.Extensions.Hosting.Systemd`.

4. Run `dotnet run`: which looks like this:

```
c:\Code\Book\Chapter_02_Workers>dotnet run
info: Chapter_02_Workers.Worker[0]
      Worker running at: 07/01/2020 21:47:36 +02:00
info: Microsoft.Hosting.Lifetime[0]
      Application started. Press Ctrl+C to shut down.
info: Microsoft.Hosting.Lifetime[0]
      Hosting environment: Development
info: Microsoft.Hosting.Lifetime[0]
      Content root path: c:\Code\Book\Chapter_02_Workers
info: Chapter_02_Workers.Worker[0]
      Worker running at: 07/01/2020 21:47:37 +02:00
info: Chapter_02_Workers.Worker[0]
      Worker running at: 07/01/2020 21:47:38 +02:00
```

Figure 2.24 – Using dotnet run for a worker service

5. Run `code .` to load the project in Visual Studio Code.

This works nicely, but there is a missing piece. The project currently runs as a console app, meaning that it must be started and run in a console window. This is not suitable for a website, where it's supposed to be done completely in the background.

In Windows, this is done by installing the app as a Windows service (see *Figure 2.25*):

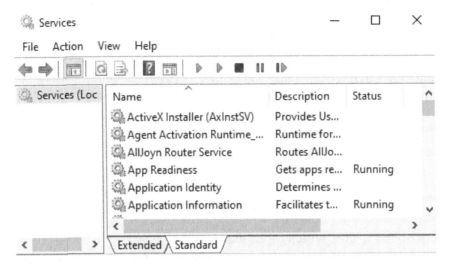

Figure 2.25 – Windows Services

It is probably not surprising that this does not sound like it's cross-platform.

Linux has a similar construct called **systemd**, so on an operating system level, you're not blocked. In Linux, services are implemented through the systemd daemon, which is supported by .NET.

> **WSL and systemd**
>
> Note that at the time of writing this book, systemd is not supported by Windows Subsystem for Linux. This means that in order to fully test this code on Linux, you will need either a Linux virtual machine running locally or an instance of a Linux virtual machine running in Azure.

In other words, we need to modify our application to support two operating system concepts. This sounds complicated, but in reality, it's fairly simple.

Going back to Visual Studio Code, open up `Program.cs` and make some minor changes, so it looks like this:

```
using Microsoft.Extensions.DependencyInjection;
using Microsoft.Extensions.Hosting;
namespace Chapter_02_Workers
{
    public class Program
```

```
{
    public static void Main(string[] args)
    {
        CreateHostBuilder(args).Build().Run();
    }
    public static IHostBuilder CreateHostBuilder(string[] args)
    =>
        Host.CreateDefaultBuilder(args)
            .UseWindowsService()
            .UseSystemd()
            .ConfigureServices((hostContext, services) =>
            {
                services.AddHostedService<Worker>();
            });
    }
}
```

The two important pieces here are `UseWindowsService` and `UseSystemd`. The .NET runtime is able to understand whether it is executing on Windows or Linux, and then it will use the corresponding version. It will ignore the other one, so you do not need to have additional logic on your behalf to figure out which one to use.

Running the previous code will produce the same output as before, so you will not immediately notice a change. It is important to understand that while the preceding code will make the code cross-platform, it will not automatically install itself as a Windows service or systemd daemon.

To get a Windows service installed on your developer machine, run the following commands in a command-line window:

1. `dotnet publish -configuration Release`
2. `sc create dotnetService binPath = c:\code\foo.exe` (where `foo.exe` is the file generated by the previous command)
3. `sc start dotnetService`

This should see you through development purposes, but it might not work when moving the code to a different environment that's not running on your local developer machine. It might be a more elaborate process to set up the service in these cases, so if you need to do that, there is an alternative configuration process. There are instructions in the appendix for this chapter on how to set up the services.

For Linux, the instructions are as follows:

1. Run `sudo nano /etc/systemd/system/dotnetd.service` to create a service.

2. Make sure the contents are similar to this:

```
[Unit]
Description=.NET Chapter 02 systemd daemon

[Service]
WorkingDirectory=/var/www/dotnetd
ExecStart=/usr/local/bin/dotnet /var/www/dotnetd/dotnetd.
dll
Restart=always
# Restart service after 10 seconds if the dotnet service
# crashes.
RestartSec=10
KillSignal=SIGINT
SyslogIdentifier=dotnet-daemon
User=apache
Environment=ASPNETCORE_ENVIRONMENT=Production

[Install]
WantedBy=multi-user.target
```

3. Enable the service: `sudo systemctl enable kestrel-dotnetd.service`.

4. Start the service: `sudo systemctl start kestrel-dotnetd.service`.

5. Verify that the service is running: `sudo systemctl status kestrel-dotnetd.service`.

   The output will be similar to this:

```
kestrel-dotnetd.service - .NET Chapter 02 systemd daemon
    Loaded: loaded (/etc/systemd/system/kestrel-dotnetd.
    service; enabled)
    Active: active (running) since Thu 2020-10-18
    04:09:35 CET; 35s ago
Main PID: 9021 (dotnet)
```

```
CGroup: /system.slice/kestrel-dotnetd.service
        └─9021 /usr/local/bin/dotnet /var/www/
dotnetd/dotnetd.dll
```

This is a great example of how .NET can help you along the way, but not all use cases can be solved that easily. Next, we will walk through a more elaborate example of cross-platform functionality.

A more complicated cross-platform example

There are scenarios where you need to deal with cross-platform that have more bits and pieces to it than .NET can handle automatically. We've already mentioned how Linux would not understand c:\WebApp\HelloWorld.txt, so let's look at a slightly more complicated example.

Let's say we have a website where we depend on encrypting and/or signing strings of text. (This could be part of a larger identity system.) We recommend doing this by using certificates. We want this code to work both for Windows and Linux, and most methods for working with certificates should be entirely cross-platform compatible. However, Windows and Linux have different ways to work with certificates on the operating system level. More specifically, they are generated differently and accessed differently. We will implement both options.

To generate a certificate on Windows, perform the following steps:

1. Open Windows Terminal with a PowerShell tab.

2. Run the following command:

```
$cert = New-SelfSignedCertificate -Type Custom -Subject
"CN=Chapter_2_Certificate" -TextExtension @("2.5.29.37={text}
1.3.6.1.5.5.7.3.3") -KeyUsage DigitalSignature -KeyAlgorithm
RSA -KeyLength 2048 -NotAfter (Get-Date).AddYears(2)
-CertStoreLocation "Cert:\CurrentUser\My"
$cert.Thumbprint
```

3.   Take a note of the thumbprint, because we need it in the code. See *Figure 2.26*:

Figure 2.26 – Generating a certificate on Windows

You can also verify the presence of the certificate in the **User Certificate** store in Windows 10 (see *Figure 2.27*). (It can be located by starting to type `certificate` on the search bar in Windows.):

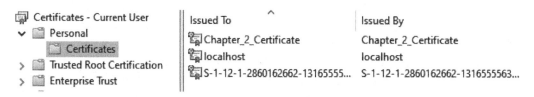

Figure 2.27 – The User Certificate store in Windows 10

To generate a certificate on Linux, perform the following steps:

1.   Open Windows Terminal with an Ubuntu 20.04 tab.

2.   Run the following commands:

```
openssl req -x509 -newkey rsa:4096 -keyout myKey.pem -out cert.
pem -days 365 -nodes
```

```
openssl pkcs12 -export -out keyStore.p12 -inkey myKey.pem -in
cert.pem
```

```
openssl x509 -in cert.pem -noout -fingerprint
```

You will need to provide some values when generating the certificate, but for the purposes of this chapter, these values do not need to adhere to any actual data.

Do not enter a password when prompted—just press *Enter* to set a blank/null password.

3.   Take a note of the thumbprint, as we will need it afterward.

You may notice that the thumbprint looks different in Windows and Linux. Windows uses the format *12AB...*, whereas Linux outputs *12:AB:...* instead. This is purely a matter of visual representation. Linux prints in a more readable format, but the actual thumbprint is not formatted differently. If you remove the colons from the Linux version, you will see that the number of characters is the same as the Windows version (as shown in *Figure 2.28*):

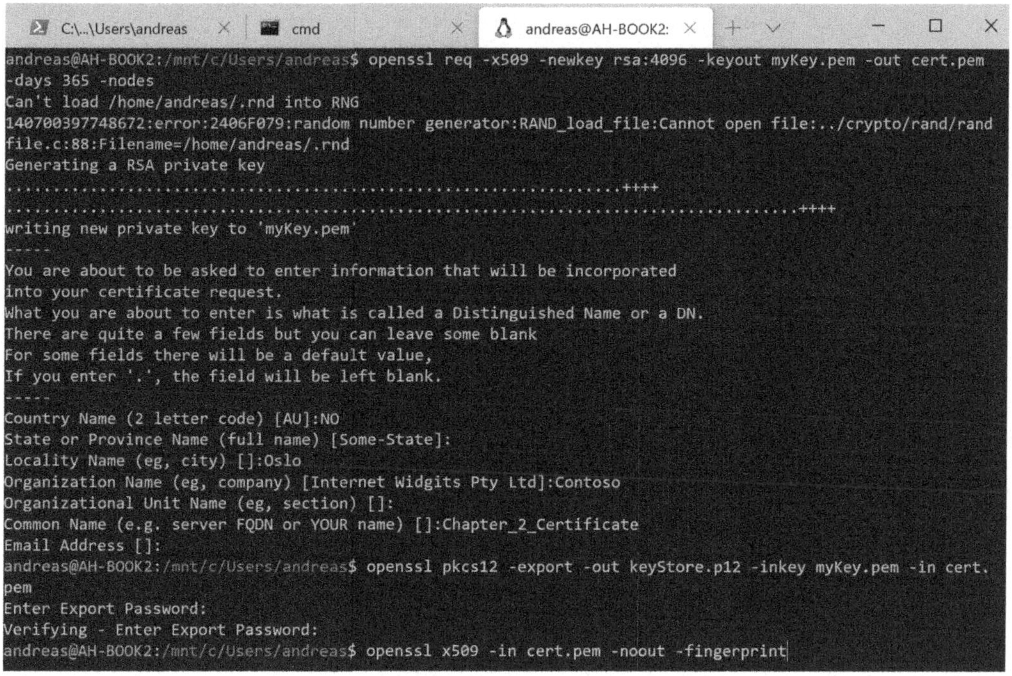

Figure 2.28 – Generating a certificate on Linux

With the certificates in place for both Windows and Ubuntu, we will create a web app that will use it. So as not to complicate matters, this code just loads the certificate and prints out the thumbprint and the common name to verify that the code is able to read (and use) certificates. The steps to create an app that work with certificates are as follows:

1. Open Windows Terminal and create a new directory: `C:\Code\Book\Chapter_02_Certificates`.

2. Change into the directory and run `dotnet new mvc`.

3. Run `dotnet add package Microsoft.IdentityModel.Tokens`.

4. Start Visual Studio Code with `code ..`

5. Open `HomeController.cs`.

6. Add the following two using lines at the top:

```
using System.Security.Cryptography.X509Certificates;
using Microsoft.IdentityModel.Tokens;
```

7. Edit the controller to look like this (some parts are omitted for readability):

```
public class HomeController : Controller
{
    private readonly ILogger<HomeController> _logger;
    private static Lazy<X509SigningCredentials>
        SigningCredentials;
    public HomeController(ILogger<HomeController> logger)
    {
        _logger = logger;
    }
    public IActionResult Index()
    {
        var SigningCertThumbprint = "WindowsThumbprint";
        SigningCredentials = new
            Lazy<X509SigningCredentials>(() =>

        {
            X509Store certStore = new X509Store(StoreName.My,
            StoreLocation.CurrentUser);
            certStore.Open(OpenFlags.ReadOnly);
            X509Certificate2Collection certCollection =
                certStore.Certificates.Find(
                X509FindType.FindByThumbprint,
                SigningCertThumbprint,
                false);
            // Get the first cert with the thumbprint
            if (certCollection.Count > 0)
            {
                return new
                    X509SigningCredentials(certCollection[0]);
            }
            throw new Exception("Certificate not found");
```

```
        });

        var myCert = SigningCredentials.Value;
        ViewBag.myCertThumbprint =
          myCert.Certificate.Thumbprint.ToString()
        ViewBag.myCertSubject =
          myCert.Certificate.SubjectName.Name.ToString();;


        return View();
    }
...
```

The important bit here is that the controller attempts to use .NET libraries that are specific for reaching into the certificate store of Windows (compatible with Windows 10 and Windows Server). The certificates are loaded into an array. We specified a thumbprint that should be unique to only one certificate. If you have the incorrect thumbprint defined, or for some reason the app cannot access the certificate store, an error will be thrown that no certificate could be found.

If a certificate is found, then the values are read. The thumbprint and subject name attributes are stored in the `ViewBag` for easy retrieval in the view.

8. Edit the `Index.cshtml` file to look like this:

```
@{
    ViewData["Title"] = "Home Page";
}


<div class="text-center">
    <h1 class="display-4">Certificate info</h1>
    <p>Certificate thumbprint: @ViewBag.
        myCertThumbprint</p>
    <p>Certificate subject: @ViewBag.myCertSubject</p>
</div>
```

9. Run the app. You will see the certificate info, as shown in *Figure 2.29*:

Certificate info

Certificate thumbprint: DEAF2B8A4864C51B5BEEFEF7BADA7CB5C6DAE995

Certificate subject: CN=Chapter_2_Certificate

Figure 2.29 – Output for the Windows certificate

The next logical step would be to switch to Linux, execute `dotnet run`, and refresh the browser. Sadly, this will give you an error, as shown in *Figure 2.30*:

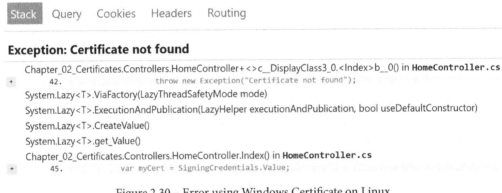

| Stack | Query | Cookies | Headers | Routing |

Exception: Certificate not found

```
Chapter_02_Certificates.Controllers.HomeController+<>c__DisplayClass3_0.<Index>b__0() in HomeController.cs
   42.            throw new Exception("Certificate not found");
System.Lazy<T>.ViaFactory(LazyThreadSafetyMode mode)
System.Lazy<T>.ExecutionAndPublication(LazyHelper executionAndPublication, bool useDefaultConstructor)
System.Lazy<T>.CreateValue()
System.Lazy<T>.get_Value()
Chapter_02_Certificates.Controllers.HomeController.Index() in HomeController.cs
   45.            var myCert = SigningCredentials.Value;
```

Figure 2.30 – Error using Windows Certificate on Linux

There are two reasons why this fails:

* We didn't change the thumbprint.

* We tried looking up the certificate through the Windows Certificate store.

We will fix this, but first we need to prepare the certificate in Linux. When we previously generated the certificates in Linux, we were in the home directory (if you were in a different directory, replace it accordingly in the instructions).

By executing `ls -l`, we see that there are a couple of files for the certificate. See *Figure 2.31*:

```
andreas@AH-BOOK2:~$ ls -l
total 20
-rw-r--r-- 1 andreas andreas 1992 Jul 12 14:27 cert.pem
drwxr-xr-x 3 andreas andreas 4096 Jun 30 18:35 dotnet_install
-rw------- 1 andreas andreas 4181 Jul 12 14:27 keyStore.p12
-rw------- 1 andreas andreas 3272 Jul 12 14:26 myKey.pem
andreas@AH-BOOK2:~$
```

Figure 2.31 – Listing certificate files in Linux

We want to make this friendlier for our code, as well as deployment purposes. Rename the certificate, as per the following steps:

1. Rename the `.p12` file, using `mv keyStore.p12 LinuxThumbprint.p12`.

2. Rename the `cert.pem` file, using `mv cert.pem LinuxThumbprint.pem`.

3. These files should be moved to a more appropriate location. For the purposes of this chapter, that would be the directory where our code exists:

```
mv LinuxThumbprint.p12/mnt/c/Code/Book/Chapter_02_
Certificates/LinuxThumbprint.p12
```

```
mv LinuxThumbprint.cert /mnt/c/Code/Book/Chapter_02_
Certificates/LinuxThumbprint.cert
```

This means our code will be able to easily locate the certificate files.

> **Integrating certificates for apps that are deployed to the cloud**
>
> A word of advice here. This approach works, as long as we manage the life cycle of the certificates inside the code's life cycle. It is not the best solution for cloud deployments where you often manage the certificates separately.
>
> Azure recommends storing private certificates (`.p12` files) in `/var/ssl/private`, if you run your app in Azure App Services and store the certificates in Azure Key Vault.

Now that the certificates are in place, we can fix our code. Perform the following steps:

1. Return to Visual Studio Code (you can still edit in Windows if you like) and open `HomeController.cs`.

2. Change the code here:

```
var SigningCertThumbprint = "WindowsThumbprint";
```

To the following:

```
var SigningCertThumbprint = "LinuxThumbprint";
```

3. Comment out the current certificate loading:

```
/*
SigningCredentials = new Lazy<X509SigningCredentials>(()
=>

...

    throw new Exception("Certificate not found");
```

```
    });
    */
    var myCert = SigningCredentials.Value;
```

4. Insert the following code instead:

```
public IActionResult Index()
{
    /*
    Windows Certificate Loading
    */
    var SigningCertThumbprint = "LinuxThumbprint";
    var bytes = System.IO.File.ReadAllBytes(
        $"{SigningCertThumbprint}.p12");
    var cert = new X509Certificate2(bytes);
    SigningCredentials = new Lazy<X509SigningCredentials>(()
    =>
    {
        if (cert != null)
        {
            return new X509SigningCredentials(cert);
        }
        throw new Exception("Certificate not found");
    });
    var myCert = SigningCredentials.Value;
```

The purpose of this code is the same as the Windows version. It reads the certificate and writes two of the attributes into the ViewBag for rendering. Where it differs from the code that handles Windows is that Linux does not have a certificate store. The code simply attempts to locate a file and read the byte values. If the file does not exist, or the contents cannot be converted to a certificate, then an error is thrown about how the certificate was not found.

5. Run the app.

Opening the browser, you should see a similar view, but with other values as shown in the following screenshot:

Certificate info

Certificate thumbprint: EC2E03FAC84E570CADE1020E08165279AD79A59B

Certificate subject: CN=Chapter_02_Certificates, O=Contoso, L=Oslo, S=Some-State, C=NO

Figure 2.32 – Output for the Linux certificate

If you want to have a true cross-platform application, you can go the extra mile and add checks for which platform the code runs on. Add a few checks:

```
public IActionResult Index()
{
    //Windows
    if (Environment.OSVersion.Platform.ToString() == "Win32NT")
    {
        //Windows logic
        ...
    }
    //Linux
    if (Environment.OSVersion.Platform.ToString() == "Unix")
    {
        //Linux logic
        ...
    }
    var myCert = SigningCredentials.Value;
    ViewBag.myCertThumbprint =
        myCert.Certificate.Thumbprint.ToString();
    ViewBag.myCertSubject =
        myCert.Certificate.SubjectName.Name.ToString();
    return View();
}
```

This illustrates that there might be some extra work involved in building cross-platform apps, other than just making sure you run .NET 5. However, it is possible and might be worth it. With the example shown here, it means that you can have developers doing their work primarily on Windows and still deploy to Linux hosts in production (provided you test for these edge cases).

Self-contained .NET apps

The discussion so far in this chapter has revolved around making sure everything works across different platforms. There are, however, times when you do not have that need, and you might want to be more specific as to what you will support.

Two examples where this may apply are as follows:

- You create a web app that is to be deployed on Windows servers. You do not control these servers, and the operations team that own the servers have not deployed the .NET 5 runtime yet. Unfortunately, their update schedule does not coincide with your planned release.

- You have a temperature sensor that is connected to a Raspberry Pi, and a .NET application is responsible for sending the data to Azure, for building a graph over time. Compiling the application on the device is not an option.

Both these use cases can be solved by creating self-contained .NET apps. If an application is self-contained, this means it has everything it needs to run without installing the .NET runtime.

Generating files for Windows Server

For a case where you don't control the operating system on a Windows server, it means you can deploy .NET 5 applications, even if the server only has .NET Core 3.1 installed, or even if there is no .NET runtime at all.

To generate files for this, run the `dotnet publish -r win-x64` command. The files generated can be copied to the server and executed without complaints about the .NET runtime.

Generating files for the Raspberry Pi

For the Raspberry Pi, even though your developer machine runs Windows 10, you can compile for a different operating system. (This is known as cross-compilation.) The resulting bits can be copied to the device and run immediately.

To generate these files, run the `dotnet publish -r linux-arm64` command.

If you want to generate files for other platforms, there is a list of valid identifiers you can use, which you can find at `https://docs.microsoft.com/en-us/dotnet/core/rid-catalog`.

A drawback of this approach is that the application is larger, since there are no shared components. If your server/device only runs one application, then this might not be an issue, but if you have 20 different .NET apps that are all self-contained, then there is a lot of overhead. This might not be an issue with rack servers that have plenty of storage, but for a Raspberry Pi, this might be a concern.

It is hard to put exact numbers on this. The .NET team continually iterates on improving everything regarding size, whether it is self-contained or not. After testing with the certificate reading sample application (in the previous section), we established the amounts given in the following figure:

Command	Size
dotnet publish	6.5 MB
dotnet publish -r win-x64	175 MB
dotnet publish -r linux-arm64	228 MB

Figure 2.33 – Size comparison of the dotnet publish commands

You will probably not see the exact same numbers when testing on your machine, but it gives a general idea of the difference in size. It is possible to trim the output, but even then, it is clear that using self-contained apps is not a space saver on a per-app basis.

For a storage-constrained device that has the .NET runtime already installed, you may want to employ a strategy that combines the best of two strategies. You make it runtime-dependent and platform-specific. This means that you create one file with the cross-platform components and a different file with the components that are specific for the target platform.

You can do this by running the `dotnet publish -r linux-arm64 --self-contained false` command.

Cross-platform for mobile devices

Developing mobile apps is not covered in this book, and you are not likely to deploy web applications to mobile devices either. It is, however, a part of the cross-platform discussion, so a brief look is warranted.

We covered the history of the different .NET frameworks in the previous chapter and touched upon the fact that support for running .NET code on mobile devices was not originally a Microsoft initiative. In other words, although you could use C# for creating mobile apps, it was not officially part of the .NET technology stack. Since Microsoft bought Xamarin, it has become official, and significant effort has been made in making the tools integrated with .NET and Visual Studio.

We already asked why you should consider cross-platform capabilities in general, but the question can also be repeated for with mobile devices. Apple provides tooling and frameworks for iOS, and Google provides tooling and frameworks for Android, so why would you use .NET?

To answer this, you should look at a couple of aspects.

First, what kind of application are you writing? Is it a fairly generic data entry line-of-business app, or is it highly optimized for the Apple or Android ecosystem? There will always be some gap between what Xamarin supports and what the native tooling supports (just like it is for .NET in Windows), and sometimes Xamarin will not cover what you need.

What skill set do your developers have, and how many developers are on your team? Xamarin is great if you are proficient in C#, since you don't have to learn a new language. If, however, you have a strong Java background, it is probably easier to get started with Kotlin for creating Android apps.

If your development team is large enough to support having dedicated iOS developers, there's nothing wrong with them using Apple's Xcode either.

Even though there are bonuses, such as reusing code across platforms, you should reflect on these things before starting a new mobile app project, but for the purposes of learning, you are, of course, encouraged to take a look at how it works.

To install Xamarin, you will need to check **Mobile development with .NET** in **Visual Studio Installer**. When you click on this topic in Visual Studio Installer, it should look like *Figure 2.34*. (You can do this either during the initial installation or by reopening it later to modify your installation.):

Figure 2.34 – Enabling Mobile development for Visual Studio

This will install the necessary bits for both Android and iOS.

For Android, you can choose to install an Android emulator and get going fairly quickly.

For iOS, there are some extra hurdles. You can develop an application for iOS on a Windows machine, but to build and publish your code, you need a device with macOS. Visual Studio supports connecting to a Mac remotely to do this task, so that you don't need to use the Mac as the developer experience. However, that is one more thing to sort out, especially if you are
a one-man development team. You can share a Mac among developers on a team, and you can also pay for "Macs in the cloud."

Creating a HelloWorld iOS application

For this reason, in order to create an iOS app, it is easier to step back to your Mac and start Visual Studio 2019 for Mac. Perform the following steps:

1. Create a new solution and choose iOS-App-Single View App.

2. Fill in the app name, the organization identifier, which devices to support (iPhone, iPad, or both), and the operating system level required. See *Figure 2.35*:

● ● ●	New Project

Configure your iOS app

App Name:	HelloWorld
Organization Identifier:	com.companyname
Bundle Identifier:	com.companyname.HelloWorld
	Sign in and select a team to enable Automatic Provisioning
Team:	Sign In

Figure 2.35 – Configuring your iOS app

3. Fill in the solution name, as shown in *Figure 2.36*:

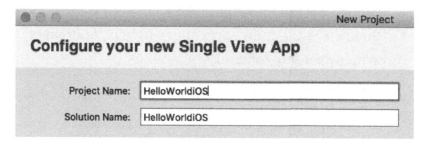

Figure 2.36 – Configuring the Single View app

4. Open `LaunchScreen.storyboard` and add a label with a short message. See *Figure 2.37*:

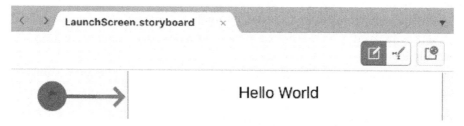

Figure 2.37 – Creating a launch screen label for an iOS app

5. You can also take a look the `Main.cs` file, to make sure everything is in order:

```csharp
using UIKit;
namespace HelloWorldiOS
{
    public class Application
    {
        // This is the main entry point of the application.
        static void Main(string[] args)
        {
            // if you want to use a different Application
            // Delegate class
            // from "AppDelegate" you can specify it here.
            UIApplication.Main(args, null, "AppDelegate");
        }
    }
}
```

6. Click the Play icon to start debugging. An emulator will be loaded, as shown in *Figure 2.38*:

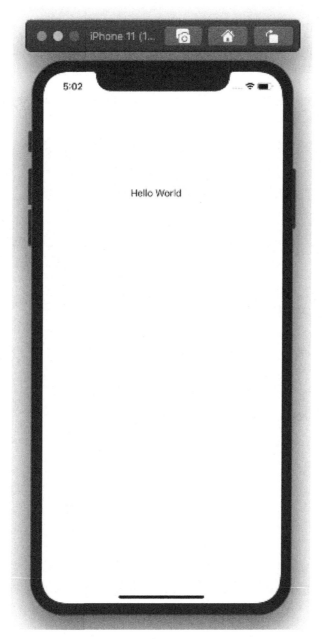

Figure 2.38 – Launching the HelloWorldiOS app

For this to work, you should already have downloaded and installed Xcode on your Mac.

To continue covering the cross-platform mobile experience, let's create something similar on Android.

Creating a HelloWorld Android app

Go back to Windows, and once you have ensured that you have the necessary components installed for Visual Studio, you can follow these steps to create an Android app:

1. Create a new `HelloWorldAndroid` project in Visual Studio by using the `Mobile App` template. See *Figure 2.39*:

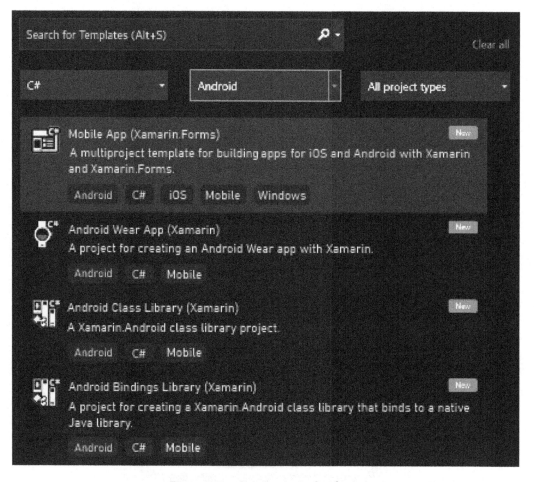

Figure 2.39 – Creating an Android app

2. Choose a name for the project, as shown in *Figure 2.40*:

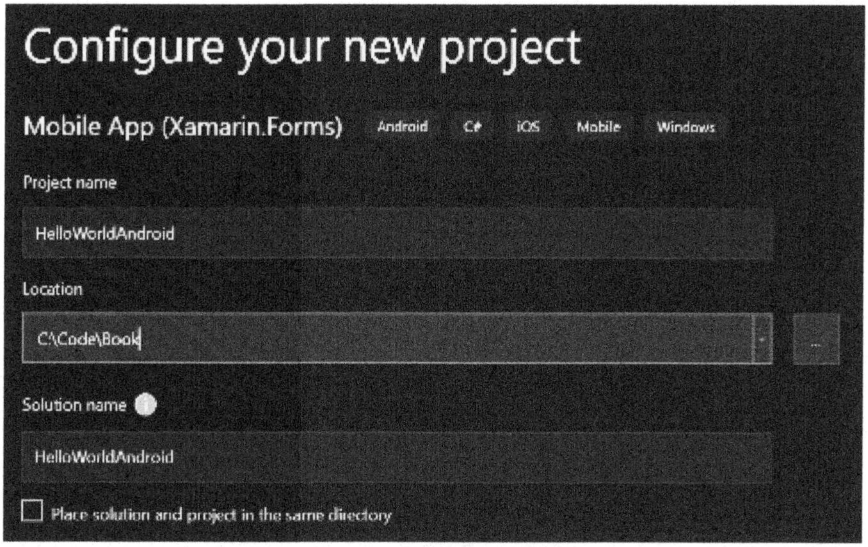

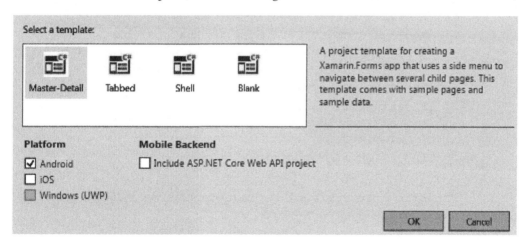

Figure 2.40 – Configuring your Android project

3. Select a new UI template, as shown in *Figure 2.41*:

Figure 2.41 – Setting up a UI template

4. You can also take a look the `MainActivity.cs` file (parts omitted for readability) to make sure that everything is ready:

```
using System;
using Android.App;
using Android.OS;
using Android.Runtime;
```

```
using Android.Support.Design.Widget;
using Android.Support.V7.App;
using Android.Views;
using Android.Widget;
namespace AndroidApp
{
    [Activity(Label = "@string/app_name",
      Theme = "@style/AppTheme.NoActionBar", MainLauncher =
        true)]
    public class MainActivity : AppCompatActivity
    {
        protected override void OnCreate(Bundle
          savedInstanceState)
        {
            base.OnCreate(savedInstanceState);
            Xamarin.Essentials.Platform.Init(this,
              savedInstanceState);
            SetContentView(Resource.Layout.activity_main);
            Android.Support.V7.Widget.Toolbar toolbar =
            FindViewById<Android.Support.V7.Widget.Toolbar>
              (Resource.Id.toolbar);
            SetSupportActionBar(toolbar);
            FloatingActionButton fab =
              FindViewById<FloatingActionButton>(Resource.
                Id.fab);
            fab.Click += FabOnClick;
        }
        public override bool OnCreateOptionsMenu(IMenu menu)
        {
            ...
        }
        public override bool OnOptionsItemSelected(IMenuItem
          item)
        {
            ...
        }

        private void FabOnClick(object sender, EventArgs
          eventArgs)
```

```
        {
            ...
        }
        ...
    }
}
```

5. Run the app through the debugger, as shown in *Figure 2.42*:

Figure 2.42 – Launching the HelloWorldAndroid app

After taking a look at the code for both iOS and Android, we can see that it is recognizable as C# code, but the boilerplate code does not look like what is generated when you use the web app template. This highlights another important point, with regard to cross-platform on mobile. If you're interested in Italian sports cars, saving up money to be able to buy a Ferrari might be a good start, but having a Ferrari does not mean you are able to drive it at maximum speed. You will be able to perform basic tasks by knowing how to drive a car in general, but it takes training to drive at high speeds (if you want to do it safely). It's the same with mobile devices—there are nuances from the platform that you need to learn before you have performant code.

.NET is not able to fix the non-coding issues for a platform either. Apple for instance, has fairly strict rules for what they allow apps running on their devices to do. So, if you want to minimize the odds of rejection, when publishing on the App Store, you have some guidelines to read through first.

This is not to discourage you from creating mobile apps or from using .NET for this purpose, but rather we want to highlight how cross-platform can still be complicated, even with the assistance .NET gives you.

Even if you have not been able to test everything that we covered here, you can always refer back to these instructions if you find yourself having more devices for development purposes. While we covered a lot of testing and experimentation, there are some details we did not go into, such as how to debug code that's running on Linux, when you're not using the combination of Visual Studio Code and WSL2. So, next, we will set up things for those use cases where the debugging process requires some extra steps to get working.

Debugging Linux on Windows with Visual Studio 2019

Earlier in this chapter, we created a worker that could run as a worker service, and we ran it through the Remote extension in Visual Studio Code. There are, however, cases where you either cannot do everything you need through Visual Studio Code, or where the Linux host is not even running on the same machine that you will debug from.

This doesn't prevent you from debugging the code running in Linux, but there are an extra couple of hoops to jump through. We will look at using Visual Studio 2019 and connecting over SSH, which is a common protocol for remote connections to a Linux system.

We can still test using WSL2, so in this case we will still connect to our local machine. It is possible to do a similar setup for other Linux distributions. The following instructions are for enabling SSH on the Ubuntu 20.04 that we have already set up:

1. Enable the SSH serve by running the following code:

```
sudo apt-get install openssh-server unzip curl
```

2. Edit sshd_config to allow a password login as following:

```
sudo vi /etc/ssh/sshd_config
```

3. Find the line PasswordAuthentication no and change it to #PasswordAuthentication no. (Press *Insert* to allow editing.)

4. Exit vi by pressing *Esc*, followed by entering :wq.

5. Start the ssh service:

```
sudo service ssh restart
```

6. To check the IP address of the Ubuntu installation that we are using, use the command ip addr. This is the one found attached to inet. In *Figure 2.43*, it is 172.28.88.220:

```
andreas@AH-BOOK2:~$ ip addr
1: lo: <LOOPBACK,UP,LOWER_UP> mtu 65536 qdisc noqueue state UNKNOWN group default
qlen 1000
    link/loopback 00:00:00:00:00:00 brd 00:00:00:00:00:00
    inet 127.0.0.1/8 scope host lo
       valid_lft forever preferred_lft forever
    inet6 ::1/128 scope host
       valid_lft forever preferred_lft forever
2: bond0: <BROADCAST,MULTICAST,MASTER> mtu 1500 qdisc noop state DOWN group defaul
t qlen 1000
    link/ether 8e:16:82:86:c3:b4 brd ff:ff:ff:ff:ff:ff
3: dummy0: <BROADCAST,NOARP> mtu 1500 qdisc noop state DOWN group default qlen 100
0
    link/ether 92:37:7d:7e:84:7e brd ff:ff:ff:ff:ff:ff
4: eth0: <BROADCAST,MULTICAST,UP,LOWER_UP> mtu 1500 qdisc mq state UP group defaul
t qlen 1000
    link/ether 00:15:5d:37:a5:a9 brd ff:ff:ff:ff:ff:ff
    inet 172.28.88.220/20 brd 172.28.95.255 scope global eth0
       valid_lft forever preferred_lft forever
    inet6 fe80::215:5dff:fe37:a5a9/64 scope link
       valid_lft forever preferred_lft forever
5: sit0@NONE: <NOARP> mtu 1480 qdisc noop state DOWN group default qlen 1000
    link/sit 0.0.0.0 brd 0.0.0.0
andreas@AH-BOOK2:~$
```

Figure 2.43 – Verifying the IP address in WSL2

7.   Test that you can connect to the SSH server with the Windows 10 SSH client. See Figure 2.44. The SSH client is an optional feature in Windows, so make sure you have installed it. Then, enter the following command, either from PowerShell or from the command line:

```
ssh user@ipaddress
```

Here's how the output looks like:

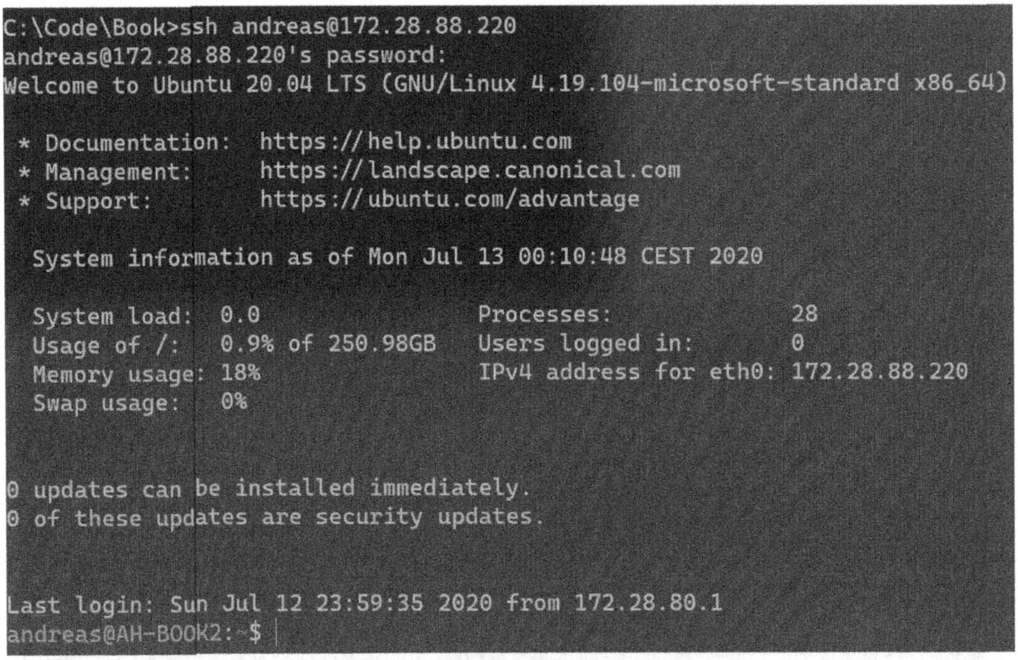

```
C:\Code\Book>ssh andreas@172.28.88.220
andreas@172.28.88.220's password:
Welcome to Ubuntu 20.04 LTS (GNU/Linux 4.19.104-microsoft-standard x86_64)

 * Documentation:  https://help.ubuntu.com
 * Management:     https://landscape.canonical.com
 * Support:        https://ubuntu.com/advantage

  System information as of Mon Jul 13 00:10:48 CEST 2020

  System load:  0.0                Processes:            28
  Usage of /:   0.9% of 250.98GB   Users logged in:       0
  Memory usage: 18%                IPv4 address for eth0: 172.28.88.220
  Swap usage:   0%


0 updates can be installed immediately.
0 of these updates are security updates.


Last login: Sun Jul 12 23:59:35 2020 from 172.28.80.1
andreas@AH-BOOK2:~$
```

Figure 2.44 – Testing the Windows SSH client

Notice that the first line in the screenshot shows a Windows prompt (C:\), whereas the last line shows an Ubuntu shell (andreas@AH-BOOK).

Once this is in place, you can open Visual Studio 2019 and connect to our code:

1.   To start the app you want to debug, open the Linux instance in Windows Terminal and run dotnet run inside the correct folder—in our example, /mnt/c/Code/Book/Chapter_02_Workers.

2.   Make sure it runs without any issues, and then open the same solution in Visual Studio 2019.

3.   Press *Ctrl+Alt+P* to open the **Attach Process** window.

4.   Select SSH as the Connection type.

5. Connect to the same SSH server as when we were testing it. Connect to user@ ipaddress. Refer to *Figure 2.45* as an example of the username and IP address:

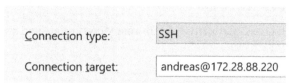

Figure 2.45 – Attach to Process dialog

6. You will be prompted to enter your password as well, and if things work you should see a list of running processes. See the following screenshot:

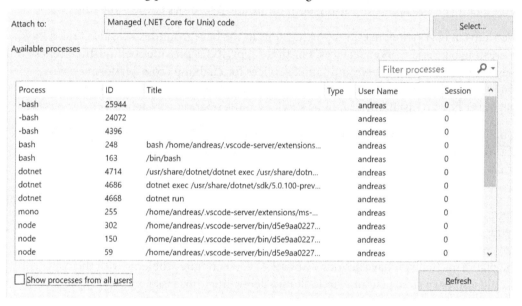

Figure 2.46 – Running processes on the remote host

7. Locate `dotnet run` and click **Attach**.

8. If everything went to plan, you should be able to hit breakpoints, read variables, output, and so on, directly from Visual Studio 2019 on Windows.

> **Windows Firewall**
>
> The first time you open the remote debug dropdown (after opening the **Attach to Process** window), you will be prompted to allow the connections through the Windows Firewall. Accept this to allow the debugger to establish connectivity.

In this case, the Linux instance was running on WSL2, but Visual Studio 2019 does not recognize this as a special case, so it doesn't matter if you attach to a different host. This may not be as simple as Visual Studio Code, but it is useful for the use cases where you need to do more complicated things.

We have gone through cross-platform .NET in many combinations, and this wraps up the current chapter.

Summary

We saw in this chapter that cross-platform can be a complicated topic, but we covered the basic use cases with simple web apps for Linux and macOS, as well as more advanced cross-platform web apps supporting both Linux and Windows at the same time.

Web apps may very well need supporting apps in the background, so we also took a look at creating backend worker services. For these apps, .NET provides behind-the-scenes magic for handling Windows and Linux services for enabling cross-platform services. There were some extra steps involved in installing the application as a service, and we went over how to install these apps as services in the operating system.

Mobile apps for iOS and Android devices are popular, and although they are not the focus of this book, we explored how to get up and running on both of those platforms with the cross-platform capabilities of .NET. We also explained some of the quirks involved in the process.

Rounding off the chapter, we took a look at how you can enable more advanced Linux debugging use cases by demonstrating how Visual Studio 2019 running on Windows can connect to a remote Linux system over SSH. You are now ready to run your code on the platforms that you have at your disposal. If you run into problems with the code, you should also have an idea of how to look into debugging those issues.

In the next chapter, we will go deeper into best practices for the C# language when we explore dependency injection.

Questions

1. On which operating systems can you run .NET 5?

2. What is Windows Subsystem for Linux?

3. What is a self-contained .NET app?

4. When is a time where a cross-platform implementation (with .NET) could become complicated?

Appendix

Earlier in this chapter, we showed you how to install a Windows service on your development machine. This approach was a simplified method that might not work for environments outside your machine. So, here is a more advanced way of configuring an app as a Windows service.

Installing your app as a Windows service – the advanced method

For production use, it is likely that permissions are more fine-grained and locked down. Perform the following steps instead to set up an app as a service:

1. Log on to the Windows server where you will deploy the service.

2. Open a PowerShell prompt, and run the following command: `New-LocalUser -Name dotnetworker`.

3. You need to grant permissions to the service account you just created in order to enable it to start the services. Follow these steps:

    a. Open the **Local Security Policy** editor by running `secpol.msc`.

    b. Expand the **Local Policies** node and select `User Rights Assignment`.

    c. Open the **Login as a service** policy.

    d. Select `Add User` or `Group`.

    e. Provide the name of the service account (`dotnetworker`) using either of the following approaches.

    f. Type the user account (`{DOMAIN OR COMPUTER NAME\USER}`) in the object name field and select `OK` to add the user to the policy.

    g. Select `Advanced`. Select `Find Now`. Select the user account from the list. Select `OK`. Select `OK` again to add the user to the policy.

    h. Select `OK` or `Apply` to accept the changes.

4. Copy the files to the server, such as `C:\dotnetworker\`.

5. Run the following PowerShell cmdlets:

```
$acl = Get-Acl "C:\dotnetworker"

$aclRuleArgs = dotnetworker, "Read,Write,ReadAndExecute",
"ContainerInherit,ObjectInherit", "None", "Allow"

$accessRule = New-Object System.Security.AccessControl.
FileSystemAccessRule($aclRuleArgs)

$acl.SetAccessRule($accessRule)

$acl | Set-Acl "C:\dotnetworker"
```

```
New-Service -Name DotnetWorker -BinaryPathName C:\
dotnetworker\dotnetworker.exe -Credential {SERVERNAME\
dotnetworker} -Description ".NET Worker Service"
-DisplayName ".NET Worker Service" -StartupType Automatic
```

Wait a couple of seconds, and it should have started.

3
Dependency Injection

This chapter talks about **Dependency Injection (DI)** in the context of ASP.NET Core. Moreover, this chapter will get you up to speed with the concept of DI, its capabilities, and how it is used in ASP.NET Core applications. We will review the different types of DI by following code examples so that you will be able to understand how and when to apply them in situations where they may be required. We will also be looking at DI containers, service lifetimes, and how to handle complex scenarios as you progress throughout the chapter. By the end of this chapter, you'll be able to understand how DI works by following some practical examples. You should then be able to apply the knowledge and skills that you have learned to build real-world and powerful ASP.NET Core applications, and take advantage of the benefits that DI has to offer.

Here is the list of topics that we will be covering in this chapter:

- Learning dependency injection in ASP.Net Core
- Reviewing types of dependency injection
- Understanding dependency injection containers
- Understanding dependency lifetimes
- Handling complex scenarios

Technical requirements

This chapter contains code snippets written in C# for demonstrating various scenarios. Please verify that you have installed the required software and tools listed in *Chapter 1, Introduction to ASP.NET Core 5*.

Check out the source code for this chapter at `https://github.com/ PacktPublishing/ASP.NET-Core-5-for-Beginners/tree/master/ Chapter%2003/Chapter_03_DI_Examples`.

Before diving into this chapter, make sure that you read the first two chapters so that you have a basic understanding of ASP.NET Core and C# in general, and how each of them works together.

Please visit the following link to check the CiA videos: `https://bit.ly/3qDiqYY`

If you're ready, let's jump right into it.

Learning dependency injection in ASP.NET Core

To give you a bit of a background, before .NET Core existed, the only way to get DI in your applications was through the use of third-party frameworks such as Autofac, LightInject, Unity, and many others. The good news is that DI is now treated as a first-class citizen in ASP.NET Core. This means that you don't need to do much to make it work.

The built-in Microsoft DI container does have its limitations though. For example, the default DI doesn't enable advanced capabilities, such as property injection decorators, injections based on name, child containers, convention-based registration, and custom lifetime management. So, if you can't find features that you're looking for available in the default DI container, you'll need to consider other third-party DI frameworks mentioned earlier as an alternative. However, it is still recommended to use the default DI framework for building ASP.NET Core applications that don't require you to carry out any specific features. This will reduce your application package dependencies and make your code appear cleaner and more manageable without having to rely on third-party frameworks. The .NET Core team did a pretty good job of providing us with the most common features and you probably won't need anything else.

In this section, we'll do some hands-on coding for you to enable a better understand the advantages of DI. We'll start by looking at a common problem and then apply DI to solve the problem.

Understanding what DI is

There is a plethora of information on the web that defines DI, but a simple definition is as follows:

"Dependency injection is a design pattern that enables developers to write loosely coupled code."

In other words, DI helps you to write clean and more maintainable code by solving dependency problems. DI makes it easy to mock object dependencies for unit testing and makes your application more flexible by swapping or replacing dependencies without having to change the consuming classes. In fact, the core foundation of ASP.NET Core frameworks relies heavily on DI, as shown in the following diagram:

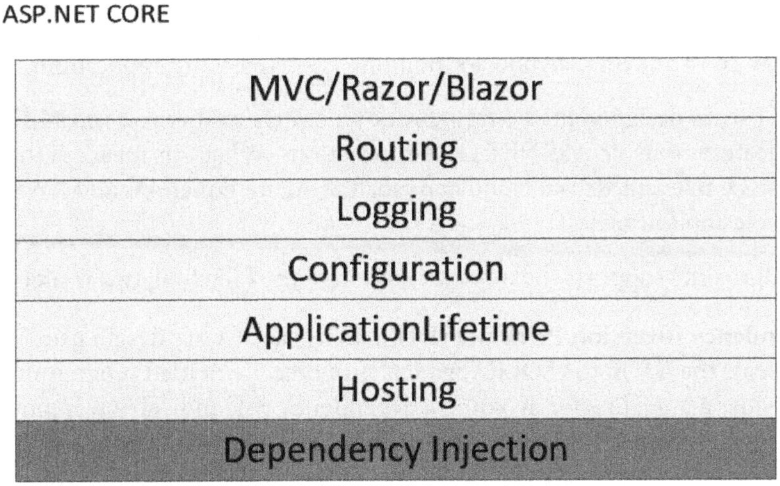

ASP.NET CORE

MVC/Razor/Blazor
Routing
Logging
Configuration
ApplicationLifetime
Hosting
Dependency Injection

Figure 3.1 – ASP.NET Core framework-provided services

All framework-provided services, such as **Hosting**, **Configuration**, **ApplicationLifetime**, **Logging**, **Routing**, and many others use DI under the hood, and they are, by default, registered to the DI container when the application web host is built.

The default DI in .NET Core sits under the `Microsoft.Extensions.DependencyInjection` namespace, whose implementation is packed into a separate NuGet package (you can learn more at `https://www.nuget.org/packages/Microsoft.Extensions.DependencyInjection/`).

When you create an ASP.NET Core application from the default template, the application references the `Microsoft.AspNetCore.App` NuGet package, as shown in the following screenshot:

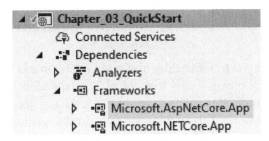

Figure 3.2 – Microsoft.AspNetCore.App NuGet package

This assembly provides a set of APIs, including the `Microsoft.Extensions.DependencyInjection` assembly for building ASP.NET Core applications.

The ASP.NET team designed the DI framework separately so that you will still be able to leverage its features outside ASP.NET Core applications. What this means is that you will be able to use DI in event-driven cloud apps such as Azure Functions and AWS Lamda, or even in console applications.

The use of DI mainly supports the implementation of the following two related concepts:

- **Dependency Inversion Principle (DIP)**: This is a software design principle and represents the "D" in the SOLID principles of object-oriented programming. It provides a guideline for avoiding a dependency risk and solving common dependency problems. However, this principle doesn't state any specific technique for you to implement.

- **Inversion of Control (IoC)**: This is a technique that follows the DIP guidelines. This concept is the process of creating application components in a detached state, preventing higher-level components from having direct access to lower-level components, and allowing them to only interact via abstractions.

DI is an implementation technique that follows the concept of IoC. It enables you to access lower-level components from a higher-level component through component injections. DI follows two SOLID principles: DIP and the **Single Responsibility Principle (SRP)**. These concepts are crucial for creating well-designed and well-decoupled applications, and you should consider applying them in any situation where required. Check out the *Further reading* section at the end of this chapter to learn more about the SOLID principles.

You may have heard these terms and concepts and you still find them confusing. Well, here is an analogy that might help you better understand them.

Let's say you are making your own song and you wanted to upload it on the web so that your friends can watch and hear it. You can think of the DIP as a way to record music. It doesn't matter how you record the song. You could use a video recorder, a camera, a smartphone, or a studio recorder. IoC is choosing how you would actually record your music and polish it with the help of some tools. For example, you can use a combination of audio and camera recorders to record your song. Typically, they are recorded as raw files. You would then use an editor tool to filter and polish the raw files to come up with a great output. Now, if you wanted to add some effects, text visualization, or graphics background, then that's where DI comes into play. It allows you to inject whatever files your file depends on to generate the output you expect. Keep in mind that in this analogy, both IoC and DI rely on using the editor tool to generate the ultimate output (high-level component) based on raw files (low-level component). In other words, both IoC and DI refer to the same concept by using the editor tools to improve your video output.

To illustrate this, let's look at a brief example.

The common dependency problem

Consider we have the following page that displays a list of music in a typical MVC web application:

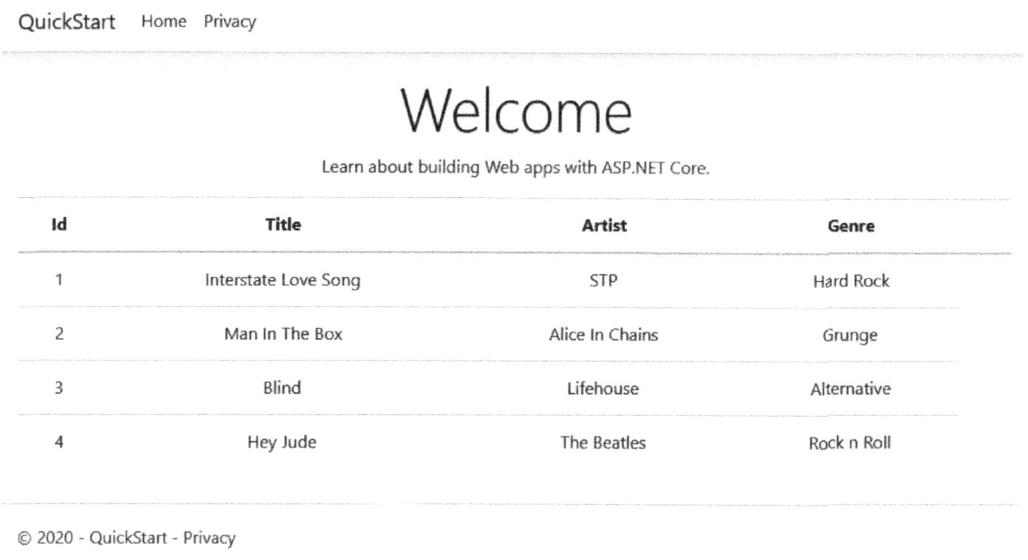

Figure 3.3 – The music list page

Let's break down how we came up with the result shown in the previous screenshot. For your quick reference, here's the class called `MusicManager`, which exposes a method for obtaining the list of music:

```csharp
using Chapter_03_QuickStart.Models;
using System.Collections.Generic;


namespace Chapter_03_QuickStart.DataManager
{
    public class MusicManager
    {
        public List<SongModel> GetAllMusic()
        {
            return new List<SongModel>
            {
                new SongModel { Id = 1, Title = "Interstate
                Love Song", Artist ="STP",
                Genre = "Hard Rock" },
                new SongModel { Id = 2, Title = "Man In The
                Box", Artist ="Alice In Chains",
                Genre = "Grunge" },
                new SongModel { Id = 3, Title = "Blind", Artist
                ="Lifehouse", Genre = "Alternative" },
                new SongModel { Id = 4, Title = "Hey Jude",
                Artist ="The Beatles", Genre = "Rock n Roll" }
            };
        }
    }
}
```

The preceding code is nothing but a plain class that contains a method, `GetAllMusic()`. This method is responsible for returning all music entries from the list. The implementation could vary depending on your data store, and you could be pulling them from a database or via an API call. However, for this example, we just return a static list of data for simplicity's sake.

The SongModel class lives inside the Models folder with the following structure:

```
namespace Chapter_03_QuickStart.Models
{
    public class SongModel
    {
        public int Id { get; set; }
        public string Title { get; set; }
        public string Artist { get; set; }
        public string Genre { get; set; }
    }
}
```

Nothing fancy. The preceding code is just a dumb class that houses some properties that the View expects.

Without DI, we would normally call a method from a class directly into the Controller class to render View, as shown in the following code block:

```
public IActionResult Index()
{
    MusicManager musicManager = new MusicManager();
    var songs = musicManager.GetAllMusic();

    return View(songs);
}
```

The Index() method in the preceding code will be invoked when you perform an HTTP GET request. The method is responsible for rendering the data into the View. You can see that it creates an instance of the MusicManager class by invoking the new operator. This is known as a "dependency" because the Index() method is now dependent on the MusicManager object for fetching the required data.

Here is a high-level graphical representation of what the code logic is doing:

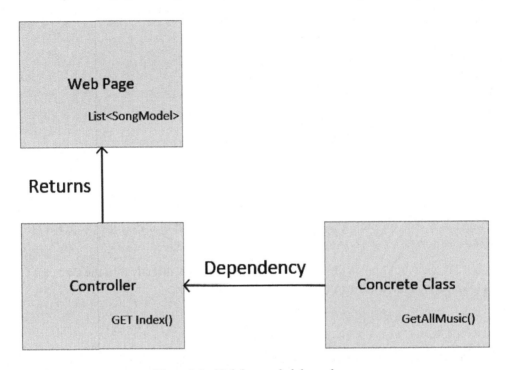

Figure 3.4 – Tightly-coupled dependency

In the preceding diagram, the Controller box represents the higher-level component where it refers to the concrete class implementation as a direct dependency, which represents the lower-level component.

While the existing implementation works, this approach could result in making your code difficult to manage because the object is tightly coupled to the method itself. Imagine you have a bunch of methods that rely on the MusicManager object and when you rename it or change its implementation in the future, you would be forced to update all your methods that depend on that object, which could be harder to maintain and problematic when it comes to unit testing your Controllers. Be aware that refactoring bad code can be time-consuming and expensive, so it is better do it correctly from the outset.

The ideal approach for avoiding such a mess is to clean up our code and take advantage of using interfaces and DI.

Making use of DI

To resolve the dependency problem that our `HomeController` had, we need to do a little bit of code refactoring. Here's a graphical illustration of the goal that we are aiming for:

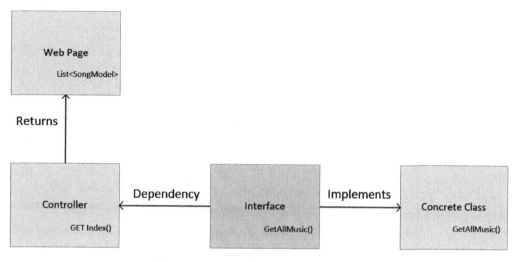

Figure 3.5 – Loosely-coupled dependency

As you can see from the preceding diagram, we just need to create an interface to resolve the dependency problem. This approach avoids the direct dependency to the lower-level component and instead, it creates an abstraction that both components depend on. This now makes the `Controller` class more testable and extensible, and makes the application more maintainable.

Let's proceed and start creating an interface. There are two ways to create an interface: Either you create it yourself or use the built-in refactoring features provided by Visual Studio 2019. Since we already have an existing class that we wanted to extract as an interface, using the refactoring feature makes a lot of sense. To do this, you need to perform the following steps:

1. Just simply right-click on the `MusicManager` class and select **Quick Actions and Refactorings...**, as shown in the following screenshot:

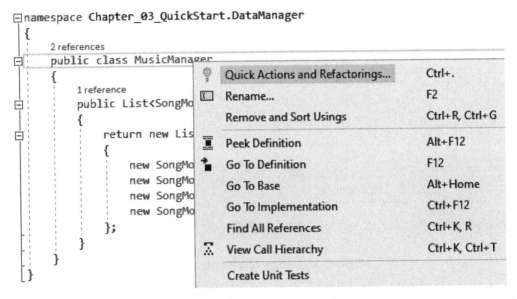

Figure 3.6 – The built-in Quick Actions and Refactorings feature

2. Then, select **Extract interface…**:

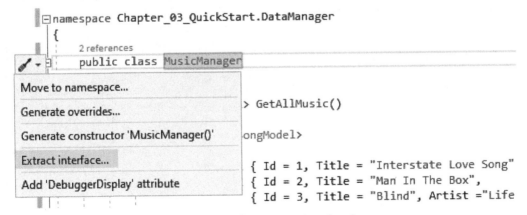

Figure 3.7 – The built-in Extract interface feature

3. Now, you should be presented with a pop-up dialog to configure the interface, as shown in the following screenshot:

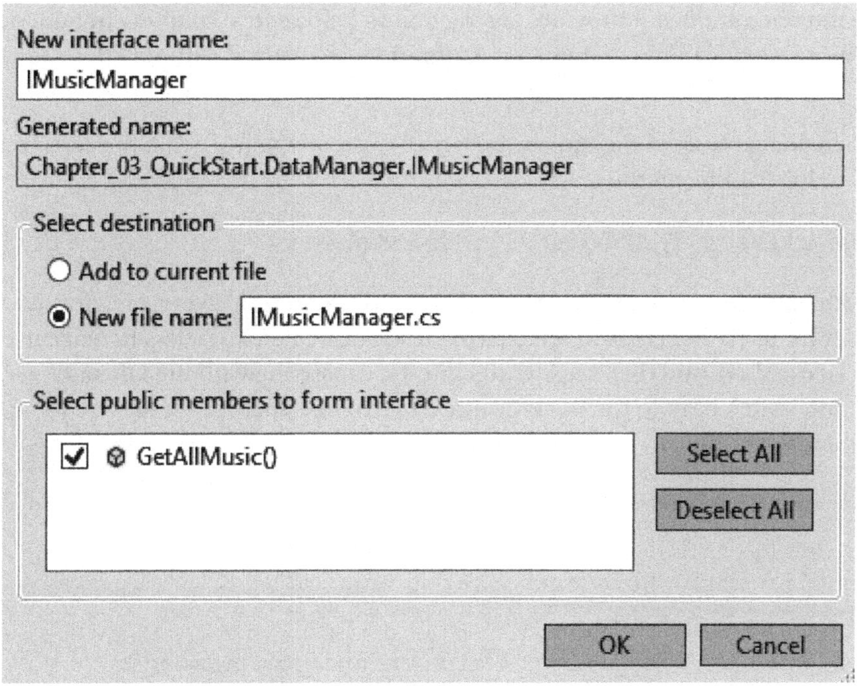

New interface name:

IMusicManager

Generated name:

Chapter_03_QuickStart.DataManager.IMusicManager

Select destination

○ Add to current file

◉ New file name: IMusicManager.cs

Select public members to form interface

☑ ⊗ GetAllMusic()   Select All

Deselect All

OK   Cancel

Figure 3.8 – The Extract Interface pop-up window

4. You could change the default configuration if you like, but for this exercise, let's just stick with the defaults and click on **OK**. Here's the generated code that is created automatically by Visual Studio:

```
using Chapter_03_QuickStart.Models;
using System.Collections.Generic;


namespace Chapter_03_QuickStart.DataManager
{
    public interface IMusicManager
    {
        List<SongModel> GetAllMusic();
    }
}
```

The preceding code is just a simple interface with the `GetAllMusic()` method signature that returns a type of `List<SongModel>`. We won't deep dive into the details of interfaces in this book, but to give you a brief overview, a couple of benefits associated with the interface are that it provides abstraction to help reduce coupling in our code and enables us to provide different implementations for the method without affecting other classes.

Now, when you go back to the `MusicManager` class, you will see that the class has been updated to inherit the interface:

```
public class MusicManager : IMusicManager
```

Neat! With just a few clicks, Visual Studio automatically sets up everything for us. What's left for us to do here is to refactor the `HomeController` class to make use of the interface and DI, and then register the interface mapping with the DI container. Let's proceed and switch back to the `HomeController` class and update the code so that it will look similar to this:

```
namespace Chapter_03_QuickStart.Controllers
{
    public class HomeController : Controller
    {
        private readonly IMusicManager _musicManager;
        public HomeController(IMusicManager musicManager)
        {
            _musicManager = musicManager;
        }

        public IActionResult Index()
        {
            var songs = _musicManager.GetAllMusic();
            return View(songs);
        }
    }
}
```

The preceding code first defines a private `read-only` field of the `IMusicManager` interface type. Making it `read-only` and `private` is considered the best practice, as this prevents you from accidentally assigning the field to a different value within your `class`. The next line of code defines the `constructor` class and uses the "constructor injection" approach to initialize the dependency object. In this case, any methods within the `HomeController` class will be able to access the `_musicManager` field and invoke all its available methods and properties. We'll talk more about the different types of DI later in this chapter.

The current code now supports the DI pattern since we are no longer passing concrete dependency to the `Controller` methods when the class is constructed. With the interface abstraction, we no longer need to create a new instance of the concrete class to directly reference the `GetAllMusic()` method. But instead, we reference the `interface` field to access the method. In other words, our method is now loosely coupled with the actual class implementation. This helps us to maintain our code more easily and perform unit tests conveniently. Let's move on and register the interface mapping with the DI container next.

Registering the service

Go ahead and navigate to the `Startup.cs` file and then add the following code within the `ConfigureServices()` method:

```
public void ConfigureServices(IServiceCollection services)
{
    services.AddTransient<IMusicManager, MusicManager>();

    //register other services here
}
```

The preceding code registers the `IMusicManager` interface as the service type and maps the `MusicManager` concrete class as the implementation type in the DI container. This tells the framework to resolve the required dependency that has been injected into the `HomeController` class constructor at runtime. The beauty of DI is that it allows you to change whatever component that you want for as long as it implements the interface. What this means is that you can always replace the `MucisManager` class mapping to something else for as long as it implements the `IMusicManager` interface without impacting the `HomeController` implementation.

The `ConfigureServices()` method is responsible for defining the services that the application uses, including platform features, such as Entity Framework Core, authentication, your own service, or even third-party services. Initially, the `IServiceCollection` interface provided to the `ConfigureServices()` method has services defined by the framework, including `Hosting`, `Configuration`, and `Logging`. We'll talk more about DI containers later in this chapter.

Benefits of DI

As you have learned from our previous example, DI entails many benefits that make your ASP.NET Core application easy to maintain and evolve. These benefits include the following:

- It promotes the loose coupling of components.
- It helps in separation of concerns.
- It promotes the logical abstractions of components.
- It facilitates unit testing.
- It promotes clean and more readable code, which makes code maintenance manageable.

Having learned what DI is and discussed its benefits, we'll now move on to discuss its types in the next section.

Reviewing types of dependency injection

There are a few options when it comes to implementing DI within your ASP.NET Core applications, and these include the following approaches:

- Constructor injection
- Method injection
- Property injection
- View injection

Let's talk about each type in detail in the coming sections.

Constructor injection

We've seen how we can implement **constructor injection** earlier in our music list example. But to recap, this approach basically allows you to inject lower-level dependent components into your class by passing them into the `constructor` class as arguments.

This approach is the most commonly used when building ASP.NET Core applications. In fact, when you create an ASP.NET Core MVC project from the default template, you will see that DI is, by default, integrated. You can verify this yourself by looking into the `HomeController` class and you should see the `ILogger` interface being injected into the class constructor, as shown in the following code:

```
public class HomeController : Controller
{
    private readonly ILogger<HomeController> _logger;

    public HomeController(ILogger<HomeController> logger)
    {
        _logger = logger;
    }
}
```

In the preceding code, notice that the concept is very much similar to our previous example when we swapped out the `MusicManager` class reference with the `IMusicManager` interface to perform DI.

The `ILogger<HomeController>` interface is registered by the logging abstraction's infrastructure and is registered by default in the framework as a `Singleton` as follows:

```
services.AddSingleton(typeof(ILogger<>), typeof(Logger<>));
```

The preceding code registers the service as a `Singleton` and uses the generic open types technique. This allows the DI container to resolve dependencies without having to explicitly register services with generic constructed types.

Method injection

Method injection is another DI approach that allows you to inject lower-level dependent components as arguments into the method. In other words, dependent objects will be passed into the method instead of passing them into the class constructor. Implementing method injection is very helpful when various methods in your class need to invoke a child object dependency to complete their job. A typical example is writing to different log formats based on which methods are invoked. Let's take an actual example for you to better understand this approach.

Let's extend our previous example about the music list, but this time, we are going to implement something like a notifier to demonstrate method or function injection.

To start off, create a new interface called `INotifier`, as shown in the following code block:

```
namespace Chapter_03_QuickStart.DataManager
{
    public interface INotifier
    {
        bool SendMessage(string message);
    }
}
```

In the preceding code, we have defined a simple interface that contains a single method called `SendMessage`. The method accepts a `string` parameter that represents a message, and returns a `boolean` type to determine whether the operation has succeeded or failed. It is as simple as that.

Now, let's proceed by creating a concrete class that implements the `INotifier` interface. Here's what the class declaration looks like:

```
namespace Chapter_03_QuickStart.DataManager
{
    public class Notifier : INotifier
    {
        public bool SendMessage(string message)
        {
            //some logic here to publish the message

            return true;
```

```
        }
    }
}
```

The preceding code shows how the `SendMessage()` method is implemented. Notice that there's really no logic implemented within the method other than returning the `boolean` value of `true`. That was intentional because the implementation is irrelevant to this topic, and we don't want to draw your attention to that area. However, in real applications, you might create different classes to implement the logic for sending the message. For example, you could use message queues, pub/sub, Event Bus, email, SMS, or even a REST API call to broadcast the messages.

Now that we have our notifier object abstracted via an interface. Let's modify the `IMusicManager` interface to include a new method called `GetAllMusicThenNotify`. The updated `IMusicManager.cs` file should now look like this:

```
using Chapter_03_QuickStart.Models;
using System.Collections.Generic;


namespace Chapter_03_QuickStart.DataManager
{
    public interface IMusicManager
    {
        List<SongModel> GetAllMusic();
        List<SongModel> GetAllMusicThenNotify(INotifier
            notifier);
    }
}
```

Notice that the `GetAllMusicThenNotify()` method also returns a `List` of `SongModel` objects, but this time, we are passing the `INotifier` interface as an argument.

Let's continue by implementing the `GetAllMusicThenNotify()` method within the `MusicManager` class. Here's the code implementation of the method:

```
public List<SongModel> GetAllMusicThenNotify(INotifier
notifier)
{
    //invoke the notifier method
```

```
var success = notifier.SendMessage("User viewed the music
    list page.");


//return the response
return success
        ? GetAllMusic()
        : Enumerable.Empty<SongModel>().ToList();


}
```

The preceding code invokes the `SendMessage()` method of the `INotifier` interface and then passes the message as the parameter/argument. This process is called method injection because we have injected the `INotifier` interface into the `GetAllMusicThenNotify()` method, without having to instantiate the concrete implementation of the notifier object. Keep in mind that in this particular example, the `SendMessage()` method will always return `true` just to simulate the process and doesn't contain any actual implementation. This simply means that the value of the `success` variable will always be `true`.

The second line in the preceding code returns the response and uses the C# *ternary conditional operator* (`? :`) to evaluate what data the method should return based on the expression value. The `Ternary` operator is the simplified syntax of the `if-else` statement. In this case, we invoke the `GetAllMusic()` method to return the entire list of music if the value of the `success` variable is true, otherwise we return an empty list using the `Enumerable.Empty<T>` method.

For more information about ternary operators and the `Enumerable.Empty` LINQ extension method, refer to `https://docs.microsoft.com/en-us/dotnet/api/system.linq.enumerable.empty`.

Now, the final step to perform is to update the `Index()` action method in the `HomeController` class to make use of the `GetAllMusicThenNotify()` method. Here's the updated version of the method:

```
public IActionResult Index()
{

    var songs = _musicManager.GetAllMusicThenNotify(new
        Notifier());
    return View(songs);

}
```

Notice in the preceding code that we are now passing the concrete instance of the notifier object. The `GetAllMusicThenNotify()` method will automatically resolve it because the concrete instance implements the `INotifier` interface.

To better understand how the dots connect to the picture, here's a high-level graphical representation of what we just did:

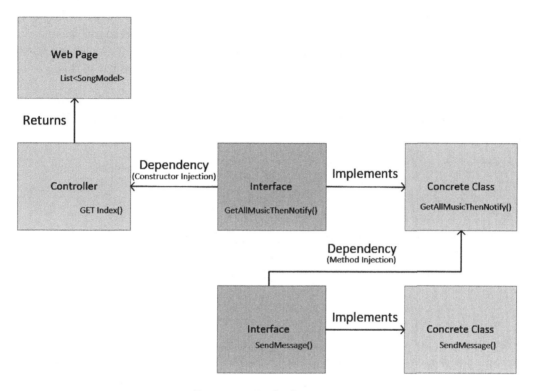

Figure 3.9 – Method injection

The important boxes in the preceding diagram are the *Interface* boxes. This is because abstracting your implementation via the interface enables you to avoid direct class access, and decouples various implementations in different classes. For example, if business requirements arise and ask you to implement different forms of notification based on different events, you could easily create `SMSNotifier`, `MessageQueueNotifier`, and `EmailNotifier` that implement the `INotifier` interface. Then, perform whatever logic it requires to fulfill the business needs separately. While you may still be able to accomplish method injection without the use of an interface, chances are that it makes your code messy and very difficult to manage. Without using an interface, you would end up creating different methods for each of your notification classes, which leads you to back to unit tests and code maintenance issues.

Property injection

Property injection (or **setter injection**) allows you to reference a lower-level dependent component as a `property` in your class. You would only use this approach in case the dependency is truly optional. In other words, your service can still work properly without these dependencies provided.

Let's take another example using our existing music list sample. This time, we will update the `Notifier` sample to use property injection instead of method injection. The first thing that we need to do in order to make this happen is to update the `IMusicManager` interface. Go ahead and replace the existing code so that it will look similar to this:

```
using Chapter_03_QuickStart.Models;
using System.Collections.Generic;


namespace Chapter_03_QuickStart.DataManager
{
    public interface IMusicManager
    {
        INotifier Notify { get; set; }
        List<SongModel> GetAllMusic();
        List<SongModel> GetAllMusicThenNotify();
    }
}
```

What we did in the preceding code is that we added a new property called `Notify` and then modified the `GetAllMusicThenNotify()` method by removing the `INotifier` parameter.

Next, let's update the `MusicManager` class to reflect the changes in the `IMusicManager` interface. The updated class should now look like this:

```
using Chapter_03_QuickStart.Models;
using System.Collections.Generic;
using System.Linq;


namespace Chapter_03_QuickStart.DataManager
{
    public class MusicManager : IMusicManager
    {
        public INotifier Notify { get; set; };
```

```
public List<SongModel> GetAllMusic()
{
    //removed code for brevity
}

public List<SongModel> GetAllMusicThenNotify()
{
    // Check if the Notify property has been set
    if (Notify != default)
    {
        //invoke the notifier method
        Notify.SendMessage("User viewed the music list
            page.");

    }

    //return list of music
    return GetAllMusic();
    }
    }
}
```

In the preceding code, we've implemented the Notify property, which returns an INotifier interface type using C#'s **auto-implemented property** feature. If you are not familiar with auto-properties, it basically makes property declaration more concise when no additional logic is required in the property accessors. What this means is that the following line of code:

```
public INotifier Notify { get; set; }
```

Is equivalent to the following code:

```
private INotifier _notifier;
public INotifier Notify
{
    get { return _notifier };
    set { _notifier = value };
}
```

The preceding code can also be rewritten using **Expression-Bodied Property Accessors**, which was introduced in C# 7.0 as follows:

```
private INotifier _notifier;
public INotifier Notify
{
    get => _notifier;
    set => _notifier = value;
}
```

You may use the preceding code when you need to set properties with different implementations. However, in the case of our example, using auto-properties makes more sense as it's cleaner.

Going back to our example, we need to implement the Notify property so that the HomeController class would be able to set its value before invoking the GetAllMusicThenNotify() method.

The GetAllMusicThenNotify() method is pretty much straightforward. First, it checks whether the Notify property has been set or is not null. The default keyword value of any reference type is null. In other words, validating against null or default doesn't matter here. Without the null validation check, you will end up getting a NullReferenceException error when the property is not set. So, it's a best practice to always check for nulls. Now, if the Notify property is not null, we then invoke the SendMessage() method. Finally, we return the list of music to the caller.

The final step that we need to modify is the Index() method of HomeController. Here's what the updated code looks like:

```
public IActionResult Index()
{
    _musicManager.Notify = new Notifier();
```

```
    var songs = _musicManager.GetAllMusicThenNotify();
    return View(songs);
}
```

The preceding code sets the Notify property with a new instance of the Notifier class. It then invokes the GetAllMusicThenNotify() method and finally returns the result to the View.

Here's a high-level graphical representation of what we just did:

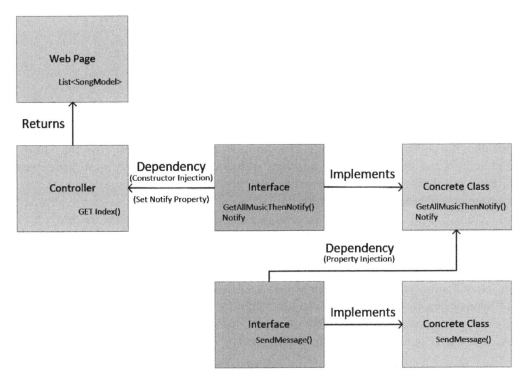

Figure 3.10 – Property injection

The important thing to note in this approach is that even if we don't set the Notify property, the Index() method will still work and returns the data to View. In summary, you should only use property injection when integrating optional features in your code.

View injection

View injection is another DI approach supported by ASP.NET Core. This feature was introduced in ASP.NET MVC 6, the first version of ASP.NET Core (previously known as ASP.NET 5), using the `@inject` directive. The `@inject` directive allows you to inject some method calls from a class or service directly into your `View`. This can be useful for view-specific services, such as localization or data required only for populating view elements.

Let's jump ahead with some examples. Now, add the following method within the `MusicManager` class:

```
public async Task<int> GetMusicCount()
{
    return await Task.FromResult(GetAllMusic().Count);
}
```

The preceding code is an asynchronous method that returns a `Task` of `int`. While this book does not cover C# asynchronous programming in depth, perhaps providing a little bit of background about it is useful. The logic within the method simply returns the count of items from the `GetAllMusic()` result. The value of `Count` is obtained using the `Count` property of the `List` collection. Since the method expects a `Task` to be returned, and the `GetAllMusic()` method returns a `List` type, then the result is wrapped inside the `Task.FromResult()` call. It then uses the `await` operator to wait for the `async` method to complete the task, and then asynchronously returns the result to the caller when the process is complete. In other words, the `await` keyword is where things can get asynchronous. The `async` keyword enables the `await` keyword in that method and changes how method results are handled. In other words, the `async` keyword only enables the `await` keyword. For more information about C#'s `async` and `await` keywords, check out the reference links at the end of this chapter.

The next step that we need to perform in order for it to work is to register the `MusicManager` class as a service in the `ConfigureServices()` method of the `Startup.cs` file:

```
public void ConfigureServices(IServiceCollection services)
{
    services.AddTransient<MusicManager>();

    //register other services here
}
```

In the preceding code, we have registered the service as `Transient`. This means that every time the dependency is requested, a new instance of the service will be created. We'll talk more about service lifetimes in the *Understanding dependency lifetimes* section of this chapter.

Now, here's how you would inject the `MusicManager` class as a service in the `View`:

```
@inject Chapter_03_QuickStart.DataManager.MusicManager
MusicService
```

And here's the code for referencing the `GetMusicCount()` method that we added earlier:

```
Total Songs: <h2>@await MusicService.GetMusicCount()</h2>
```

The `@` symbol is a **Razor implicit syntax** that allows you to use C# code in the `View`. We'll deep dive into Razor in the next chapter.

Here is a sample screenshot of the output after a service has been injected into the `View`:

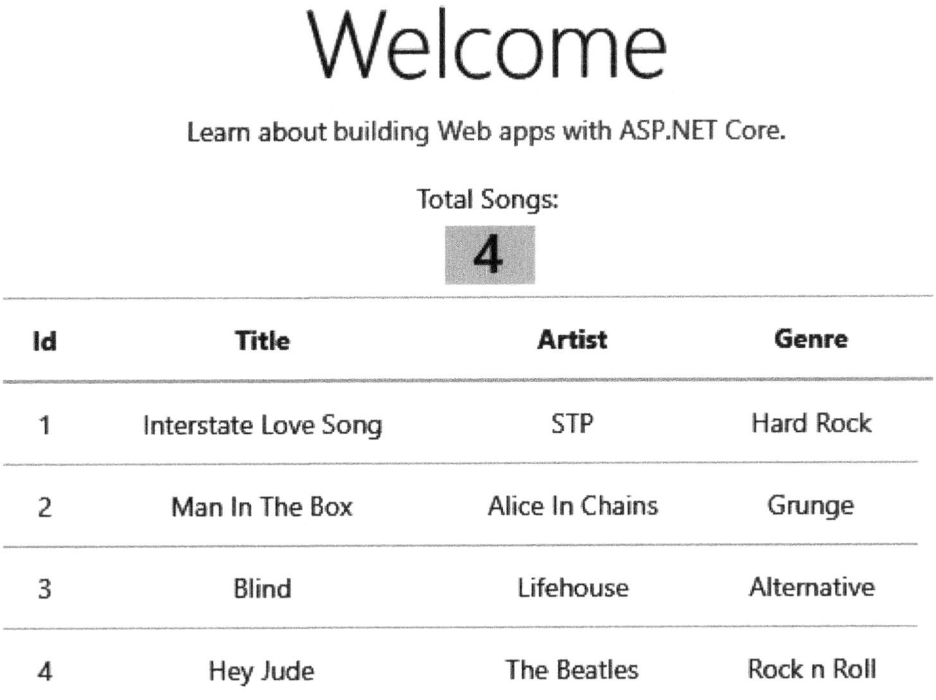

Welcome

Learn about building Web apps with ASP.NET Core.

Total Songs:
4

Id	Title	Artist	Genre
1	Interstate Love Song	STP	Hard Rock
2	Man In The Box	Alice In Chains	Grunge
3	Blind	Lifehouse	Alternative
4	Hey Jude	The Beatles	Rock n Roll

Figure 3.11 – View injection output

Notice that the value of 4 has been printed on the page. That's the value returned from the `GetMusicCount()` method. Keep in mind that while using this technique might be useful, you should consider separating your `View` and `Controller` logic to value the separation of concerns. In practice, it's recommended to generate the data from your `Controller`; the `View` should not care how and where the data was processed.

Now that we've seen the different types of DI and learned when to use them, we'll move on to discuss DI containers in the next section.

Understanding dependency injection containers

The **dependency injection container** is not really a requirement to apply the DI technique. However, using it can simplify the management of all of your dependencies, including their lifetimes, as your application grows and becomes more complex.

.NET Core comes with a built-in DI/IoC container that simplifies DI management. In fact, the default ASP.NET Core application template uses DI extensively. You can see it by looking at the `Startup` class of your ASP.NET Core application:

```
public class Startup
{
    public IConfiguration Configuration { get; }

    public Startup(IConfiguration configuration)
    {
        Configuration = configuration;
    }

    public void ConfigureServices(IServiceCollection services)
    {
        // This method gets called by the runtime.
        // Use this method to add services to the container.
    }

    public void Configure(IApplicationBuilder app,
                          IWebHostEnvironment env)
    {
        // This method gets called by the runtime.
```

```
            // Use this method to configure the HTTP request
            // and middleware pipeline.
    }
}
```

In the preceding code, the IConfiguration interface has been passed to the Startup class constructor using the constructor injection approach. This allows you to get access to the configuration values defined in the appsettings.json file. You don't need to register IConfiguration yourself as the framework takes care of this for you when the Host is configured. You can see how this is being done by looking at the CreateHostBuilder() method of the Program class:

```
public static IHostBuilder CreateHostBuilder(string[] args) =>
    Host.CreateDefaultBuilder(args)
        .ConfigureWebHostDefaults(webBuilder =>
        {
            webBuilder.UseStartup<Startup>();
        });
```

The CreateDefaultBuilder() method in the preceding code initializes a new instance of the WebHostBuilder class with pre-configured defaults, including Hosting, Configurations, and Logging. Ultimately, the ConfigureWebHostDefaults() method adds everything else needed for a typical ASP.NET Core application, such as configuring Kestrel and using the Startup class to configure your DI container and middleware pipeline.

Keep in mind that you can only inject certain services into the Startup class constructor, and these include IWebHostEnvironment, IhostEnvironment, and IConfiguration.

Other services must be registered to the DI container when the application starts. This process is done by adding services to `IServiceCollection`:

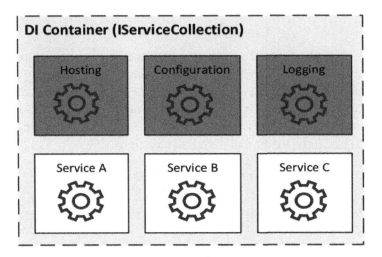

Figure 3.12 – The DI container

In .NET Core, the dependencies managed by the container are called services. Any services that we expect to be injected into the container must be added to `IServiceCollection` so that the service provider will be able to resolve the services at runtime. Under the hood, the Microsoft built-in DI container implements the `IServiceProvider` interface. It's really not ideal to build your own IoC/DI container framework, but if you do, the `IServiceProvider` interface is what you should look at.

`IServiceCollection` has two main types of services:

- **Framework-provided services**: These represent the purple boxes from the preceding diagram, which are part of the .NET Core framework and registered by default. These services include `Hosting`, `Configuration`, `Logging`, `HttpContext`, and many others.

- **Application services**: These represent the white boxes. This type of services refers to the services that you create and use in your ASP.NET Core application that is not part of the framework itself. Since these services are typically created by you, then you need to manually register them in the DI container so that they will be resolved when the application starts. An example of this type of service is our `IMusicManager` interface sample.

The DI container manages the instantiation and configuration of the services registered. Typically, this process is executed in three steps:

1. **Registration**: The services that you want to be injected into different areas of your application need to be registered first so that the DI container framework will know which implementation type to map the service to. A great example of this is when we mapped the IMusicManager interface to the concrete class implementation called MusicManager. Generally, service registrations are configured in the ConfigureServices() method of the Startup.cs file, as in the following code:

```
public void ConfigureServices(IServiceCollection
services)
{
    services.AddTransient<IMusicManager, MusicManager>();
}
```

2. **Resolution**: This is where the DI container automatically resolves the dependency when the application starts by creating an object instance and injecting it into the class. Based on our previous example, this is where we inject the IMusicManager interface into the HomeController class constructor using the constructor injection approach, as shown in the following code:

```
private readonly IMusicManager _musicManager;

public HomeController(IMusicManager musicManager)
{
    _musicManager = musicManager;
}
```

3. **Disposition**: When registering services, the DI container framework also needs to know the lifetime of the dependencies so it can manage them correctly. Based on our previous example regarding the constructor injection approach, this is where we register the interface mapping as a Transient service in the ConfigureServices() method of the Startup.cs file.

For more information about the ASP.NET Core fundamentals and how the default Microsoft DI container works under the hood, refer to the official documentation here: https://docs.microsoft.com/en-us/aspnet/core/fundamentals/dependency-injection.

Now that we've understood how the DI works, let's move on to the next section to talk about service lifetimes.

Understanding dependency lifetimes

If you're completely new to ASP.NET Core, or haven't worked with ASP.NET Core for a long time, or if you're an experienced ASP.NET developer but don't really look into dependency lifetimes in detail, the chances are you might be using just one type of dependency lifetime to register all your services when building ASP.NET Core applications. This is because you are confused as to which service lifetime to use, and you wanted to play it safe. Well, that's understandable, because choosing which type of service lifetime to use can be confusing sometimes. Hopefully, this section will give you a better understanding of the different types of lifetimes that you can use within your application and decide when to use each option.

There are primarily three service lifetimes in ASP.NET Core DI:

- Transient

- Scoped

- Singleton

Transient service

The `AddTransient()` method is probably what you were using most often. If that is the case, then that's a good call because this type is the safest option to use when in doubt. **Transient** services are created each time they are requested. In other words, if you register your service with a transient lifetime, you will get a new object whenever you invoke it as a dependency, regardless of whether it is a new request or the same. This lifetime works best for lightweight and stateless services as they are disposed at the end of the request.

Let's take a look at an example for you to better understand how transient service lifetime works. We'll use the existing music list example for ease of reference. The first thing we need to do is add the following property to the `IMusicManager` interface:

```
Guid RequestId { get; set; }
```

The preceding code is just a simple property that returns a **Globally Unique Identifier (GUID)**. We'll use this property to determine how each dependency behaves.

Now, let's implement the `RequestId` property in the `MusicManager` class by adding the following code to the existing code:

```
public Guid RequestId { get; set; }
```

```
public MusicManager(): this(Guid.NewGuid()) {}
```

```
public MusicManager(Guid requestId)
{
    RequestId = requestId;
}
```

In the preceding code, we've implemented the `RequestId` property from the `IMusicManager` interface and then defined two new constructors. The first constructor sets a new `GUID` value, and the second constructor initializes the `GUID` value to the `RequestId` property by applying the constructor injection approach. Without the first `constructor`, the DI container won't be able to resolve the dependency that we've configured in the `HomeController` class when the application starts.

To demonstrate multiple dependency references, let's create a new class called `InstrumentalMusicManager` and then copy the following code:

```
using System;

namespace Chapter_03_QuickStart.DataManager
{
    public class InstrumentalMusicManager
    {

        private readonly IMusicManager _musicManager;

        public Guid RequestId { get; set; }

        public InstrumentalMusicManager(IMusicManager
            musicManager)
        {
            RequestId = musicManager.RequestId;
        }
```

```
        }
}
```

In the preceding code, we've also applied the `Constructor Injection` approach by injecting the `IMusicManager` interface as an object dependency into the class. We then initialized the value of the `RequestId` property, just like what we did in the `MusicManager` class. The only differences between the `InstrumentalMusicManager` and `MusicManager` classes are the following:

1. The `InstrumentalMusicManager` class doesn't implement the `IMusicManager` interface. This was intentional because we are only interested in the `RequestId` property and to make this demo as simple as possible.

2. The `InstrumentalMusicManager` class doesn't have a setter constructor. The reason for this is that we will let the `MusicManager` class set the value. By injecting the `IMusicManager` interface into the constructor, we will be able to reference the value of the `RequestId` property from it since the `MusicManager` class implements this interface, although the value of the property will vary depending on how the service is registered with the type of lifetime, which we will see in action later.

Now, navigate to the `Startup` class and update the `ConfigureServices()` method so that it will look similar to the following code:

```
public void ConfigureServices(IServiceCollection services)
{
    services.AddTransient<IMusicManager, MusicManager>();
    services.AddTransient<InstrumentalMusicManager>();

    // Removed for brevity. Register other services here
}
```

In the preceding code, we've registered both services as transient services. Notice that we opted out of the second parameter of the `AddTransient()` method. This is because the `InstrumentalMusicManager` class doesn't implement any interface.

The final step that we need to perform is to update the HomeController class to inject the InstrumentalMusicManager concrete class as a dependency and reference both RequestId values from each service that we have registered earlier. Here's what the HomeController class code looks like:

```
public class HomeController : Controller
{
    private readonly IMusicManager _musicManager;
    private readonly InstrumentalMusicManager _insMusicManager;

    public HomeController(IMusicManager musicManager,
                          InstrumentalMusicManager
                          insMusicManager)
    {
        _musicManager = musicManager;
        _insMusicManager = insMusicManager;
    }

    public IActionResult Index()
    {
        var musicManagerReqId = _musicManager.RequestId;
        var insMusicManagerReqId = _insMusicManager.RequestId;

        _musicManager.Notify = new Notifier();
        var songs = _musicManager.GetAllMusicThenNotify();
        return View(songs);
    }
}
```

In the preceding code, we injected an instance of the InstrumentalMusicManager class and IMusicManager interface as a dependency using the Constructor Injection approach. We then get each RequestId value from both object instances.

Now, when you run the application and set a break point at the `Index()` method, we should see the different values for the `musicManagerReqId` and `insMusicManagerReqId` variables, as shown in the following screenshot:

```
0 references
public IActionResult Index()
{
    var musicManagerReqId = _musicManager.RequestId;
    var in ▶ ● musicManagerReqId    {b50f0518-6849-47cb-9f22-5d93394d59a7} ⇷ s elapsed
```

Figure 3.13 – The RequestId value from the IMusicManager interface instance

In the preceding screenshot, we can see that the `musicManagerReqId` variable holds the GUID value of `b50f0518-8649-47cb-9f22-59d3394d59a7`. Let's take a look at the value of `insMusicManagerReqId` in the following screenshot:

```
0 references
public IActionResult Index()
{
    var musicManagerReqId = _musicManager.RequestId;
    var insMusicManagerReqId = _insMusicManager.RequestId;
            ▶ ● insMusicManagerReqId    {f96020f4-a86b-4fa2-ab84-7e9d4403398b} ⇷
```

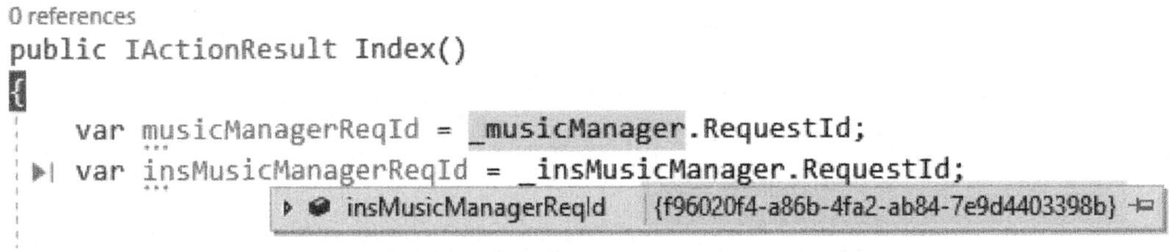

Figure 3.14 – The RequestId value from the InstrumentalMusicManager class instance

As you can see, each variable has different values, even if the `RequestId` has only been set in the `MusicManager` class implementation. This is how the `Transient` services work, and the DI container framework creates a new instance for every dependency each time they are requested. This ensures the uniqueness of each dependent object instance for every request. While this service lifetime has its own benefits, be aware that using this type of lifetime can potentially impact the performance of your application, especially if you are working on a huge monolith app where dependency reference is massive and complex.

Scoped service

Scoped service lifetimes are services created at the lifetime of each client request. In other words, an instance is created per web request. A common example of using a `Scoped` lifetime is when using an **Object Relational Mapper (ORM)** such as Microsoft's **Entity Framework Core (EF)**. By default, the `DbContext` in EF will be created once per client web request. This is to ensure that related calls to process the data will be contained in the same object instance for each request. Let's take a look at how this approach works by modifying our existing previous example.

Let's go ahead and update the `ConfigureServices()` method of the `Startup` class so that it will look similar to the following code:

```
public void ConfigureServices(IServiceCollection services)
{
    services.AddScoped<IMusicManager, MusicManager>();
    services.AddTransient<InstrumentalMusicManager>();
}
```

All that we actually changed in the preceding code is just the `MusicManager` class registration being added as a scoped service. The `InstrumentalMusicManager` interface remains transient because this class depends on the `MusicManager` class, which implemented the `IMusicManager` interface. This means that the DI container will automatically apply whatever service lifetime is being used in the main component.

Now, when you run the application again, you should see that both the `musicManagerReqId` and `insMusicManagerReqId` variables now hold the same `RequestId` value, as shown in the following screenshot:

```
0 references
public IActionResult Index()
{
 ▶| var musicManagerReqId = _musicManager.RequestId;
    var insM ▶ ● musicManagerReqId    {50b6b498-f09d-4640-b5dc-c06d9e3c2cd1} ⁑ psed
```

Figure 3.15 – The RequestId value from the IMusicManager interface instance

In the preceding screenshot, we can see that the `musicManagerReqId` variable holds the GUID value of `50b6b498-f09d-4640-b5dc-c06d9e3c2cd1`. The value of the `insMusicManagerReqId` variable is shown in the following screenshot:

```
0 references
public IActionResult Index()
{
    var musicManagerReqId = _musicManager.RequestId;
 ▶| var insMusicManagerReqId = _insMusicManager.RequestId;
        ▶ ● insMusicManagerReqId    {50b6b498-f09d-4640-b5dc-c06d9e3c2cd1} ⁑
```

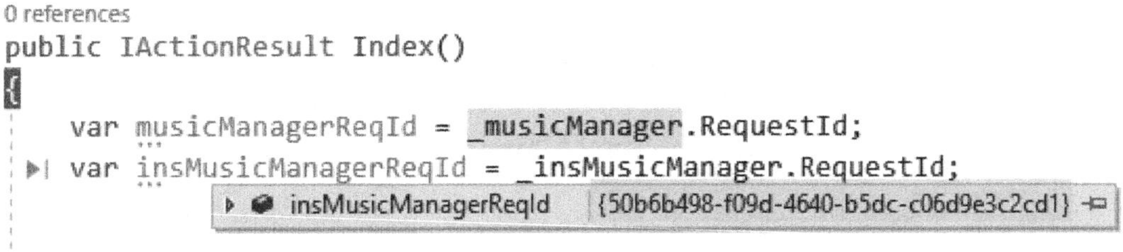

Figure 3.16 – The RequestId value from the InstrumentalMusicManager interface instance

Notice in the preceding screenshot that both `musicManagerReqId` and `insMusicManagerReqId` now have the same value. This is how `Scoped` services work; the values will remain the same throughout the entire client request.

Singleton service

Singleton service lifetimes are services created only once and all dependencies will share the same instance of the same object during the entire lifetime of the application. You would use this type of lifetime for services that are expensive to instantiate because objects will be stored in memory and can be reused for all injections within your application. A typical example of a singleton service is `ILogger`. The `ILogger<T>` instances for a certain type, `T`, are kept around for as long as the application is running. What this means is that when injecting an `ILogger<HomeController>` instance into your `Controller`, the same logger instance will be passed to it every time.

Let's take a look at another example to better understand this type of service lifetime. Let's update the `ConfigureServices()` method in the `Startup` class and add `MusicManager` as a singleton service, just as in the following code:

```
public void ConfigureServices(IServiceCollection services)
{
    services.AddSingleton<IMusicManager, MusicManager>();
    services.AddTransient<InstrumentalMusicManager>();
}
```

The `AddSingleton()` method in the preceding code enables the service to be created only once. When we run the application again, we should be able to see that both the `musicManagerReqId` and `insMusicManagerReqId` variables now hold the same `RequestId` value, as shown in the following screenshots:

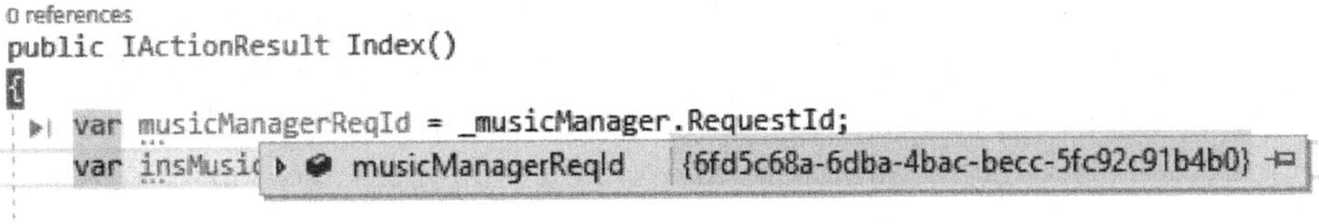

Figure 3.17 – The RequestId value from the IMusicManager interface instance

In the preceding screenshot, we can see that the `musicManagerReqId` variable holds the GUID value of `6fd5c68a-6dba-4bac-becc-5fc92c91b4b0`. Now, let's take a look at the value of the `insMusicManagerReqId` variable in the following screenshot:

Figure 3.18 – The RequestId value from the InstrumentalMusicManager interface instance

As you notice in the preceding screenshot, the value of each variable is also the same. The only difference to this approach compared with `Scoped` services is that no matter how many times you make a request to the `Index()` action method, you should still be getting the same value. You can verify this by refreshing the page to simulate multiple HTTP requests. In the web context, this means that every subsequent request will use the same object instance as it was first created. This also means that it spans across web requests, so regardless of which users made the request, they will still be getting the same instance.

Keep in mind that since singleton instances are kept in memory during the entire application's lifetime, you should watch out for your application memory usage. The good thing though is that the memory will be allocated just once, so the garbage collector will have less to do and may provide you with some performance gain. However, I would recommend that you only use a singleton when it makes sense and don't make things a singleton because you think it's going to save on performance. Moreover, don't mix a singleton service with other service lifetime types, such as transient or scoped, because it may affect how complex scenarios your application behaves.

For more advance and complex scenarios, visit the official documentation relating to DI in ASP.NET Core at `https://docs.microsoft.com/en-us/aspnet/core/fundamentals/dependency-injection`.

Learning and understanding how each service lifetime works is very important in order for your application to behave correctly. Now, let's take a quick look at how we can manage services for handling complex scenarios in the next section.

Handling complex scenarios

If you've made it this far, then we can assume that you now have a better understanding of how the DI works and how you could implement them in different scenarios as required. In this section, we are going to look at some complex situations that you might face when writing your applications. We will see how we can apply the available options provided by the default DI containers to solve complex scenarios. Finally, we are going to look at how we can improve the organization of services when registering them in the DI container

Service descriptors

It's important to understand what service descriptors are before we dive into various complex scenarios.

Service descriptors contain information about the registered services that have been registered in the DI container, including the type of service, implementation, and lifetime. These are used internally by both `IServiceCollection` and `IServiceProvider`. It's very uncommon for us to work directly against service descriptors since they are typically created automatically by the various extension methods of `IServiceCollection`. However, situations may arise that may require you to work directly with service descriptors.

Let's take a look at some examples to make sense of this. In our previous example, we've registered the `IMusicManager` interface mapping as a service using the `AddSingleton()` generic extension method:

```
services.AddSingleton<IMusicManager, MusicManager>();
```

Using the generic extension method in the preceding code is very convenient to use when registering our services in the DI container. However, there may be scenarios where you would want to add services manually using service descriptors. Let's see how we can achieve this by looking at some examples.

There are four possible ways to create service descriptors. The first one is to use the `ServiceDescriptor` object itself, and pass the required arguments in the constructor, as shown in the following code snippet:

```
var serviceDescriptor = new ServiceDescriptor
(
    typeof(IMusicManager),
    typeof(MusicManager),
    ServiceLifetime.Singleton
);

services.Add(serviceDescriptor);
```

In the preceding code, we've passed `IMusicManager` in the first argument as the service type. We then set the corresponding implementation type as `MusicManager` and finally, set the service lifetime to a singleton. The `ServiceDescriptor` object has another two overload constructors that you can use. You can read more about them at `https://docs.microsoft.com/en-us/dotnet/api/microsoft.extensions.dependencyinjection.servicedescriptor`.

The second option is to use the static `Describe()` method of the `ServiceDescriptor` object, as shown in the following code snippet:

```
var serviceDescriptor = ServiceDescriptor.Describe
(
    typeof(IMusicManager),
    typeof(MusicManager),
    ServiceLifetime.Singleton
);

services.Add(serviceDescriptor);
```

In the preceding code, we are passing the same arguments to the method, which is pretty much the same as what we did earlier using the `ServiceDescriptor` object constructor option. You can read more about the `Describe()` method and its available overload methods at `https://docs.microsoft.com/en-us/dotnet/api/microsoft.extensions.dependencyinjection.servicedescriptor.describe`.

You may have noticed that both options in the preceding examples require us to pass the service lifetime. In this case, we are forced to pass the `ServiceLifetime.Singleton` enum value. To simplify them, we can use the available `static` methods to create service descriptors with lifetimes.

The following code demonstrates the remaining options:

```
var serviceDescriptor = ServiceDescriptor.Singleton
(
    typeof(IMusicManager),
    typeof(MusicManager)
);

services.Add(serviceDescriptor);
```

The preceding code makes use of the `Singleton()` static method by simply passing both the service type and the corresponding implementation type. While the code seems much cleaner now, you can simplify the creation further by using the generic method to make your code more concise, as shown in the following code snippet:

```
var serviceDescriptor = ServiceDescriptor
    .Singleton<IMusicManager,MusicManager>();


services.Add(serviceDescriptor);
```

Add versus TryAdd

We've learned how to create service descriptors in the previous example. In this section, let's take a look at the various ways in which we can register them in the DI container.

Earlier in this chapter, we've seen how to use the generic `Add` extension methods, such as the `AddTransient`, `AddScoped`, and `AddSingleton` methods for registering a service in the DI container with a specified lifetime. Each of these methods has various overloads that accept different arguments based on your needs. However, as your application becomes more complex and you have a lot of services to deal with, using these generic methods can potentially cause your application to behave differently when you accidentally register the same type of service.

For example, register the following service multiple times:

```
services.AddSingleton<IMusicManager, MusicManager>();
services.AddSingleton<IMusicManager, AwesomeMusicManager>();
```

The preceding code registers two services that refer to the `IMusicManager` interface. The first registration maps to the `MusicManager` concrete class implementation, and the second one maps to the `AwesomeMusicManager` class.

If you run the application, you will see that the implementation type being injected into the `HomeController` class is the `AwesomeMusicManager` class, as shown in the following screenshot:

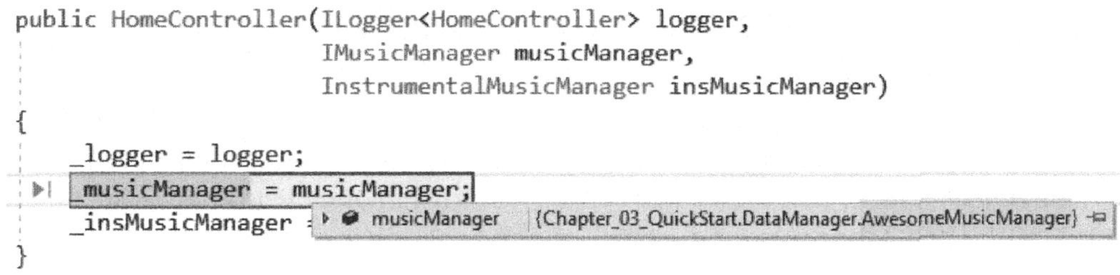

```
public HomeController(ILogger<HomeController> logger,
                      IMusicManager musicManager,
                      InstrumentalMusicManager insMusicManager)
{
    _logger = logger;
▶| _musicManager = musicManager;
    _insMusicManager ▶ ● musicManager    {Chapter_03_QuickStart.DataManager.AwesomeMusicManager} ⮫
}
```

Figure 3.19 – The HomeController class constructor injection

This simply means that the DI container will use the last registered entry for situations where you register multiple services of the same type. Therefore, the order of service registrations in the `ConfigureServices()` method can be quite important. To avoid this kind of situation, we can use the various `TryAdd()` generic extension methods that are available for registering the service.

So, if you want to register multiple implementations of the same service, you can simply do something like this:

```
services.AddSingleton<IMusicManager, MusicManager>();
services.TryAddSingleton<IMusicManager, AwesomeMusicManager>();
```

In the preceding code, we've changed the second registration to make use of the `TryAddSingleton()` method. When you run the application again, you should now see that the `MusicManager` class implementation is the one that gets injected as shown in the following figure:

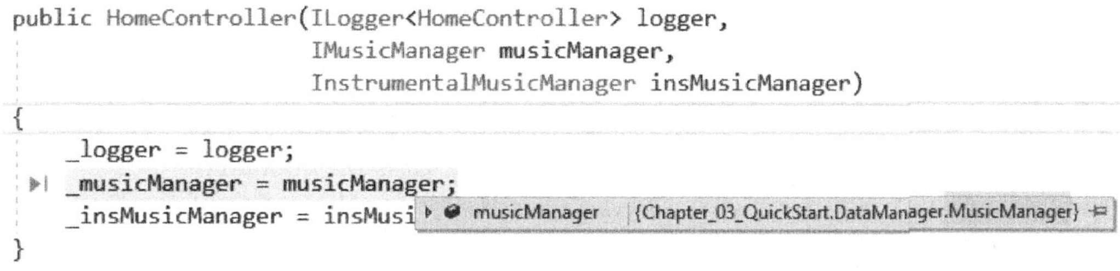

```
public HomeController(ILogger<HomeController> logger,
                      IMusicManager musicManager,
                      InstrumentalMusicManager insMusicManager)
{
    _logger = logger;
▶| _musicManager = musicManager;
    _insMusicManager = insMusi ▶ ● musicManager    {Chapter_03_QuickStart.DataManager.MusicManager} ⮫
}
```

Figure 3.20 – The HomeController class constructor injection

When using `TryAdd()` methods, the DI container will only register services when there is no implementation already defined for a given service type. This makes things convenient for you, especially when you have complicated applications, because you can express your intent more clearly when registering your service and it prevents you from accidentally replacing previously registered services. So, if you want to register your services safely, then consider using the `TryAdd()` method instead.

Dealing with multiple service implementations

Previously, we've seen the effect of using the `Add()` methods for registering multiple services of the same service type with the DI container. While the DI container uses the last implementation type defined for the same service type, you should know that the first service defined is still kept in the service collections entry. In other words, invoking the `Add()` method multiple times for the same interface will create multiple entries in the service collection. This means that the last registration in our previous example does not replace the first registration.

To utilize the multiple implementations of the same interface, then you must first change how you define your services with having the same service type. This is to avoid potential side effects when having duplicate instances of the implementation. Therefore, when registering multiple instances of an interface, it's recommended to use the `TryAddEnumerable()` extension method, just as in the following example:

```
services.TryAddEnumerable(ServiceDescriptor
                    .Singleton<IMusicManager,
                    MusicManager>());
services.TryAddEnumerable(ServiceDescriptor
                    .Singleton<IMusicManager,
                    AwesomeMusicManager>());
```

In the preceding code, we've replaced the `AddSingleton()` and `TryAddSingleton()` calls to the `TryAddEnumerable()` method. The `TryAddEnumerable()` method accepts a `ServiceDescriptor` argument type. This method prevents duplicate registrations of the same implementation. For more information, see `https://docs.microsoft.com/en-us/dotnet/api/microsoft.extensions.dependencyinjection.extensions.servicecollectiondescriptorextensions.tryaddenumerable`.

Now, the next step is to modify the `HomeController` class and contain the dependencies in an `IEnumerable` generic collection type to allow all implementations to be evaluated and resolved.

Here's an example of how to do that using our previous example:

```
private readonly IEnumerable<IMusicManager> _musicManagers;
public HomeController(IEnumerable<IMusicManager> musicManagers)
{
    _musicManagers = musicManagers;
}
```

In the preceding code, we've changed the `HomeController` constructor argument to accept an `IEnumerable<IMusicManager>` service type. When the DI container is resolving services for this class, it will now attempt to resolve all instances of `IMusicManager` and inject them as an `IEnumerable`, as shown in the following screenshot:

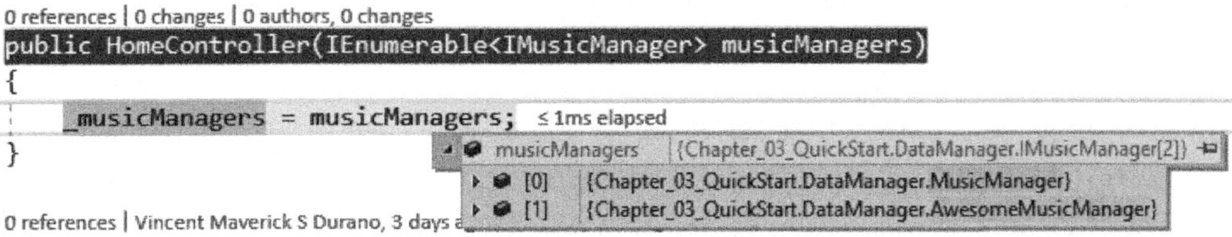

```
0 references | 0 changes | 0 authors, 0 changes
public HomeController(IEnumerable<IMusicManager> musicManagers)
{
    _musicManagers = musicManagers;   ≤ 1ms elapsed
}                                    musicManagers    {Chapter_03_QuickStart.DataManager.IMusicManager[2]}
                                       [0]    {Chapter_03_QuickStart.DataManager.MusicManager}
                                       [1]    {Chapter_03_QuickStart.DataManager.AwesomeMusicManager}
0 references | Vincent Maverick S Durano, 3 days a
```

Figure 3.21 – Resolving all instances of IMusicManager

Keep in mind that the DI container will only resolve multiple instances of service implementations when the type is `IEnumerable`.

Replacing and removing service registrations

In this section, we'll take a look at how we can replace and remove service registrations. To replace a service registration, you can use the `Replace()` extension method of the `IServiceCollection` interface, as shown:

```
services.AddSingleton<IMusicManager, MusicManager>();
services.Replace(ServiceDescriptor
            .Singleton<IMusicManager,
            AwesomeMusicManager>());
```

The `Replace()` method also accepts a `ServiceDescriptor` argument type. This method will look for the first service registration for the `IMusicManager` service type and then remove it if it finds one. The new implementation type will then be used to create a new registration in the DI container. In this case, the `MusicManager` implementation type will be replaced with the `AwesomeMusicManager` class implementation. One thing to keep in mind here is that the `Replace()` method will only support removing the first service type entry in the collection.

In situations where you would need to remove all prior service registrations of a service type, you can use the `RemoveAll()` extension method and pass the type of the service that you wish to remove. Here's an example:

```
services.AddSingleton<IMusicManager, MusicManager>();
services.AddSingleton<IMusicManager, AwesomeMusicManager>();
services.RemoveAll<IMusicManager>();
```

The preceding code removes both registrations of the `IMusicManager` service type in the service collection.

Replacing or removing services in the DI container is quite a rare scenario, but it may be useful if you want to provide your own implementation for the framework or other third-party services.

Summary

DI is a huge topic, but we've tackled most of the major topics that should help you as a beginner as you progress on your journey to learning ASP.NET Core.

We've covered the concepts of DI, how it works under the hood, and its basic usage in the context of ASP.NET Core. These concepts are crucial for creating well-designed and well-decoupled applications. We've learned that DI offers a few benefits that help us to build robust and powerful applications. By following some detailed examples, we've learned how we can effectively use DI to solve potential problems in a variety of scenarios.

DI is a very powerful technique for building highly extensible and maintainable applications. By taking advantage of the abstractions, we can easily swap out dependencies without affecting the behavior of your code. This gives you greater flexibility in terms of integrating new features easily, and makes your code more testable, which is also crucial for building well-crafted applications. While the DI container is not really a requirement to apply the DI pattern, using it can simplify the management of all of your dependencies, including their lifetimes, as your application grows and becomes more complex.

In the next chapter, we are going to explore Razor View Engines for building powerful ASP.NET Core web applications. We will do some hands-on coding by building the application from scratch so that you have a better understanding of the topics as you progress.

Questions

1. What are the types of DI?

2. When should dependency lifetimes be used?

3. What's the difference between the `Add` and `TryAdd` extension methods?

Further reading

Prerequisites:

- Understanding the basic fundamentals of ASP.NET Core: `https://docs.microsoft.com/en-us/aspnet/core/fundamentals`

- Understanding the SOLID principles: `https://en.wikipedia.org/wiki/SOLID`

- Understanding the basic fundamentals of DI in ASP.NET Core: `https://docs.microsoft.com/en-us/aspnet/core/fundamentals/dependency-injection`

- Understanding view injections in MVC: `https://docs.microsoft.com/en-us/aspnet/core/mvc/views/dependency-injection`

Basic:

- C# guide to open and closed types: `https://docs.microsoft.com/en-us/dotnet/csharp/language-reference/language-specification/types#open-and-closed-types`

- C# guide to constructed types: `https://docs.microsoft.com/en-us/dotnet/csharp/language-reference/language-specification/types#constructed-types`

- Understanding the LINQ enumerable `empty`: `https://docs.microsoft.com/en-us/dotnet/api/system.linq.enumerable.empty`

- Understanding the C# ternary conditional operator: `https://docs.microsoft.com/en-us/dotnet/csharp/language-reference/operators/conditional-operator`

- Understanding C# auto-implemented properties: `https://docs.microsoft.com/en-us/dotnet/csharp/programming-guide/classes-and-structs/auto-implemented-properties`

Advanced:

- Understanding service descriptors: `https://docs.microsoft.com/en-us/dotnet/api/microsoft.extensions.dependencyinjection.servicedescriptor`

- Understanding the `TryAddEnumerable` method: `https://docs.microsoft.com/en-us/dotnet/api/microsoft.extensions.dependencyinjection.extensions.servicecollectiondescriptorextensions.tryaddenumerable`

- Understanding `async` and `await` in C#: `https://docs.microsoft.com/en-us/dotnet/csharp/language-reference/operators/await`

4
Razor View Engine

Building dynamic and data-driven web applications is pretty easy; however, things can sometimes be confusing, especially if you are new to the technology. As a beginner, you might find yourself having a hard time understanding how the stateless nature of the web works. The main reason for this is either you have never been exposed to how to apply the framework or simply because you are completely new to web development and you have no idea where to begin.

Even though there are many tutorials that you can use as a reference to learn, you may still find it hard to connect pieces, which could result in you losing interest. The good news is that ASP.NET Core makes things easier for you to learn how to carry out web development. As long as you understand C#, basic HTML, and CSS, you should be able to learn web development in no time. If you are new, confused, and have no idea how to start building an ASP.NET Core application, then this chapter is for you.

This chapter is mainly targeted at beginner to intermediate .NET developers who want to jump into ASP.NET Core 5, get a feel of the different web frameworks, and get their hands dirty with coding examples.

As you may know, there are lots of technologies that you can choose to integrate certain capabilities with ASP.NET Core, as shown in Figure 4.1.:

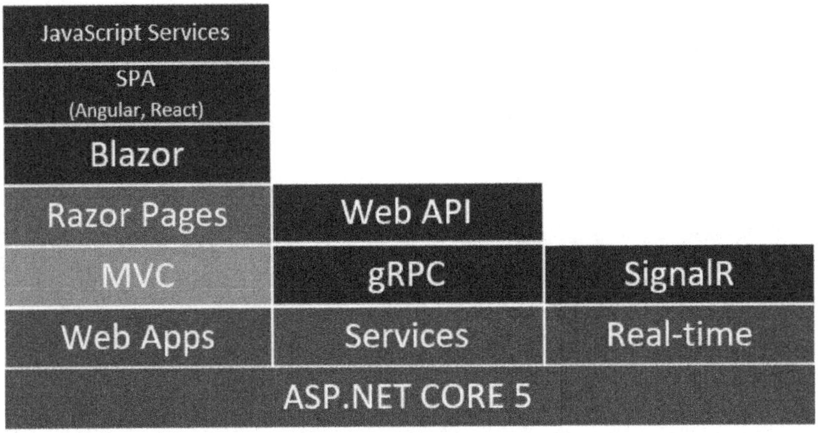

Figure 4.1 – ASP.NET Core technology stacks

In the preceding diagram, you can see that ASP.NET Core provides most of the common capabilities that you can integrate with your application. This gives you the flexibility to choose whatever framework and services you want to use when building your application. In fact, you can even combine any of these frameworks to produce powerful applications. Bear in mind though that we won't be covering all the technologies shown in the preceding diagram in this chapter.

In this chapter, we will mainly be focusing on the **Web Apps** stack by looking at a couple of web framework flavors that you can choose for building web applications in ASP. NET Core. We'll cover the basics of MVC and Razor Pages by doing some hands-on coding exercises so that you get a feel of how each of them works and understand their differences.

Here is a list of the main topics that we'll go through in this chapter:

- Understanding the Razor view engine
- Learning the basics of Razor syntax
- Building a to-do application with MVC
- Building a to-do application with Razor Pages
- Differences between MVC and Razor Pages

By the end of this chapter, you should understand the fundamentals of the Razor view engine and its syntax and know how to build a basic, interactive, data-driven web application using two of the popular web frameworks that ship with ASP.NET Core. You should then be able to weigh in on their pros and cons and decide which web framework is best suited for you. Finally, you'll understand when to use each web framework when building real-world ASP.NET Core applications.

Technical requirements

This chapter uses Visual Studio 2019 to demonstrate various examples, but the process should be the same if you're using Visual Studio Code.

Check out the source code for this chapter at `https://github.com/ PacktPublishing/ASP.NET-Core-5-for-Beginners/tree/master/ Chapter%2004/Chapter_04_RazorViewEngine_Examples`.

Before diving into this chapter, make sure that you have a basic understanding of ASP. NET Core and C# in general and how each of them works separately, as well as together. Though it's not required, having a basic knowledge of HTML and CSS is helpful for you to easily understand how the pages are constructed.

Please visit the following link to check the CiA videos: `https://bit.ly/3qDiqYY`

If you're ready, let's jump right into it.

Understanding the Razor view engine

Before we deep dive into the Razor view engine in the context of ASP.NET Core, let's talk a bit about the history of the various view engines in ASP.NET.

The previous versions of the ASP.NET frameworks had their own view/markup engines for rendering dynamic web pages. Back in the old days, **Active Server Pages** (Classic ASP) used a `.ASP` file extension. ASP.NET Web Forms, which is commonly known as the **Web Forms view engine**, used a `.ASPX` file extension. These file types were markup engines that contained server-side code, such as VBScript, VB.NET, or C#, which were processed by the web server (IIS) to output HTML in the browser. A few years later, after ASP.NET Web Forms became popular, Microsoft introduced ASP.NET MVC 1.0 as a new, alternative web framework for building dynamic web applications in the full .NET Framework. Bringing MVC into .NET opened it up to a wider audience of developers, because it values the clean separation of concerns and friendly URL routings, allows deeper extensibility, and follows real web development experience.

While the early versions of MVC addressed most of the Web Forms downsides, they still used the .ASPX-based markup engine to serve up pages. Many were not glad about the integration of the .ASPX markup engine in MVC, because as it was too complex to work with the UI. It could potentially affect the overall performance of the application due to its processing overhead. When Microsoft released ASP.NET MVC 3.0 in early January 2011, the **Razor view engine** came to life as a new view engine addition to power ASP.NET MVC views. The Razor view engine in the ASP.NET full .NET Framework supports both VB.NET (.vbhtml) and C# (.cshtml) as the server-side language.

When ASP.NET Core was introduced, a lot of things were changed for the better. Since the framework was redesigned to be modular, unified, and cross-platform, many features and capabilities from the full .NET framework were discontinued, such as Web Forms and VB.NET support. Because of these changes, the Razor view engine also dropped support for the .vbhtml file extension, leaving it to only support C# code.

Now that you have a little bit of background about the various view engines in the different ASP.NET web frameworks, let's move on to the next section. There, you will better understand why the ASP.NET team came to the decision to use the **Razor view engine** as the default markup engine to power all ASP.NET Core web frameworks.

Reviewing the Razor view engine

As the ASP.NET Core framework has evolved, the ASP.NET Core team has been working hard to provide a better view engine that offers a lot of benefits and productivity. The new Razor view engine is the default view engine for all ASP.NET Core web frameworks, and it has been optimized to provide us with faster HTML generation using a code-focused templating approach.

The Razor view engine, often referred to as **Razor**, is a C#-based template markup syntax for generating HTML with dynamic content. It's the view engine that powers not just the ASP.NET Core MVC, but all other ASP.NET Core web frameworks for generating dynamic pages (as shown in Figure 4.2).

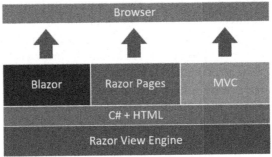

Figure 4.2 – Razor view engine

In the preceding diagram, we can see that the **Blazor**, **Razor Pages**, and **MVC** web frameworks rely on Razor view engines to generate content pages and components. Blazor differs a bit from MVC and Razor Pages because it a **single-page application** (**SPA**) web framework that uses a component-based approach. Blazor components are files that use the `.razor` extension, which still uses the Razor engine under the hood. Content pages, often referred to as the **UI**, are simply Razor files with the `.cshtml` extension. Razor files are mainly composed of the HTML and Razor syntax, which enables you to embed C# code in the content itself. So, if you request a page, the C# code gets executed on the server. It then processes whatever logic it requires, takes data from somewhere, and then returns the generated data, along with the HTML that makes up the page, to the browser.

Having the ability to use the same templating syntax for building up your UI enables you to easily transition from one web framework to another without much of a learning curve. In fact, you can combine any of the web frameworks for building web applications. However, it's not recommended to do so, as things can get messy and it may cause your application code to be difficult to maintain. One exception, though is if you are migrating your whole application from one web framework to another, and you want to start replacing portions of your application to use other web frameworks; then, it makes a lot of sense to combine them.

Razor offers a lot of benefits, including the following:

- **Easy to learn**: As long as you know basic HTML and a little bit of C#, then learning Razor is quite easy and fun. Razor was designed to enable C# developers to take advantage of their skills and boost productivity when building UIs for their ASP. NET Core applications.

- **Clean and fluid**: Razor was designed to be compact and simple and does not require you to write a lot of code. Unlike other view templating engines, where you need to specify certain areas within your HTML to denote a server-side code block, the Razor engine is smart enough to detect server code in your HTML, which enables you to write clean and more manageable code.

- **Editor-agnostic**: Razor isn't tied to a specific editor like Visual Studio. This enables you to write code in whatever text editor you prefer to improve productivity.

- **IntelliSense support**: While you can write Razor-based code in any text editor, using Visual Studio can boost your productivity even more because of the statement completion support built into it.

- **Ease of unit testing**: Razor-based pages/views support unit tests.

Understanding how the Razor view engine works is very important when building dynamic and interactive pages in ASP.NET Core. In the next section, we'll discuss some of the basic syntaxes of Razor.

Learning the basics of Razor syntax

The beauty of Razor, compared to other templating view engines, is that it minimizes the code required when constructing your views or content pages. This enables a clean, fast, and fluid coding workflow to boost your productivity when composing UIs.

To embed C# code into your Razor files (.cshtml), you need to tell the engine that you are injecting a server-side code block by using the @ symbol. Typically, your C# code block must appear within the @{...} expression. This means that as soon as you type @, the engine is smart enough to know that you are starting to write C# code. Everything that follows after the opening { symbol is assumed to be server-side code, until it reaches the matching closing block } symbol.

Let's take a look at some examples for you to better understand the Razor syntax basics.

Rendering simple data

In a typical ASP.NET Core MVC web application generated from the default template, you'll see the following code within the Index.cshtml file for the home page:

```
@{
    ViewData["Title"] = "Home Page";
}
```

The preceding code is referred to as a **Razor code block**. Razor code blocks normally start with the @ symbol and are enclosed by curly braces {}. In the preceding example, you'll see that the line starts with the @ symbol, which tells the Razor engine that you are about to embed some server code. The code within the open and close curly braces are assumed to be C# code. The code within the block will be evaluated and executed from the server, allowing you to access the value and reference it in your view. This example is the same as setting a variable in the Controller class.

Here's another example of creating a new ViewData variable and assigning a value to it in the Index() method of the HomeController class, as shown in the following code block:

```
public IActionResult Index()
{
```

```
    ViewData["Message"] = "Razor is Awesome!";
    return View();
}
```

In the preceding example, we've set the ViewData["Message"] value to "Razor is Awesome!". ViewData is nothing but a dictionary of objects, and it is accessible by using string as the key. Now, let's try to display the values of each ViewData object by adding the following code:

```
<h1>@ViewData["Title"]</h1>
<h2>@ViewData["Message"]</h2>
```

The preceding code is an example of **implicit Razor expressions**. These expressions normally start with the @ symbol and are then followed by C# code. Unlike **Razor code blocks**, Razor expression code is rendered into the browser.

In the preceding code, we've referenced the values of both ViewData["Title"] and ViewData["Message"], then contained them within the <h1> and <h2> HTML tags. The value of any variable is rendered along with the HTML. Figure 4.3 shows you the sample output of what we just did.

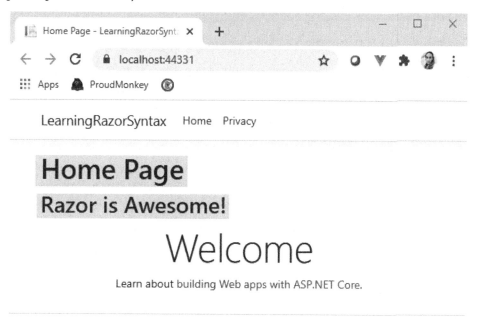

Figure 4.3 – Implicit Razor expression output

In the preceding screenshot, we can see that each value from `ViewData` is printed on the page. This is what Razor is all about; it enables you to mix HTML with server-side code using a simplified syntax.

The **Razor implicit expressions** described in the previous example typically should not contain spaces, with the exception of using the C# `await` keyword:

```
<p>@await SomeService.GetSomethingAsync()</p>
```

The `await` keyword in the preceding code denotes an asynchronous call to the server by invoking the `GetSomethingAsync()` method of the `SomeService` class. Razor allows you to inject a server-side method into your content page using **view injection**. For more information about **dependency injection**, you can review *Chapter 3, Dependency Injection*.

Implicit expressions also do not allow you to use C# generics, as in the following code:

```
<p>@SomeGenericMethod<T>()</p>
```

The reason why the preceding code won't work and will throw an error is that data type `T` within the `<>` brackets is parsed as an HTML tag. To use generics in Razor, you would need to use a **Razor code block** or **explicit expressions**, just like in the following code:

```
<p>@(SomeGenericMethod<T>())</p>
```

Razor explicit expressions start with the `@` symbol with balanced matching parentheses. Here's an example of an explicit expression that displays the date from yesterday:

```
<p>@((DateTime.Now - TimeSpan.FromDays(1)).
    ToShortDateString())</p>
```

The preceding code gets yesterday's date and uses the `ToShortDateString()` extension method to convert the value into a short date format. Razor will process the code within the `@()` expression and render the result to the page.

Razor will ignore any content containing the `@` symbol in between text. For example, the following line remains untouched by Razor parsing:

```
<a href="mailto:user@email.com">user@email.com</a>
```

Explicit expressions are useful for string concatenation as well. For example, if you want to combine static text with dynamic data and render it, you can do something like this:

```
<p>Time@(DateTime.Now.Hour) AM</p>
```

The preceding code will render something like `<p>Time@10 AM</p>`. Without using the explicit `@()` expression, the code will render as `<p>Time@DateTime.Now.Hour AM</p>` instead. Razor will evaluate it as plain text like an email address.

If you want to display static content that includes an @ symbol before the text, then you can simply append another @ symbol to escape it. For example, if we want to display the text @vmsdurano on the page, then you can simply do something such as the following:

```
<p>@@vmsdurano</p>
```

Now that you've learned how the basic syntax of Razor works, let's move on to the next section and take a look at some advanced examples.

Rendering data from a view model

In most cases, you would typically be dealing with real data to present dynamic content on a page when working with a real application. This data would normally come from `ViewModel`, which holds some information related to the content that you are interested in.

In this section, we'll see how we can present data that comes from the server on your page using the Razor syntax. Let's start off by creating the following class in the `Models` folder of your MVC application:

```
public class BeerModel
{
    public int Id { get; set; }
    public string Name { get; set; }
    public string Type { get; set; }
}
```

The preceding code is just a plain class that represents `ViewModel`. In this case, `ViewModel` is called `BeerModel`, which houses some properties that the view expects. Next, we'll create a new class that will populate the view model. The new class would look something like this:

```
public class Beer
{
    public List<BeerModel> GetAllBeer()
    {
        return new List<BeerModel>
        {
```

```
        new BeerModel { Id =1, Name="Redhorse",
            Type="Lager" },
        new BeerModel { Id =2, Name="Furious",
            Type="IPA" },
        new BeerModel { Id =3, Name="Guinness",
            Type="Stout" },
        new BeerModel { Id =4, Name="Sierra", Type="Ale" },
        new BeerModel { Id =5, Name="Stella",
            Type="Pilsner" },
    };
  }
}
```

The preceding code is nothing but a plain class that represents the model. This class contains a `GetAllBeer()` method, which is responsible for returning all items from the list. In this case, we are returning a `List<BeerModel>` type. The implementation could vary depending on your datastore and what data access framework you're using. You could be pulling the data from a database or via an API call. However, for this example, we will just return a static list of data for simplicity's sake.

You can think of `ViewModel` as a placeholder to hold properties that are only required for your views. `Model`, on the other hand, is a class that implements the domain logic for your application. Often, these classes are retrieved and store data in databases. We'll talk more about these concepts later in this chapter.

Now that we already modeled some sample data, let's modify our `Index()` method of the `HomeController` class so that it looks something like this:

```
public IActionResult Index()
{
    var beer = new Beer();
    var listOfBeers = beer.GetAllBeer();
    return View(listOfBeers);
}
```

The preceding code initializes an instance of the `Beer` class and then invokes the `GetAllBeer()` method. We then set the result to a variable called `listOfBeers` and then pass it to the view as an argument to return the response.

Now, let's see how we can display the result on the page. Go ahead and switch back to the `Index.cshtml` file that is located in the `Views/Home` folder.

The first thing that we need to do for us to access the data from the view model is to declare a class reference using the @model directive:

```
@model IEnumerable<Chapter_04_LearningRazorSyntax.Models.
    BeerModel>
```

The preceding code declares a reference to the view model as a type of IEnumerable<BeerMode>, which makes the view a strongly typed view. The @model directive is one of the **Razor reserved keywords**. This particular directive enables you to specify the type of class to be passed in the view or page. Razor directives are also expressed as *implicit expressions* by using the @ symbol, followed by the directive name or Razor reserved keywords.

At this point, we now have access to the view model that we created earlier. Since we are declaring the view model as enumerable, you can easily iterate to each item in the collection and present the data however you want. Here's an example of displaying just the Name property of the BeerModel class:

```
<h1>My favorite beers are:</h1>
<ul>
    @foreach (var item in Model)
    {
        <li>@item.Name</li>
    }
</ul>
```

In the preceding code, we've used the <ul> HTML tag to present the data in a bulleted list format. Within the <ul> tag, you should notice that we've used the @ symbol to start manipulating the data in C# code. The foreach keyword is one of the **C# reserved keywords**, which are used for iterating data in a collection. Within the foreach block, we have constructed the items to be displayed in the <li> tag. In this case, the Name property is rendered using *implicit expressions*.

Notice how fluid and easy it is to embed C# logic into the HTML. The way it works is that Razor will look for any HTML tags within the expression. If it sees one, it jumps out of the C# code and will only jump back in when it sees a matching closing tag.

Here's the output when rendered in the browser:

My favorite beers are:

- Redhorse
- Furious
- Guinness
- Sierra
- Stella

Figure 4.4 – Implicit Razor expression output

The preceding is just an example of how we can easily display a formatted list of data on a page. If you want to filter the list based on some condition, you can do something like this:

```
<ul>
    @foreach (var item in Model)
    {
        if (item.Id == 2)
        {
            <li>@item.Name</li>
        }
    }
</ul>
```

In the preceding code, we've used the C# `if-statement` within the `foreach` loop to filter only the item that we need. In this case, we checked to see whether the `Id` property is equal to `2` and then constructed an `<li>` element to display the value when the condition is met.

There are many ways to present information on the page depending on your requirements. In most cases, you may be required to present a complex UI to display information. In such cases, that's where HTML and tag helpers can be useful.

Introduction to HTML helpers and tag helpers

Before **tag helpers** were introduced, **HTML helpers** were used to render dynamic HTML content in Razor files. Typically, you will find code that looks similar to this in the view of MVC applications:

```
<h1>List of beers:</h1>
<table class="table">
```

```
    <thead>
        <tr>
            <th>
                @Html.DisplayNameFor(model => model.Id)
            </th>
            @* Removed other headers for brevity *@
        </tr>
    </thead>
    <tbody>
        @foreach (var item in Model)
        {
            <tr>
                <td>
                    @Html.DisplayFor(modelItem => item.Id)
                </td>
                @* Removed other rows for brevity *@
            </tr>
        }
    </tbody>
</table>
```

The preceding code uses a `<table>` tag to present data in a tabular form. In the `<thead>` section, we've used the `DisplayNameFor` HTML helper to display each property name from the view model. We then iterated to each item within the `<tbody>` section using the C# `foreach` iterator. This is pretty much the same as what we did in our previous example. The difference now is we've constructed the data to be presented in tabular format.

The `<tr>` element represents the rows and the `<td>` element represents the columns. In each column, we've used the `DisplayFor` HTML helper to display the actual data in the browser. Keep in mind though that the `DisplayFor` helper doesn't generate any HTML tags when rendered; instead, it will just display the value in plain text. So, use `DisplayFor` only when there's a reason for you to use it. Ideally, the `foreach` block from the preceding code can be replaced with this code:

```
<tbody>
    @foreach (var item in Model)
    {
        <tr>
```

```
            <td>@item.Id</td>
            @* Removed other rows for brevity *@
        </tr>
    }
</tbody>
```

The preceding code is much cleaner and will render much faster, compared to using the `DisplayFor` HTML helper. Running the code should result an output like Figure 4.5.

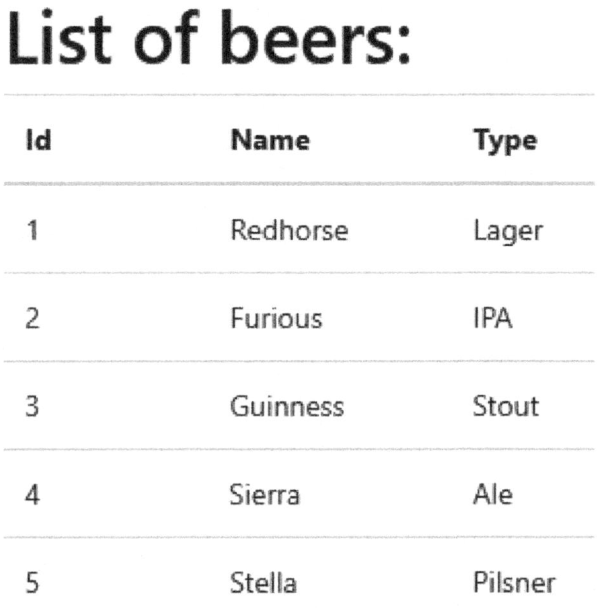

List of beers:

Id	Name	Type
1	Redhorse	Lager
2	Furious	IPA
3	Guinness	Stout
4	Sierra	Ale
5	Stella	Pilsner

Figure 4.5 – HTML helpers output

While other HTML helpers are useful when dealing with collections, complex objects, templates, and other situations, there are certain cases where things can become cumbersome, especially when dealing with UI customization. For example, if we want to apply some CSS style to elements that were generated by HTML helpers, then we will have to use the overload method to do that without any IntelliSense help. Here's a quick example:

```
<h1>My most favorite beer:</h1>
@{ var first = Model.FirstOrDefault(); }

@* Removed other line for brevity *@
@Html.LabelFor(model => first.Name, new
```

```
{ @class = "font-weight-bold" })
: @first.Name
@* Removed other line for brevity *@
```

The preceding code uses the `LabelFor` HTML helper to display information. In this example, we were only displaying the first item set from the `ViewModel` collection using the LINQ `FirstOrDefault` extension method. The second argument in the `LabelFor` method represents the `htmlAttributes` parameter, where we are forced to pass an anonymous object just to set the CSS class. In this case, we applied the CSS class attribute to `font-weight-bold` for the label element. The reason for this is that the `class` keyword is a *reserved keyword* in C#, thus we need to tell Razor to evaluate `@class=expression` as an element attribute by using the @ symbol before it. This kind of situation makes it a little bit harder to maintain and not quite friendly to read as your page gets bigger, especially to frontend developers who are not familiar with C#. To address this, we can use **tag helpers**.

ASP.NET Core offers a bunch of built-in **tag helpers** that you can use to help improve your productivity when creating and rendering HTML elements in the Razor markup. Unlike **HTML helpers**, which are invoked as C# methods, **tag helpers** are attached directly to HTML elements. This makes tag helpers much more friendly and fun to use for frontend developers because they can have full control over HTML.

While **tag helpers** is a huge topic to cover, we'll try to look at a common example for you to understand their purpose and benefits.

Going back to our previous example, we can rewrite the code using **tag helpers** with the following code:

```
<h1>My most favorite beer:</h1>
@* Removed other line for brevity *@
<label asp-for="@first.Name" class="font-weight-bold"></label>
: @first.Name
@* Removed other line for brevity *@
```

In the preceding code, notice that we have now used a standard `<label>` HTML tag and used the `asp-for` tag helper to display the `Name` property from `ViewModel`. Note that the closing tag is required. If you use a self-closing tag, such as `<label asp-for="@first.Id" />`, the value will not be rendered.

In cases where you want to change the property name to be rendered in the HTML, you can use the [Display] attribute. For example, if we want to display the value Beer Id for the property ID, we can simply do something like the following code:

```
Display(Name = "Beer Id")]
public int Id { get; set; }
```

What we did in the preceding code is called **data annotation**. This enables you to define certain metadata that you want to apply for properties in the model/view model, such as conditions, validations, custom formatting, and so on. For more information about data annotation, see https://docs.microsoft.com/en-us/dotnet/api/system.componentmodel.dataannotations.

Figure 4.6 displays the sample output when running the code.

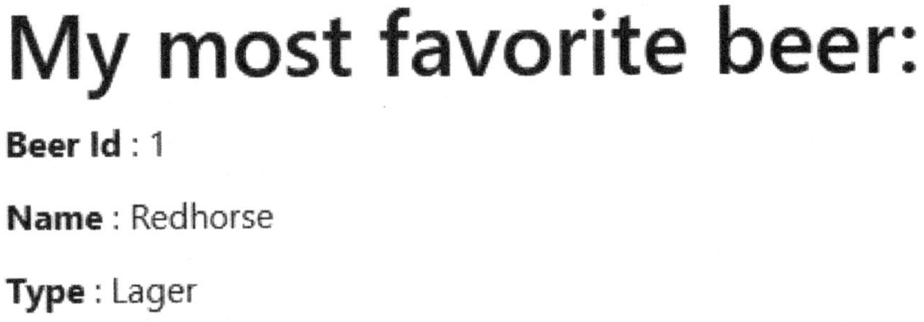

My most favorite beer:

Beer Id : 1

Name : Redhorse

Type : Lager

Figure 4.6 – Tag helpers output

There are many things that you can do with **tag helpers**. ASP.NET Core provides most of the tag helpers that are common for building up your pages, such as form actions, input controls, routings, validations, components, scripts, and many others. In fact, you can even create your own or extend tag helpers to customize your needs.

Tag helpers give you a lot of flexibility when generating HTML elements, provide rich IntelliSense support, and provide an HTML-friendly development experience, which helps you save some development time when building UIs.

For more information about tag helpers in ASP.NET Core, see https://docs.microsoft.com/en-us/aspnet/core/mvc/views/tag-helpers.

Learning the basic fundamentals of the **Razor view engine** and understanding how the syntax works are crucial for building any ASP.NET Core web applications. In the following sections, we will do some hands-on exercises by building a to-do application in various web frameworks. This is to give you a better understanding of how each web framework works and help you decide which approach to choose when building real-world web applications.

Building a to-do application with MVC

A to-do application is a great example to demonstrate how to perform adding and modifying information on a web page. Understanding how this works in the stateless nature of the web is of great value when building real-world, data-driven web applications.

Before we get started, let's take a quick refresher on MVC first so that you have a better understanding of what it is.

Understanding the MVC pattern

To better understand the MVC pattern approach, Figure 4.7 illustrates an attempt that describes the high-level process in a graphical way:

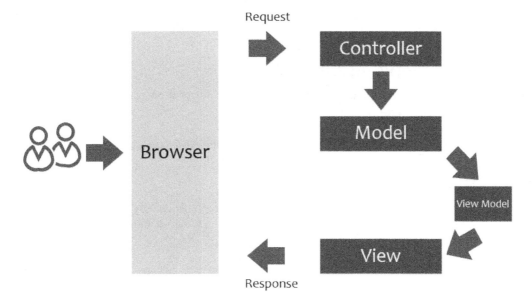

Figure 4.7 – The MVC request and response flow

The preceding diagram is pretty much self-explanatory by just looking at the request flow. But to verify your understanding, it might be helpful to give a brief explanation of the process. The term MVC represents the three components that make up the application: **M** for **Models**, **V** for **Views**, and **C** for **Controllers**. In the preceding diagram, you can see that the controller is the very first entry that is invoked when a user requests a page in the browser. Controllers are responsible for handling any user interactions and requests, processing any logic that is required to fulfill the request, and ultimately, returning a response to the user. In other words, controllers orchestrate the flow of logic.

Models are components that actually implement domain-specific logic. Often, models contain entity objects, your business logic, and data access code that retrieves and stores data. Bear in mind though that in real applications, you should consider separating your business logic and data access layer to value the separation of concerns and single responsibility. `ViewModel` is simply a class that houses some properties that are only needed for the view. `ViewModel` is optional because you can technically return a model to a view directly. In fact, it is not part of the MVC term. However, it's worth including it in the flow because it is very useful and recommended when building real applications. Adding this extra layer enables you to expose only the data that you need instead of returning all data from your entity object via models. Finally, views are components that make up your UI or page. Typically, views are just Razor files (`.cshtml`) that contain HTML, CSS, JavaScript, and C#-embedded code.

Now that you have an idea of how MVC works, let's start building a web application from scratch to apply these concepts and get a feel of the framework.

Creating an MVC application

Let's go ahead and fire up Visual Studio 2019, and then select the **Create a new project** box, as shown Figure 4.8.

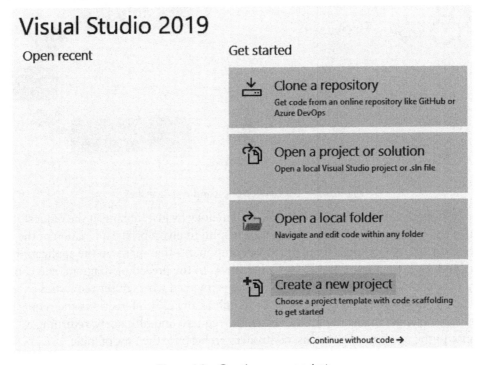

Figure 4.8 – Creating a new project

The **Create a new project** dialog should show up. In the dialog, select **Web** as the project type, and then find the **ASP.NET Core Web Application** project template, as shown in in Figure 4.9.

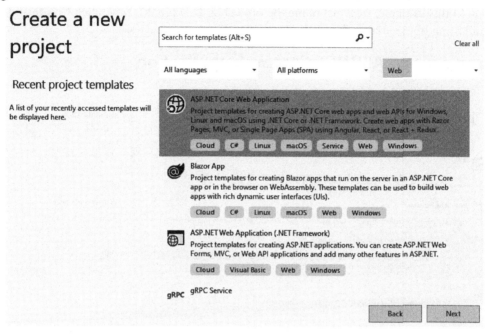

Figure 4.9 – Creating a new ASP.NET Core web app

To continue, double-click the **ASP.NET Core Web Application** template or simply click the **Next** button. The **Configure your new project** dialog should show up, as shown in Figure 4.10.

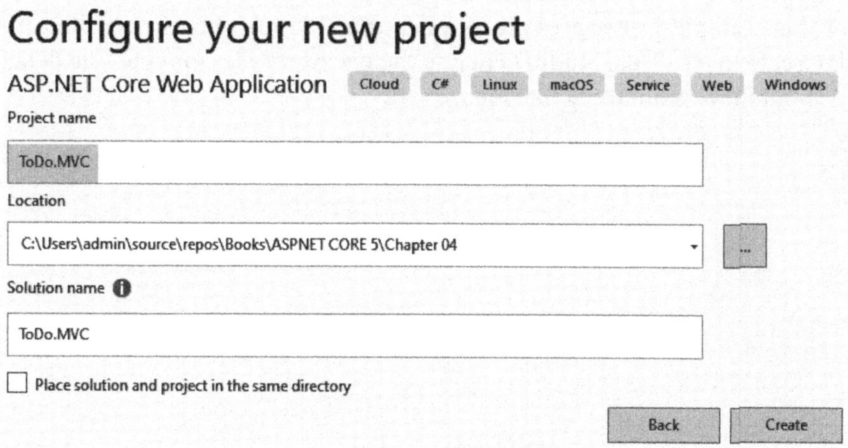

Figure 4.10 – Configuring the new project

The preceding dialog allows you to configure your project name and the location path to where you would want the project to be created. In a real application, you should consider giving a meaningful name to your project that clearly suggests what the project is all about. In this example, we'll just name the project as ToDo.MVC. Now, click **Create** and it should bring up the dialog shown in Figure 4.11.

Create a new ASP.NET Core web application

| .NET Core | ▾ | ASP.NET Core 5.0 | ▾ |

Empty
An empty project template for creating an ASP.NET Core application. This template does not have any content in it.

API
A project template for creating an ASP.NET Core application with an example Controller for a RESTful HTTP service. This template can also be used for ASP.NET Core MVC Views and Controllers.

Web Application
A project template for creating an ASP.NET Core application with example ASP.NET Razor Pages content.

Web Application (Model-View-Controller)
A project template for creating an ASP.NET Core application with example ASP.NET Core MVC Views and Controllers. This template can also be used for RESTful HTTP services.

Angular
A project template for creating an ASP.NET Core application with Angular

React.js
A project template for creating an ASP.NET Core application with React.js

Get additional project templates

Authentication
No Authentication
Change

Advanced
☑ Configure for HTTPS
☐ Enable Docker Support
   (Requires Docker Desktop)
Linux ▾
☐ Enable Razor runtime compilation

Author: Microsoft
Source: Templates 5.0.0-preview.6.20318.15

| Back | Create |

Figure 4.11 – Creating a new MVC project

The preceding dialog allows you to choose what type of web framework you want to create. For this example, just select **Web Application (Model-View-Controller)** and then click **Create** to let Visual Studio generate the necessary files for you. The default files generated should look something like Figure 4.12.

Figure 4.12 – Default MVC project structure

The preceding screenshot shows the default structure of the MVC application. You will notice that the template automatically generates the `Models`, `Views`, and `Controllers` folders. The names of each folder don't really matter in order for the application to function, but it's recommended and good practice to name the folders that way to conform with the MVC pattern. In MVC applications, functionalities are grouped into functions. This means that each folder that represents MVC will contain its own dedicated logical functions. `Models` contains data and validation; `Views` contains UI-related elements for displaying data, and `Controllers` contains actions that handle any user interactions.

If you already know the significant changes of the ASP.NET Core project structure, then you can skip this part, but if you are new to ASP.NET Core, then it's worth covering a few of the core files generated so that you have a better understanding of their purpose. Here's the anatomy of the core files aside from the MVC folders:

- `Connected Services`: Allows you to connect to services such as Application Insights, Azure Storage, mobile, and other ASP.NET Core services that your application depends on, without you having to manually configure their connection and configurations.

- `Dependencies`: This is where project dependencies are located, such as NuGet packages, external assemblies, the SDK, and framework dependencies needed for the application.

- `Properties`: This folder contains the `launchSettings.json` file, where you can define application variables and profiles for running the app.

- `wwwroot`: This folder contains all your static files, which will be served directly to the clients, including HTML, CSS, images, and JavaScript files.

- `appsettings.json`: This is where you configure application-specific settings. Keep in mind though that sensitive data should not be added to this file. You should consider storing secrets and sensitive information in a vault or secrets manager.

- `Program.cs`: This file is the main entry point for the application. This is where you build the host for your application. By default, the ASP.NET Core app builds a generic host that encapsulates all framework services needed to run the application.

- `Startup.cs`: This file is the heart of any .NET application. This is where you configure the services and dependencies required for your application.

Running the app for the first time

Let's try to build and run the default generated template to ensure that everything is working. Go ahead and press the *Ctrl + F5* keyboard keys or simply click the play button located on the Visual Studio menu toolbar, as shown in Figure 4.13.

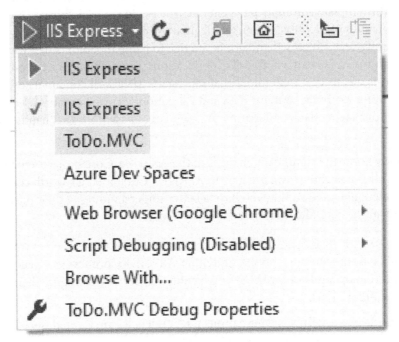

Figure 4.13 – Running the application

In the preceding screenshot, you will see that the default template automatically configures two web server profiles for running the app in localhost from inside Visual Studio: **IIS Express** and **ToDo.MVC**. The default profile used is IIS Express and the ToDo.MVC profile runs on the Kestrel web server. You can see how this was configured by looking at the launchSettings.json file. For more information about configuring ASP.NET Core environments, see https://docs.microsoft.com/en-us/aspnet/core/fundamentals/environments.

Visual Studio will compile, build, and automatically apply whatever configuration you've set up for each profile in the application. If everything builds successfully, then you should be presented with the output shown in Figure 4.14.

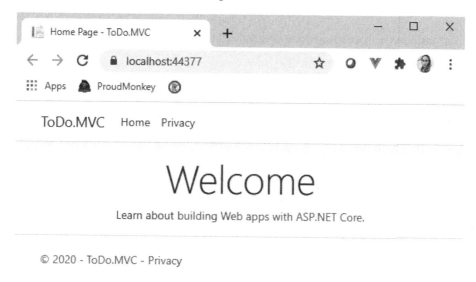

Figure 4.14 – First run output

Cool! Now, let's move on to the next step.

Configuring in-memory databases

One of the great features of ASP.NET Core is that it allows you to create a database in memory. This enables you to easily create a data-driven app without the need to spin up a real server for storing your data. With that said, we are going to take advantage of this feature in concert with **Entity Framework (EF)** Core so that we can play around with the data and dispose of it when no longer needed.

Working with a real database will be covered in *Chapter 7, APIs and Data Access,* as it mainly focuses on APIs and data access. For now, let's just use an in-memory working database for the sole purpose of this demo application.

Installing EF Core

The first thing we need to do is to add the `Microsoft.EntityFrameworkCore` and `Microsoft.EntityFrameworkCore.InMemory` NuGet packages as project references, so that we will be able to use EF as our data access mechanism to query data against the in-memory datastore. To do this, navigate to the Visual Studio menu, then go to **Tools | NuGet Package Manager | Package Manager Console**. In the console window, install each package by running the following commands:

```
Install-Package Microsoft.EntityFrameworkCore -Version 5.0.0
Install-Package Microsoft.EntityFrameworkCore.InMemory -Version 5.0.0
```

Each command in the preceding code will pull all the required dependencies needed for the application.

> **Note**
>
> The latest official version of `Microsoft.EntityFrameworkCore` as of the time of writing is 5.0.0. Future versions may change and could impact the sample code demonstrated in this chapter. So, make sure to always check for any breaking changes when deciding to upgrade to newer versions.

Another way to install NuGet dependencies in your project is using the **Manage NuGet Packages for Solution…** option, or by simply right-clicking on the **Dependencies** folder of the project and then selecting the **Manage NuGet Packages…** option. Both options provide a UI where you can easily search for and manage your project dependencies.

After successfully installing both packages, make sure to check your project **Dependencies** folder and verify whether they were added, just like in Figure 4.15.

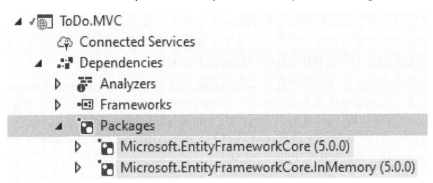

Figure 4.15 – NuGet package dependencies

Now that we have EF Core in place, let's move on to the next step.

Creating a view model

Next, we need to create a model that will contain some properties needed for our to-do page. Let's go ahead and create a new class called Todo in the Models folder and then copy the following code:

```
namespace ToDo.MVC.Models
{
    public class Todo
    {
        public int Id { get; set; }
        public string TaskName { get; set; }
        public bool IsComplete { get; set; }
    }
}
```

The preceding code is nothing more than a plain class that houses some properties.

Defining DbContext

EF Core requires DbContext for us to query the datastore. This is typically done by creating a class that inherits from the DbContext class. Now, let's add another class to the Models folder. Name the class TodoDbContext and then copy the following code:

```
using Microsoft.EntityFrameworkCore;
namespace ToDo.MVC.Models
{
    public class TodoDbContext: DbContext
    {
        public TodoDbContext(DbContextOptions<TodoDbContext>
            options)
        : base(options) { }
        public DbSet<Todo> Todos { get; set; }
    }
}
```

The preceding code defines DbContext and a single entity that exposes Model as DbSet. DbContext requires an instance of DbContextOptions. We can then override the OnConfiguring() method to implement our own code, or just pass DbContextOptions to the DbContext base constructor, as we've done in the preceding code.

Seeding test data in memory

Now, since we don't have an actual database for us to pull some data, we need to create a helper function that will initialize some data when the application starts. Let's go ahead and create a new class called `TodoDbSeeder` in the `Models` folder, and then copy the following code:

```
public class TodoDbSeeder
{
    public static void Seed(IServiceProvider serviceProvider)
    {
        using var context = new TodoDbContext(serviceProvider.
        GetRequiredService<DbContextOptions<TodoDbContext>>());

        // Look for any todos.
        if (context.Todos.Any())
        {
            //if we get here then the data already seeded
            return;
        }

        context.Todos.AddRange(
            new Todo
            {
                Id = 1,
                TaskName = "Work on book chapter",
                IsComplete = false
            },
            new Todo
            {
                Id = 2,
                TaskName = "Create video content",
                IsComplete = false
            }
        );
        context.SaveChanges();
    }
}
```

The preceding code looked for the `TodoDbContext` service from `IServiceCollection` and created an instance of it. The method is responsible for generating a couple of test `Todo` items on application startup. This is done by adding the data to the `Todos` entity of `TodoDbContext`.

At this point, we now have `DbContext` that enables us to access our `Todo` items and a helper class that will generate some data. What we need to do next is to wire them into the `Startup.cs` and `Program.cs` files to get our data populated.

Modifying the Startup class

Let's update the `ConfigureServices()` method of the `Startup` class to the following code:

```
public void ConfigureServices(IServiceCollection services)
{
    services.AddDbContext<TodoDbContext>(options => options.
        UseInMemoryDatabase("Todos"));
    services.AddControllersWithViews();
}
```

The preceding code registers `TodoDbContext` into `IServiceCollection` and defines an in-memory database called `Todos`. We need to do this so that we can reference an instance of `DbContext` in the `Controller` class or anywhere in our code within the application via **dependency injection**.

Now, let's move on to the next step by invoking the seeder helper function to generate the test data.

Modifying the Program class

Update the `Main()` method of the `Program.cs` file so that it looks similar to the following code:

```
public static void Main(string[] args)
{
    var host = CreateHostBuilder(args).Build();
    using (var scope = host.Services.CreateScope())
    {
        var services = scope.ServiceProvider;
        TodoDbSeeder.Seed(services);
    }
```

```
        host.Run();
    }
```

The preceding code creates a scope within the `Host` lifetime and looks for a service provider that is available from `Host`. Finally, we invoke the `Seed()` method of the `TodoDbSeeder` class and pass the service provider as an argument to the method.

At this point, our test data should be loaded into our memory "database" when the application starts and is ready for use in our application.

Creating the to-do controller

Now, let's create a new `Controller` class for our `Todo` page. Go ahead and navigate to the `Controllers` folder and create a new **MVC Controller-Empty** class called `TodoController`. Replace the default-generated code so that it looks similar to the following code:

```
public class TodoController : Controller
{
    private readonly TodoDbContext _dbContext;
    public TodoController(TodoDbContext dbContext)
    {
        _dbContext = dbContext;
    }
    [HttpGet]
    public IActionResult Index()
    {
        var todos = _dbContext.Todos.ToList();
        return View(todos);
    }
}
```

The preceding code first defines a `private` and `read-only` field of `TodoDbContext`. The next line of code defines the `constructor` class and uses the **constructor injection** approach to initialize the dependency object. In this case, any methods within the `TodoController` class will be able to access the instance of `TodoDbContext` and can invoke all its available methods and properties. For more information about dependency injection, review *Chapter 3, Dependency Injection*.

The `Index()` method is responsible for returning all `Todo` items from our in-memory datastore to the view. You can see that the method has been decorated with the `[HttpGet]` attribute, which signifies that the method can only be invoked in an HTTP GET request.

Now, that we have `TodoController` configured, let's move on to the next step and create the view for displaying all items on the page.

Creating a view

Before creating a view, make sure to build your application first to verify any compilation errors. After a successful build, right-click on the **Index()** method and then select **Add View…**. In the window dialog, select **Razor View** and it should bring up the dialog shown in Figure 4.16.

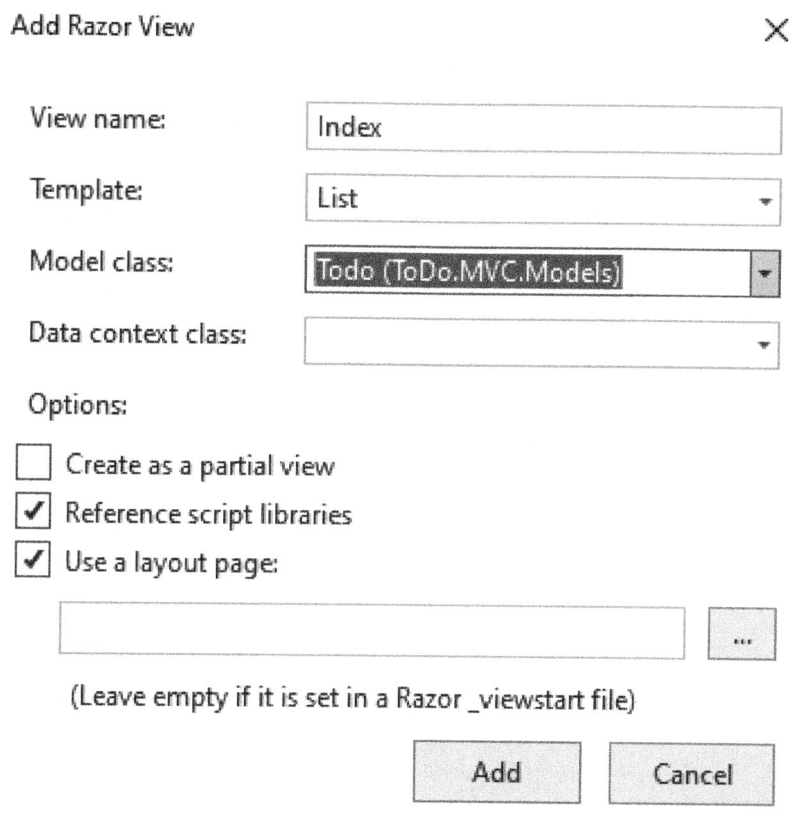

Add Razor View   ✕

View name: Index

Template: List

Model class: Todo (ToDo.MVC.Models)

Data context class:

Options:

☐ Create as a partial view
☑ Reference script libraries
☑ Use a layout page:

                                                              ...

(Leave empty if it is set in a Razor _viewstart file)

                              Add   Cancel

Figure 4.16 – Adding a new view

In the preceding dialog, select **List** for **Template** and select **Todo (ToDo.MVC.Models)** for **Model class**. Finally, click **Add** to generate the views (as shown in Figure 4.17).

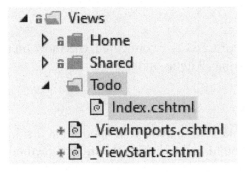

Figure 4.17 – The generated views

In the preceding screenshot, notice that the scaffolding engine automatically creates the views in a way that conforms to the MVC pattern. In this case, the `Index.cshtml` file was created under the `Todo` folder.

Note

You are free to manually add view files if you'd like. However, using the scaffolding template is much more convenient to generate simple views that match your controller action methods.

Now that we have wired our model, controllers, and views together, let's run the application to see the result.

Running the to-do app

Press the *Ctrl + F5* keys to launch the application in the browser, and then append `/todo` to the URL. You should be redirected to the to-do page and be presented with the output shown in Figure 4.18.

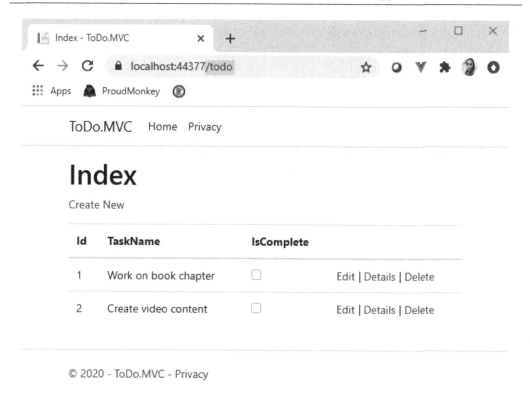

Figure 4.18 – The to-do list page

Notice in the preceding screenshot that the test data that we configured earlier has been displayed and the scaffolding template automatically constructs the HTML markup based on ViewModel. This is very convenient and definitely saves you some development time when creating simple pages in your application.

To know how the MVC routing works and how it was configured, just navigate to the Startup class. You should find the following code within the Configure() method:

```
app.UseEndpoints(endpoints =>
{
    endpoints.MapControllerRoute(
        name: "default",
        pattern: "{controller=Home}/{action=Index}/{id?}");
});
```

The preceding code configures a default routing pattern for your application using the `UseEndpoints()` middleware. The default pattern sets a value of `Home` as the default controller, `Index` as the default `Action` value, and `id` as the optional parameter holder for any routes. In other words, the `/home/index` path is the default route when the application starts. The MVC pattern follows this routing convention to route URL paths into `Controller` actions. So, if you want to configure custom routing rules for your application, then this is the middleware that you should look at. For more information about ASP.NET Core routing, see `https://docs.microsoft.com/en-us/aspnet/core/fundamentals/routing`.

At this point, we can confirm that our to-do page is up and running with test data. Now, let's take a look at how to extend the application by implementing some basic functionalities, such as adding, editing, and deleting items.

Implementing add item functionality

Let's modify our `TodoController` class and add the following code snippet for the add new item functionality:

```
[HttpGet]
public IActionResult Create()
{
    return View();
}


[HttpPost]
public IActionResult Create(Todo todo)
{
    var todoId = _dbContext.Todos.Select(x => x.Id).Max() + 1;
    todo.Id = todoId;
    _dbContext.Todos.Add(todo);
    _dbContext.SaveChanges();

    return RedirectToAction("Index");
}
```

As you will notice in the preceding code, there are two methods with the same name. The first `Create()` method is responsible for returning the view when a user requests the page. We will create this view in the next step. The second `Create()` method is an overload method that accepts a `Todo` view model as an argument, which is responsible for creating a new entry in our in-memory database. You can see that this method has been decorated with the `[HttpPost]` attribute, which signifies that the method can be invoked only for `POST` requests. Keep in mind that we are generating an ID manually by incrementing the existing maximum ID from our datastore. In real applications where you use a real database, you may not need to do this as you can let the database auto-generate the ID for you.

Now, let's create the corresponding view of the `Create()` method. To create a new view, just follow the same steps as we did for the `Index()` method, but this time select **Create** as the scaffolding template. This process should generate a Razor file called `Create.cshtml` in the `View/Todo` folder.

If you look at the generated view, the `Id` property of the `Todo` view model has been generated as well. This is normal as the scaffolding template will generate a Razor view based on the view model/model provided. We don't want the `Id` property to be included in the view as we are generating it in the code. So, remove the following HTML markup from the view:

```
<div class="form-group">
    <label asp-for="Id" class="control-label"></label>
    <input asp-for="Id" class="form-control" />
    <span asp-validation-for="Id" class="text-danger"></span>
</div>
```

Now, run the application again and navigate to /todo/create, and you should be presented with a page that looks similar to Figure 4.19.

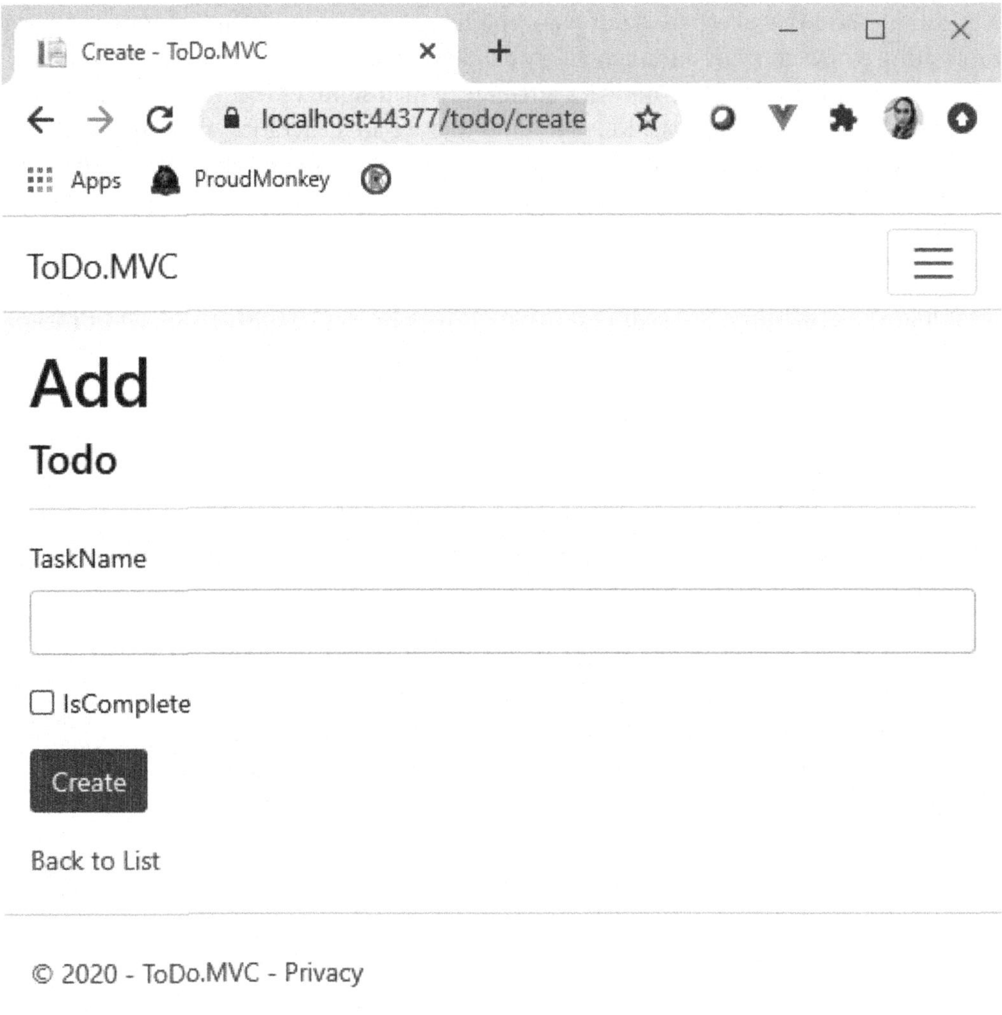

Figure 4.19 – The to-do Add page

Now, type the value Write Tech Blog in the **TaskName** textbox and tick the **IsComplete** checkbox. Clicking the **Create** button should add a new entry to our in-memory database and redirect you to the **Index** page, as shown in Figure 4.20.

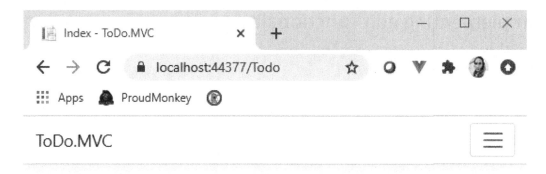

Figure 4.20 – The to-do list page

Sweet! To add more items, you can click the **Create New** link at the top of the list and you should be redirected back to the create view. Keep in mind though that we are not implementing any input validation here for simplicity's sake. In real applications, you should consider implementing model validations using either **data annotation** or **FluentValidation**. You can read more about these by referring to the following links:

- `https://docs.microsoft.com/en-us/aspnet/core/mvc/models/validation`

- `https://docs.fluentvalidation.net/en/latest/aspnet.html`

Now, let's move on to the next step.

Implementing edit functionality

Switch back to the `TodoController` class and add the following code snippet for the edit functionality:

```
[HttpGet]
public IActionResult Edit(int id)
{
    var todo = _dbContext.Todos.Find(id);
    return View(todo);
}


[HttpPost]
public IActionResult Edit(Todo todo)
{
    _dbContext.Todos.Update(todo);
    _dbContext.SaveChanges();
    return RedirectToAction("Index");
}
```

The preceding code also has just two action methods. The first `Edit()` method is responsible for populating the fields in the view based on the ID being passed to the route. The second `Edit()` method will be invoked during an HTTP POST request, which handles the actual update to the datastore.

To create the corresponding view for the `Edit` action, just follow the same steps as we did in the previous functionality, but this time, select **Edit** as the scaffolding template. This process should generate a Razor file called `Edit.cshtml` in the `View/Todo` folder.

The next step is to update our `Index` view to map the routes for edit and delete actions. Go ahead and update the `Action` link to the following:

```
@Html.ActionLink("Edit", "Edit", new { id = item.Id }) |
@Html.ActionLink("Delete", "Delete", new { id = item.Id })
```

The preceding code defines a couple of `ActionLink` HTML helpers for navigating between views with parameters. The changes we made in the preceding code are passing the ID as the parameter to each route and removing the details link, as we won't be covering that here. Anyway, implementing the details page should be pretty straightforward. You can also view the GitHub code repository of this chapter to see how it was implemented.

Now, when you run the application, you should be able to navigate from the to-do `Index` page to the `Edit` page by clicking the **Edit** link. Figure 4.21 shows you a sample screenshot of the **Edit** page.

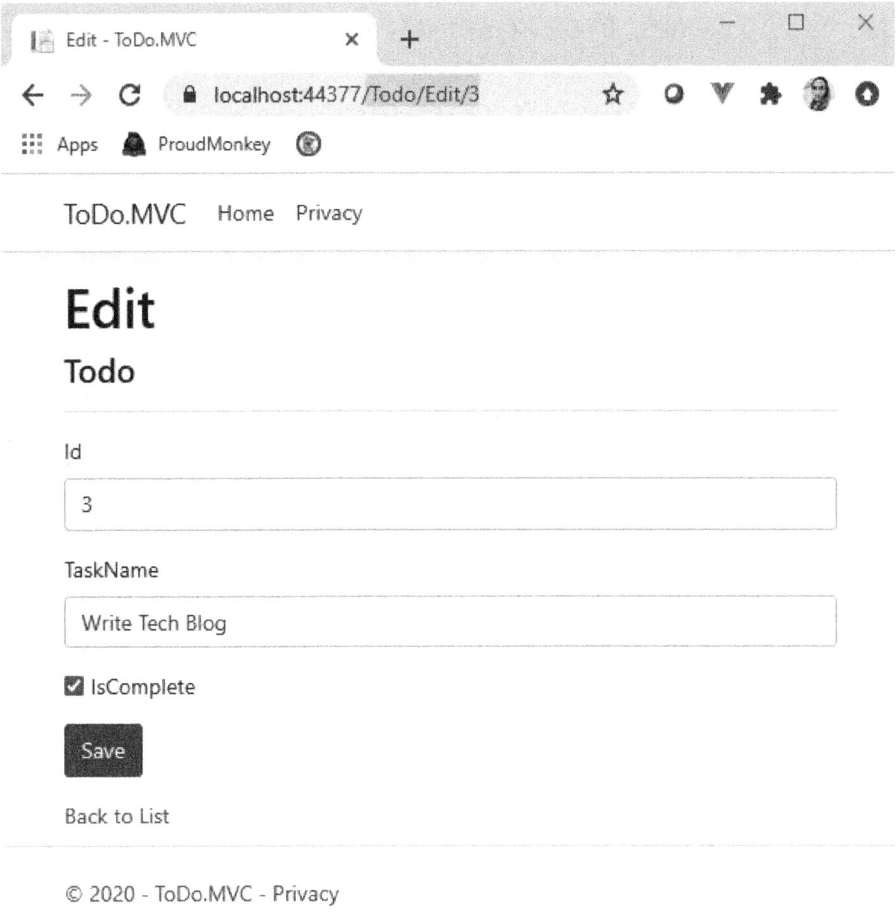

Figure 4.21 – The to-do Edit page

In the preceding screenshot, notice that the ID is now included in the route and the page is automatically being populated with the corresponding data. Now, let's move on to the next step.

Implementing the delete functionality

Switch back to the `TodoController` class and add the following code snippet for the delete functionality:

```
public IActionResult Delete(int? id)
{
    var todo = _dbContext.Todos.Find(id);
    if (todo == null)
    {
        return NotFound();
    }
    return View(todo);
}


[HttpPost]
public IActionResult Delete(int id)
{
    var todo = _dbContext.Todos.Find(id);
    _dbContext.Todos.Remove(todo);
    _dbContext.SaveChanges();

    return RedirectToAction("Index");
}
```

The first `Delete()` method in the preceding code is responsible for populating the page with the corresponding data based on the ID. If the ID does not exist in our in-memory datastore, then we simply return a `NotFound()` result. The second `Delete()` method will be triggered when clicking the **Delete** button. This method executes the deletion of the item from the datastore. Figure 4.22 shows you a sample screenshot of the **Delete** page.

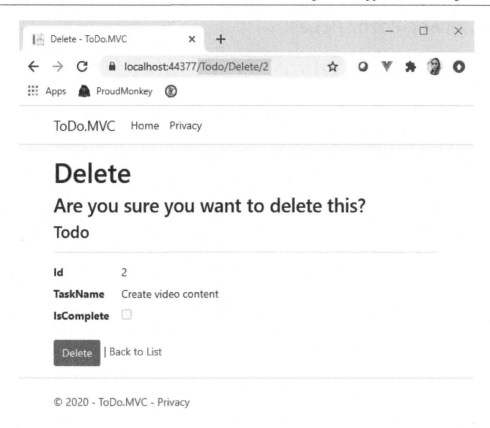

Figure 4.22 – The to-do Delete page

At this point, you should have a better understanding of how MVC works and how we can easily implement **Create**, **Read**, **Update**, and **Delete** (**CRUD**) operations on a page. There are a lot of things that we can do to improve the application, so take a moment to add the missing features as an extra exercise. You could try integrating model validations, logging, or any features that you want to see in the application. You can also refer to the following project template to help you get up to speed on using MVC in concert with other technologies to build web applications:

`https://github.com/proudmonkey/MvcBoilerPlate`

Let's move on to the next section and take a look at Razor Pages.

Building a to-do app with Razor Pages

Razor Pages is another web framework for building ASP.NET Core web applications. It was first introduced with the release of ASP.NET Core 2.0 and became the default web application template for ASP.NET Core.

Reviewing Razor Pages

To better understand the Razor Pages approach, Figure 4.23 provides a high-level diagram of the process that describes the HTTP request and response flow.

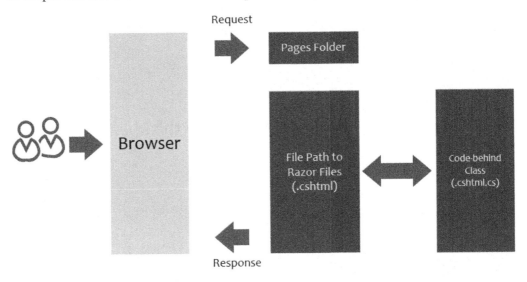

Figure 4.23 – Razor Pages request and response flow

If you've worked with ASP.NET Web Forms before, or any web framework that follows a page-centric approach, then you should find Razor Pages familiar. Unlike MVC, where requests are handled in the controller, the routing system in Razor Pages is based on matching URLs to the physical file path. In other words, all requests default to the root folder, which is named `Pages` by default.

The route collection will then be constructed based on the file and folder paths within the root folder. For example, if you have a Razor file that sits under `Pages/Something/MyPage.cshtml`, then you can navigate to that page in the browser using the `/something/mypage` route. Routing in Razor Pages is flexible as well, and you can customize it however you want. Take a look at the following resource for detailed references about Razor Pages routing:

`https://www.learnrazorpages.com/razor-pages/routing`

Razor Pages still uses the **Razor view engine** to generate HTML markup, just like you would do with MVC. One of the main differences between the two web frameworks is that Razor Pages doesn't use controllers anymore, and instead uses individual pages. Typically, Razor Pages consists of two main files: a `.cshtml` file and a `.cshtml.cs` file. The `.cshtml` file is a Razor file containing Razor markup, and the `.cshtml.cs` file is a class that defines the functionality for the page.

For you to better understand how Razor Pages differs from MVC, let's mimic the to-do app that we built earlier with MVC. Note that we will only be covering the significant differences in this example, and common things such as configuring an in-memory datastore and running the app to see the output will not be covered. This is because the process and implementation are pretty much the same as with MVC. The source code for this exercise can be found here:

```
https://github.com/PacktPublishing/ASP.NET-Core-5-for-
Beginners/tree/master/Chapter%2004/Chapter_04_RazorViewEngine_
Examples/ToDo.RazorPages
```

Creating a Razor Pages application

Go ahead and fire up Visual Studio 2019, and then create a new project. This time, select **Web Application** from the ASP.NET Core web application project templates, as shown in Figure 4.24.

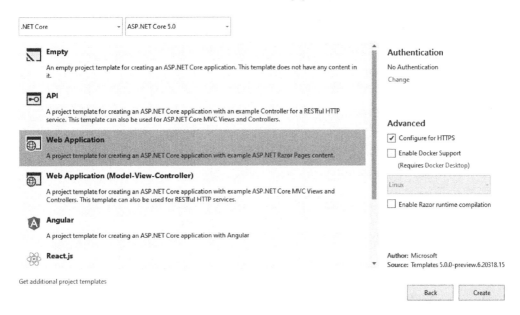

Figure 4.24 – Creating a new Razor Pages web app

Click the **Create** button to generate the default files. Figure 4.25 shows you how the Razor Pages project structure is going to look.

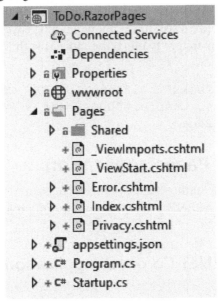

Figure 4.25 – The Razor Pages project structure

In the preceding screenshot, you'll immediately notice that there are no `Controllers`, `Models`, and `Views` folders anymore. Instead, you only have the `Pages` folder. Razor Pages applications are configured using the `AddRazorPages()` service in the `ConfigureServices()` method of the `Startup` class:

```
public void ConfigureServices(IServiceCollection services)
{
    services.AddRazorPages();
}
```

Now, let's take a look at the `Index.cshtml` file to see how the page structure differs from MVC views.

Understanding the Razor Pages structure

Here's how the `Index.cshtml` markup looks:

```
@page
@model IndexModel
@{
```

```
        ViewData["Title"] = "Home page";
}
<div class="text-center">
    <h1 class="display-4">Welcome</h1>
</div>
```

We can see that the preceding markup is very similar to MVC views, except for two things:

- It uses the @page directive at the very beginning of the file. This directive tells the Razor engine to treat the page as Razor Pages so that any page interactions will be properly routed to the correct handler method. In other words, the @page directive indicates that actions and routes should not be handled in Controllers.

- Unlike in MVC, where @model represents the ViewModel or Model class to be used in the view, the @model directive in Razor Pages represents the name of the "code-behind" class for the Razor file instead. In this case, the Index.cshtml file refers to the IndexModel class defined within the Index.cshtml.cs file, as shown in the following code:

```
public class IndexModel : PageModel
{
    private readonly ILogger<IndexModel> _logger;
    public IndexModel(ILogger<IndexModel> logger)
    {
        _logger = logger;
    }
    public void OnGet() { }
}
```

The preceding code shows the typical code-behind class structure of Razor Pages. Every class that represents a model for the page should inherit from the PageModel base class. This class encapsulates several features and functions needed for executing things such as ModelState, HttpContext, TempData, Routing, and many others.

Creating the to-do pages

Let's go ahead create a new folder called Todos in the Pages folder. We'll start with the Index page for displaying the list of to-do items.

Building the Index page

To create a new Razor page, just right-click on the Todos folder and then select **Add | Razor Pages...**. Set the page name to Index and click the **Add** button. This process should generate both Index.cshtml (Razor markup) and Index.cshtml.cs (code-behind class) files in the Todos folder.

Now, copy the following code snippet into the code-behind class:

```
public class IndexModel : PageModel
{
    private TodoDbContext _dbContext;
    public IndexModel(TodoDbContext dbContext)
    {
        _dbContext = dbContext;
    }

    public List<Todo> Todos { get; set; }
    public void OnGet()
    {
        Todos = _dbContext.Todos.ToList();
    }
}
```

The preceding code is somewhat similar to the Controllers code in MVC, except for the following:

- It now uses the OnGet() method to fetch the data. PageModel exposes a few handler methods for executing requests, such as OnGet(), OnPost(), OnPut(), OnDelete(), and more. The Razor Pages framework uses a naming convention for matching the appropriate HTTP request methods (HTTP verbs) to execute. This is done by prefixing the handler method with On followed by the HTTP verb name. In other words, Razor Pages doesn't use HTTP verb attributes such as [HttpGet], [HttpPost], and so on when executing a request.

- It exposes a public property as ViewModel. In this case, the Todos property will be populated with data from the datastore when you request the Index page in the browser. This property will then be consumed or used in the Razor markup to present the data. Take the following example:

```
<tbody>
    @foreach (var item in Model.Todos)
```

```
        {
            <tr>
                @*Removed other rows for brevity*@
                <td>
                    <a asp-page="Edit" asp-route-id="@item.
                        Id">Edit</a> |
                    <a asp-page="Details" asp-route-id="@item.
                        Id">Details</a> |
                    <a asp-page="Delete" asp-route-id="@item.
                        Id">Delete</a>
                </td>
            </tr>
        }
    </tbody>
```

The preceding markup uses the same structure as what we did in MVC, except that we now reference the data from the `Model.Todos` property. Also, we now used the `asp-page` and `asp-route` tag helpers to navigate between pages with route parameters.

Now, when you run the application and navigate to `/todos`, you should be presented with the following output shown in Figure 4.26.

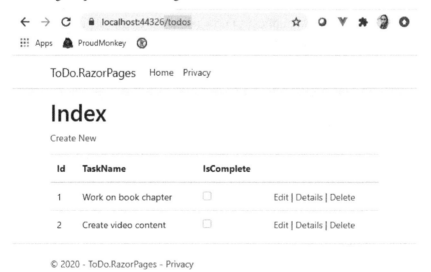

Figure 4.26 – The Razor Pages to-do list page

Sweet! Now, let's move on by adding the remaining functionalities.

Add item implementation

The following code snippet is the equivalent of adding a new Todo item in Razor Pages:

```
public class CreateModel : PageModel
{
    //removed constructor and private field for brevity
    [BindProperty]
    public Todo Todo { get; set; }
    public IActionResult OnGet()
    {
        return Page();
    }

    public IActionResult OnPost()
    {
        _dbContext.Todos.Add(Todo);
        _dbContext.SaveChanges();
        return RedirectToPage("./Index");
    }
}
```

The preceding code contains a public property called Todo that represents ViewModel and two main handler methods. The Todo property is decorated with the [BindProperty] attribute so that the server will be able to reference the values from the page on POST. The OnGet() method simply returns a page. The OnPost() method takes the Todo object that was posted, inserts a new record into the datastore, and finally, redirects you back to the Index page.

For more information about model binding in Razor Pages, see https://www.learnrazorpages.com/razor-pages/model-binding.

Edit item implementation

The following is the code snippet for the edit functionality in Razor pages:

```
public class EditModel : PageModel
{
    //removed constructor and private field for brevity
    [BindProperty]
```

```
    public Todo Todo { get; set; }
    public void OnGet(int id)
    {
        Todo = _dbContext.Todos.Find(id);
    }


    public IActionResult OnPost()
    {
        _dbContext.Todos.Update(Todo);
        _dbContext.SaveChanges();
        return RedirectToPage("./Index");
    }
}
```

The preceding code is somewhat similar to the Create page except that the OnGet() method now accepts an ID as an argument. The Id value is used to look up the associated data from the datastore and if it finds it, it populates the Todo object. The Todo object is then bound to the page and any changes on the associated properties will be captured when the page is submitted. The OnPost() method takes care of updating the data to the datastore.

The id value is added to the route data. This is done by setting the {id} template holder in the @page directive, as shown in the following code:

```
@page "{id:int}"
```

The preceding code will create the /Edit/{id} route, where id represents a value. The : int expression signifies a route constraint, which means that the id value must be an integer.

Delete item implementation

The following is the code snippet for the delete functionality in Razor Pages:

```
[BindProperty]
public Todo Todo { get; set; }
public void OnGet(int id)
{
    Todo = _dbContext.Todos.Find(id);
}
```

```
public IActionResult OnPost()
{
    _dbContext.Todos.Remove(Todo);
    _dbContext.SaveChanges();
    return RedirectToPage("./Index");
}
```

The preceding code is very similar to the Edit page. The only difference is the line where we remove the item within the OnPost() handler method.

Now that you've learned the core differences between MVC and Razor Pages and have a feel for both web frameworks by following hands-on exercises, you should be able to decide which approach to use when building real-world applications.

Differences between MVC and Razor Pages

To summarize, here are the key differences between MVC and Razor Pages:

- Both are great web frameworks for building dynamic web applications. They have their own benefits. You just have to use which approach is better suited in certain situations.

- Both MVC and Razor Pages value the separation of concerns. MVC is just more strict as it follows a specific pattern.

- Learning MVC may take you more time due to its complexity. You have to understand the underlying concept behind it.

- Learning Razor Pages is easier as it's less magical, more straightforward, and more organized. You don't have to switch between folders just to build a page.

- The MVC structure is grouped by functionality. For example, all actions in the view should sit within the Controller class to follow the convention. This makes MVC very flexible, especially when dealing with complex URL routings.

- The Razor Pages structure is grouped by features and purpose. For example, any logic for the to-do page is contained within a single location. This enables you to easily add or remove features in your application without modifying different areas in your code. Also, code maintenance is much easier.

Summary

This chapter was huge! We learned about the concept of the Razor view engine and how it powers different web frameworks to generate HTML markup using a unified markup syntax. This is one of the main reasons why ASP.NET Core is powerful; it gives you the flexibility to choose whatever web framework you prefer without you having to learn a different markup syntax for building UIs.

We've covered two of the hot web frameworks to date that ship with ASP.NET Core. MVC and Razor Pages probably each deserve their own dedicated chapter to cover their features in detail. However, we still managed to tackle them and explore their common features and differences by building an application from scratch, using an in-memory database. Learning the basics of creating a simple data-driven web application is a great start to becoming a full-fledged ASP.NET Core developer.

We can conclude that Razor Pages is ideal for beginners or for building simple dynamic web applications as it minimizes complexity. MVC, on the other hand, is a great candidate for building large-scale and more complex applications.

Understanding the different web frameworks is crucial for building real-world applications, because it helps you understand the pros and cons that allows you to choose which approach you should take, based on the project scope and requirements.

In the next chapter, we are going to explore Blazor as a new, alternative approach for building modern web applications.

Further reading

- ASP.NET Core web apps: `https://dotnet.microsoft.com/apps/aspnet/web-apps`

- Razor syntax: `https://docs.microsoft.com/en-us/aspnet/core/mvc/views/razor`

- Learn ASP.NET Core: `https://dotnet.microsoft.com/learn/aspnet`

- ASP.NET Core built-in tag helpers: `https://docs.microsoft.com/en-us/aspnet/core/mvc/views/tag-helpers/built-in`

- ASP.NET Core tag helpers: `https://docs.microsoft.com/en-us/aspnet/core/mvc/views/tag-helpers/intro`

- C# => operator: `https://docs.microsoft.com/en-us/dotnet/csharp/language-reference/operators/lambda-operator`

- ASP.NET Core fundamentals: `https://docs.microsoft.com/en-us/aspnet/core/fundamentals`

- Razor Pages page model class: `https://docs.microsoft.com/en-us/dotnet/api/microsoft.aspnetcore.mvc.razorpages.pagemodel`

- Learn Razor Pages: `https://www.learnrazorpages.com/razor-pages`

- EF Core: `https://docs.microsoft.com/en-us/ef/core/`

- EF Core in-memory provider: `https://docs.microsoft.com/en-us/ef/core/providers/in-memory`

5
Getting Started with Blazor

In the previous chapter, we learned about the fundamentals of Razor View Engine and understood how it powers different web frameworks to render web UIs. We covered hands-on coding exercises to get a feel for both the MVC and Razor Pages web frameworks that ship with ASP.NET Core for building powerful web applications. In this chapter, we are going to look at the latest addition to the ASP.NET Core web framework – Blazor.

The Blazor web framework is a huge topic; this book splits the topic into two chapters for you to easily grasp the core concepts and fundamentals needed for you to get started with the framework. By the time you've finished both chapters, you will know how Blazor applications can be used in concert with various technologies to build powerful and dynamic web applications.

Here are the topics that we'll cover in this chapter:

- Understanding the Blazor web framework
- Understanding the goal of what we are going to build using various technologies
- Building a tourist spot application
- Creating the backend application

This chapter is mainly targeted at beginner- and intermediate-level .NET developers with prior C# experience, who want to jump into Blazor and get their hands dirty with practical examples. It will help you learn the basics of the Blazor programming model, for you to build your first web application from scratch.

Technical requirements

This chapter uses Visual Studio 2019 to build the project. You can view the source code for this chapter at `https://github.com/PacktPublishing/ASP.NET-Core-5-for-Beginners/tree/master/Chapter%2005%20and%2006/Chapter_05_and_06_Blazor_Examples/TouristSpot`.

Before diving into this chapter, make sure that you have a basic understanding of ASP. NET Core and C# in general, because we're not going to cover their fundamentals in this chapter.

Please visit the following link to check the CiA videos: `https://bit.ly/3qDiqYY`

Understanding the Blazor web framework

Blazor was introduced as an experimental project in early 2018. It's the latest addition to the **Single-Page Application (SPA)**-based ASP.NET Core web frameworks. You can think of it as similar to React, Angular, Vue, and other SPA-based frameworks, but it is powered by C# and the Razor markup language, enabling you to create web applications without having to write JavaScript. Yes, you heard that right – without JavaScript! Though Blazor doesn't require you to use JavaScript, it offers a feature called **JavaScript interoperability (JS interop)**, which allows you to invoke JavaScript code from your C# code and vice versa. Pretty neat!

Regardless of whether you are coming from a Windows, Xamarin, Web Forms, or traditional ASP.NET MVC development background, or are completely new to ASP. NET Core and want to take your skills to the next level, Blazor is definitely a great choice for you since it enables you to use your existing C# skills to write web UIs. Learning the framework itself is easy, as long as you know basic HTML and CSS. It was designed to enable C# developers to take advantage of their skills to easily transition to the web paradigm for building SPA-based web applications.

Reviewing the different flavors of Blazor

Before we talk about the different flavors of Blazor, let's have a quick overview of Razor components.

Razor components are the building blocks for Blazor applications. They are self-contained chunks of UI that are composed of HTML, CSS, and C# code using **Razor** markup. These components can be a whole page, a section in a page, a form, or a dialog box. Components are very flexible, lightweight, and easy to reuse, nest, or even share across different applications, such as Razor Pages or MVC apps. Any changes that happen in a component, such as a button click that affects the state of an app, will render a graph and a UI `diff` is calculated. This `diff` contains a set of DOM edits that are required to update the UI and is applied by the browser.

Blazor has gained a lot of popularity, even if the framework is still pretty much new to the market. In fact, big UI providers, such as Telerik, Syncfusion, and DevExpress, already offer a bunch of Razor components that you can integrate into your application. There are also other open source projects that provide ready-made components that you can use for free, such as MatBlazor and RadZen.

Blazor comes with two main hosting models:

- Blazor Server
- Blazor **WebAssembly (WASM)**

Let's do a quick rundown of each.

Blazor Server

Blazor Server, often referred to as server-side Blazor, is a type of Blazor application that runs on a server. It was the first Blazor model to be officially shipped in .NET Core and is ready for production use. Figure 5.1 shows how Blazor Server works under the hood.

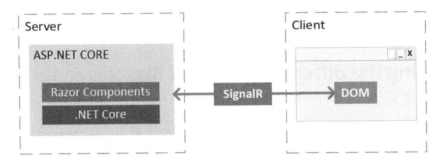

Figure 5.1 – Blazor Server

In the preceding diagram, we can see that the server-based Blazor application is wrapped within the ASP.NET Core application, allowing it to run and be executed on the server. It mainly uses SignalR to manage and drive real-time server updates to the UI and vice versa. This means that maintaining the application state, DOM interactions, and rendering of the components happens in the server, and SignalR will notify the UI via a hub with a `diff` to update the DOM when the application state changes.

The pros of this are as follows:

- No need for you to write JavaScript to run the app.
- Your application code stays on the server.
- Since the application runs on the server, you can take advantage of ASP.NET Core features, such as hosting a Web API in a shared project, integrating other middleware, and connecting to a database and other external dependencies via DI.
- Enables fast load times and small download sizes, since the server takes care of heavy workloads.
- Runs on any browser.
- Great debugging capability.

The cons are as follows:

- It requires a server to bootstrap the application.
- No offline support. SignalR requires an open connection to the server. The moment the server goes down, so does your application.

- There is higher network latency, since every UI interaction needs to call the server to re-render the component state. This can be resolved if you have a geo-replicated server that hosts your app in various regions.

- Maintaining and scaling can be costly and difficult. This is because every time you open an instance of a page, a separate SignalR connection is created, which can be hard to manage. This can be resolved when using the Azure SignalR service when deploying your app to Azure. For non-Azure cloud providers, you may have to rely on your traffic manager to get around this challenge.

Blazor WebAssembly

WASM, in simple terms, is an abstraction that enables high-level programming languages, such as C#, to run in the browser. This process is done by downloading all the required WASM-based .NET assemblies and application DLLs in the browser, so that the application can run independently in the client browser. Most major browsers nowadays, such as Google Chrome, Microsoft Edge, Mozilla Firefox, and Apple's Safari and WebKit, support WASM technology.

Blazor WASM has recently been integrated into Blazor. Under the hood, Blazor WASM uses WASM-based .NET runtimes to execute an application's .NET assemblies and DLLs. This type of application can run on a browser that supports WASM web standards with no plugins required. That said, Blazor WASM is not a new form of Silverlight.

Figure 5.2 shows you how a Blazor WASM application works under the hood.

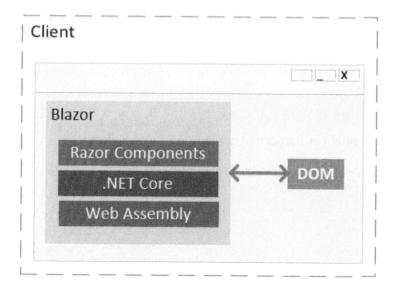

Figure 5.2 – Blazor WASM

In the preceding illustration, we can see that the Blazor WASM application doesn't depend on ASP.NET Core; the application is directly executed on the client. Client-side Blazor is running using WASM technology. By default, a Blazor WASM application runs purely on the client; however, there's an option for you to turn it into an ASP.NET-hosted app to get all the benefits of Blazor and full-stack .NET web development.

The pros of this are as follows:

- No need for you to write JavaScript to run the app.

- No server-side dependency, which means no latency or scalability issues since the app runs on the client machine.

- Enables offline support, since the app is offloaded to the client as a self-contained app. This means you can still run the application while being disconnected from the server where your application is hosted.

- Support for **Progressive Web Applications (PWAs)**. PWAs are web applications that use modern browser APIs and capabilities to behave like native ones.

These are the cons:

- The initial loading of a page is slow, and the download size is huge because all the required dependencies need to be pulled upfront to offload your application to the client's browser. This can be optimized in the future, when caching is implemented to reduce the size of downloads and the amount of time that subsequent requests take to process.

- Since DLLs are downloaded to the client, your application code is exposed. So, you must be very careful about what you put there.

- Requires a browser that supports WASM. Note that most major browsers now support WASM.

- It's a less mature runtime as it's new.

- Debugging might be harder and limited, compared to Blazor Server.

For more information about Blazor hosting models, see `https://docs.microsoft.com/en-us/aspnet/core/blazor/hosting-models`.

Mobile Blazor Bindings

Blazor also provides a framework for building native and hybrid mobile applications for Android, iOS, Windows, and macOS, using C# and .NET. **Mobile Blazor Bindings** uses the same markup engine for building UI components. This means that you can use Razor syntax to define UI components and their behaviors. Under the hood, the UI components are still based on **Xamarin.Forms**, as it uses the same XAML-based structure to build components. What makes this framework stand out over Xamarin.Forms is that it allows you to mix in HTML, giving developers the choice to write apps using the markup they prefer. With hybrid apps, you can mix in HTML to build components just as you would build web UI components. This makes it a great stepping stone for ASP.NET developers looking to get into cross-platform native mobile application development using their existing skills. With that being said, Mobile Blazor Bindings is still in its experimental stage and there is no guarantee about anything until it is officially released.

We won't be covering Mobile Blazor Bindings development in this chapter. If you want to learn more about it, you can refer to the official documentation here: `https://docs.microsoft.com/en-us/mobile-blazor-bindings`.

Understanding the goal of what we are going to build using various technologies

As we've learned from the previous section, Blazor is only a framework for building UIs. To make learning Blazor fun and interesting, we are going to use various technologies to build a whole web application to fulfill a goal. That goal is to build a simple data-driven web application with real-time capability using cutting-edge technologies: **Blazor Server**, **Blazor WASM**, **ASP.NET Core Web API**, **SignalR**, and **Entity Framework Core**.

Figure 5.3 illustrates the high-level process of how each technology connects.

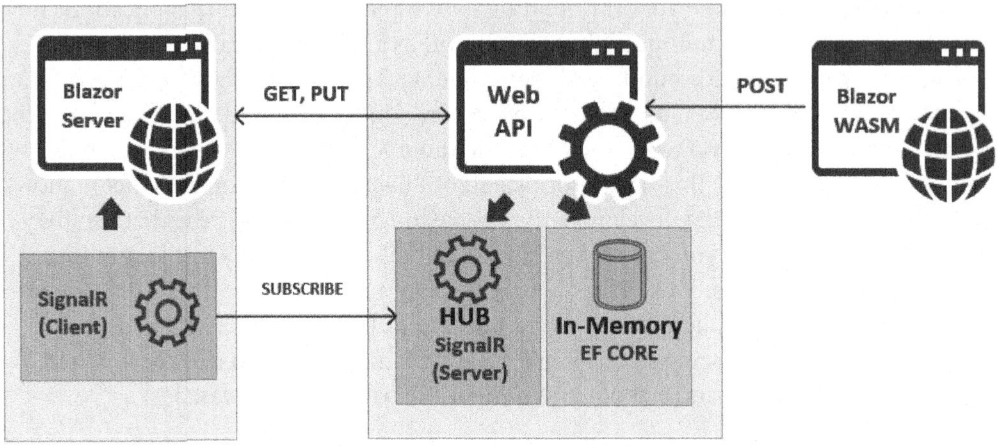

Figure 5.3 – Five players, one goal

Based on the preceding diagram, we are going to need to build the following applications:

- A web app that displays and updates information on the page via API calls. This application will also implement a SignalR subscription that acts as the client to perform real-time data updates to the UI.

- A Web API app that exposes GET, PUT, and POST public-facing API endpoints. This application will also configure an in-memory data store to persist data and implement SignalR to broadcast a message to the hub where clients can subscribe and get data in real time.

- A PWA that submits a new record via an API call.

Now that you already have an idea of what to build and which sets of technologies to use, let's start getting our hands dirty with coding.

Building a tourist spot application

In order to cover real-world scenarios in a typical data-driven web application, we will build a simple tourist spot application that composes various applications to perform different tasks. You can think of this application as a wiki for tourist destinations, where users can view and edit information about places. Users can also see the top places, based on reviews, and they also see new places submitted by other similar applications in real time. By real time, we mean without the user having to refresh the page to see new data.

Figure 5.4 describes the applications needed and the high-level flow of the process for our tourist spot application example

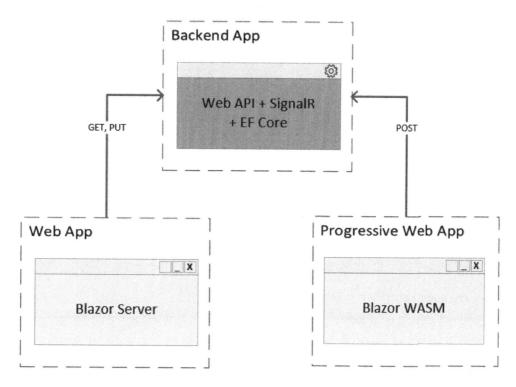

Figure 5.4 – The applications to be built

If you're ready, then let's get cracking. We'll start by building the backend application, which exposes the API endpoints to serve data so that other applications can consume it.

Creating the backend application

For the tourist spot application project, we are going to use ASP.NET Core Web API as our backend application.

Let's go ahead and fire up Visual Studio 2019 and then select the **Create a new project** option. On the next screen, select **ASP.NET Core Web Application** and then click **Next**. The **Configure your new project** dialog should appear as it does in Figure 5.5.

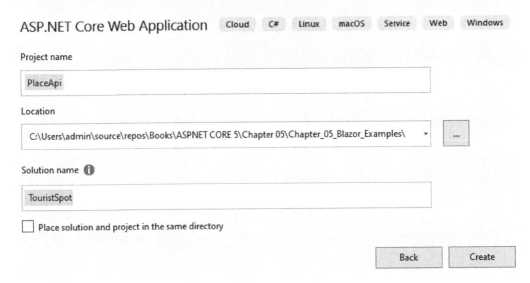

Figure 5.5 – Configure your new project

This dialog allows you to configure your project and solution name, as well as the location path to where you want the project to be created. For this particular example, we'll just name the project `PlaceApi` and set the solution name to `TouristSpot`. Now, click **Create** and you should see the dialog shown in Figure 5.6.

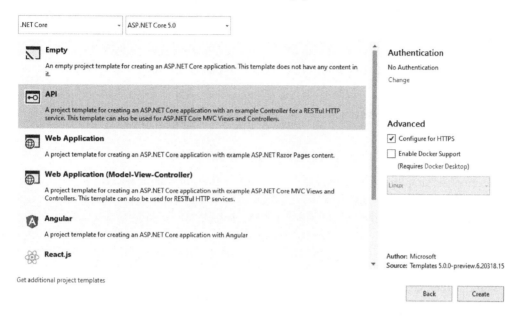

Figure 5.6 – Create a new ASP.NET Core web application

This dialog allows you to choose the type of web framework that you want to create. For this project, just select **API** and then click **Create** to let Visual Studio generate the necessary files for you. The default files generated should look something like it does in Figure 5.7.

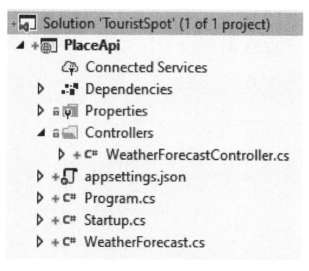

Figure 5.7 – Web API default project structure

The preceding screenshot shows the default structure of an ASP.NET Core Web API application. Please note that we won't dig into the details about Web API in this chapter, but to give you a quick overview, Web API works the same way as the traditional ASP.NET MVC, except that it was designed for building RESTful APIs that can be consumed over HTTP. In other words, Web API doesn't have **Razor View Engine** and it wasn't meant to generate pages. We'll deep dive into the details of Web API in *Chapter 7, APIs and Data Access*.

Now, let's move on to the next step.

Configuring an in-memory database

In the previous chapter, we learned how to use an in-memory database with Entity Framework Core. If you've made it this far, you should now be familiar with how to configure an in-memory data store. For this demonstration, we will be using the technique you're now familiar with to easily create a data-driven app, without the need to spin up a real database server to store data. Working with a real database in Entity Framework Core will be covered in *Chapter 7, APIs and Data Access*; for now, let's just make use of an in-memory database, for the simplicity of this exercise.

Installing Entity Framework Core

Entity Framework Core was implemented as a separate NuGet package to allow developers to easily integrate it when needed. There are many ways to integrate NuGet package dependencies in your application. We could either install it via the **command line (CLI)** or via the NuGet package management interface (the UI) integrated into Visual Studio. To install dependencies using the UI, simply right-click on the `Dependencies` folder of the project and then select the **Manage NuGet Packages…** option. Figure 5.8 shows you how the UI should come up.

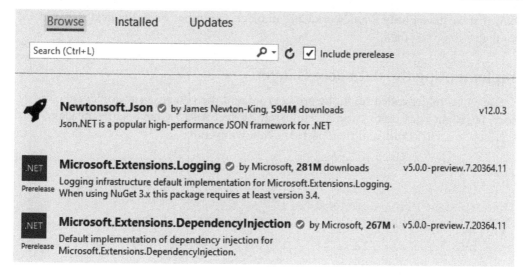

Figure 5.8 – NuGet package management UI

In the **Browse** tab, type in the package names listed here and install them:

- `Microsoft.EntityFrameworkCore`

- `Microsoft.EntityFrameworkCore.InMemory`

After successfully installing both packages, make sure to check your project's `Dependencies` folder and verify that they were added (as shown in Figure 5.9).

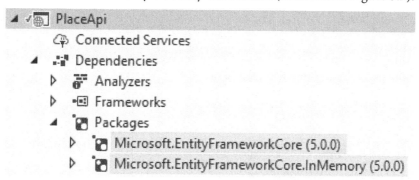

Figure 5.9 – Installed project NuGet dependencies

Note:

The latest official version of `Microsoft.EntityFrameworkCore` at the time of writing is `5.0.0`. Future versions may change and could impact the sample code used in this chapter. So, make sure to always check for any breaking changes when deciding to upgrade to newer versions.

Now that we have Entity Framework Core in place, let's move on to the next step and configure some test data.

Implementing the data access layer

Create a new folder called `Db` in the project root and then create a sub-folder called `Models`. Right-click on the `Models` folder and select **Add** > **Class**. Name the class `Places.cs`, click **Add**, and then paste the following code:

```csharp
using System;

namespace PlaceApi.Db.Models
{
    public class Place
    {
        public int Id { get; set; }
        public string Name { get; set; }
        public string Location { get; set; }
        public string About { get; set; }
        public int Reviews { get; set; }
        public string ImageData { get; set; }
        public DateTime LastUpdated { get; set; }
    }
}
```

The preceding code is just a plain class that houses some properties. We will use this class later to populate each property with test data.

Now, create a new class called `PlaceDbContext.cs` in the `Db` folder and copy the following code:

```csharp
using Microsoft.EntityFrameworkCore;
using PlaceApi.Db.Models;
namespace PlaceApi.Db
{
    public class PlaceDbContext : DbContext
    {
        public PlaceDbContext(DbContextOptions<PlaceDbContext>
        options)
        : base(options) { }
```

```
        public DbSet<Place> Places { get; set; }
    }
}
```

The preceding code defines a `DbContext` instance and a single entity that exposes a `Places` property (*entity*) as a `DbSet` instance. `DbSet<Place>` represents a collection of data in memory and is the gateway to performing database operations. For example, any changes to `DbSet<Place>` will be committed to the database, right after invoking the `SaveChanges()` method of `DbContext`.

Let's continue by adding another new class called `PlaceDbSeeder.cs` in the Db folder. The first thing that we need to do is to declare the following namespace references:

```
using Microsoft.EntityFrameworkCore;
using Microsoft.Extensions.DependencyInjection;
using PlaceApi.Db.Models;
using System;
using System.IO;
using System.Linq;
```

The preceding code enables us to access the methods and members from each namespace that are required when we implement our methods to seed the test data.

Now, paste the following method into the class:

```
private static string GetImage(string fileName, string
fileType)
{
    var path = Path.Combine(Environment.CurrentDirectory, "Db/
        Images", fileName);
    var imageBytes = File.ReadAllBytes(path);
    return $"data:{fileType};base64,{Convert.
        ToBase64String(imageBytes)}";
}
```

The `GetImage()` method, in the preceding code, gets the image files stored within the `Db/Images` folder and converts the image to a `byte` array. It then converts the bytes to the `base64` string format and returns the formatted data as an image. We are going to reference this method in the next step.

Now, paste the following code into the class:

```
public static void Seed(IServiceProvider serviceProvider)
{
    using var context = new PlaceDbContext(serviceProvider.
    GetRequiredService<DbContextOptions<PlaceDbContext>>());
    if (context.Places.Any()){ return; }
    context.Places.AddRange(
        new Place
        {
            Id = 1,
            Name = "Coron Island",
            Location = "Palawan, Philippines",
            About = "Coron is one of the top destinations for
            tourists to add to their wish list.",
            Reviews = 10,
            ImageData = GetImage("coron_island.jpg", "image/
            jpeg"),
            LastUpdated = DateTime.Now
        },
        new Place
        {
            Id = 2,
            Name = "Olsob Cebu",
            Location = "Cebu, Philippines",
            About = "Whale shark watching is the most popular
            tourist attraction in Cebu.",
            Reviews = 3,
            ImageData = GetImage("oslob_whalesharks.png",
            "image/png"),
            LastUpdated = DateTime.Now
        }
    );

    context.SaveChanges();
}
```

The Seed() method in the preceding code will initialize a couple of Place data sets when the application starts. This is done by adding the data into the Places entity of PlaceDbContext. You can see that we set the value of the ImageData property by calling the GetImage() method created earlier.

Now that we have implemented our seeder class, the next thing we need to do is to create a new class that will house a couple of extension methods for registering our in-memory database and using our seeder class as a middleware. Within the Db folder, go ahead and add a new class called PlaceDbServiceExtension.cs and paste in the following code:

```csharp
using Microsoft.AspNetCore.Builder;
using Microsoft.EntityFrameworkCore;
using Microsoft.Extensions.DependencyInjection;

namespace PlaceApi.Db
{
    public static class PlaceDbServiceExtension
    {
        public static void AddInMemoryDatabaseService(this
        IServiceCollection services, string dbName)
            => services.AddDbContext<PlaceDbContext>(options
            => options.UseInMemoryDatabase(dbName));

        public static void InitializeSeededData (this
            IApplicationBuilder app)
        {
            using var serviceScope = app.ApplicationServices.
                GetRequiredService<IServiceScopeFactory>().
                CreateScope();
            var service = serviceScope.ServiceProvider;
            PlaceDbSeeder.Seed(service);
        }
    }
}
```

The preceding code defines two main `static` methods.
`AddInMemoryDatabaseService()` is an `IServiceCollection` extension method
that registers `PlaceDbContext` as a service in the **dependency injection (DI)** container.
Notice that we are configuring the `UseInMemoryDatabase ()` extension method as
a parameter to the `AddDbContext()` method call. This tells the framework to spin up
an in-memory database with a given database name. The `InitializeSeededData()`
extension method is responsible for generating test data when the application runs. It
uses the `GetRequiredService()` method of the `ApplicationServices` class to
reference the service provider used to resolved dependencies from the scope. It then calls
the `PlaceDbSeeder.Seed()` method that we created earlier and passes the service
provider to initialize the test data.

The `this` keyword, before the object type in each method's parameters,
denotes that a method is an extension method. **Extension methods** enable
you to add a method to an existing type. For this particular example, we are
adding the `AddInMemoryDatabaseService()` method to an object of type
`IServiceCollection` and adding the `InitializeSeededData()` method to
an object of type `IApplicationBuilder`. For more information about extension
methods, see `https://docs.microsoft.com/en-us/dotnet/csharp/`
`programming-guide/classes-and-structs/extension-methods`.

At this point, we now have a `DbContext` instance that enables us to access our `Places`
`DbSet`, a helper class that will generate some data, and a couple of extension methods to
register our in-memory service. What we need to do next is to wire them into `Startup.`
`cs` to populate our data when the application starts.

Modifying the Startup class

Let's update the `ConfigureServices()` method of the `Startup` class to the
following code:

```
public void ConfigureServices(IServiceCollection services)
{
    services.AddInMemoryDatabaseService("PlacedDb");
    services.AddControllers();
}
```

In the preceding code, we've invoked the `AddInMemoryDatabaseService()` extension method that we created earlier. Again, this process registers `PlaceDbContext` in `IServiceCollection` and defines an in-memory database called `PlacedDb`. Registering `DbContext` as a service into the DI container enables us to reference an instance of this service in any class within the application via DI.

Now, the final step that we need to do is to call the `InitializeSeededData()` extension method in the `Configure()` method as follows:

```
public void Configure(IApplicationBuilder app,
IWebHostEnvironment env)
{

    app.InitializeSeededData();


    //removed other middlewares for brevity
}
```

At this point, our test data should now be loaded into our in-memory database when the application starts and should be ready for use in our application.

Implementing real-time functionality with SignalR

Adding real-time functionality to any ASP.NET Core server application is pretty easy nowadays, because SignalR is fully integrated into the framework. This means that there's no need to download or reference a separate NuGet package just to be able to implement real-time capability.

ASP.NET SignalR is a technology that offers a clean set of APIs that enables real-time behavior for your web application, where the server pushes data to the client, as opposed to the traditional way of having the client continuously pull data from the server to get updated.

To start working with **ASP.NET Core SignalR**, we need to create a **hub** first. Hub is a special class in SignalR that enables us to call methods on connected clients from the server. The server in this example is our Web API, for which we will define a method for clients to invoke. The client in this example is the **Blazor Server application**.

Let's create a new class called `PlaceApiHub` under the root of the application and then paste in the following code:

```
using Microsoft.AspNetCore.SignalR;


namespace PlaceApi
```

```
{
    public class PlaceApiHub : Hub
    {
    }
}
```

The preceding code is just a class that inherits from the Hub class. We'll leave the Hub class empty, as we are not invoking any methods from the client. Instead, the API will send the events over the hub.

Next, we are going to register SignalR and the ResponseCompression service in the DI container. Add the following code within the ConfigureServices() method of the Startup class:

```
public void ConfigureServices(IServiceCollection services)
{
    services.AddSignalR();
    services.AddResponseCompression(opts =>
    {
        opts.MimeTypes = ResponseCompressionDefaults.MimeTypes.
        Concat(
            new[] { "application/octet-stream" });
    });

    // Removed other services for brevity
}
```

Next, we need to add the ResponseCompression middleware in the pipeline and map our Hub. Add the following code within the Configure() method:

```
public void Configure(IApplicationBuilder app,
IWebHostEnvironment env)
{
    // Removed other code for brevity

    app.UseResponseCompression();

    app.UseEndpoints(endpoints =>
    {
```

```
        endpoints.MapControllers();
        endpoints.MapHub<PlaceApiHub>("/PlaceApiHub");
    });
}
```

The preceding code defines a route for the SignalR hub by mapping the `PlaceApiHub` class. This enables the client application to connect to the hub and listen to events being sent from the server.

That was simple. We will implement sending an event in the next section when creating the Web API endpoints.

Creating the API endpoints

Now that our in-memory database is all set and we've configured SignalR for our real-time capability, it's time for us to create the API controller and expose some endpoints to serve data to the client. In this particular example, we are going to need the following API endpoints to handle fetching, creating, and updating data:

- `GET: api/places`

- `POST: api/places`

- `PUT: api/places`

Go ahead and right-click on the `Controllers` folder and then select **Add** > **Controller** > **API Controller Empty**, and then click **Add**.

Name the class `PlacesController.cs` and then click **Add**. Now, replace the default generated code so that what you have looks like the following code:

```
using Microsoft.AspNetCore.Mvc;
using PlaceApi.Db;
using PlaceApi.Db.Models;
using System;
using System.Linq;


namespace PlaceApi.Controllers
{
    [ApiController]
    [Route("api/[controller]")]
    public class PlacesController : ControllerBase
```

```
{
        private readonly PlaceDbContext _dbContext;
        private readonly IHubContext<PlaceApiHub> _hubContext;


        public PlacesController(PlaceDbContext dbContext,
                        IHubContext<PlaceApiHub> hubContext)
        {
            _dbContext = dbContext;
            _hubContext = hubContext;
        }


        [HttpGet]
        public IActionResult GetTopPlaces()
        {
            var places = _dbContext.Places.OrderByDescending(
                o => o.Reviews).Take(10);
            return Ok(places);
        }
    }
}
```

The preceding code shows the typical structure of an API Controller class. An API should implement the ControllerBase abstract class to utilize the existing functionalities built into the framework for building RESTful APIs. We'll talk in more depth about APIs in the next chapter. For the time being, let's just walk through what we did in the preceding code. The first two lines of the PlacesController class define private and read-only fields for PlaceDbContext and IHubContext<PlaceApiHub>. The next line defines the class constructor and injects PlaceDbContext and IHubContext<PlaceApiHub> as dependencies to the class. In this case, any methods within the PlacesController class will be able to access the instance of PlaceDbContext and IHubContext, allowing us to invoke all its available methods and properties.

Currently, we have only defined one method in our PlaceController. The GetTopPlaces() method is responsible for returning the top 10 rows of data from our in-memory datastore. We've used the **LINQ** OrderByDescending() and Take() extension methods, of the Enumerable type, to get the top rows based on the Reviews value. You can see that the method has been decorated with the [HttpGet] attribute, which signifies that the method can only be invoked by an HTTP GET request.

Now, let's add another method for handling new record creation. Append the following code within the class:

```
[HttpPost]
public IActionResult CreateNewPlace([FromBody] Place place)
{
    var newId = _dbContext.Places.Select(x => x.Id).Max() + 1;
    place.Id = newId;
    place.LastUpdated = DateTime.Now;

    _dbContext.Places.Add(place);
    int rowsAffected = _dbContext.SaveChanges();

    if (rowsAffected > 0)
    {
        _hubContext.Clients.All.SendAsync("NotifyNewPlaceAdded",
            place.Id, place.Name);
    }

    return Ok("New place has been added successfully.");
}
```

The preceding code is responsible for creating a new `Place` record in our in-memory database and at the same time broadcasting an event to the hub. In this case, we are invoking the `Clients.All.SendAsync()` method of the `Hub` class and passing `place.Id` and `place.Name` to the `NotifyNewPlaceAdded` event. Note that you can also pass an object to the `SendAsync()` method instead of passing individual parameters, just like what we did in this example. You can see that the `CreateNewPlace()` method has been decorated with the `[HttpPost]` attribute, which signifies that the method can be invoked only by HTTP POST requests. Keep in mind that we are generating `Id` manually by incrementing the existing maximum ID from our data store. In a real application using a real database, you may not need to do this as you can let the database auto-generate `Id` for you.

Let's create the last endpoint that we need for our application. Add the following code block to the class:

```
[HttpPut]
public IActionResult UpdatePlace([FromBody] Place place)
{
    var placeUpdate = _dbContext.Places.Find(place.Id);

    if (placeUpdate == null)
    {
        return NotFound();
    }

    placeUpdate.Name = place.Name;
    placeUpdate.Location = place.Location;
    placeUpdate.About = place.About;
    placeUpdate.Reviews = place.Reviews;
    placeUpdate.ImageDataUrl = place.ImageDataUrl;
    placeUpdate.LastUpdated = DateTime.Now;

    _dbContext.Update(placeUpdate);
    _dbContext.SaveChanges();

    return Ok("Place has been updated successfully.");
}
```

The preceding code is responsible for updating an existing Place record in our in-memory database. The UpdatePlace() method takes a Place object as a parameter. It first checks whether the record exists based on the ID. If the record isn't in the database, we return a NotFound() response. Otherwise, we update the record in the database and then return an OK() response with a message. Notice that the method in this case is decorated with the [HttpPut] attribute, which denotes that this method can only be invoked by an HTTP PUT request.

Enabling CORS

Now that we have our API ready, the next step that we are going to take is to enable **Cross-Origin Resource Sharing (CORS)**. We need to configure this so that other client applications that are hosted in different domains/ports can access the API endpoints. To enable CORS in ASP.NET Core Web API, add the following code in the `ConfigureServices()` method of the `Startup` class:

```
services.AddCors(options =>
{
    options.AddPolicy("AllowAll",
    builder =>
    {
        builder.AllowAnyOrigin()
                .AllowAnyHeader()
                .AllowAnyMethod();
    });
});
```

The preceding code adds a CORS policy to allow any client applications access to our API. In this case, we've set up a CORS policy with the `AllowAnyOrigin()`, `AllowAnyHeader()`, and `AllowAnyMethod()` configurations. Bear in mind, though, that you should consider setting the allowable origins, methods, headers, and credentials before exposing your APIs publicly in real-world applications. For details about CORS, see the official documentation here: `https://docs.microsoft.com/en-us/aspnet/core/security/cors`.

Now, add the following code in the `Configure()` method after the `UseRouting()` middleware:

```
app.UseCors("AllowAll");
```

That's it.

Testing the endpoints

Now that we have implemented the required API endpoints for our application, let's do a quick test to ensure that our API endpoints are working. Press *Ctrl + F5* to launch the application in the browser and then navigate to the `https://localhost:44332/api/places` endpoint. You should be presented with the output shown in Figure 5.10.

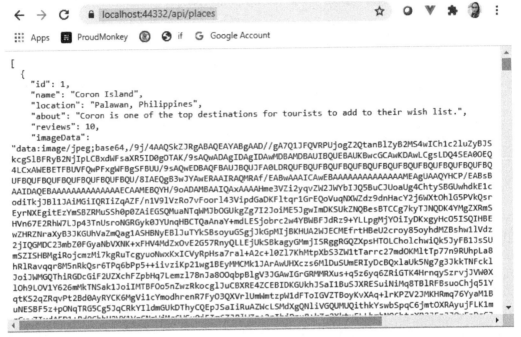

Figure 5.10 – API's HTTP GET request output

The preceding screenshot shows the result of our `GetTopPlaces()` GET endpoint in JSON format. Keep note of the localhost port value on which our API is currently running, as we are going to use the exact same port number when invoking the endpoints in our Blazor applications. In this case, our API is running on port `44332` locally in IIS Express. You can see how this was defined by looking at the `launchSettings.json` file within the `Properties` folder, as shown in the following code:

```
{
    "$schema": "http://json.schemastore.org/launchsettings.json",
    "iisSettings": {
        "windowsAuthentication": false,
        "anonymousAuthentication": true,
        "iisExpress": {
            "applicationUrl": "http://localhost:60766",
```

```
        "sslPort": 44332
      }
    },
    //Removed other configuration for brevity
}
```

The preceding code shows the profile configurations when running the application locally, including IIS Express. You can update the configuration and add new profiles to run the application on different environments. In this example, we'll just leave the default configuration as is for simplicity's sake. The default IIS Express configuration sets the `applicationUrl` port to `60766` when running in `http` and sets the port to `44332` when running in `https`. By default, the application uses the `UseHttpsRedirection()` middleware in the `Configure()` method of the `Startup` class. This means that when you try to use the `http://localhost:60766` URL, the application will automatically redirect you to a secured port, which in this case is port `44332`.

Using the browser only allows us to test HTTP `GET` endpoints. To test the remaining endpoints, such as `POST` and `PUT`, you may have to install a browser app extension. In Chrome, you can install the **Advanced REST client** extension. You can also download **Postman** to test out the API endpoints that we created earlier. Postman is a really handy tool for testing APIs without having to create a UI, and it's absolutely free. You can get it here: `https://www.getpostman.com/`.

Figure 5.11 shows you a sample screenshot of the API tested in Postman.

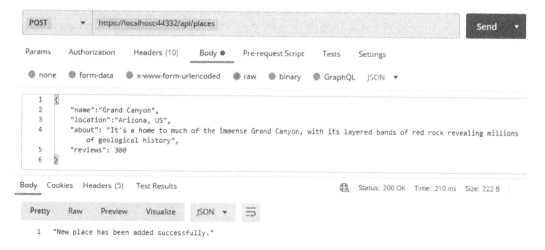

Figure 5.11 – Testing with POSTMAN

At this point, we have working API endpoints that we can use to present data on our page. Learning the basics of creating a Web API is very important for the overall implementation of our project.

Summary

In this chapter, we've learned about the concepts behind the different types of Blazor hosting model. We've identified the goal of the application that we are going to build while learning about Blazor, and we've identified the various technologies needed to reach it. We started creating the backend application using the ASP.NET Core API, and we saw how we can easily configure test data, without having to set up a real database, using Entity Framework Core's in-memory provider feature. This enables us to easily spin up data-driven applications when doing **proof-of-concept** (**POC**) projects. We also learned how to create simple REST Web APIs to serve data and learned how to configure SignalR to perform real-time updates. Understanding the basic concepts of the technologies and frameworks used in this chapter is very important to successfully working with real applications.

We've learned that both of the Blazor models we saw in this chapter are great choices, despite their cons. The programming behind Blazor allows C# developers, who want to avoid JavaScript hurdles, to build SPAs without having to learn a new programming language. Despite being fairly new, it's clear that Blazor is going to be an incredible hit and a great contender among other well-known SPA frameworks, such as Angular, React, and Vue, and that's because of how WASM essentially supersedes JavaScript. Sure, JavaScript and its frameworks aren't going anywhere, but being able to use an existing C# skillset to build a web application that produces the same output as a JavaScript web application is a great advantage, in terms of avoiding having to learn a new programming language just to build web UIs. On top of that, we've learned that Blazor isn't limited to web applications only; Mobile Blazor Bindings is in the works to provide a framework for developers to write cross-platform native mobile applications.

In the next chapter, we are going to continue exploring Blazor and build the remaining pieces to complete our tourist spot application.

Questions

1. What are the different types of Blazor applications?

2. Why use Blazor over other SPA web frameworks?

Further reading

- Introduction to ASP.NET Core Blazor: `https://docs.microsoft.com/en-us/aspnet/core/blazor`

- ASP.NET Core Blazor hosting model configuration: `https://docs.microsoft.com/en-us/aspnet/core/blazor/fundamentals/additional-scenarios`

- Create Web APIs in ASP.NET Core: `https://docs.microsoft.com/en-us/aspnet/core/web-api`

- Get started with ASP.NET Core SignalR: `https://docs.microsoft.com/en-us/aspnet/core/tutorials/signalr`

- EF Core In-Memory Database Provider: `https://docs.microsoft.com/en-us/ef/core/providers/in-memory`

Section 2 – Walking

Now that you can crawl, let's learn how to walk! After we demonstrate the Blazor web frameworks, we'll explore creating a web API project, accessing data, identity authentication and authorization for your solution, and how to leverage containers in this section.

This section includes the following chapters:

- *Chapter 6, Exploring the Blazor Web Framework*
- *Chapter 7, APIs and Data Access*
- *Chapter 8, Identity*
- *Chapter 9, Containers*

6

Exploring the Blazor Web Framework

In the previous chapter, we learned what Blazor is all about and also learned about the different hosting models that the framework offers. We started building the backend application using the ASP.NET Core web API, EF Core, and SignalR. In this chapter, we will build the remaining pieces to complete our goal.

Here is a list of the main topics that will be covered in this chapter:

- Creating the Blazor Server Project
- Creating the Blazor Web Assembly project

By the end of this chapter, you will have learned how to build a tourist spot application to learn Blazor in conjunction with various technologies with the aid of hands-on practical examples.

Technical requirements

This chapter follows on from the previous chapter, so before diving into this chapter, make sure that you've read *Chapter 5*, *Getting Started with Blazor*, and understand the goal of what we are going to achieve for building a sample application. It's also recommended to review *Chapter 4*, *Razor View Engine*, because Blazor uses the same markup engine for generating pages. Although not mandatory, a basic knowledge of HTML and CSS will be beneficial in helping you to easily understand how the page is constructed.

You can view the source code for this chapter at `https://github.com/PacktPublishing/ASP.NET-Core-5-for-Beginners/tree/master/Chapter%2005%20and%2006/Chapter_05_and_06_Blazor_Examples/TouristSpot`.

Please visit the following link to check the CiA videos: `http://bit.ly/3qDiqYY`

Creating the Blazor Server project

Let's go ahead and add a new **Blazor Server** project within the existing project solution. In the Visual Studio menu, select **File | New | Project**. Alternatively, you can also right-click on the solution to add a new project. In the **Create a new project** dialog field, select **Blazor App**, as shown in the following screenshot:

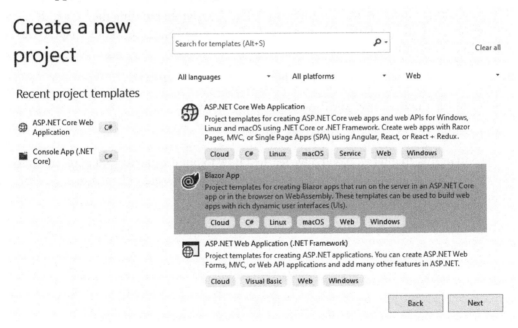

Figure 6.1 – Creating a new Blazor app project

Click **Next**. In the next screen, you can configure the name and location path for your project. In this example, we will just name the project `BlazorServer.Web`. Click **Create** and you should be presented with the following dialog:

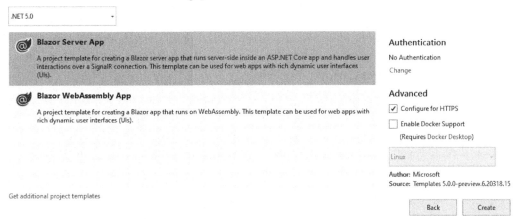

Figure 6.2 – Creating a new Blazor Server app project

Select the **Blazor Server App** template, leave the default configuration as is, and then click **Create**. Visual Studio should scaffold the necessary files needed to build the Blazor Server app, as shown in the following screenshot:

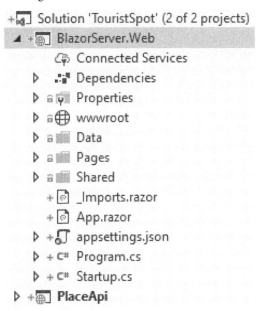

Figure 6.3 – Blazor Server app default project structure

If you've read *Chapter 4, Razor View Engine*, you'll notice that the Blazor Server project structure is very similar to Razor Pages, except for the following:

- It uses the `.razor` file extension instead of `.cshtml`, the reason being that the Blazor application is mainly based on components. The `.razor` files are **Razor components** that enable you to build the UI using HTML and C#. It's basically the same as building UIs in a `.cshtml` file. In Blazor, components are pages themselves, or they could be a page with child components. Razor components can also be used in MVC or Razor Pages as they all use the same markup language, called **Razor View Engine**.

- Blazor applications contain an `App.razor` component. Just like any other SPA web framework, Blazor uses a main component to load the application UI. The `App.razor` component serves as the master component for the application and enables you to configure the routes for your components. Here is the default implementation of the `App.razor` file:

```
<Router AppAssembly="@typeof(Program).Assembly">
    <Found Context="routeData">
        <RouteView RouteData="@routeData" DefaultLayout="@
            typeof(MainLayout)" />
    </Found>
    <NotFound>
        <LayoutView Layout="@typeof(MainLayout)">
            <p>Sorry, there's nothing at this address.</p>
        </LayoutView>
    </NotFound>
</Router>
```

The preceding code defines a `Router` component and configures a default layout to be rendered in the browser when the application starts. In this case, the default layout will render the `MainLayout.razor` component. For more information about **Blazor routing**, refer to the following link: `https://docs.microsoft.com/en-us/aspnet/core/blazor/fundamentals/routing`.

The Blazor Server project also contains a `Host.cshtml` file that serves as the main entry point for the application. In a typical client-based SPA framework, the `_Host.cshtml` file represents the `Index.html` file, where the main `App` component is being referenced and bootstrapped. In this file, you can see that the `App.razor` component is being called within the `<body>` section of the HTML document, as shown in the following code block:

```
<body>
    <app>
        <component type="typeof(App)"
            render-mode="ServerPrerendered" />
    </app>
    @*Removed other code for brevity*@
</body>
```

The preceding code renders the `App.razor` component with `ServerPrerendered` as the default rendering mode. This mode tells the framework to render the component in static HTML first and then bootstrap the app when the browser starts.

Creating the model

The first thing that we are going to do in this project is to create a class that will contain some properties that match with what we expect from the web API response. Let's go ahead and create a new class called `Place.cs` under the `Data` folder. The class definition should look like the following:

```
using System;
using System.ComponentModel.DataAnnotations;


namespace BlazorServer.Web.Data
{
    public class Place
    {
        public int Id { get; set; }
        [Required] public string Name { get; set; }
        [Required] public string Location { get; set; }
        [Required] public string About { get; set; }
        public int Reviews { get; set; }
        public string ImageData { get; set; }
        public DateTime LastUpdated { get; set; }
    }
}
```

As you will observe, the preceding code is identical to the `Place` class that we've created in the web API project, except that we've used **data annotation** to decorate a few properties with the `[Required]` attribute. We are going to populate these properties with the result from the web API and use it in the Blazor components to display information. The required properties ensure that these fields will not be empty when updating the form. We are going to see how this is done later in this chapter.

Implementing a service for web API communication

Now that we have our `Model` in place, let's implement a service for invoking a couple of web API endpoints to fetch and update data. First, install the `Microsoft.AspNetCore.SignalR.Client` NuGet package in order for us to be able to connect to `Hub` and listen to an event.

After installing the SignalR client package, create a new class called `PlaceService.cs` under the `Data` folder and copy the following code:

```
public class PlaceService
{
    private readonly HttpClient _httpClient;
    private HubConnection _hubConnection;

    public PlaceService(HttpClient httpClient)
    {
        _httpClient = httpClient;
    }

    public string NewPlaceName { get; set; }
    public int NewPlaceId { get; set; }
    public event Action OnChange;
}
```

The preceding code defines a couple of private fields for `HttpClient` and `HubConnection`. We'll use these fields later to invoke methods. The `PlaceService` constructor takes an `HttpClient` object as a dependency to the class and assigns the `_httpClient` field. At runtime, the `HttpClient` object will be resolved by the DI container.

The `NewPlaceName` and `NewPlaceId` properties will be populated once the application receives the newly added record from `Hub`. The `OnChange` event is a special type of delegate in C# that allows you to subscribe to it when a certain action raises the event.

Now, let's implement the `SignalR` configuration for subscribing to `Hub`. Go ahead and append the following code within the `PlaceService` class:

```
public async Task InitializeSignalR()
{
    _hubConnection = new HubConnectionBuilder()
        .WithUrl($"{_httpClient.BaseAddress.AbsoluteUri}
        PlaceApiHub")
        .Build();

    _hubConnection.On<int, string>("NotifyNewPlaceAdded",
        (placeId, placeName) =>
```

```
    {
        UpdateUIState(placeId, placeName);
    });

    await _hubConnection.StartAsync();
}

public void UpdateUIState(int placeId, string placeName)
{
    NewPlaceId = placeId;
    NewPlaceName = placeName;
    NotifyStateChanged();
}

private void NotifyStateChanged() => OnChange?.Invoke();
```

The `InitializeSignalR()` method is responsible for creating a connection to Hub by setting the `HubConnection.WithUrl()` method. We've used the value of `_httpClient.BaseAddress.AbsoluteUri` to avoid hardcoding the base URL of the web API endpoint. We'll configure the base URL later when we register the `PlaceService` class with the typed instance of `HttpClient`. The value of the `WithUrl` parameter is actually equivalent to `https://localhost:44332/PlaceApiHub`. If you recall, the `/PlaceApiHub` URL segment is the Hub route that we configured earlier when we created the API project. In the next line, we've used the `On` method of `HubConnection` to listen to the `NotifyNewPlaceAdded` event. When a server broadcasts data to this event, `UpdateUIState()` will be invoked, which sets the `NewPlaceId` and `NewPlaceName` properties and then ultimately invokes the `NotifyStateChanged()` method to trigger the `OnChange` event.

Next, let's implement the methods for connecting to the web API endpoints. Append the following code:

```
public async Task<IEnumerable<Place>> GetPlacesAsync()
{
    var response = await _httpClient.GetAsync("/api/places");

    response.EnsureSuccessStatusCode();

    var json = await response.Content.ReadAsStringAsync();
```

```
    var jsonOption = new JsonSerializerOptions
    {
        PropertyNameCaseInsensitive = true
    };

    var data = JsonSerializer.Deserialize<IEnumerable<Place>>(
        json, jsonOption);

    return data;
}

public async Task UpdatePlaceAsync(Place place)
{
    var response = await _httpClient.PutAsJsonAsync(
        "/api/places", place);
    response.EnsureSuccessStatusCode();
}
```

The GetPlacesAsync() method calls the /api/places HTTP GET endpoint to fetch data. Notice that we are passing JsonSerializerOptions with PropertyNameCaseInsensitive set to true when deserializing the result to a Place model. This is to correctly map the properties in the Place model because the default JSON response from the API call is in camel case format. Without setting this option, you will not be able to populate the Place model properties with data because the format is in Pascal case.

The UpdatePlaceAsync() method is very straightforward. It takes a Place model as a parameter and then calls the API to save the changes to the database. The EnsureSuccessStatusCode() method call will throw an exception if the HTTP response was unsuccessful.

Next, add the following entry to the appSettings.json file:

```
"PlaceApiBaseUrl": "https://localhost:44332"
```

Defining common configuration values within appSettings.json is a good practice to avoid hardcoding any static values in your C# code.

Note: The ASP.NET Core project template will generate both `appSettings.json` and `appSettings.Development.json` files. If you are deploying your application in different environments, you can take advantage of the configuration and create specific configuration files targeting each environment. For local development, you can put all your local configuration values in the `appSettings.Development.json` file and the common configurations in the `appSettings.json` file. At runtime, and depending on which environment your application is running, the framework will automatically override whatever values you configured in the `appSettings.json` file with the values you configured in your environment-specific configuration file. For more information, check out the *Further reading* section of this chapter.

The final step for this to work is to register `PlaceService` in `IServiceCollection`. Go ahead and add the following code to the `ConfigureServices()` method of the `Startup` class:

```
services.AddHttpClient<PlaceService>(client =>
{
    client.BaseAddress = new Uri(
        Configuration["PlaceApiBaseUrl"]);
});
```

The preceding code registers a typed instance of `HttpClientFactory` in the DI container. Notice that the `BaseAddress` value is being pulled from `appSettings.json` via the `Configuration` object.

Implementing the application state

Blazor applications are made up of components and, in order to effectively communicate between the changes that are happening in dependent components, we need to implement some sort of state container to keep track of the changes. Create a new class called `AppState.cs` under the **Data** folder and copy the following code:

```
public class AppState
{
    public Place Place { get; private set; }
    public event Action OnChange;

    public void SetAppState(Place place)
    {
        Place = place;
        NotifyStateChanged();
    }
}
```

```
    }

    private void NotifyStateChanged() => OnChange?.Invoke();
}
```

The preceding code consist of a property, an event, and methods. The `Place` property is used to hold the current `Place` model that has been modified. The `OnChange` event is used to trigger some logic when the application state has changed. The `SetAppState()` method handles the current state of the component. This is where we set the properties to keep track of the change and call the `NotifyStateChanged()` method to invoke the `OnChanged` event.

The next step is to register the `AppState` class as a service so that we can inject it into any component. Go ahead and add the following code to the `ConfigureServices()` method of the `Startup` class:

```
public void ConfigureServices(IServiceCollection services)
{
    services.AddScoped<AppState>();

    //removed other services for brevity
}
```

The preceding code registers the `AppState` class as a scoped service in the DI container because we wanted an instance of this service to be created for each web request.

At this point, we now have what we need to build the UIs: a service to consume data and a service to keep track of the component state. Now, let's move on to the next step and start building the UIs for the application.

Creating Razor components

We are going to split the page implementation into components. With that said, we are now going to create the following Razor components:

- `Main.razor`
- `ViewTouristSpot.razor`
- `EditTouristSpot.razor`

The following diagram shows a graphical representation of how we are going to lay out our web page:

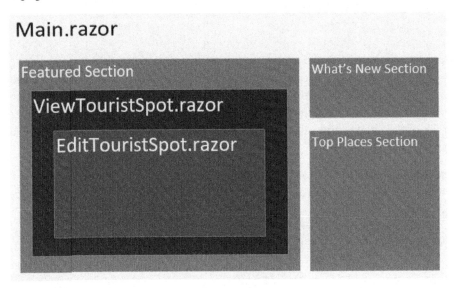

Figure 6.4 – The Main layout

The `Main.razor` component will contain three main sections for displaying various data representations. These sections are just `<div>` elements in the component. Under **Featured Section**, we will render the `ViewTouristSpot.razor` component as a child to the `Main.razor` component. `ViewTouristSpot.razor` will contain `EditTouristSpot.razor` as a child component.

Now that you already have an idea of how the page is going to look, let's start building the required components.

Composing the EditTouristSpot component

Let's start creating the inner child component. Create a new folder called **Spots** under the **Pages** folder. Right-click on the **Place** folder and then select **Add | Razor Component**. A window dialog should appear for you to name the component. In this example, just set the name to `EditTouristSpot.razor` and then click **Add**. Delete the generated code because we are going to replace it with our code implementation.

A Razor component is typically divided into three main parts:

- The first part is for declaring class and service references that are required in order for us to invoke methods and members.

- The second part is for constructing the actual UI using Razor syntax by combining HTML, CSS, and C#.

- The third part is for handling any user interaction logic contained within the @ code{} block.

Here's a quick summary of a typical component composition:

```
@*Routing, Namespace, Class and Service references goes here*@
```

```
@*HTML generation and UI construction goes here*@
```

```
@*UI logic and C# code block goes here*@
```

Let's start integrating the first part. Add the following code:

```
@using BlazorServer.Web.Data
@inject PlaceService _placeService
@inject AppState _appState
```

The preceding code uses the @using and @inject Razor directives to reference a server-side class and service within the Blazor component. This enables us to access members and methods that are available. For this specific example, declaring the @using BlazorServer.Web.Data reference allow us to access the Place class defined within that namespace. The same goes for the @inject directive. When injecting the AppState and PlaceService services, it allows us to access all the methods that they expose within the markup.

Now, let's integrate the second part. Append the following code:

```
@if (IsReadOnlyMode)
{
    <ViewTouristSpot Place="Place" />
}
else
{
    <EditForm Model="@Place" OnValidSubmit="HandleValidSubmit">
```

```
            <div class="card">
                <div class="card-body">
                    <DataAnnotationsValidator />
                    <ValidationSummary />
                    Name:
                    <InputText class="form-control"
                               @bind-Value="Place.Name" />
                    Location:
                    <InputText class="form-control"
                               @bind-Value="Place.Location" />
                    About:
                    <InputTextArea class="form-control"
                               @bind-Value="Place.About" />

                    <br />
                    <button type="submit" class="btn btn-outline-
                        primary">Save</button>
                    <button type="button" class="btn btn-outline-
                        primary" @onclick="UndoChanges">Cancel
                    </button>
                </div>
            </div>
        </EditForm>
    }
```

The preceding code is referred to as a **Razor code block**. Razor code blocks normally start with the @ symbol and are enclosed by curly braces, { }. The if-else statement determines which HTML block to render in the browser based on the IsReadOnlyMode Boolean property defined within the @code section. By default, it's set to false, so the HTML block within the else part gets evaluated and displays the edit form. Otherwise, it renders the ViewTouristSpot.razor component to turn the display back into a read-only state.

In the read-only state, we've passed the `Place` object as a parameter to the `ViewTouristSpot` component so it can display the data without re-invoking the API. Keep in mind that the `ViewTouristSpot` component doesn't yet exist and we are going to create it in the next section. In the edit state, we've used the `EditForm` component to take advantage of its built-in features and form validations. The `EditForm` component takes a model to be validated. In this case, we've passed the `Place` object as the model and wired up the `HandleValidSubmit()` method to the `OnValidSubmit` event handler. We have also used various built-in components, such as `DataAnnotationsValidator`, `ValidationSummary`, `InputText`, and `InputTextArea` to handle input validations and model property bindings. In this example, we are using *two-way data binding* to bind the `Place` properties to input elements using the `@bind-Value` attribute. The `EditForm` component will render as an HTML `<form>` element in the browser and submit all form values when an HTML `<input>` of `type="submit"` is clicked. When the `Save` button is clicked, this triggers the `DataAnnotationsValidator` component and checks whether all validations are passed. If you recall, in the *Creating the model* section of this chapter, we only validated the `Name`, `Location`, and `About` properties to be required, and the `HandleValidSubmit()` method won't be triggered if any of those properties are left empty.

The form uses Boostrap 4 CSS classes to define the look and feel of the component. **Bootstrap** is part of the default template when creating any ASP.NET Core web frameworks and you can see that the CSS file sits under the `wwwroot/css/bootstrap` folder.

Now, let's integrate the last part of this component. Append the following code:

```
@code {
    [Parameter] public Place Place { get; set; }
    private Place PlaceCopy { get; set; }
    bool IsReadOnlyMode { get; set; } = false;
}
```

The preceding code is referred to as a **C# code block**. The `@code` directive is unique to `.razor` files, and allows you to add C# methods, properties, and fields to a component. You can think of the code block as a code-behind file (`cshtml.cs`) in Razor Pages or a `Controller` class in MVC, where you can implement C# code logic based on UI interactions.

The `Place` property is decorated with the `[Parameter]` attribute with a `public` access modifier to allow the parent component to set a value to this property. The `PlaceCopy` property is a holder property that contains the original values being passed from the parent component. In this case, the parent component is `ViewTouristSpot.razor`. The `IsReadOnlyMode` property is a Boolean flag used to determine which HTML block to render.

Let's continue by implementing the methods that are needed for this component. Append the following code within the `@code{ }` block:

```
protected override void OnInitialized()
{
    PlaceCopy = new Place
    {
        Id = Place.Id,
        Name = Place.Name,
        Location = Place.Location,
        About = Place.About,
        Reviews = Place.Reviews,
        ImageData = Place.ImageData,
        LastUpdated = Place.LastUpdated
    };
}
```

The `OnInitialized()` method is part of the Blazor framework, which allow us to override it to perform certain operations. This method is triggered during component initialization and is a perfect place to configure object initialization and assignments. As you will notice, this is where we assign the property values from the original `Place` model to a new `Place` object called `PlaceCopy`. The main reason why we keep the original state of the `Place` object is because we wanted to reset the data to its default state when cancelling the edit. We could have just set the `IsReadOnlyMode` flag to `true` for the cancel action. However, doing this alone would not reset the values to the original state when switching back to the read-only state. The reason for this is that we were using two-way data binding for our `Place` model, and any property changes made to the form will be kept.

The process of two-way data binding works like this:

- The input elements in the UI automatically reflect the changes when properties in the `Place` model get updated from the server.

- When UI elements get updated, the changes get propagated back to the `Place` model as well.

If you don't want to keep an original state of the `Place` model, you can inject the `NavigationManager` class and then simply redirect to the `Main.razor` component using the following code:

```
NavigationManager.NavigateTo("/main", true);
```

The preceding code is the quickest and easiest way to switch to the read-only state. However, doing this would cause the page to reload and invoke the API again to fetch the data, which can be expensive.

Let's move on and append the following code within the `@code{}` block:

```
private void NotifyStateChange(Place place)
{
    _appState.SetAppState(place);
}
```

The `NotifyStateChange()` method takes a `Place` model as an argument. This is where we invoke the `SetAppState()` method of `AppState` to notify the main component of the change. This way, when we modify the form or perform an update, the main component can perform certain actions to act on it; for example, refreshing the data or updating some UI in the main component.

Next, append the following code within the `@code{}` block:

```
protected async Task HandleValidSubmit()
{
    await _placeService.UpdatePlaceAsync(Place);
    IsReadOnlyMode = true;
    NotifyStateChange(Place);
}
```

The `HandleValidSubmit()` method in the preceding code will be triggered when clicking the `Save` button and when no model validation error occurred. This method calls the `UpdatePlaceAsync()` method of `PlaceService` and invokes the API to update a `Place` record.

Finally, append the following code within the `@code{}` block:

```
private void UndoChanges()
{
    IsReadOnlyMode = true;
    if (Place.Name.Trim() != PlaceCopy.Name.Trim() ||
    Place.Location.Trim() != PlaceCopy.Location.Trim() ||
    Place.About.Trim() != PlaceCopy.About.Trim())
    {
        Place = PlaceCopy;
        NotifyStateChange(PlaceCopy);
    }
}
```

The `UndoChanges()` method in the preceding code will be triggered when clicking the `Cancel` button. This is where we revert back to the values from the `PlaceCopy` object when any of the `Place` properties have been modified.

Let's move on to the next step and create the `ViewTouristSpot` component for displaying a read-only state of data.

Composing the ViewTouristSpot component

Go ahead and create a new Razor component within the `Spots` folder and name it `ViewTouristSpot.razor`. Replace the code generated so that it will look like the following:

```
@using BlazorServer.Web.Data

@if (IsEdit)
{
    <EditTouristSpot Place="Place" />
}
else
{
```

```
    <div class="card">
        <img class="card-img-top" src="@Place.ImageData"
            alt="Card image cap">
        <div class="card-body">
            <h5 class="card-title">@Place.Name</h5>
            <h6 class="card-subtitle mb-2 text-muted">
                Location: <b>@Place.Location</b>
                Reviews: @Place.Reviews
                Last Updated: @Place.LastUpdated.
                    ToShortDateString()
            </h6>
            <p class="card-text">@Place.About</p>
            <button type="button" class="btn btn-outline-
                primary"
                    @onclick="(() => IsEdit = true)">
                Edit
            </button>
        </div>
    </div>
}


@code {
    [Parameter] public Place Place { get; set; }
    bool IsEdit { get; set; } = false;
}
```

There really isn't much going on in the preceding code. Since this component is
meant to be a read-only view, there's really no complex logic here. Just like in the
EditTouristSpot.razor file, we also implemented an if-else statement to
determine which HTML block to render. In the @code section, we only have two
properties; the Place property is used to pass the model to the EditTouristSpot
component. The IsEdit Boolean property is used as a flag to render HTML. We only set
this property to true when clicking the Edit button.

Composing the Main component

Now that we are already familiar with the components for editing and viewing data, the last thing that we need to do is to create the main component to contain them in a single page. Let's go ahead and create a new Razor component under the `Pages` folder and name it `Main.razor`. Now, replace the generated code with the following:

```
@page "/main"
@using BlazorServer.Web.Data
@using BlazorServer.Web.Pages.Spots
@inject PlaceService _placeService
@inject AppState _appState
@implements IDisposable
```

The preceding code defines a new route using the `@page` directive. At runtime, the `/main` route will be added to the route data collection, enabling you to navigate to this route and render its associated components. We've used the `@using` directive to reference a class from the server and used the `@inject` directive to reference a service. We also used the `@implements` directive to implement a disposable component. We'll see how this is used later.

Now, let's continue composing our `main` component. Append the following code:

```
@if (Places == null)
{
    <p><em>Loading...</em></p>
}
else
{
    <div class="container">
        <div class="row">
            <div class="col-8">
                <h3>Featured Tourist Spot</h3>
                <ViewTouristSpot Place="Place" />
            </div>
            <div class="col-4">
                <div class="row">
                    <h3>What's New?</h3>
                    <div class="card" style="width: 18rem;">
                        <div class="card-body">
```

```
                    <h5 class="card-title">@_
                        placeService.NewPlaceName</h5>
                </div>
            </div>
        </div>
        <div class="row">
            <h3>Top Places</h3>
            <div class="card" style="width: 18rem;">
                <div class="card-body">
                    <ul>
                        @foreach (var place in Places)
                        {
                            <li>
                                <a href="
                                    javascript:void(0)"
                                @onclick="(() =>
                                    ViewDetails(
                                    place.Id))">
                                    @place.Name
                                </a>
                            </li>
                        }
                    </ul>
                </div>
            </div>
        </div>
    </div>
</div>
}
```

The preceding code is responsible for rendering HTML. Once again, we've used **Bootstrap** CSS to set up the layout. The layout is basically composed of two columns' `<div>` elements. In the first column, we render the `ViewTouristSpot` component and pass the `Place` model as the parameter to the component. We are going to see how the model is populated in the next section. The second column renders two rows. The first row displays the `NewPlaceName` property from `PlaceService`, and the second column displays the list of places presented using the `<ul>` HTML element. Within the `<ul>` tag, we've used the `@` symbol to start manipulating the data in C# code. The `foreach` keyword is one of the C# reserved keywords, which is used for iterating data in a collection. Within the `foreach` block, we have constructed the items to be displayed in the `<li>` tag. In this case, the `Name` property of the `Place` model is rendered using implicit expressions.

To complete the `Main.razor` component, let's implement the server-side logic to handle user interactions and application states. Go ahead and append the following code:

```
@code {
    private IEnumerable<Place> Places;
    public Place Place { get; set; }
}
```

The preceding code defines two properties for storing the list of places and the current place being viewed.

Next, append the following code within the `@code { }` block:

```
protected override async Task OnInitializedAsync()
{
    await _placeService.InitializeSignalR();

    Places = await _placeService.GetPlacesAsync();
    Place = Places.FirstOrDefault();

    _placeService.NewPlaceName = Place.Name;
    _placeService.NewPlaceId = Place.Id;

    _placeService.OnChange += HandleNewPlaceAdded;
    _appState.OnChange += HandleStateChange;
}
```

In the `OnInitializedAsync()` method, we've invoked the `InitializeSignalR()` method of `PlaceService` to configure the **SignalR** and `Hub` connections. We've also populated each property in the component. The `Places` property contains the data from the `GetPlacesAsync()` method call. Under the hood, this method invokes an API call to fetch data. The `Places` property is used to display the list of places in the *Top Places* section. The `Place` property, on the other hand, contains the first result from the `Places` collection and is used for displaying the data in the `ViewTouristSpot` component. We also set the `NewPlaceName` and `NewPlaceId` properties of `PlaceService` so that we will have a default display for the *What's new* section. We've also wired up both `OnChange` events from the `PlaceService` and `AppState` services to each corresponding method.

Next, append the following code within the `@code{}` block:

```
private async void HandleNewPlaceAdded()
{
    Places = await _placeService.GetPlacesAsync();
    StateHasChanged();
}
```

The `HandleNewPlaceAdded()` method will be invoked when a server sends the event to Hub. This process is done when a new record is added via an API `POST` request. This method is responsible for updating the data in the component to reflect the new record in real time.

Next, append the following code within the `@code{}` block:

```
private async void HandleStateChange()
{
    Places = await _placeService.GetPlacesAsync();
    Place = _appState.Place;

    if (_placeService.NewPlaceId == _appState.Place.Id)
    {
        _placeService.NewPlaceName = _appState.Place.Name;
    }

    StateHasChanged();
}
```

The HandleStateChange() method in the preceding code is responsible for keeping the Models state up to date. You can see in this method that we are repopulating the Places, Place, and NewPlaceName properties when the state has been changed. Note that we are only updating the NewPlaceName value if NewPlaceId matches the Place records that are being modified. This is because we don't want to change this value when we are editing a record that is not new. The StateHasChanged() call is responsible for re-rendering the component with the new state.

Next, append the following code within the @code{ } block:

```
private void ViewDetails(int id)
{
    Place = Places.FirstOrDefault(o => o.Id.Equals(id));
}
```

The ViewDetails() method in the preceding code takes an integer as a parameter. This method is responsible for updating the current Place model based on Id.

Finally, append the following code within the @code{ } block:

```
public void Dispose()
{
    _appState.OnChange -= StateHasChanged;
    _placeService.OnChange -= StateHasChanged;
}
```

In the preceding code, we will unsubscribed to the OnChange event when the Dispose() method is invoked. The Dispose() method is automatically called when the component is removed from the UI. It is very important to always unhook the component's StateHasChanged method from the OnChange event to avoid potential memory leaks.

Updating the NavMenu component

Now, let's add the /main route to the existing navigation component. Go ahead and open the NavMenu.razor file, which resides under the Shared folder. Append the following code within the <ul> element:

```
<li class="nav-item px-3">
    <NavLink class="nav-link" href="main">
        <span class="oi oi-list-rich" aria-hidden="true">
        </span> Tourist Spots
```

```
    </NavLink>
  </li>
```

The preceding code adds a **Tourist Spots** link from the existing menu. This enable us to easily navigate to the main component page without having to manually type the route in the browser.

Running the application

One of the many great features built into Visual Studio is that it provides a capability for us to run multiple projects simultaneously in our local machine. Without this feature, we would have to deploy all applications in a web server where each of them can talk to one another. Otherwise, our Blazor web applications won't be able to connect to the web API.

To run multiple projects at the same time in Visual Studio, perform the following steps:

1. Right-click on the **Solution** project and then select **Set startup projects**.

2. Select the **Multiple startup projects** radio button, as shown in the following screenshot:

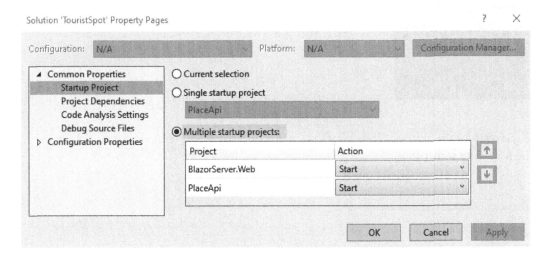

Figure 6.5 – Setting multiple startup projects

3. Select **Start** as the action for both projects.

4. Click **Apply** and then **OK**.

Now, build and run the application using *Ctrl + F5*. From the navigation sidebar menu, click the **Tourist Spots** link and the `Main` component page should display just like in the following screenshot:

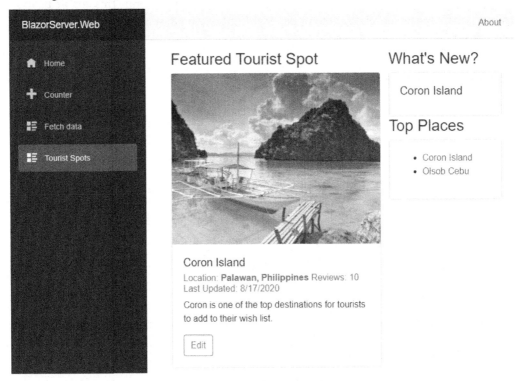

Figure 6.6 – The main page

Clicking the **Edit** button will display the `EditTouristSpot` component, as shown in the following screenshot:

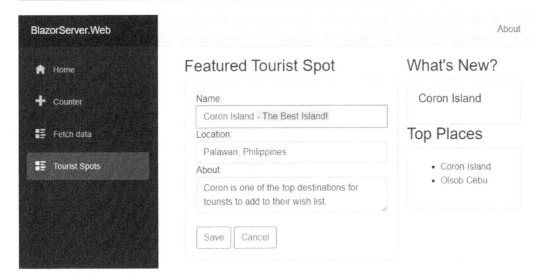

Figure 6.7 – The main page showing edit mode

In the preceding screenshot, the **Name** property was modified. Clicking the **Cancel** button will discard the changes and bring you back to the default view. Clicking **Save** will update the record in our in-memory database, update the state, and reflect the changes to the **Main** component, as shown in the following screenshot:

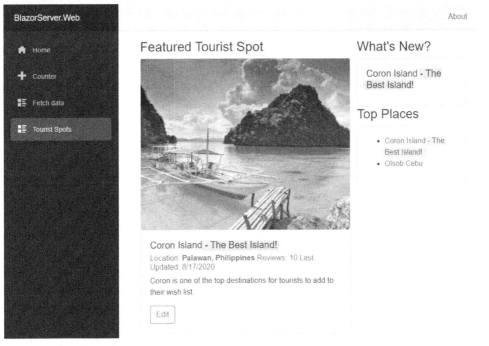

Figure 6.8 – The main page showing readonly mode

You can also select any items from the **Top Places** section, and this should bring up the corresponding details on the page. For example, clicking on the **Oslob Cebu** item will update the page to the following:

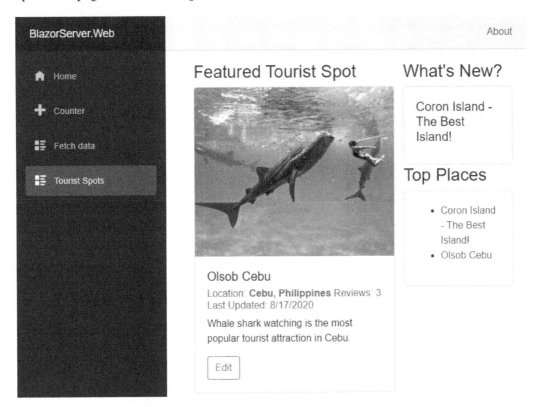

Figure 6.9 – The main page showing readonly mode

Notice that all the details information has been updated except for the **What's New?** section. This was intentional because we only want to update it when there's a new record posted in the database. We are going to see how this section will be updated in the next section.

If you've made it this far, congratulations! You just had your first Blazor web application running with live data connected to an API! Now, let's continue the fun and create a Blazor WebAssembly WASM (app) where we can submit new tourist spot records and reflect the changes in the Blazor Server app in real time.

Creating the Blazor Web Assembly project

In the previous project, we learned how to create a web app with basic functionalities such as fetching and updating records via a web API call. In this project, we will build the frontend **Progressive Web Application (PWA)** to create a new record. This process is executed by invoking an API endpoint to post data and sends an event to Hub to automatically update the Blazor Server UI in real time when a new record is submitted.

Here's an attempt showing how the process works:

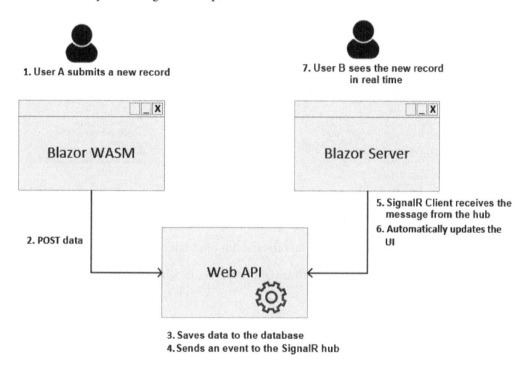

Figure 6.10 – Real-time data update flow

The preceding diagram shows the high-level process of how the real-time functionality works. The steps are pretty much self-explanatory, and it should give you a better understanding of how each application connects to one another. Without further ado, let's start building the last project to complete the whole application.

Go ahead and add a new Blazor WebAssembly project within the existing project solution. To do this, just right-click on **Solution** and then select **Add | New Project**. In the window dialog, select **Blazor App** and then click **Next**. Set the name of the project to BlazorWasm.PWA and then click **Create**.

In the next dialog, select **Blazor WebAssembly App** and then check the **Progressive Web Application** checkbox, as shown in the following screenshot:

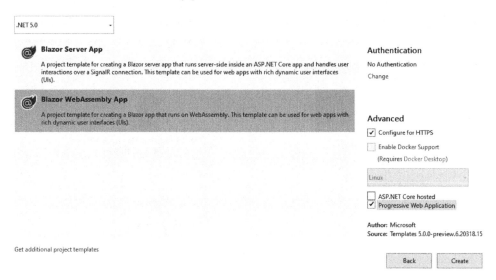

Figure 6.11 – Creating a new Blazor WASM project

Click **Create** to let Visual Studio generate the default template.

The project structure of the Blazor WebAssembly project is somewhat similar to Blazor Server except for the following:

- It doesn't have a Startup.cs file. This is because a Blazor WASM project is configured differently and uses its own host to run the application.

- The Progam.cs file now contains the following code:

```
public static async Task Main(string[] args)
{
    var builder = WebAssemblyHostBuilder.CreateDefault(args);
    builder.RootComponents.Add<App>("app");

    builder.Services.AddTransient(sp => new HttpClient {
BaseAddress = new Uri(builder.HostEnvironment.BaseAddress) });

    await builder.Build().RunAsync();
}
```

In the preceding code, we can see that it uses `WebAssemblyHostBuilder` instead of using the typical ASP.NET Core `IHostBuilder` to configure a web `Host`. It also configures `HttpClient` with `BaseAddress` set to `HostEnvironment.BaseAddress`, which is the host address where the application itself is running, for example, `localhost:<port>`.

- It doesn't have the `_Host.chtml` file in the **Pages** folder. If you recall, in the Blazor Server project, the `_Host.chtml` file is the main entry point for the application where it bootstraps the `App.razor` component. In Blazor WASM, `App.razor` is added to the application start instead, as you can see in the `Program.cs` file.

- It doesn't have the **Data** folder where it configures sample data for the default `Weatherforecast` service. The sample data is now moved to the `weather.json` file under the **wwwroot/sample-data** folder.

- A few other new files have been added to **wwwroot** as well, such as `index.html`, `manifest.json`, and `service-worker.js`. `index.html` is the one that actually replaces the `_Host.chtml` file, which contains the main HTML document for the application. You can see that this file contains the `<head>` and `<body>` tags, as well as rendering the `<app>` component, CSS, and the JavaScript framework. The `manifest.json` and `service-worker.js` files enable the Blazor WASM app to turn into a PWA.

I am pretty sure that there are many other differences between Blazor Server and WebAssembly, but the items highlighted in the list are the key differences.

Creating the model

Now, let's start adding the feature we need for this project. Create a new folder called **Dto** in the project root. Within the **Dto** folder, add a new class called `CreatePlaceRequest.cs` and copy the following code:

```
using System.ComponentModel.DataAnnotations;

namespace BlazorWasm.PWA.Dto
{
    public class CreatePlaceRequest
    {
        [Required]
        public string Name { get; set; }
        [Required]
        public string Location { get; set; }
```

```
    [Required]
    public string About { get; set; }
    [Required]
    public int Reviews { get; set; }
    public string ImageData { get; set; }
}
}
```

The preceding code defines a class that houses some properties. Notice that the class resembles the `Place` class from the web API, except that we've used **data annotations** by decorating a few properties with the `[Required]` attribute. This attribute ensures that the properties will not be posted to the database if they are left empty.

Let's move on to the next step and create the component for adding new records to the database.

Composing the Index component

Now, navigate to the `Index.razor` component. Delete the existing code within it and add the following code:

```
@page "/"

@using Dto
@inject HttpClient client
```

The preceding code sets the route to the root using the `@page` directive. The next line declares a reference to the C# namespace using the `@using` directive. We are going to use the `Dto` namespace to access a class and populate the component with values from the properties in the class. The last line injects an `HttpClient` object for us to communicate with the web API.

Next, append the following code block:

```
<h1>Submit a new Tourist Destination Spot</h1>
<EditForm Model="@NewPlace" OnValidSubmit="HandleValidSubmit">
    <div class="card" style="width: 30rem;">
        <div class="card-body">
            <DataAnnotationsValidator />
            <ValidationSummary />
            Browse Image:
```

```
<InputFile OnChange="HandleSelection" />
<p class="alert-danger">@errorMessage</p>
<p>@status</p>
<p>
    <img src="@imageData" style="width:300px;
        height:200px;">
</p>


Name:
<InputText class="form-control" id="name" @bind-
    Value="NewPlace.Name" />
Location:
<InputText class="form-control" id="location" @
    bind-Value="NewPlace.Location" />
About:
<InputTextArea class="form-control" id="about" @
    bind-Value="NewPlace.About" />
Review:
<InputNumber class="form-control" id="review" @
    bind-Value="NewPlace.Reviews" />


<br/>
<button type="submit" class="btn btn-outline-
    primary oi-align-right">Post</button>
        </div>
    </div>
</EditForm>
```

The preceding code is the HTML code that renders the form with input elements and a button to upload an image. It also uses an EditForm component to handle form submission and model validations. We're not going to elaborate on how the code works because we've already covered this in the previous section when we built the components for the Blazor Server project.

In this example, we are using the `InputFile` Blazor component to upload an image and configure the `OnChange` event that is wired to the `HandleSelection` method. By default, the `InputFile` component only allows single-file selection. To support multiple-file selection and uploading, set the `multiple` attribute just like in the following code snippet:

```
<InputFile OnChange="HandleSelection" multiple />
```

For more information about the `InputFile` component, check out the *Further reading* section of this chapter.

Let's continue by implementing the server-side code logic. Append the following code:

```
@code {
    string status;
    string imageData;
    string errorMessage;
}
```

The preceding code defines a few private fields that are required in the component UI. The `status` field is a variable for storing the uploaded status text. `imageData` is for storing the encodedimage data, and `errorMessage` is for storing the error text.

Next, append the following code within the `@code{}` block:

```
async Task HandleSelection(InputFileChangeEventArgs e)
{
    errorMessage = string.Empty;
    int maxFileSize = 2 * 1024 * 1024;
    var acceptedFileTypes = new List<string>() { "image/png",
        "image/jpeg", "image/gif" };
    var file = e.File;

    if (file != null)
    {
        if (!acceptedFileTypes.Contains(file.ContentType))
        {
            errorMessage = "File is invalid.";
            return;
        }
```

```
        if (file.Size > maxFileSize)
        {
            errorMessage = "File size exceeds 2MB";
            return;
        }


        var buffer = new byte[file.Size];
        await file.OpenReadStream().ReadAsync(buffer);


        status = $"Finished loading {file.Size} bytes from
            {file.Name}";


        imageData = $"data:{file.ContentType};base64,{Convert.
            ToBase64String(buffer)}";


    }
}
```

The HandleSelection() method in the preceding code takes
InputFileChangeEventArgs as the parameter. In this method, we only allow a single
file to be uploaded instead of multiple files by reading the e.File property. If you accept
multiple files, then use the e.GetMultipleFiles() method instead. We also defined
a couple of pre-validation values for the maximum file size and file types. In this example,
we only allow 2 MB as the maximum file size and only accept .PNG, .JPEG, and .GIF file
types to be uploaded. We then perform some validation checks and display an error if any
condition is not met. If all conditions are met, we copy the file being uploaded in a stream
and convert the resulting bytes into Base64String so we can set the image data to an
<img> HTML element.

Now, append the following code within the @code{} block:

```
private CreatePlaceRequest NewPlace = new CreatePlaceRequest();
async Task HandleValidSubmit()
{
    NewPlace.ImageData = imageData;
    var result = await client.PostAsJsonAsync(
        "https://localhost:44332/api/places", NewPlace);
}
```

The `HandleValidSubmit()` method in the preceding code will be invoked when clicking the `Post` button and if no model validation errors occurred. This method takes the `NewPlace` object and passes it the API call to perform `HTTP POST`.

That's it! Now, let's try to run the application.

Running the application

Now, include the Blazor WASM project as a startup project and then click *Ctrl + F5* to run the application. You should see three browser tabs running each application. You can minimize the tab that runs the web API because we don't need to do anything with it. Now, look for the Blazor WASM tab.

To turn the Blazor WebAssembly page into a PWA, you simply click the + sign located in the browser navigation bar, as shown in the following screenshot:

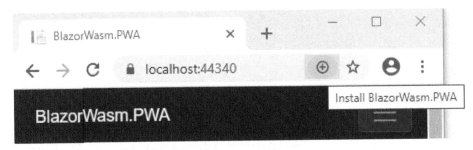

Figure 6.12 – Blazor WASM

Clicking the + sign will prompt a dialog asking you whether you want to install Blazor as a standalone app on your desktop or mobile device, as shown in the following screenshot:

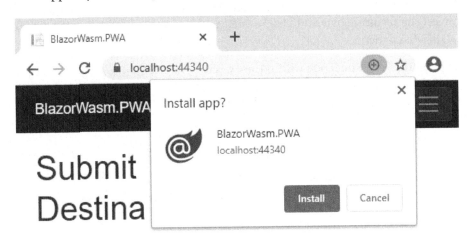

Figure 6.13 – Installing Blazor WASM as a PWA

Clicking **Install** will create an icon on your desktop or mobile device as if it's a regular native app that has been installed and turns the web page into a window without the URL bar, like this:

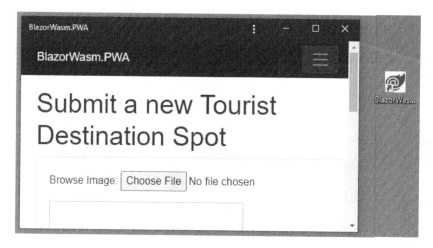

Figure 6.14 – Blazor WASM as a PWA

Pretty cool!

Now, open both the Blazor Server app and Blazor PWA app side by side so you'll see how a real-time update works:

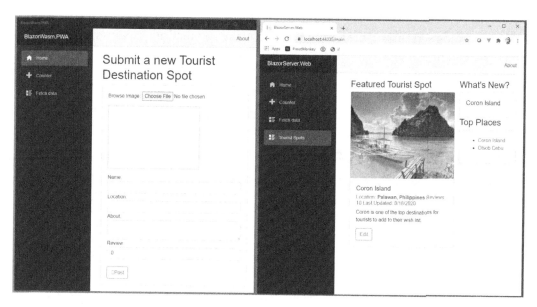

Figure 6.15 – Blazor Server and PWA side by side

Now, browse an image and enter the required fields to submit a new `Place` record. When you click **Submit**, you'll notice in the Blazor Server app (the right-hand window in the preceding screenshot) that the **What's New?** and **Top Places** sections are automatically updated with the newly added `Place` name without you having to refresh the page. Here's an example of what it looks like:

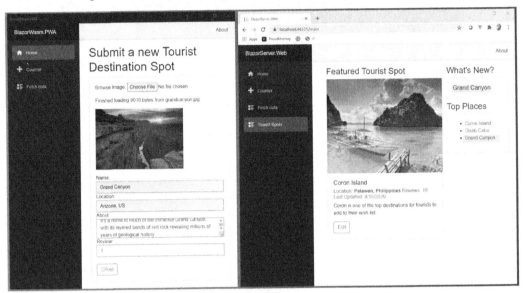

Figure 6.16 – Blazor Server and PWA real-time communication

In the preceding screenshot, the **Grand Canyon** name automatically appears in the Blazor Server web UI in real time right after clicking the **Post** button. You can view it live here:

```
https://github.com/PacktPublishing/ASP.NET-Core-5-for-
Beginners/blob/master/Chapter%2005%20and%2006/Chapter_05_
and_06_Blazor_Examples/TouristSpot/AwesomeBlazor.gif
```

Uninstalling the PWA app

To completely uninstall the PWA app from your local machine or device, make sure to exit all the apps that are running in IIS Express. You can access the IIS Express manager in the bottom-right corner of your Windows machine task bar, as shown here:

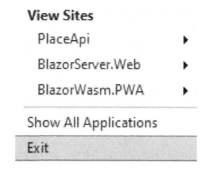

Figure 6.17 – IIS Express manager

After exiting all the apps, you can uninstall the PWA app just like you would normally uninstall an application on your machine.

Summary

In this chapter, we learned about the different flavors of the Blazor web framework by doing some hands-on coding. We learned how we can easily build a powerful web application in Blazor in concert with other ASP.NET Core technology stacks by just applying our C# skills and without the need to write JavaScript. We saw how we can easily integrate features and capabilities that are already available in .NET, such as real-time functionality. We also learned how to perform basic form data bindings, state management, routing, and how to interact with the backend REST APIs to consume and pass data. Having to learn these basic concepts and fundamentals is crucial when you will be building real-world applications.

In the next chapter, you are going to explore web APIs in depth and data access for working with real databases.

Further reading

- Introduction to ASP.NET Core Blazor: `https://docs.microsoft.com/en-us/aspnet/core/blazor`

- ASP.NET Core Blazor hosting model configuration: `https://docs.microsoft.com/en-us/aspnet/core/blazor/fundamentals/additional-scenarios`

- Using multiple environments in ASP.NET Core: `https://docs.microsoft.com/en-us/aspnet/core/fundamentals/environments`

- Enumerable class: `https://docs.microsoft.com/en-us/dotnet/api/system.linq.enumerable`

- Razor components: `https://docs.microsoft.com/en-us/aspnet/core/blazor/components`

- Blazor cascading values and parameters: `https://docs.microsoft.com/en-us/aspnet/core/blazor/components/cascading-values-and-parameters`

- Blazor life cycle: `https://docs.microsoft.com/en-us/aspnet/core/blazor/components/lifecycle`

- Blazor routing: `https://docs.microsoft.com/en-us/aspnet/core/blazor/fundamentals/routing`

- Blazor debugging: `https://docs.microsoft.com/en-us/aspnet/core/blazor/debug`

- WebAssembly: `https://webassembly.org/`

- Understanding the `InputFile` component: `https://docs.microsoft.com/en-us/aspnet/core/blazor/file-uploads`

7
APIs and Data Access

In real-world scenarios, whether it's a mobile app, desktop, service, or web apps, they heavily rely on **Application Programming Interfaces (APIs)** to interact with systems to submit or fetch data. APIs typically act as a gateway between client applications and a database to perform any data operations between systems. Often, APIs provide instructions and a specific format to clients on how to interact with the system to perform data transactions. Thus, APIs and data access work together to achieve two main goals: serving and taking data.

Here is the list of the main topics that we'll go through in the chapter:

- Understanding ORM and Entity Framework Core
- Learning database-first development
- Learning code-first development and migrations

In this chapter, we are going to learn about the different approaches to working with a real database in **Entity Framework (EF)** Core. We will take a look at how to use EF Core with an existing database, as well as implementing APIs that talk to a real database using the EF Core code-first approach. We will look into ASP.NET Core Web APIs in concert with Entity Framework Core to perform data operations in an SQL Server database. We will also learn how to implement the most commonly used HTTP methods (verbs) for exposing some API endpoints.

It is important to understand that ASP.NET Core is not only limited to Entity Framework Core and SQL Server. You can always use whatever data access frameworks you prefer. For example, you can always use Dapper, NHibernate, or even use the good old plain ADO.NET as your data access mechanism. You can also use MySQL or Postgres as your database provider if you'd like.

Technical requirements

This chapter uses Visual Studio 2019 to demonstrate building different applications. Some of the code snippets demonstrated in this chapter were omitted for brevity. Make sure to check the source code at `https://github.com/PacktPublishing/ASP.NET-Core-5-for-Beginners/tree/master/Chapter%2007/Chapter_07_API_EFCore_Examples`.

Please visit the following link to check the CiA videos: `https://bit.ly/3qDiqYY`

A basic understanding of databases, ASP.NET Core, and C# in general, is required because we're not going to cover their fundamentals in this chapter.

Understanding ORM and Entity Framework Core

In the software engineering world, most applications require a database to store data. So, we all need code to read/write the data stored in a database. Creating and maintaining code for a database is tedious work and it is a real challenge for us as developers. That's where **Object Relational Mappers (ORMs)** like Entity Framework come into play.

Entity Framework Core is an ORM and a data access technology that enables C#
developers to interact with a database without having to manually write SQL scripts.
ORMs like EF Core help you build data-driven applications quickly by working through
.NET objects instead of interacting directly with the database schema. These .NET objects
are simply classes, which are typically referred to as **Entities**. With EF Core, C# developers
can take advantage of their existing skills and leverage the power of **Language Integrated
Query** (**LINQ**) to manipulate the dataset against the conceptual Entity Models, otherwise
simply referred to as Models. We'll be using the term *models* from here on as shown in
Figure 7.1.

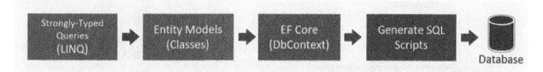

Figure 7.1 – EF Core high-level process

The preceding diagram depicts the process of interacting with a database using EF Core.
In the traditional ADO.NET, you would typically write SQL queries by hand to perform
database operations. While performance varies according to how your queries are written,
still, the ADO.NET way brings a performance advantage over ORMs as you can inject
your SQL queries directly into your code and run it against the database. However, this
leads to your code becoming hard to maintain because any SQL query changes will result
in changing your application code as well; with the exception of using **stored procedures**.
Also, debugging your code can be painful as you will be dealing with a plain string to
write your SQL queries and any typos or syntax errors can be easily overlooked.

With EF Core, you don't have to worry about writing SQL scripts yourself. Instead, you
will use LINQ to query strongly-typed objects and let the framework handle the rest, such
as generating and executing SQL queries.

Keep in mind that EF Core is not limited to SQL Server databases. The framework
supports various database providers that you can integrate with your application, such as
Postgres, MySQL, SQLite, Cosmos, and many others.

Reviewing EF Core design workflows

There are two main design workflows supported by EF Core: the database-first approach and the code-first approach.

The following *Figure 7.2* depicts the difference between the two design workflows:

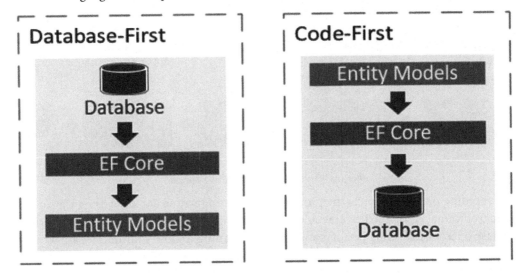

Figure 7.2 – EF Core design workflows

In the preceding figure, we can see that the database-first workflow begins with an existing database and EF Core will generate models based on the database schema. The code-first workflow, on the other hand, begins with writing models and EF Core will generate the corresponding database schema via EF migrations. Migration is a process that keeps your models and database schema in sync without losing existing data.

The following table outlines recommendations for which design workflow to consider when building an application:

	Database-First	Code-First
Code Generation	You create table definitions in the database and import them using a script to scaffold everything for you.	You write classes that represent the entity models that you want to keep track of as well as defining relationships between other models.
Syncing Changes	You write SQL migration scripts for the changes and run them against the database. You then manually configure your application code to sync models with your database changes.	Use the EF migration tool when you need to sync model changes to your database. This lets you manage database schema changes without you having to write any SQL manually.
Type of project best suited for	You may use database-first for projects where you have full control over databases or when a database is developed and owned by another team.	You may use the code-first approach if you're building applications from scratch where business requirements change constantly. This enables you to evolve your models as you develop.

It's very important to understand the differences between the design workflows so you know when to apply them to your projects.

Now that you've learned the difference between the two design workflows, let's move on to the next section and learn how to implement each approach with hands-on coding exercises.

Learning database-first development

In this section, we will build a .NET Core console application to explore the database-first approach and see how entity models are created from an existing database (reverse engineering).

Creating a .NET Core console app

To create a new .NET Core console app, follow these steps:

1. **Open** Visual Studio 2019 and select **Create a new project**.

2. Select the **Console App (.NET Core)** project template.

3. Click **Next**. On the next screen, name the project `EFCore_DatabaseFirst`.

4. Click **Create** to let Visual Studio generate the default files for you.

Now, we are going to add the required Entity Framework Core packages in our application for us to work with our existing database using the database-first approach.

Integrating Entity Framework Core

The Entity Framework Core feature was implemented as a separate NuGet package to allow developers to easily integrate features that the application needs.

As you may have already learned from *Chapter 4*, *Razor View Engine*; *Chapter 5*, *Getting Started with Blazor*; and *Chapter 6*, *Exploring Blazor Web Frameworks*, there are many ways to add NuGet package dependencies in Visual Studio; you could either use the **Package Manager Console (PMC)** or **NuGet Package Manager (NPM)**. In this exercise, we are going to use the console.

By default, the PMC window is `enabled` and you can find it in the bottom-left portion of Visual Studio.

If, for some reason, you can't find the PMC window, you can manually navigate to it by going to the **Visual Studio** menu under **Tools** > **NuGet Package Manager** > **Package Manager Console**.

Now, let's install a few NuGet packages by running the following commands in the console individually:

```
PM> Install-Package Microsoft.EntityFrameworkCore.Tools
PM> Install-Package Microsoft.EntityFrameworkCore.SqlServer
PM> Install-Package Microsoft.EntityFrameworkCore.SqlServer.
Design -Pre
```

The commands in the preceding code will install the NuGet packages as dependencies in your application. The `-Pre` command instructs to install the latest preview version of Entity Framework Core packages. In this case, the current version as of this time of writing is **5.0.0** for the SQL Server and Tools packages, and **2.0.0-preview1-final** for the `SqlServer.Design` package.

Now that we have installed the necessary tools and dependencies for us to work with an existing database, let's move on to the next step.

Creating a database

To simulate working with an existing database, we will need to create a database from scratch. In this example, we will just be creating a single table that houses some simple columns for simplicity. You can use SQL Server Express if you have it installed or use the local database built into Visual Studio.

To create a new database in Visual Studio, follow these simple steps:

1. Go to **View** > **SQL Server Object Explorer**.
2. Drill down to **SQL Server** > **(localdb)\MSSQLLocalDB**.
3. Right-click on the Databases folder.
4. Click **Add New Database**.
5. Name it DbFirstDemo and click **OK**.
6. Right-click on the DbFirstDemo database and then select **New Query**.
7. Copy the following SQL script:

```
CREATE TABLE [dbo].[Person]
(
       [Id] INT NOT NULL PRIMARY KEY IDENTITY(1,1),
       [FirstName] NVARCHAR(30) NOT NULL,
       [LastName] NVARCHAR(30) NOT NULL,
       [DateOfBirth] DATETIME NOT NULL
)
```

8. Run the script and it should create a new table called Person in your local database.

Now that we have a database, let's move on to the next section and create .NET class objects for us to work with the data using EF Core.

Generating models from an existing database

As of the time of writing, there are two ways to generate models from an existing database. You can either use PMC or .NET Core **Command-Line Interface** (**CLI**) commands. Let's see how we can do this in the following section.

Using the Scaffold-DbContext command

The first thing that you need to do is to grab the `ConnectionString` value for you to connect to the database. You can get this value from the **Properties** window of the `DbFirstDemo` database in Visual Studio.

Now navigate back to the PMC and run the following command to create the corresponding `Models` from the existing database:

```
PM> Scaffold-DbContext "INSERT THE VALUE OF CONNECTION STRING
HERE" Microsoft.EntityFrameworkCore.SqlServer -o Db
```

The `Scaffold-DbContext` command in the preceding code is part of the `Microsoft.EntityFrameworkCore.Tools` package, which is responsible for the reverse engineering process. This process will create a `DbContext` and `Model` classes based on the existing database.

We've passed in three main parameters in the `Scaffold-DbContext` command:

- **Connection string**: The first parameter is the connection string that instructs how to connect to the database.

- **Provider**: The database provider that will be used to execute the connection string against. In this case, we've used `Microsoft.EntityFrameworkCore.SqlServer` as the provider.

- **Output directory**: The `-o` option is shorthand for `–OutputDir`, which enables you to specify the location of the files to be generated. In this case, we've set it to `Db`.

Using the dotnet ef dbcontext scaffold command

The second option to generate `Models` from an existing database is using the EF Core tools via .NET Core CLI. In order to do this, we need to use the command-line prompt. In Visual Studio, you can go to **Tools** > **Command Line** > **Developer Command Prompt**. This process will launch a Command Prompt window at the folder where the solution file (`.sln`) is located. Since we need to execute the command at the level where the project file (`.csproj`) is located, then we need to move the directory one folder down. So, in Command Prompt, do the following:

```
cd EFCore_DatabaseFirst
```

The preceding command will set the current directory to where the project file is located.

Another approach is to navigate to the EFCore_DatabaseFirst folder outside Visual Studio and then press *Shift + Right-click* and select **Open command window here** or **Open PowerShell window here.** This process will directly open Command Prompt in the project file directory.

In Command Prompt, let's first install the EF Core CLI tools by running the following command:

```
Dotnet tool install--global dotnet-ef
```

The preceding code will install the EF Core tools globally on your machine. Now, run the following command:

```
dotnet ef dbcontext scaffold "INSERT THE VALUE OF CONNECTION
STRING HERE" Microsoft.EntityFrameworkCore.SqlServer -o Db
```

The preceding code is quite similar to using the Scaffold-DbContext command, except we've used the dotnet ef dbcontext scaffold command, which is specific to CLI-based EF Core tools.

Both options will give you the same results and will create a DbContext and Model classes within the Db folder, as shown in *Figure 7.3*:

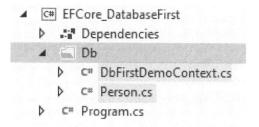

Figure 7.3 – EF Core generated files

Take a moment to examine each file generated and see what code is generated.

When you open the DbFirstDemoContext.cs file, you can see that the class is declared as partial class and it derives from the DbContext class. DbContext is the main requirement in Entity Framework Core. In this example, the DbFirstDemoContext class represents the DbContext that manages the connection with the database and provides various capabilities such as building models, data mapping, change tracking, database connections, caching, transaction management, querying, and persisting data.

You'll also see the following code within the `DbFirstDemoContext` class:

```
public virtual DbSet<Person> People { get; set; }
```

The preceding code represents an entity. Entities are defined as the type of `DbSet` that represents your model. EF Core requires an `Entity` so it can read, write, and migrate data to the database. To put it in simple terms, `DbSet<Person>` represents your database table called `Person`. Now, instead of you writing SQL script to perform database operations such as `insert`, `update`, `fetch` or `delete`, you will simply perform database operations against the `DbSet` called `People` and leverage the power of LINQ to manipulate data with strongly-typed code. This helps you, as a developer, boost productivity by programming against a conceptual application model with full IntelliSense support, instead of programming directly against a relational storage schema. Notice how EF automatically sets the `DbSet` property name to its plural form. It's just awesome!

The other thing that you'll see within the `DbFirstDemoContext` class is `OnConfiguring()`. This method configures the application to use Microsoft SQL Server as the provider using the `UseSqlServer()` extension method and passing the `ConnectionString` value. In the actual generated code, you will see that the value is being passed directly to the `UseSqlServer()` method.

> **Note**
> In real-world applications, you should avoid injecting the actual value directly and instead store your `ConnectionString` value in a key vault or secrets manager for security's sake.

Finally, you will see a method called `OnModelCreating()` within the `DbFirstDemoContext` class. The `OnModelCreating()` method configures a `ModelBuilder` for your `Models`. The method is defined from the `DbContext` class and marked as `virtual`, allowing us to override its default implementation. You'll use this method to configure `Model` relationships, data annotations, column mappings, data types, and validations. In this particular example, when EF Core generates the models, it applies the corresponding configuration that we have in our `dbo.Person` database table.

> **Note**
> Any changes you've made to the `DbContext` class and `Entity` models will be lost when running the database-first command again.

Now that we have a `DbContext` configured, let's move on to the next section and run some tests to perform some simple database operations.

Performing basic database operations

Since this is a console application, we are going to perform simple insert, update, select, and delete database operations in the Program.cs file for the simplicity of this exercise.

Let's start by inserting new data into the database.

Adding a record

Go ahead and add the following code within the Program class:

```
static readonly DbFirstDemoContext _dbContext = new
DbFirstDemoContext();

static int GetRecordCount()
{
    return _dbContext.People.ToList().Count;
}

static void AddRecord()
{
    var person = new Person { FirstName = "Vjor", LastName =
    "Durano", DateOfBirth = Convert.ToDateTime("06/19/2020") };
    _dbContext.Add(person);
    _dbContext.SaveChanges();
}
```

The preceding code defines a static readonly instance of the DbFirstDemoContext class. We need the DbContext so that we can access the DbSet and perform database operations against it.

The GetRecordCount() method simply returns the number of record counts stored in the database. The AddRecord() method is responsible for inserting a new record into the database. In this example, we just defined some static values for the Person Model for simplicity. The _dbContext.Add() method takes a Model as the parameter. In this case, we've passed the person variable to it and then invoked the SaveChanges() method of the DbContext class. Any changes you've made to the DbContext won't be reflected in the underlying database – not unless you call the SaveChanges() method.

Now, what's left for us to do here is to call the methods in the preceding code. Go ahead and copy the following code in the `Main` method of the `Program` class:

```
static void Main(string[] args)
{
    AddRecord();
    Console.WriteLine($"Record count: {GetRecordCount()}");
}
```

Running the preceding code will insert a new record into the database and output the value 1 as the record count.

You can verify that the record has been created in the database by going to the **SQL Server Object Explorer** pane in Visual Studio. Drill down to the `dbo.Person` table, right-click on it, and select **View Data**. It should show the newly added record in the database, as shown in *Figure 7.4*:

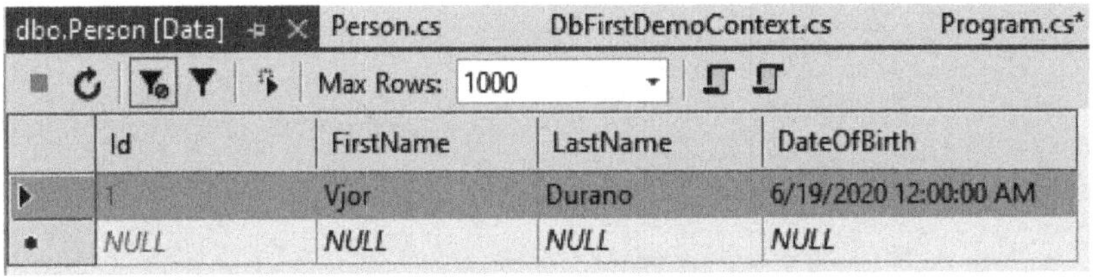

Figure 7.4 – Showing data in the dbo.Person table

Cool! Now, let's continue and do some other database operations.

Updating a record

Let's perform a simple update to an existing record in the database. Append the following code within the `Program` class:

```
static void UpdateRecord(int id)
{
    var person = _dbContext.People.Find(id);
    // removed null check validation for brevity
    person.FirstName = "Vynn Markus";
    person.DateOfBirth = Convert.ToDateTime("11/22/2016");

    _dbContext.Update(person);
    _dbContext.SaveChanges();
}
```

The preceding code takes an id as an argument. It then queries the database using the Find() method of the DbContext. We then check whether the id that we passed in has an associated record in the database. If the Find() method returns null, we simply do nothing and return directly to the caller. Otherwise, if the given id existed in the database, we perform a database update. In this case, we've simply replaced the value of the FirstName and DateOfBirth properties.

Now, let's call the UpdateRecord() method in the Main method of the Program class as in the following:

```
static void Main(string[] args)
{
    UpdateRecord(1);
}
```

In the preceding code, we manually pass the value of 1 as the id. That value represents an existing record in the database when we performed insertion in the previous section.

Running the code should update the values for the FirstName and DateOfBirth columns as shown in *Figure 7.5*:

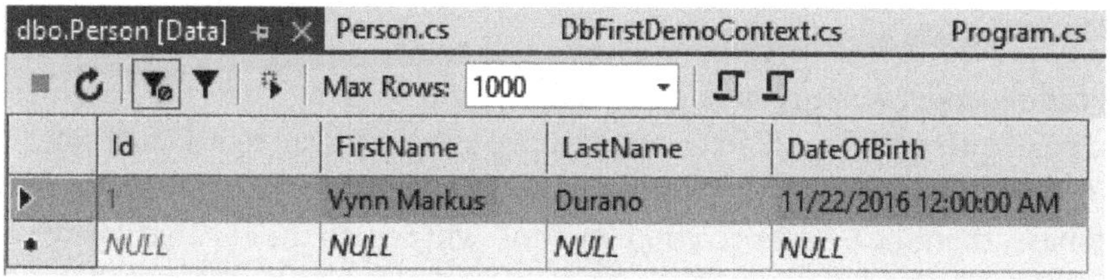

Figure 7.5 – Showing updated data in the dbo.Person table

Great! Now, let's continue with other database operations.

Querying a record

Go ahead and copy the following code within the Program class:

```
static Person GetRecord(int id)
{
    return _dbContext.People.SingleOrDefault(p => p.Id.
        Equals(id));
}
```

The preceding code also takes an `id` as an argument so it can identify which record to fetch. What it does is it queries the database using the LINQ `SingleOrDefault()` extension method and uses a **lambda expression** to perform value comparisons with the given `id` value. If the `id` matches with a record from the database, then we return a `Person` object to the caller.

Now, let's invoke the `GetRecord()` method by copying the following code within the `Main` method of the `Program` class:

```
static void Main(string[] args)
{
    var p = GetRecord(1);
    if (p != null)
    {
        Console.WriteLine($"FullName: {p.FirstName}
            {p.LastName}");
        Console.WriteLine($"Birth Date: {p.DateOfBirth.
            ToShortDateString()}");
    }
}
```

In the preceding code, we've manually passed the value of 1 again as the parameter to the `GetRecord()` method. This is to ensure that we are getting a record back since we only have one record in the database at the moment. If you pass an `id` value that doesn't exist in the database, then the `GetRecord()` method will return `null`. That's why you see we have implemented a basic validation to check against `null` so that the application won't break. We then print the values to the console window.

Running the code will result in the following as shown in *Figure 7.6*:

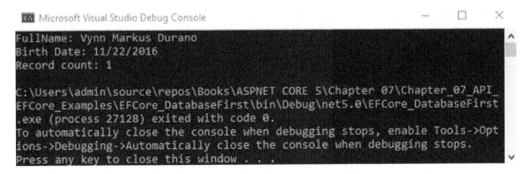

Figure 7.6 – Fetching a record console output

It's that simple! There are many things that you can do with LINQ to query data, especially complex data. In this example, we are just doing basic querying with a single database for you to better understand how it works.

Now, let's move on to the last example.

Deleting a record

Now, let's see how we can easily perform deletion with EF Core. Copy the following code within the `Program` class:

```
static void DeleteRecord(int id)
{
    var person = _dbContext.People.Find(id);
    // removed null check validation for brevity
    _dbContext.Remove(person);
    _dbContext.SaveChanges();
}
```

Just like in the database `update` operation, the preceding code checks for the existing record first using the `Find()` method. If the record exists, we invoke the `Remove()` method of the `DbContext` and save the changes to reflect the deletion in the database.

Now, copy the following code in the `Main` method of the `Program` class:

```
static void Main(string[] args)
{
    DeleteRecord(1);
    Console.WriteLine($"Record count: {GetRecordCount()}");
}
```

Running the code will delete the record in the database with an `id` value equal to 1. The call to the `GetRecordCount()` method will now return 0 as we don't have any other records in the database.

Now that you've learned about implementing a database-first approach with EF Core, let's move on to the next section and explore the EF Core code-first approach in concert with ASP.NET Core Web API.

Learning code-first development and migrations

In this section, we are going to explore EF Core code-first development by building a simple ASP.NET Core Web API application to perform basic database operations.

Before we get our hands dirty with coding, let's first review what ASP.NET Core Web API is.

Reviewing ASP.NET Core Web API

There are many ways to enable various systems to access data from one application to another. A few examples of communications are HTTP-based APIs, web services, WCF servers, event-based communication, message queues, and many others. Nowadays, HTTP-based APIs are the most commonly used means of communication between applications. There are a few ways to use HTTP as the transport protocol for building APIs: OpenAPI, **Remote Procedure Call (gRPC)**, and **REpresentational State Transfer (REST)**.

ASP.NET Core Web API is an HTTP-based framework for building RESTful APIs that allow other applications on different platforms to consume and pass data over HTTP. In the ASP.NET Core application, Web APIs are very similar to MVC except that they return data as the response to the client instead of a `View`. The term *client* in the context of APIs refers to either a web app, mobile app, desktop app, another Web API, or any other type of service that supports the HTTP protocol.

Creating a Web API project

Now that you know what Web API is all about, let's see how we can build a simple, yet realistic RESTFul API application that serves data from a real database. Keep in mind though that we're not going to cover all the constraints and guidelines of REST as it would be a huge task to cover them all in a single chapter. Instead, we will just be covering some of the basic guidelines for you to be able to get a good grasp and a headstart with building APIs in ASP.NET Core.

To create a new Web API project, fire up Visual Studio 2019 and follow the steps given here:

1. Select the **Create a new project** option.
2. On the next screen, select **ASP.NET Core Web Application** and then click **Next**.

3. On the **Configure your new project** dialog, set the project name to `EFCore_CodeFirst` and choose the location that you want the project to be created at.

4. Click **Create**. On the next screen, select the **API** project template and click **Create**.

You should see the default files generated by Visual Studio for the Web API template. The default generated template includes `WeatherForecastController` to simulate a simple `HTTP GET` request using static data. To ensure that the project works, run the application by pressing the *Ctrl + F5* keys and you should be presented with the following output when everything is fine as shown in *Figure 7.7*:

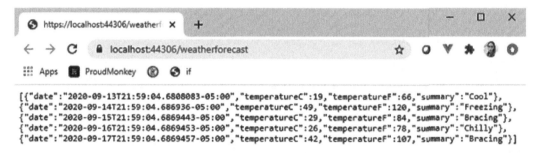

Figure 7.7 – Weather forecast HTTP GET response output

At this point, we can conclude that the default project is working properly. Now let's move on to the next step and set up the data access part of the application.

Configuring data access

The first thing that we need to do here is to integrate the required NuGet package dependencies for the application. Just like what we did in the *Integrating Entity Framework Core* section, install the following NuGet packages:

- `Microsoft.EntityFrameworkCore`
- `Microsoft.EntityFrameworkCore.Design`
- `Microsoft.EntityFrameworkCore.SqlServer`

At the minimum, we need to add these dependencies so we can work with EF Core, use SQL Server as the database provider, and finally, use EF Core commands to create migrations and database synchronization.

After successfully installing the required NuGet package dependencies, let's jump to the next step and create our `Models`.

Creating entity models

As we learned in the code-first workflow, we are going to begin creating the conceptual Models that represent entities.

Create a new folder called Db at the root of the application and create a sub-folder called Models. To make this exercise more fun, we are going to define a few Models that contain relationships. We are going to be building an API where music players can submit their information along with the musical instruments that they play. To achieve this requirement, we are going to need a few models to hold different information.

Now, create the following classes within the Models folder:

- InstrumentType.cs
- PlayerInstrument.cs
- Player.cs

The following is the class definition of the InstrumentType.cs file:

```
public class InstrumentType
{
    public int InstrumentTypeId { get; set; }
    public string Name { get; set; }
}
```

The following is the class definition of the PlayerInstrument.cs file:

```
public class PlayerInstrument
{
    public int PlayerInstrumentId { get; set; }
    public int PlayerId { get; set; }
    public int InstrumentTypeId { get; set; }
    public string ModelName { get; set; }
    public string Level { get; set; }
}
```

The following is the class definition of the Player.cs file:

```
public class Player
{
    public int PlayerId { get; set; }
    public string NickName { get; set; }
```

```
    public List<PlayerInstrument> Instruments { get; set; }
    public DateTime JoinedDate { get; set; }
}
```

The classes in the preceding code are nothing but plain classes that house some properties that are required for us to build some API endpoints. These classes represent our `Models` that we are going to migrate as database tables later on. Keep in mind that, for simplicity's sake, we are using an `int` type as identifiers in this example. In a real application, you may want to consider using the **Globally Unique Identifier (GUID)** type instead so that it can't be easily guessed when you expose these identifiers in your API endpoints.

Seeding data

Next, we'll create an extension method to demonstrate preloading data into our lookup table called `InstrumentType`. Go ahead and create a new class called `DbSeeder` within the `Db` folder, then copy the following code:

```
public static class DbSeeder
{
    public static void Seed(this ModelBuilder modelBuilder)
    {
        modelBuilder.Entity<InstrumentType>().HasData(
            new InstrumentType { InstrumentTypeId = 1, Name =
                "Acoustic Guitar" },
            new InstrumentType { InstrumentTypeId = 2, Name =
                "Electric Guitar" },
            new InstrumentType { InstrumentTypeId = 3, Name =
                "Drums" },
            new InstrumentType { InstrumentTypeId = 4, Name =
                "Bass" },
            new InstrumentType { InstrumentTypeId = 5, Name =
                "Keyboard" }
        );
    }
}
```

The preceding code initializes some data for the `InstrumentType Model` using the `HasData()` method of the `EntityTypeBuilder<T>` object. We will invoke the `Seed()` extension method in the next step when we configure our `DbContext`.

Defining a DbContext

Create a new class called `CodeFirstDemoContext.cs` and copy the following code:

```
public class CodeFirstDemoContext : DbContext
{
    public CodeFirstDemoContext(
        DbContextOptions<CodeFirstDemoContext> options)
    : base(options) { }
    public DbSet<Player> Players { get; set; }
    public DbSet<PlayerInstrument> PlayerInstruments { get;
        set; }
    public DbSet<InstrumentType> InstrumentTypes { get; set; }


    protected override void OnModelCreating(ModelBuilder
        modelBuilder)
    {
        modelBuilder.Entity<Player>()
                .HasMany(p => p.Instruments)
                .WithOne();

        modelBuilder.Seed();
    }
}
```

The preceding code defines a few `DbSet` entities for the `Player`, `PlayerInstrument`, and `InstrumentType` Models. In the `OnModelCreating()` method, we've configured a one-to-many relationship between the `Player` and `PlayerInstrument` Models. The `HasMany()` method instructs the framework that the `Player` entity can contain one or more `PlayerInstrument` entries. The call to the `modelBuilder.Seed()` method will prepopulate the `InstrumentType` table in the database with data at the time it is created.

Keep in mind that the `DbContext` features extension methods to do database CRUD operations and already manages transactions. So, there's really no need for you to create a generic repository and unit of work pattern, not unless it's really needed to add more value.

Registering the DbContext as a service

Within the Db folder, go ahead and create a new class called DbServiceExtension. cs and copy the following code:

```
public static class DbServiceExtension
{
    public static void AddDatabaseService(this
        IServiceCollection services, string connectionString)
            => services.AddDbContext<CodeFirstDemoContext>(
            options => options.UseSqlServer(connectionString));
}
```

The preceding code defines a static method called AddDatabaseService(), which is responsible for registering the DbContext that uses the SQL Server database provider in the DI container.

Now that we have our DbContext, let's move on to the next step and wire up the remaining pieces to make the database migration work.

Setting the database ConnectionString

In this exercise, we will also use a local database built into Visual Studio. However, this time, we won't be injecting the ConnectionString value into our code. Instead, we'll use a configuration file to store it. Now, open the appsettings.json file and append the following configuration:

```
"ConnectionStrings": {
  "CodeFirstDemoDb": "Data Source=(localdb)\\MSSQLLocalDB;
    Initial Catalog=CodeFirstDemo;Integrated Security=True;
    Connect Timeout=30;Encrypt=False;
    TrustServerCertificate=False;
    ApplicationIntent=ReadWrite;MultiSubnetFailover=False"
}
```

The preceding code uses the same ConnectionStrings value that we used in the previous example about **learning database-first development**, except that we are changing the Initial Catalog value to CodeFirstDemo. This value will automatically become the database name once the migration has been executed in SQL Server.

> **Note**
>
> As a reminder, always consider storing the `ConnectionStrings` value and other sensitive data in a key vault or secrets manager when developing a real application. This is to prevent exposing sensitive information to malicious users when hosting your source code in a version control repository.

Modifying the Startup class

Let's update the `ConfigureServices()` method of the `Startup` class to the following code:

```
public void ConfigureServices(IServiceCollection services)
{
    services.AddDatabaseService(
        Configuration.GetConnectionString("CodeFirstDemoDb"));
    //Removed other code for brevity
}
```

In the preceding code, we've invoked the `AddDatabaseService()` extension method that we created earlier. Registering the `DbContext` as a service in the DI container enables us to reference an instance of this service in any class within the application via DI.

Managing database migrations

In real-world development scenarios, business requirements often change and so do your `Models`. In cases like this, the migration features in EF Core come in handy to keep your conceptual `Model` in sync with the database.

To recap, migrations in EF Core are managed by executing commands either using the PMC or via .NET Core CLI. In this section, we are going to learn how we can perform the commands to do migrations.

First, let's start with creating a migration.

Creating a migration

Open the PMC in Visual Studio and run the following command:

```
PM> Add-Migration InitialMigration -o Db/Migrations
```

Alternatively, you can also run the following command using the .NET Core CLI:

```
dotnet ef migrations add InitialMigration -o Db/Migrations
```

Both migration commands should generate the migration files under the Db/ Migrations folder, as shown in *Figure 7.8*:

Figure 7.8 – Generated migration files

EF Core will use the generated migration files in the preceding screenshot to apply migrations in the database. The 20200913063007_InitialMigration.cs file contains Up() and Down() methods that accept MigrationBuilder as an argument. The Up() method gets executed when you apply Model changes to the database. The Down() method discards any changes and restores the database state based on the previous migration. The CodeFirstDemoContextModelSnapshot file contains a snapshot of the database every time you add a migration.

You may have noticed that the naming convention for the migration files is prefixed with a timestamp. This is because the framework will use these files in comparing the current state of the Models against the previous database snapshot when you create a new migration.

Now that we have the migration files, the next thing that we need to do is to apply the created migration to reflect the changes in the database.

Applying Migration

Navigate back to the PMC window and run the following command:

```
PM> Update-Database
```

The .NET Core CLI equivalent command is the following:

```
dotnet ef database update
```

The preceding commands will generate a database called `CodeFirstDemo` with the corresponding tables based on the `Models` along with a special migrations history table named `_EFMigrationsHistory` as shown in *Figure 7.9*:

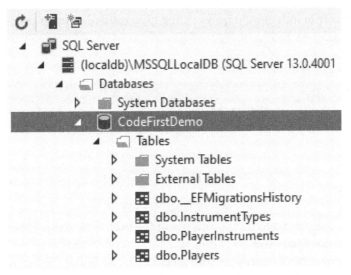

Figure 7.9 – The generated CodeFirstDemo database

The `dbo._EFMigrationsHistory` table stores the name of the migration file and EF Core version used to execute the migration. This table will be used by the framework to automatically apply changes based on the new migration. The `dbo.InstrumentTypes` table will also be preloaded with data.

At this point, you should now have the data access all set up and ready for use in the application.

Reviewing DTO classes

Before we deep dive into the implementation details. Let's first review what DTOs are, as we will be creating them later in this exercise.

Data Transfer Objects (DTOs) are classes that define a `Model` with sometimes predefined validation in place for HTTP responses and requests. You can think of DTOs as `ViewModels` in MVC where you only want to expose relevant data to the `View`. The basic idea of having DTOs is to decouple them from the actual `Entity Model` classes that are used by the data access layer to populate the data. This way, when a requirement changes or if your `Entity Model` properties are changed, they won't be affected and won't break your API. Your `Entity Model` classes should only be used for database related processes. Your DTOs should only be used for taking requests input and response output, and should only expose properties that you want your client to see.

Now, let's move on to the next step and create a few API endpoints for serving and consuming data.

Creating Web API endpoints

Most examples on the internet teach you how to create Web API endpoints by implementing the logic directly inside the `Controllers` for simplicity. For this exercise, we won't do that, instead, we will create APIs by applying some recommended guidelines and practices. This way, you will be able to use the techniques and apply them when building real-world applications.

For this exercise, we are going to cover the most commonly used **HTTP methods** (verbs) for implementing Web API endpoints, such as `GET`, `POST`, `PUT`, and `DELETE`.

Implementing an HTTP POST endpoint

Let's start off by implementing a `POST` API endpoint for adding a new record in the database.

Defining DTOs

First, go ahead and create a new folder called `Dto` at the root of the application. The way you want to structure your project files is based on preference and you are free to organize them however you want. For this demo, we wanted to have a clean separation of concerns so we can easily navigate and modify code without affecting other code. So, within the `Dto` folder, create a subfolder called `PlayerInstruments` and then create a new class called `CreatePlayerInstrumentRequest` with the following code:

```
public class CreatePlayerInstrumentRequest
{
    public int InstrumentTypeId { get; set; }
    public string ModelName { get; set; }
    public string Level { get; set; }
}
```

The preceding code is a class that represents a `DTO`. Remember, DTOs should only contain properties that we need to expose from the outside world or consumers. In essence, DTOs are meant to be light classes.

Create another sub-folder called `Players` and copy the following code:

```
public class CreatePlayerRequest
{
    [Required]
    public string NickName { get; set; }
    [Required]
    public List<CreatePlayerInstrumentRequest>
        PlayerInstruments { get; set; }
}
```

The preceding code contains a couple of properties. Notice that we've referenced the `CreatePlayerInstrumentRequest` class in a `List` type representation. This is to enable a one-to-many relation when you create a new player with multiple instruments. You can see that each property has been decorated with the `[Required]` attribute to ensure that the properties will not be left empty when submitting a request. The `[Required]` attribute is built into the framework and sits under the `System.ComponentModel.DataAnnotations` namespace. The process of enforcing validations to `Models` is called **data annotation**. If you want to have a clean `Model` definition and perform complex predefined validations in a fluent way, then you may try considering using `FluentValidation` instead.

Defining an interface

As you may have seen in the previous chapter's examples, we can directly pass an instance of the `DbContext` in the `Controller` via **constructor injection**. However, when building real applications, you should make your `Controllers` as thin as possible and take business logic and data processing outside your `Controllers`. Your `Controllers` should only handle things like routing, `Model` validations, and delegating the data processing to a separate service. With that said, we are going to create a service that handles the communication between the `Controllers` and `DbContext`.

Implementing the code logic in a separate service is a way of making your `Controller` thin and simple. However, we don't want the `Controller` to directly depend on the actual service implementation as it can lead to tightly coupled dependencies. Instead, we will create an `interface` abstraction to decouple the actual service dependency. This makes your code more testable, extensible, and easier to manage. You may review *Chapter 3, Dependency Injection*, for details about `interface` abstraction.

Now, create a new folder called `interfaces` at the root of the application. Within the folder, create a new interface called `IPlayerService` and copy the following code:

```
public interface IPlayerService
{
    Task CreatePlayerAsync(CreatePlayerRequest playerRequest);
}
```

The preceding code defines a method that takes the `CreatePlayerRequest` class that we created earlier. The method returns a `Task`, which denotes that the method will be invoked asynchronously.

Now that we have an `interface` defined, we should now be able to create a service that implements it. Let's see how to do that in the next step.

Implementing the service

In this section, we are going to implement the `interface` we defined earlier to build the actual logic for the method defined in the `interface`.

Go ahead and create a new folder called `Services` at the root of the application and then replace the default generated code with the following:

```
public class PlayerService : IPlayerService
{
    private readonly CodeFirstDemoContext _dbContext;
    public PlayerService(CodeFirstDemoContext dbContext)
    {
        _dbContext = dbContext;
    }
}
```

In the preceding code, we've defined a `private` and `readonly` field of the `CodeFirstDemoContext` and added a class constructor that injects the `CodeFirstDemoContext` as a dependency of the `PlayerService` class. By applying **dependency injection** in the constructor, any methods within the class will be able to access the instance of the `CodeFirstDemoContext`, allowing us to invoke all its available methods and properties.

You may also notice that the class implements the `IPlayerService` interface. Since an `interface` defines a contract that a `class` should follow, then the next step that we are going to take is to implement the `CreatePlayerAsync()` method. Go ahead and append the following code within the `PlayerService` class:

```
public async Task CreatePlayerAsync(CreatePlayerRequest
playerRequest)
{
    using var transaction = await _dbContext.Database.
        BeginTransactionAsync();
    try
    {
        var player = new Player
        {
            NickName = playerRequest.NickName,
            JoinedDate = DateTime.Now
        };

        await _dbContext.Players.AddAsync(player);
        await _dbContext.SaveChangesAsync();

        var playerId = player.PlayerId;
    }
    catch
    {
        await transaction.RollbackAsync();
        throw;
    }
}
```

In the preceding code, the method was implemented as asynchronous by marking it with the `async` keyword. What the code does is it first adds a new `Player` entry in the database and gets back the `PlayerId` that has been generated.

To complete the `CreatePlayerAsync()` method. Copy the following code within the `try` block after the `var playerId = player.PlayerId;` line:

```
var playerInstruments = new List<PlayerInstrument>();

foreach (var instrument in playerRequest.PlayerInstruments)
{
    playerInstruments.Add(new PlayerInstrument
    {
        PlayerId = playerId,
        InstrumentTypeId = instrument.InstrumentTypeId,
        ModelName = instrument.ModelName,
        Level = instrument.Level
    });
}

_dbContext.PlayerInstruments.AddRange(playerInstruments);
await _dbContext.SaveChangesAsync();
await transaction.CommitAsync();
```

The preceding code iterates through the `playerRequest.PlayerInstruments` collection and creates the associated `PlayerInstrument` in the database along with the `playerId`.

Since the `dbo.PlayerInstruments` table depends on the `dbo.Players` table, we've used the EF Core database transaction feature to ensure that records in both tables will only be created on a successful operation. This is to avoid the data being corrupted when one database operation is failing. You can see it by invoking the `transaction.CommitAsync()` method when everything runs successfully and invoking the `transaction.RollbackAsync()` method within the `catch` block to revert any changes when an error occurs.

Let's proceed to the next step and register the service.

Registering the service

We need to register the interface mapping into the DI container in order for us to inject the `interface` into any other classes within the application. Add the following code within the `ConfigureServices()` method of the `Startup.cs` file:

```
services.AddTransient<IPlayerService, PlayerService>();
```

The preceding code registers the `PlayerService` class in the DI container as an `IPlayerService` interface type with a transient scope. This tells the framework to resolve interface dependency we inject it into the `Controller` class constructor at runtime.

Now that we have implemented the service and wired up the piece in the DI container, we can now inject the `IPlayerService` as a dependency of the `Controller` class, which we are going to create in the next step.

Creating the API controller

Go ahead and right-click on the `Controllers` folder and then select **Add** > **Controller** > **API Controller Empty**, and then click **Add**.

Name the class `PlayersController.cs` and then click **Add**. Now, copy the following code so it will look similar to this:

```
[Route("api/[controller]")]
[ApiController]
public class PlayersController : ControllerBase
{
    private readonly IPlayerService _playerService;
    public PlayersController(IPlayerService playerService)
    {
        _playerService = playerService;
    }
}
```

The preceding code is the typical structure of an API `Controller` class. Web API controllers use the same routing middleware that's used for MVC except that it uses **attribute routing** to define the routes. The `[Route]` attribute enables you to specify whatever route for your API endpoints. The ASP.NET Core API default convention uses the format `api/[controller]` where the `[controller]` segment represents a token placeholder to automatically build the route based on the `Controller` class prefixed name. For this example, the route `api/[controller]` will be translated to `api/players` where `players` came from the `PlayersController` class name. The `[ApiController]` attribute enables the `Controller` to apply API-specific behaviors for your APIs, such as attribute routing requirements, automatic handling of HTTP 404 and 405 responses, problem details for errors, and more.

Web APIs should derive from the `ControllerBase abstract` class to utilize the existing functionalities built into the framework for building RESTful APIs. In the preceding code, you can see that we've now injected the `IPlayerService` as a dependency instead of the `DbContext` itself. This decouples your data access implementation from the `Controller` class, allowing more flexibility when you decide to change the underlying implementation of the service, as well as making your `Controller` thin and clean.

Now, append the following code for the `POST` endpoint:

```
[HttpPost]
public async Task<IActionResult> PostPlayerAsync([FromBody]
CreatePlayerRequest playerRequest)
{
    if (!ModelState.IsValid) { return BadRequest(); }
    await _playerService.CreatePlayerAsync(playerRequest);
    return Ok("Record has been added successfully.");
}
```

The preceding code takes a `CreatePlayerRequest` class as an argument. By marking the argument with the `[FromBody]` attribute, we tell the framework to only accept values from the body of the request for this endpoint. You can also see that the `PostPlayerAsync()` method has been decorated with the `[HttpPost]` attribute, which signifies that the method can only be invoked for HTTP POST requests. You can see that the method implementation is now much cleaner as it only validates the DTO and delegates the actual data processing to the service. `ModelState.IsValid()` will check for any predefined validation rules for the `CreatePlayerRequest Model` and returns a `Boolean` to indicate whether the validation failed or passed. In this example, it only checks whether both properties in the `CreatePlayerRequest` class are not empty by checking against the `[Required]` attribute annotated for each property.

At this point, you should now have the `POST` endpoint available. Let's do a quick test to ensure that the endpoint is working as we expect.

Testing the POST endpoint

We will use **Postman** to test our API endpoints. Postman is really a handy tool to test APIs without having to create a UI, and it's absolutely free. Go ahead and download it here: https://www.getpostman.com/.

After downloading Postman, install it on your machine so you can start testing. Now, run the application first, by pressing the *Ctrl + F5* keys to launch the application in the browser.

Open Postman and then make a POST request with the following URL: `https://localhost:44306/api/players`.

Note that port 44306 might be different in your case, so make sure to replace that value with the actual port your local application is running at. You can see `launchSettings.json` under the `Properties` folder in your project to learn more about how launch URL profiles are configured.

Let's continue with the testing. In Postman, switch to the **Body** tab, select the **raw** option, and select **JSON** as the format. Refer to the following *Figure 7.10* for a visual reference:

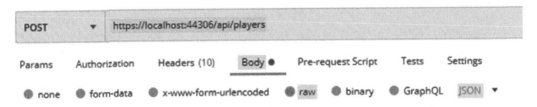

Figure 7.10 – Configuring a POST request in Postman

Now, in the **raw** textbox, copy the following JSON as the request payload:

```json
{
    "nickName":"Vianne",
    "playerInstruments" :[
        {
            "InstrumentTypeId": 1,
            "ModelName": "Taylor 900 Series",
            "Level": "Professional"
        },
        {
            "InstrumentTypeId": 2,
            "ModelName": "Gibson Les Paul Classic",
            "Level": "Intermediate"
        },
        {
            "InstrumentTypeId": 3,
            "ModelName": "Pearl EXL705 Export",
```

```
            "Level": "Novice"
        }
    ]
}
```

The preceding code is the JSON request body that the /api/players endpoint expects. If you remember, the POST endpoint expects CreatePlayerRequest as an argument. The JSON payload in the preceding code represents that.

Now, click the **Send** button in Postman to invoke the HTTP POST endpoint and you should be presented with the following result as shown in *Figure 7.11*:

Figure 7.11 – Making a POST request in Postman

The preceding screenshot returns a 200 HTTP status with a response message indicating that the record has been created successfully in the database. You can verify the newly inserted data by looking at the dbo.Players and dbo.PlayerInstruments database table.

Now, let's test the Model validation. The following *Figure 7.12* shows the result if we omit the playerInstruments attribute in the request body and hit the **Send** button:

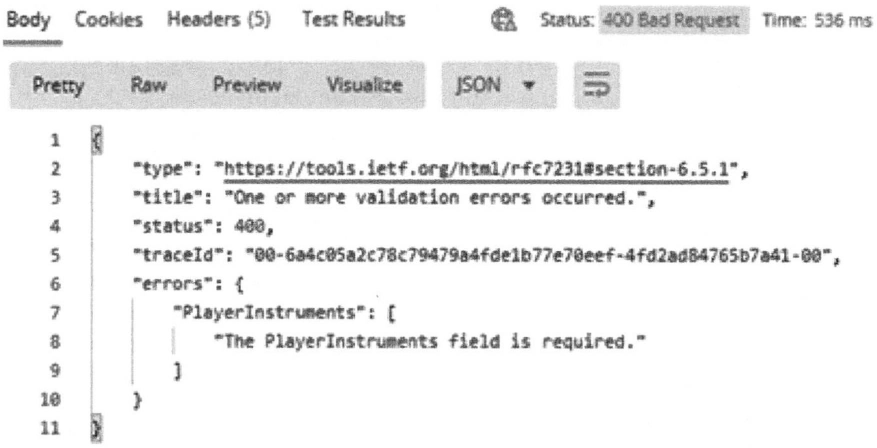

Figure 7.12 – Validation error response output

The preceding screenshot shows a validation error in ProblemDetails format with the 400 HTTP Status code. This is how the response is going to look when you annotate a Model property to be required and you don't supply it when invoking the API endpoint.

Now that you've learned the basics of creating a Web API endpoint for a POST request, let's continue to get our hands dirty by exploring other examples.

Implementing HTTP GET endpoints

In this section, we'll create a couple of HTTP GET endpoints for you to learn some of the basic ways to fetch data from the database.

Defining the DTO

Just like what we did for the POST endpoint, the first step that we need to do is to create a DTO class for us to define the properties that we need to expose. Create a new class called GetPlayerResponse within the Dto/Players folder and copy the following code:

```
public class GetPlayerResponse
{
```

```
    public int PlayerId { get; set; }
    public string NickName { get; set; }
    public DateTime JoinedDate { get; set; }
    public int InstrumentSubmittedCount { get; set; }
}
```

The preceding code is just a plain class that holds a few properties. These are the properties that we are going to return to the client as the response.

For this endpoint implementation, we are not going to return all records from the database to the client because it would be very inefficient. Imagine you have thousands or millions of records in your database and your API endpoint tries to return all of them at once. That would definitely blow down the entire performance of your application and, worse, it could make your application unusable.

Implementing GET with pagination

To prevent potential performance issues from happening, we will implement a pagination feature to value performance. This will enable us to limit the amount of data to return to the client and maintain performance even if the data in the database grows.

Now, go ahead and create a new class called `PagedResponse` within the `Dto` folder. Copy the following code:

```
public class PagedResponse<T>
{
    const int _maxPageSize = 100;
    public int CurrentPageNumber { get; set; }
    public int PageCount { get; set; }
    public int PageSize
    {
        get => 20;
        set => _ = (value > _maxPageSize) ? _maxPageSize :
            value;
    }
    public int TotalRecordCount { get; set; }
    public IList<T> Result { get; set; }

    public PagedResponse()
    {
```

```
        Result = new List<T>();
    }
}
```

The preceding code defines some basic metadata for the paged `Model`. Notice that we've set the constant `_maxPageSize` variable to `100`. This is the value of the maximum number of records that the API GET endpoint will return to the client. The `PageSize` property is set to `20` as the default in case the client won't specify the value when invoking the endpoint. Another thing to notice is we've defined a generic property `Result` of type `IList<T>`. The `T` can be of any `Model` that you want to return as paginated.

Next, let's create a new class called `UrlQueryParameters` within the `Dto` folder. Copy the following code:

```
public class UrlQueryParameters
{
    public int PageNumber { get; set; };
    public int PageSize { get; set; };
}
```

The preceding code will be used as the method argument for the GET endpoint that we are going to implement later. This is to allow clients to set the page size and number when requesting the data.

Next, create a new folder called `Extensions` at the root of the application. Within the `Extensions` folder, create a new class called `PagerExtension` and copy the following code:

```
public static class PagerExtension
{
    public static async Task<PagedResponse<T>>
        PaginateAsync<T>(
        this IQueryable<T> query,
        int pageNumber,
        int pageSize)
        where T : class
    {
        var paged = new PagedResponse<T>();
        pageNumber = (pageNumber < 0) ? 1 : pageNumber;
```

```
paged.CurrentPageNumber = pageNumber;
paged.PageSize = pageSize;
paged.TotalRecordCount = await query.CountAsync();

var pageCount = (double)paged.TotalRecordCount /
    pageSize;
paged.PageCount = (int)Math.Ceiling(pageCount);

var startRow = (pageNumber - 1) * pageSize;
paged.Result = await query.Skip(startRow).
    Take(pageSize).ToListAsync();

return paged;
    }
}
```

The preceding code is where the actual pagination and calculation is happening. The `PaginateAsync()` method takes three parameters in order to perform pagination and returns a `Task` of type `PagedResponse<T>`. The `this` keyword in the method argument denotes that the method is an extension method of the type `IQueryable<T>`. Notice that the code uses the LINQ `Skip()` and `Take()` methods to paginate the result.

Now that we have defined the `DTO` and implemented an extension method to paginate the data, let's continue to the next step and add a new method signature in the `IPlayerService` interface.

Updating the interface

Go ahead and add the following code within the `IPlayerService` interface:

```
Task<PagedResponse<GetPlayerResponse>>
GetPlayersAsync(UrlQueryParameters urlQueryParameters);
```

The preceding code defines a method that takes `UrlQueryParameters` as an argument and returns `PagedResponse` of type `GetPlayerResponse Model`. Next, we'll update the `PlayerService` to implement this method.

Updating the service

Add the following code within the `PlayerService` class:

```
public async Task<PagedResponse<GetPlayerResponse>>
GetPlayersAsync(UrlQueryParameters parameters)
{
    var query = await _dbContext.Players
                    .AsNoTracking()
                    .Include(p => p.Instruments)
                    .PaginateAsync(parameters.PageNumber,
                    parameters.PageSize);

    return new PagedResponse<GetPlayerResponse>
    {
        PageCount = query.PageCount,
        CurrentPageNumber = query.CurrentPageNumber,
        PageSize = query.PageSize,
        TotalRecordCount = query.TotalRecordCount,
        Result = query.Result.Select(p => new GetPlayerResponse
        {
            PlayerId = p.PlayerId,
            NickName = p.NickName,
            JoinedDate = p.JoinedDate,
            InstrumentSubmittedCount = p.Instruments.Count
        }).ToList()
    };
}
```

The preceding code shows the EF Core way of querying data from the database. Since we are only fetching data, we've used the `AsNoTracking()` method to improve the query performance. No tracking queries are much quicker because they eliminate the need to set up change tracking information for the entity, thus they are quicker to execute and improve query performance for read-only data. The `Include()` method allows us to load the associated data in the query results. We then call the `PaginateAsync()` extension method that we implemented earlier to chunk the data based on `UrlQueryParameters` property values. Finally, we construct the return response using a **LINQ method-based query**. In this case, we return a `PagedResponse` object with the `GetPlayerResponse.` type

To see the actual SQL script generated by EF Core, or if you prefer to use raw SQL script to query the data, check out the links in the *Further reading* section of this chapter.

Let's move on to the next step and update the `Controller` class to define the `GET` endpoint.

Updating the controller

Add the following code within the `PlayersController` class:

```
[HttpGet]
public async Task<IActionResult> GetPlayersAsync([FromQuery]
UrlQueryParameters urlQueryParameters)
{
    var player = await _playerService.GetPlayersAsync(
        urlQueryParameters);
    //removed null validation check for brevity
    return Ok(player);
}
```

The preceding code takes `UrlQueryParameters` as the request parameter. By decorating the parameter with the `[FromQuery]` attribute, we tell the framework to evaluate and get the request values from the query string. The method invokes `GetPlayersAsync()` from the `IPlayerService` interface and passes along `UrlQueryParameters` as the argument. If the result is `null`, we return `NotFound()`; otherwise, we return `Ok()` along with the result.

Now, let's test the endpoint to ensure we get what we expect.

Testing the endpoint

Now run the application and open Postman. Make an `HTTP GET` request with the following endpoint:

```
https://localhost:44306/api/players?pageNumber=1&pageSize=2
```

You can set the value of `pageNumber` and `pageSize` to whatever you want and then hit the **Send** button. The following *Figure 7.13* is a sample screenshot of the response output:

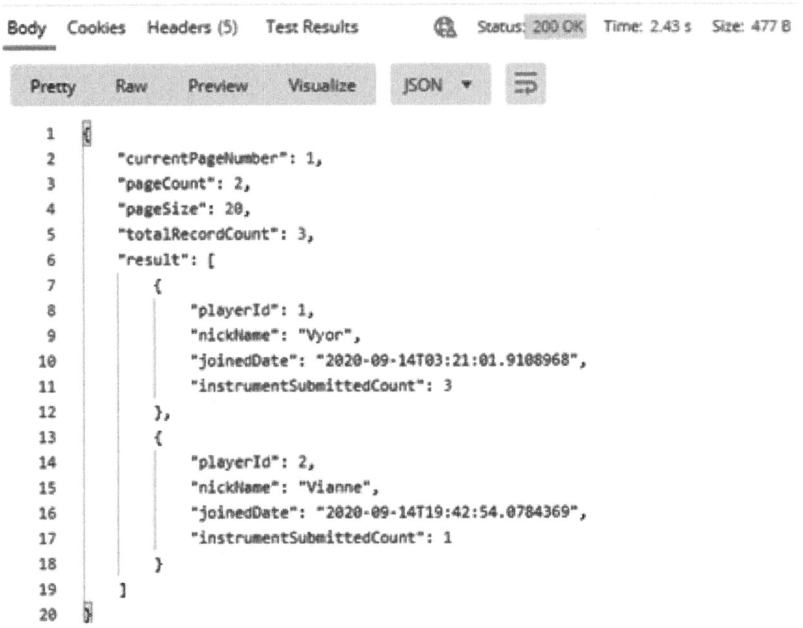

Figure 7.13 – Paginated data response output

Sweet! Now, let's try another `GET` endpoint example.

Implementing GET by ID

In this section, we will learn how to fetch data from the database by passing the ID of the record. We will see how we can query the related data from each database table and return a response to the client containing detailed information coming from the different tables.

Defining the DTOs

Without further ado, let's go ahead and create a new class called `GetPlayerInstrumentResponse` within the `Dto/PlayerInstrument` folder. Copy the following code:

```
public class GetPlayerInstrumentResponse
{
    public string InstrumentTypeName { get; set; }
    public string ModelName { get; set; }
    public string Level { get; set; }
}
```

Create another new class called `GetPlayerDetailResponse` with the `Dto/Players` folder and then copy the following code:

```
public class GetPlayerDetailResponse
{
    public string NickName { get; set; }
    public DateTime JoinedDate { get; set; }
    public List<GetPlayerInstrumentResponse> PlayerInstruments
        { get; set; }
}
```

The preceding classes represent the response `DTO` or `Model` that we are going to expose to the client. Let's move on to the next step and define a new method in the `IPlayerService` interface.

Updating the interface

Add the following code within the `IPlayerService` interface:

```
Task<GetPlayerDetailResponse> GetPlayerDetailAsync(int id);
```

The preceding code is the method signature that we are going to implement in the service. Let's go ahead and do that.

Updating the service

Add the following code within the `PlayerService` class:

```
public async Task<GetPlayerDetailResponse>
GetPlayerDetailAsync(int id)
{
    var player = await _dbContext.Players.FindAsync(id);
    //removed null validation check for brevity
    var instruments = await
            (from pi in _dbContext.PlayerInstruments
            join it in _dbContext.InstrumentTypes
                on pi.InstrumentTypeId equals
                it.InstrumentTypeId
            where pi.PlayerId.Equals(id)
            select new GetPlayerInstrumentResponse
            {
                InstrumentTypeName = it.Name,
```

```
                ModelName = pi.ModelName,
                Level = pi.Level
            }).ToListAsync();


    return new GetPlayerDetailResponse
    {
        NickName = player.NickName,
        JoinedDate = player.JoinedDate,
        PlayerInstruments = instruments
    };
}
```

The preceding code contains the actual implementation of the
GetPlayerDetailAsync() method. The method in asynchronous that takes an id as
the argument and returns a GetPlayerDetailResponse type. The code first checks
whether the given id has associated records in the database using the FindAsync()
method. If the result is null, we return default or null; otherwise, we query the
database by joining the related tables using **LINQ query expressions**. If you've written
T-SQL before, you'll notice that the query syntax is pretty much similar to SQL except that
it manipulates the conceptual Entity Models providing strongly-typed code with rich
IntelliSense support.

Now that we have our method implementation in place, let's move on to the next step and
update the Controller class to define another GET endpoint.

Updating the controller

Add the following code within the PlayersController class:

```
[HttpGet("{id:long}/detail")]
public async Task<IActionResult> GetPlayerDetailAsync(int id)
{
    var player = await _playerService.GetPlayerDetailAsync(id);
    //removed null validation check for brevity
    return Ok(player);
}
```

The preceding code defines a GET endpoint with a route configured to `"{id:long}/detail"`. The `id` in the route represents a parameter that you can set in the URL. As a friendly reminder, consider using `GUID` as record identifiers when exposing a resource ID to the outside world instead of identity seed. This is to reduce the risk of exposing data to malicious users trying to sniff your endpoints by just incrementing the `id` value.

Let's see how the output is going to look by testing the endpoint.

Testing the endpoint

Run the application and make a GET request in Postman with the following endpoint:

```
https://localhost:44306/api/players/1/detail
```

The following *Figure 7.14* is a sample screenshot of the response output:

Figure 7.14 – Detailed data response output

Now that you've learned various ways to implement HTTP GET endpoints, let's move on to the next section and see how we can implement the PUT endpoint.

Implementing an HTTP PUT endpoint

In this section, we are going to learn how to update a record in the database by utilizing the HTTP PUT method.

Defining a DTO

To make this example simple, let's just update a single column in the database. Go ahead and create a new class called UpdatePlayerRequest within the Dto/Players folder. Copy the following code:

```
public class UpdatePlayerRequest
{
    [Required]
    public string NickName { get; set; }
}
```

Next, we'll update the IPlayerService interface to include a new method for performing a database update.

Updating the interface

Add the following code within the IPlayerService interface:

```
Task<bool> UpdatePlayerAsync(int id, UpdatePlayerRequest
playerRequest);
```

The preceding code is the method signature for updating the dbo.Players table in the database. Let's move on to the next step and implement this method in the service.

Updating the service

Add the following code within the IPlayerService class:

```
public async Task<bool> UpdatePlayerAsync(int id,
UpdatePlayerRequest playerRequest)
{
    var playerToUpdate = await _dbContext.Players.
        FindAsync(id);
    //removed null validation check for brevity
    playerToUpdate.NickName = playerRequest.NickName;
    _dbContext.Update(playerToUpdate);
    return await _dbContext.SaveChangesAsync() > 0;
}
```

The preceding code is pretty much straightforward. First, it checks whether the id has an associated record in the database. If the result is null, we return false; otherwise, we update the database with the new value of the NickName property. Now, let's move on to the next step and update the Controller class to invoke this method.

Updating the controller

Add the following code within the PlayersController class:

```
[HttpPut("{id:long}")]
public async Task<IActionResult> PutPlayerAsync(int id,
[FromBody] UpdatePlayerRequest playerRequest)
{
    if (!ModelState.IsValid) { return BadRequest(); }

    var isUpdated = await _playerService.UpdatePlayerAsync(id,
        playerRequest);
    if (!isUpdated) {
        return NotFound($"PlayerId { id } not found.");
    }
    return Ok("Record has been updated successfully.");
}
```

The preceding code takes an id and an UpdatePlayerRequest Model from the request body. The method is decorated with [HttpPut("{id:long}")], which signifies that the method can only be invoked in an HTTP PUT request. The id in the route denotes a parameter in the URL.

Testing the PUT endpoint

Run the application and make a PUT request in Postman with the following endpoint:

```
https://localhost:44306/api/players/1
```

Now, just like in the POST request, copy the following code in the **raw** textbox:

```
{
    "nickName":"Vynn"
}
```

The preceding code is the required parameter for the PUT endpoint. In this particular example, we will change the `NickName` value to `"Vynn"` for `id` equal to `1`. Clicking the **Send** button should update the record in the database.

Now, when you perform a GET request by `id` via `/api/players/1/detail`, you should see that the `NickName` for `id` holding the value of `1` has been updated. In this case, the value `"Vjor"` is updated to `"Vynn"`.

Let's move on to the last example – implementing an HTTP DELETE method.

Implementing an HTTP Delete endpoint

In this section, we are going to learn how to implement an API endpoint that performs database record deletion. For this example, we don't need to create a DTO since we are just going to pass the `id` in the route for the `delete` endpoint. So, let's jump right in by updating the `IPlayerService` interface to include a new method for deletion.

Updating the interface

Add the following code within the `IPlayerService` interface:

```
Task<bool> DeletePlayerAsync(int id);
```

The preceding code is the method signature that we are going to implement in the next section. Notice that the signature is similar to the `update` method except that we are not passing a DTO or `Model` as an argument.

Let's move on to the next step and implement the method in the service.

Updating the service

Add the following code within the `PlayerService` class:

```
public async Task<bool> DeletePlayerAsync(int id)
{
    var playerToDelete = await _dbContext.Players
                               .Include(p => p.Instruments)
                               .FirstAsync(p => p.PlayerId.
                               Equals(id));

    //removed null validation check for brevity
    _dbContext.Remove(playerToDelete);
    return await _dbContext.SaveChangesAsync() > 0;
}
```

The preceding code uses the `Include()` method to perform cascading deletions with the associated records in the `dbo.PlayerIntruments` table. We then use the `FirstAsync()` method to filter the record to be deleted based on the `id` value. If the result is `null`, we return `false`; otherwise, we perform the record deletion using the `_dbContext.Remove()` method. Now, let's update the `Controller` class to invoke this method.

Updating the controller

Add the following code within the `PlayersController` class:

```
[HttpDelete("{id:long}")]
public async Task<IActionResult> DeletePlayerAsync(int id)
{
    var isDeleted = await _playerService.DeletePlayerAsync(id);
    if (!isDeleted) {
        return NotFound($"PlayerId { id } not found.");
    }
    return Ok("Record has been deleted successfully.");
}
```

The implementation in the preceding code is also similar to the update method, except that the method is now decorated with the `[HttpDelete]` attribute. Now, let's test the DELETE API endpoint.

Testing the DELETE endpoint

Run the application again and make a DELETE request in Postman with the following endpoint:

```
https://localhost:44306/api/players/1
```

Clicking the **Send** button should show a successful response output when the record with `id` equal to `1` has been deleted from the database.

That's it! If you've made it this far, then you should now be familiar with building APIs in ASP.NET Core and be able to apply the things that you've learned in this chapter when building your own APIs. As you may know, there are many things that you could do to improve this project. You could try incorporating features such as logging, caching, HTTP response consistency, error handling, validations, authentication, authorization, Swagger documentation, and exploring other HTTP methods such as PATCH.

Summary

In this chapter, we've covered the concepts and the different design workflows for implementing Entity Framework Core as your data access mechanism. Understanding how the database-first and code-first workflows work is very important when deciding how you want to design your data access layer. We've learned how APIs and data access work together to serve and consume data from various clients. Learning how to create APIs that deal with a real database from scratch gives you a better understanding of how the underlying backend application works, especially if you will be working with real applications that use the same technology stack.

We've learned how to implement the common HTTP methods in ASP.NET Core Web API with practical hands-on coding exercises. We've also learned how to design an API to make it more testable and maintainable by leveraging interface abstraction, and learned about the concepts of having DTOs to value the separation of concerns and how to make API controllers as thin as possible. Learning this technique enables you to easily manage your code, without affecting much of your application code when you decide to refactor your application. Finally, we've learned how to easily test API endpoints using Postman.

In the next chapter, you are going to learn about ASP.NET Core Identity for securing web apps, APIs, managing user accounts, and more.

Further reading

- Entity Framework Core Resource – `https://entityframeworkcore.com/`

- EF Core Overview – `https://docs.microsoft.com/en-us/ef/core/`

- EF Core Supported Database Providers – `https://docs.microsoft.com/en-us/ef/core/providers/`

- Lambda Expressions-- `https://docs.microsoft.com/en-us/dotnet/csharp/language-reference/operators/lambda-expressions`

- LINQ Query Expressions – `https://docs.microsoft.com/en-us/dotnet/csharp/programming-guide/concepts/linq/basic-linq-query-operations`

- EF Core Querying Data –`https://docs.microsoft.com/en-us/ef/core/querying/`

- EF Core Logging Commands – `https://www.entityframeworktutorial.net/efcore/logging-in-entityframework-core.aspx`

- EF Core Raw SQL – `https://docs.microsoft.com/en-us/ef/core/querying/raw-sql`

- Migrations Overview – `https://docs.microsoft.com/en-us/ef/core/managing-schemas/migrations`

- Create Web APIs with ASP.NET Core – `https://docs.microsoft.com/en-us/aspnet/core/web-api`

- C# Asynchronous Programming – `https://docs.microsoft.com/en-us/dotnet/csharp/programming-guide/concepts/async/`

- ASP.NET Core Routing – `https://docs.microsoft.com/en-us/aspnet/core/mvc/controllers/routing`

- Using FluentValidation with ASP.NET Core – `https://docs.fluentvalidation.net/en/latest/aspnet.html`

8

Working with Identity in ASP.NET

Pretty much all websites these days have a login function. Even if they work when browsing anonymously, there is usually an option to become a member or something similar. This means that these websites have some concept of identity to tell their visitors apart. In other words – if you are tasked with building a website, it is likely that you will need to deal with identities as well. The thing is, identity can be hard to get right and the consequences of getting it wrong can be less than fun. In this chapter, we will dive into the basics of identity in ASP.NET 5.

We will cover the following topics in this chapter:

- Understanding authentication concepts
- Understanding authorization concepts
- The role of middleware in ASP.NET and identity
- OAuth and OpenID Connect basics
- Integrating with Azure Active Directory
- Working with federated identity

Technical requirements

This chapter includes short code snippets to demonstrate the concepts that are explained. The following software is required to make it work:

- Visual Studio 2019: Visual Studio can be downloaded from `https://visualstudio.microsoft.com/vs/community/`. The Community edition is free and will work for the purposes of this book.

- Some of the samples require you to have an **Azure Active Directory** (**AAD**) tenant. If you don't have one already, you can either create one by going to the Azure portal (`https://portal.azure.com`) and sign up for a free account or even better, sign up for a free Office 365 Developer account, which includes the paid version of AAD as well as the Office 365 services: `https://docs.microsoft.com/en-us/office/developer-program/microsoft-365-developer-program`.

- The section on federated identity uses AAD B2C. This is a special version of AAD that you need to create separately: `https://docs.microsoft.com/en-us/azure/active-directory-b2c/tutorial-create-tenant`.

For lab purposes, all of the samples in this chapter are possible to test free of charge, but regional-specific requirements might need the use of a credit card for verification purposes.

Please visit the following link to check the CiA videos: `https://bit.ly/3qDiqYY`

Code for this chapter can be found at `https://github.com/PacktPublishing/ASP.NET-Core-5-for-Beginners/tree/master/Chapter%2008`

Understanding authentication concepts

Most of us have an understanding of what we mean when we say "identity" in everyday speech. In .NET, and coding in general, we need to be more specific before letting a user into our apps. Identity in this context encompasses multiple concepts with different actions and mechanisms along the way to establish who the user is and what they are allowed to do in our systems.

The first piece of the identity puzzle is authentication. In documentation and literature, you will often find this shortened to **AuthN**. Authentication is about answering the question of who you are. Analogous to the real world, this carries different levels of trust, depending on how this question is answered.

If you met someone you didn't know at a party and asked them what their name was, you would probably be happy with whatever they answered without further verification. You would, however, most likely not be happy with implementing a login function on a website where the user could get away with typing only a username to log in.

A real-life example would be asking someone to provide identity papers – this could be a national ID card, driver's license, passport, or something similar. On websites, the most common method is providing a combination of a username and a secret only you know (for instance, a password).

The simplest form of implementing this in a web app is to use **basic authentication**, which is part of the HTTP specification. This works by the client side appending a header to the HTTP request with credentials encoded as a Base64 value. In a console app, it would look like this:

```
static void Main(string[] args)
{
  var username = ''andreas'';
  var password = ''password'';
  var byteEncoding = System.Text.UTF8Encoding.UTF8.GetBytes(
    $''{username}:{password}'');
  var credentials = Convert.ToBase64String(byteEncoding);
  Console.WriteLine(credentials);
  HttpClient client = new HttpClient();
  client.DefaultRequestHeaders.Authorization = new
    AuthenticationHeaderValue(''Basic'', credentials);
  var response = client.GetAsync(''https://localhost:5001'');
}
```

The credentials will always be `YW5kcmVhczpwYXNzd29yZA==` with no random element, so the main benefit of transferring it this way is for encoding purposes. Let's have a quick look at what Base64 is before moving on.

Base64 encoding

All of us are familiar with Base10 (usually called decimal) as this is what we use when doing ordinary arithmetic – we use 0–9 for representing numbers. In computing, Base16 is also often used under the name hexadecimal. Since the numbers only go up to 9, we use letters in addition, so A=10, B=11, and so on up to F=15. Base64 takes this even further by using A-Z, a-z, 0-9, and the + and / characters, with = as a special padding character (to ensure a string is always of a predictable length).

We will not dive into the algorithm of how to convert characters, but as demonstrated in the previous snippet, it will turn something that is human-readable into something that, while still technically readable, is hard to interpret just by looking at it. The main benefit of encoding the data this way is that both plain text and binary data can be transferred without corruption even if you use non-printable or non-readable characters. The HTTP protocol does not, by itself, account for all characters, so for a password with special characters, it might not be correctly interpreted on the server side if you transfer it without encoding.

Base64 is not a form of encryption, so you cannot trust it for secrets as such and it can be considered plain text even though you, as a human, are not able to decode it on the fly. This also means that using basic auth without HTTPS is an insecure authentication mechanism. Using TLS/SSL to secure the transport greatly improves on this, but it still relies on sending the password over the wire.

With this in the back of our minds, it follows that we are able to decode the Base64 string on the other end of the transmission, and the corresponding server part would look like this:

```
public String Get()
{
    var authHeader = HttpContext.Request.
        Headers[''Authorization''];
    var base64Creds = AuthenticationHeaderValue.Parse
        (authHeader).Parameter;
    var byteEncoded = System.Convert FromBase64String(
        base64Creds);
    var credentials = System.Text.Encoding.UTF8.GetString(
        byteEncoded);
    if (credentials == ''andreas:password'')
    {
        return ''Hello Andreas'';
    }
    else
    {
        return ''You didn't pass authentication!'';
    }
}
```

Run the server first, then the client, and you'll get some output:

```
dotnet run
Base64 encoded: YW5kcmVhczpwYXNzd29yZA==
Response: Hello Andreas
```

It might not surprise you that this implementation is a bad one since we are hardcoding the username and password in the authentication code. The obvious choice at this point would be to move that into a database and do a lookup instead. That leads us to us calling out one of the most egregious identity implementation errors you can commit – storing passwords directly in the database. Never, ever store the password in the database. Period. You should store a hash of the password that is not reversible and calculate whether the password entered matches what is stored in the database. That way, an attacker will not as easily be able to extract the passwords should they get hold of the database.

This begs the question of what a hash is in this context, so let's cover that next.

How hashing works

A hashing function is an algorithm for converting one value into another one, commonly used for the optimization of lookups in data structures or verification of the initial value. For instance, if we were to create a very basic hashing algorithm, we could use number replacements for characters to create a hash for a given string. Let's say A=1, B=2, and so on. The Password string would then be 16 1 19 19 23 15 4 (each number represents a single character; spaces added for readability). Let's then add these digits and divide by the number of characters – (16 + 1 + 19 + 19 + 23 + 15 + 4) / 8 = 12.125. Going with the integer part only, we end up with 12.

Instead of storing your actual password, we would store the value 12. When we type in Password as the password, we are able to compute the hash again and compare it against the stored value. It's also great because it is not reversible – even if the algorithm is known, it is not possible to reverse engineer the number 12 to end up with Password, so a copy of the database is not going to help with figuring out the passwords.

Even if you're not a mathematical genius, you will probably spot that this algorithm is weak. With the simple substitution scheme we use, it is fairly easy to create a string that will also produce 12 as the value and thus be valid. A good hashing algorithm should produce unique values so that two different passwords are not likely to have the same hash. Luckily, Microsoft has implemented a number of hashing algorithms for .NET already, so you do not have to roll out your own.

If we were to illustrate this with pseudo-code (we will not compile since we have not implemented database lookups), it would look as follows:

```
var credentials = System.Text.Encoding.UTF8.GetString(
    byteEncoded);
//Split the credentials into separate parts
var username = credentials.Split('':'')[0];
var password = credentials.Split('':'')[1];
//Bad
if (db.CheckUser == true && db.CheckPassword == true)
{
    return $''Hello {username}'';
}
//Good
var myHash = System.Security.Cryptography.SHA256.Create();
var hashEncoder = System.Text.UTF8Encoding.UTF8;
var byteHashedPassword = myHash.ComputeHash(
    hashEncoder.GetBytes(password));
System.Text.StringBuilder sb = new System.Text.StringBuilder();
foreach (Byte b in byteHashedPassword)
    sb.Append(b.ToString(''x2''));
var hashedPassword = sb;
if (db.CheckUser == true && db.CheckHashedPassword == true)
{
    return $''Hello {username}'';
}
```

By now, you might be thinking that there's a lot that goes on in authentication, and you are spot on. In fact, basic authentication is not really recommended to use, but it should hopefully have given you an idea of what authentication is. We will show some better techniques after explaining a close companion of authentication, called authorization.

Understanding authorization concepts

The second piece of the identity puzzle is authorization, usually shortened to **AuthZ**. Where **AuthN** is about finding out who you are, **AuthZ** is about what you are allowed to do.

Going back to the real world and how things work there, let's for a moment consider international air travel. Assume for simplicity's sake that all international travel requires you to show a passport. If you don't have a passport with you, this will be the same as not being authenticated (unauthenticated) and you will not be allowed into the destination country.

If you have a passport, the relevant authorities will examine it by asking the following questions:

- Is it issued by an actual country? (Unfortunately, ".NET-land" is not recognized by the United Nations.)

- Does it appear genuine, with watermarks, biometric markers, and so on, or does it look like something you printed at home?

- Can the issuing country be trusted to have good procedures in place for issuing passports?

If you pass these, you will be authenticated but you might not be able to move on to baggage claims yet. There is a new round of questions:

- Are you a citizen of a country the destination accepts travelers from?

- Are you from a country requiring a visa and if so, do you have one with you?

- Are you a convicted criminal?

- Are you a known terrorist? (The airline should probably check this before letting you on the plane in the first place, but they might have missed it.)

The details will vary depending on which country you would like to get into, but the point is the same. While your identity checks out, there are still other mechanisms in place for giving an approval stamp.

You might have recognized a similar pattern in web apps. For example, if you log in with John as the username, you have the permissions of a regular user and can do database lookups, edits, and so on. Whereas if you login with JohnAdmin as the username, you are given administrative permissions and can access system-wide server settings and whatnot. Revisiting the authentication code from the previous section, we would extend the pseudo-code to something like this:

```
public String Get()
{
  var authHeader = HttpContext.Request.
    Headers[''Authorization''];
  var base64Creds = AuthenticationHeaderValue.Parse(
```

```
      authHeader).Parameter;
  var byteEncoded = System.Convert.FromBase64String(
    base64Creds);
  var credentials = System.Text.Encoding.UTF8.GetString(
    byteEncoded);
  //Split the credentials into separate parts
  var username = credentials.Split('':'')[0];
  var password = credentials.Split('':'')[1];
  //Password hashing magic omitted
  ...
  //Authentication code omitted
  ...
  var userrole;
  if (db.CheckRole == ''Admin'')
  {
    userrole = ''Admin'';
  }
  if (db.CheckRole == ''User'')
  {
    userrole = ''User''
  }
  else
  {
    return ''You didn't pass authentication!'';
  }
  return $''Hello {userrole}'';
}
```

Even though this is also pseudo-code where we're missing the role lookup, we can see how it adds an additional layer when we introduce authorization. It could be that your web app might not need to distinguish between roles, but the point we are making here is one we have been building up to over a couple of pages now.

Do not implement your own identity solution from scratch (or based on this sample code).

This is not to discredit the knowledge and competency of the readers of this book; it is a general best practice that this should be done by those who have it as a full-time job who have access to a team reviewing and testing everything with a critical eye.

Microsoft has included a template in Visual Studio for a SQL-backed web app that implements a similar identity setup:

1. Start Visual Studio and select **Create a new project**.

2. Select the **ASP.NET Core Web Application** template and hit **Next**.

3. Name the solution `Chapter_08_DB_Auth` and select a suitable location for this book's exercises (such as `C:\Code\Book\Chapter_08`) and click on **Create**.

4. Select the **Web Application (Model-View-Controller)** option and click **Change** under **Authentication**. Make sure you select **Individual User Accounts** and **Store user accounts in-app** before clicking **OK**, followed by **Create**:

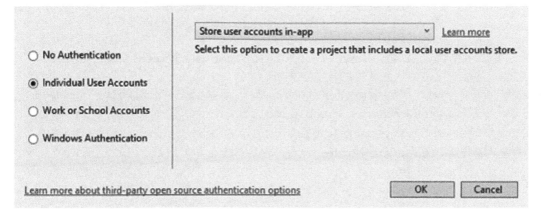

Figure 8.1 – Individual user accounts authentication

5. If you take a look at the **Data** folder, you will see the code that generates a database where the user accounts are stored as shown in *Figure 8.2*:

Figure 8.2 – Migrations files in Visual Studio

6.   Open up `00000000000000_CreateIdentitySchema.cs`. It should be 200+ lines of code, and the `user` object looks like this:

```
migrationBuilder.CreateTable(
  name: ''AspNetUsers'',
  columns: table => new
  {
    Id = table.Column<string>(nullable: false),
    UserName = table.Column<string>(maxLength: 256,
      nullable: true),
    NormalizedUserName = table.Column<string>(maxLength:
      256, nullable: true),
    Email = table.Column<string>(maxLength: 256,
      nullable: true),
    NormalizedEmail = table.Column<string>(maxLength:
      256, nullable: true),
    EmailConfirmed = table.Column<bool>(nullable: false),
    PasswordHash = table.Column<string>(nullable: true),
    SecurityStamp = table.Column<string>(nullable: true),
    ConcurrencyStamp = table.Column<string>(nullable:
      true),
    PhoneNumber = table.Column<string>(nullable:
      true),
    PhoneNumberConfirmed = table.Column<bool>(
      nullable: false),
    TwoFactorEnabled = table.Column<bool>(nullable:
      false),
    LockoutEnd = table.Column<DateTimeOffset>(
      nullable: true),
    LockoutEnabled = table.Column<bool>(nullable: false),
    AccessFailedCount = table.Column<int>(nullable:
      false)
  },
  constraints: table =>
  {
    table.PrimaryKey(''PK_AspNetUsers'', x => x.Id);
  });
```

The names should be fairly self-explanatory, but as you can see, there is a little bit more to it than a username and a hashed password.

7. Taking a quick look at the configuration in `Startup.cs`, we can see where the database is initialized and requires authentication to happen:

```
public void ConfigureServices(IServiceCollection
services)
{
  services.AddDbContext<ApplicationDbContext>(options =>
    options.UseSqlServer(
      Configuration.GetConnectionString(
      ''DefaultConnection'')));
  services.AddDefaultIdentity<IdentityUser>(options =>
    options.SignIn.RequireConfirmedAccount = true)
    .AddEntityFrameworkStores<ApplicationDbContext>();
  services.AddControllersWithViews();
}
```

8. Following this up by attempting to run the app, there should be a form for registering an email address and defining a password. *Figure 8.3* is an example of signing up:

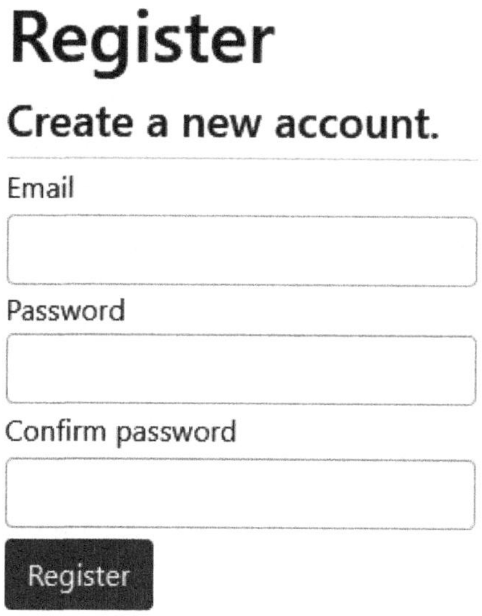

Register

Create a new account.

Email

Password

Confirm password

Register

Figure 8.3 – Registering an individual user account

If you peek into the rest of the files that were scaffolded, you will notice that there is actually a bit of code to make it all run, and then there's everything in the libraries you don't see, solidifying why you would prefer not to do all of this yourself.

Templates like these used to be very popular years ago as they took away a lot of the hard work and users were accustomed to register on every site they visited. While there's nothing inherently wrong with using this – it's secure and maintained by Microsoft – it has become less common now that there are other options.

We will resume our regular programming soon, but the previous code snippet provides an entry point for us to segue into a topic that technically is not related to identity, but is useful for understanding how different identity pieces play into .NET apps.

The role of middleware in ASP.NET and identity

A lot of technologies and products start with a code name, and when Microsoft came up with *Project Katana*, it certainly had a zing to the name. This project came about in 2013 to address a couple of shortcomings in .NET at the time.

We're not going to drag up old .NET code and point to flaws in the design here, but even without going into the details, you can probably relate to the challenge of replacing components in your code. Let's say, for instance, that you start out creating a utility for controlling some smart light bulbs you have in your home. During troubleshooting one day, you realize that it would be easier if you captured some information and logged it. The quick-and-dirty method is to append lines to a file called `log.txt`. This works nicely until you realize that you could use some insight into non-error conditions as well, such as logging when the lights were turned on and off to create some stats for yourself.

This doesn't lend itself as easily to be logged in a text file when you want to use it outside the app. So, you realize it could be nice to have in a database. Then you have to rewrite all those calls to a file to log to a database instead. You get the picture.

It would be nice to have a more generic `log.Info(''Lights out'')` method that did not care about the details. Since logging is a common concern in many apps, there are a number of logging frameworks out there, but there's still a setup ceremony to it per app.

This chapter is about identity, so what's the connection, you say? Well, authentication and authorization are also common use cases for apps. And so is URL routing in web apps, caching, and a couple of other things as well.

Another facet of these components is that you most likely want to run them as early as possible during the initialization of the app – loading the logging component when something fails might be too late.

That was an elaborate setup for saying that Microsoft has built an abstraction called *middleware*. Project Katana actually covered four components, and this carries over for the current implementation - host, server, middleware, and application.

The host part can be found in `Program.cs` and for a web app, it looks like this:

```
public class Program
{
  public static void Main(string[] args)
  {
    CreateHostBuilder(args).Build().Run();
  }
  public static IHostBuilder CreateHostBuilder(string[] args)
  =>
    Host.CreateDefaultBuilder(args)
      .ConfigureWebHostDefaults(webBuilder =>
      {
        webBuilder.UseStartup<Startup>();
      });
}
```

If you compare this to the worker service we created in *Chapter 2, Cross-Platform Setup*, you will notice similarities:

```
public class Program
{
  public static void Main(string[] args)
  {
    CreateHostBuilder(args).Build().Run();
  }
  public static IHostBuilder CreateHostBuilder(string[] args)
  =>
    Host.CreateDefaultBuilder(args)
      .UseWindowsService()
      .UseSystemd()
      .ConfigureServices((hostContext, services) =>
```

```
    {
        services.AddHostedService<Worker>();
    });
}
```

You're not able to turn any web app into a service by changing these lines, but notice how the pattern is the same.

We've already mentioned, and peeked into, the `Startup.cs` file, which is where the server and middleware components can be found.

The server and services are invoked by the runtime with this code:

```
public void ConfigureServices(IServiceCollection services)
{
    ...
    services.AddControllersWithViews();
    ...
}
```

The actual runtime might vary, as we've already seen, depending on whether you host in IIS or Kestrel (which does not matter in this context).

The middleware is found in the next section of the file:

```
public void Configure(IApplicationBuilder app,
IWebHostEnvironment env)
{
    if (env.IsDevelopment())
    {
        app.UseDeveloperExceptionPage();
    }
    else
    {
        app.UseExceptionHandler(''/Error'');
        app.UseHsts();
    }
    ...
}
```

This is called a pipeline, and it builds as a sequence – authentication goes before authorization, for instance, but not all middleware is sensitive to which step it is loaded at.

Some of the middleware has a binary behavior – `UseHttpsRedirection` enables exactly that, and if you don't want it, you simply remove it.

`UseEndpoints` lets you add specific endpoints you want to listen to:

```
app.UseEndpoints(endpoints =>
{
    endpoints.MapControllerRoute(
        name: ''default'',
        pattern: ''{controller=Home}/{action=Index}/{id?}'');
});
```

The beauty of middleware and identity is that you can add custom middleware to the mix, and since the usage is standardized, it is fairly pain-free to change afterward. We did not implement basic auth as middleware, but the boilerplate added by the wizard in Visual Studio for using a local database did.

This will become handy if we were to upgrade our identity implementation to be based on OAuth, which will be covered next.

OAuth and OpenID Connect basics

Basic authentication is simple to implement, and if you need to work with legacy systems, there's a good chance you will run into it. It's not recommended to start new projects using basic authentication though.

There is no shortage of acronyms for protocols in the identity space, and .NET Framework has relied upon different authentication and authorization protocols over the years. We are not able to delve into all of them, nor to do a comparison of the strengths and weaknesses of them.

The most popular set of protocols used for *AuthN* and *AuthZ* purposes these days is **OAuth** and **OpenID Connect (OIDC)**, so we will look at parts of both the theory and practical implementations. OAuth is the base protocol and OIDC builds on top of this, so there are some overlapping details we will get back to.

Looking back at basic authentication, we already mentioned that a drawback is the fact that the passwords are transferred over the wire. Both the client and server side have access to the actual password, which is, in many cases, more than they need. For instance, a web app will certainly care about establishing whether you have an administrator role before allowing you access to the administrative settings, but as long as the identity is established, the password doesn't provide any value in doing this authorization step. That's just extra data you need to protect.

OAuth decouples these parts so that the server side does not need to know the password. For the client, it is more a case of "it depends" for how this is handled – if a password is required, you can't avoid typing it somewhere. It all starts with what are called **JSON Web Tokens (JWTs)**, so let's cover that first.

JSON web tokens

With OAuth and OIDC, we don't rely on passing around `username:password` as the key to the kingdom, but instead, we rely on passing around tokens. These tokens are called JWTs, and pronounced *jot/jots*.

A JWT is formatted as JSON and contains three parts – a header, payload, and signature. A sample JWT could look like this:

```
{
    ''alg'': ''RS256'',
    ''kid'': ''4B92FBAE5D98B4D2AB43ACE4198026073012E17F'',
    ''x5t'': ''S5L7rl2YtNKrQ6zkGYAmBzAS4X8'',
    ''typ'': ''JWT''
}.{
    ''sub'': ''john.doe@contoso.com'',
    ''nbf'': 1596035128,
    ''exp'': 1596038728,
    ''iss'': ''contoso'',
    ''aud'': ''MyWebApp''
}.[Signature]
```

If you have not seen anything like this before, you probably have (at least) two questions:

- What do all these things mean?
- How does this actually help?

The information in this token is called *claims* – so, for instance, the `''sub''` claim is short for *subject* and has the value `john.doe@contoso.com`. This claim is usually the user/username (it does not have to be in email format, but this is common).

The rest of the claims are as follows.

The header is as follows:

- `''alg''`: The algorithm used for generating the signature
- `''kid''`: Key identifier
- `''x5t''`: Key identifier
- `''typ''`: The type of the token

The payload is as follows:

- `''nbf''`: Not before. The time from which the token is valid; usually the same time as it was issued.
- `''exp''`: Expiration time. The time the token is valid until. Usually an hour from when it was issued (but this is up to the token issuer).
- `''iss''`: Issuer. The issuer of the token.
- `''aud''`: Audience. Who the token is intended for; usually the app the token is intended for.

This is just a minimal sample token – you can have more claims if you want to, and you choose the format of these. If you want a `''foo''` claim with a value of `''bar''` that only makes sense for your application, that is OK. Just be aware that the token does not have an unlimited size – in enterprise environments, some developers try to include all the groups the user is a member of. When the user is a member of 200+ groups, you experience what is known as *token bloat*, which causes the token to be fragmented when transferring over a network. In most cases, these packets are not reassembled correctly, and things fall apart.

Passing the token to the server is similar to basic authentication in that we add an authorization header where the token is Base64-encoded (token shortened for brevity):

```
Authorization: Bearer eyJhbGciOi...PDh4ck7Q
```

This is nifty as you can send more information than when passing the username and password while still keeping the credentials out of the data transmission. It is called a *bearer token* because anyone who possesses it can use it. This brings us back to question number two – how is this better? The first impression you get is that any client can craft their own token and that doesn't sound like a good mechanism.

There are two important actions in OAuth/OIDC transactions:

- **Issuing a token**: This is about controlling who gets a token and this will be protected by one or more mechanisms.

- **Validating a token**: This is about checking that the token is trustworthy and what the contents are.

Both of them are primarily based on using certificates – signing when issuing and verifying when validating. (Note that this is not the same as certificate-based auth; we're only focusing on the token itself here.)

Let's take a look at how this works in code.

How to generate/issue a token

In *Chapter 2, Cross-Platform Setup*, we showed how to generate a certificate, install it on Windows and Linux, as well as reading it afterward. Building on this, we can use the same certificate for signing a token.

To create an app that will generate a token, do the following:

1. Open up the command line and create a new directory (`Chapter_08_BearerAuthClient`).

2. Run the `dotnet new console` command.

3. Run the `dotnet add package System.IdentityModel.Tokens.Jwt` command.

4. We then need to add some code to `Program.cs`. First, we create the token (based on a generic template):

```
static void Main(string[] args)
{
    jwt = new GenericToken
    {
        Audience = ''Chapter_08_BearerAuth'',
        IssuedAt = DateTime.UtcNow.ToString(),
```

```
  iat = DateTimeOffset.UtcNow.ToUnixTimeSeconds().
    ToString(),

  Expiration = DateTime.UtcNow.AddMinutes(60).
    ToString(),

  exp = DateTimeOffset.UtcNow.AddMinutes(60).
    ToUnixTimeSeconds().ToString(),

  Issuer = ''Chapter 08'',

  Subject = ''john.doe@contoso.com'',

};
```

Then, we set up/retrieve the certificates we use for signing:

```
SigningCredentials = new Lazy<X509SigningCredentials>(()
=>
  {
    X509Store certStore = new X509Store(StoreName.My,
      StoreLocation.CurrentUser);

    certStore.Open(OpenFlags.ReadOnly);

    X509Certificate2Collection certCollection =
      certStore.Certificates.Find(
          X509FindType.FindByThumbprint,

          SigningCertThumbprint,

          false);

    // Get the first cert with the thumbprint

    if (certCollection.Count > 0)

    {

      return new X509SigningCredentials(
        certCollection[0]);

    }

    throw new Exception(''Certificate not found'');

  });
```

The final piece is lining up the claims and creating the actual signed token:

```
IList<System.Security.Claims.Claim> claims = new
  List<System.Security.Claims.Claim>();

claims.Add(new System.Security.Claims.Claim(''sub'',
  jwt.Subject,
  System.Security.Claims.ClaimValueTypes.String,
  jwt.Issuer));

// Create the token
```

```
    JwtSecurityToken token = new JwtSecurityToken(
      jwt.Issuer,
      jwt.Audience,
      claims,
      DateTime.Parse(jwt.IssuedAt),
      DateTime.Parse(jwt.Expiration),
      SigningCredentials.Value);
    // Get the string representation of the signed token
    // and print it
    JwtSecurityTokenHandler jwtHandler = new
      JwtSecurityTokenHandler();
    output = jwtHandler.WriteToken(token);
    Console.WriteLine($''Token: {output}'');
}
```

Note that in order to focus on the important pieces, this is not the complete code – check the GitHub repo for this chapter for the complete code.

5. Run the `dotnet run` command.

   Your output will look similar to *Figure 8.4*:

```
c:\Code\Book\Chapter_07_BearerAuthClient>dotnet run
Token: eyJhbGciOiJSUzI1NiIsImtpZCI6IkRFQUYyQjhBNDg2NEM1
0b3NvLmNvbSIsIm5iZiI6MTU5NjEwNjc2NCwiZXhwIjoxNTk2MTEwMz
RiKogGtX1MH0zd0YddxV12hW0cCTHmLpuX0sL0sn16NJ0CFHGEzMqIX
jA30P6AOhbkVbps5bdjkSeqAyuaZQXQK3LveY8qz1IO3UGzC-sKXrl0
```

Figure 8.4 – A JWT

This is not intended for you to read, but it is reversible as it is just Base64-encoded. The great part is that your actual secret is not included, so even if someone were able to read it, that's not a problem.

How to validate a token

Generating a token is nice and dandy, but unsurprisingly, we need a counterpart – checking that the token is good and allowing or rejecting access based on this evaluation. For this, we will also create a server-side code sample:

1. Open up the command line and create a new directory (`Chapter_08_BearerAuthServer`).
2. Run the `dotnet new console` command.

3. Run the `dotnet add package System.IdentityModel.Tokens.Jwt` command.

4. The following code goes into `EchoController.cs`:

```
[HttpGet]
public String Get()
{
  var audience = ''Chapter_08_BearerAuth'';
  var issuer = ''Chapter 08'';
  var authHeader = HttpContext.Request.Headers
    [''Authorization''];
  var base64Token = AuthenticationHeaderValue.Parse(
    authHeader).Parameter;

  JwtSecurityTokenHandler handler = new
    JwtSecurityTokenHandler();
  TokenValidationParameters validationParameters = null;
  validationParameters = new TokenValidationParameters
  {
    ValidIssuer = issuer,
    ValidAudience = audience,
    ValidateLifetime = true,
    ValidateAudience = true,
    ValidateIssuer = true,
    //Needed to force disabling signature validation
    SignatureValidator = delegate (string token,
      TokenValidationParameters parameters)
    {
      var jwt = new JwtSecurityToken(token);
      return jwt;
    },
    ValidateIssuerSigningKey = false,
  };
  try
  {
    SecurityToken validatedToken;
    var identity = handler.ValidateToken(base64Token,
```

```
            validationParameters, out validatedToken);
    return ''Token is valid!'';
}
catch (Exception e)
{
    return $''Token failed to validate:    {e.Message}'';
}
}
```

As in the previous code sample, parts have been left out for readability.

5. Run the `dotnet run` command.

6. Step back to the client-side code and add the following code:

```
HttpClient client = new HttpClient();
client.DefaultRequestHeaders.Authorization = new
    AuthenticationHeaderValue(''Bearer'', output);
var response = client.GetAsync(
    ''https://localhost:5001/Echo'').Result;
Console.WriteLine(response.Content.ReadAsStringAsync().
    Result.ToString());
```

7. Run the `dotnet run` command in this folder while the server part is running.

    You should see an output that says `Token is valid`.

While there are terms in the server code that intuitively have a meaning, a little bit of explaining of the procedure is probably warranted.

The basics are that we configure values for the issuer (whoever issued the token) and the audience (who the intended recipient of the token is). We then configure the parameters for validating the token; the aforementioned audience and issuer as well as the time stamp of the token.

If the token is valid, we return a message indicating so, and if it fails, we return a different message.

In this code, we disabled checking the signature, and that might seem counterintuitive. You should always validate the signature – if not, anyone can generate a token that will pass as valid as long as they figure out the right values to insert. The reason for disabling this important piece of the puzzle is that the code becomes much more complex if we want to do that. We need to cover some additional topics first before returning to an approach that requires less complexity to get it right.

OAuth flows

It is all nice and dandy to be able to send a token to an API and have it validated, but you might wonder how this would actually work in an app. We can't have a user type in the details we used here, and even if we only did this on a server, there are no credentials involved. That doesn't sound like something you would actually use in real life.

JWTs are a central piece of OAuth, but there is more to the protocols than the token. OAuth consists of what we call "flows" that prescribe the steps on the journey to acquiring and using said token. We will not be able to cover all the variants of these flows here, but we will cover a few that are relevant to ASP.NET Core use cases.

There are a couple of terms we need to sort out that applies to all of the flows.

Instead of each application handling the issuing of tokens, we have a central service known as an **identity provider**. This service usually verifies the credentials (password, certificate, and so on) and takes care of issuing tokens. While this is technically something you can implement on your own, it is highly recommended to go for an established solution in the market (we will be taking a look at using **Azure AD** for this purpose).

When acquiring tokens, the client requests which permissions it would like. These permissions are known as *scopes* and are embedded in the token as claims.

The flows described here drive the login for Facebook, Google, and Microsoft, so you have most likely tried them out already even if you didn't give it much thought at the time. (These providers support multiple flows to support different use cases.)

OAuth Client Credentials grant

The easiest flow to understand is probably the Client Credentials flow as this is the closest to using a username and a password. You would register an application in the UI for the identity provider you're using and get a client ID and a client secret. When you want to acquire a token, you send these to an identity provider and indicate which permissions you would like. The flow goes like *Figure 8.5*:

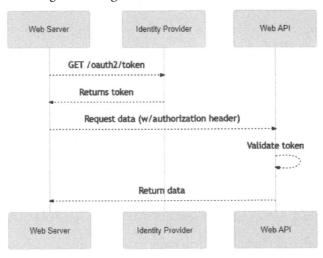

Figure 8.5 – OAuth Client Credentials flow

A very important thing to note is that this flow is only intended for *trusted clients*. A trusted client typically runs on a server where the code and configuration are not available to the end user. This is typically a service account, or server-side-rendered web apps. The client ID is not sensitive, but paired with the client secret, it potentially enables anyone possessing it to extract information they should not have. If you have a client-side app such as JavaScript that is downloaded to the browser, a mobile app, or something similar, you should never use the Client Credentials flow.

The client secret is usually too long and complex for a user to remember and type in, so for passwords, there are different flows.

OAuth Resource Owner Password Credentials

A flow that is similar to Client Credentials but intended for user credentials is the **Resource Owner Password Credentials** (**ROPC**) flow. When using an external identity provider, there will often be a predefined look and feel of the login experience and usually, it's rendered as HTML in a browser. Even if there is an option to style it to your own liking, it is not unusual that the people working with user experience will say that they need to tweak some element a certain way for them to be happy.

At this point, you might be thinking it would be great if you could create all the visual aspects yourself and deal with the authentication just like when you're implementing a server-side authentication experience. Such an option exists with this flow, but you should never admit to the designers that it exists. It is highly discouraged to use this flow, by Microsoft and the identity community, because it is inherently less secure than handling the credentials exchange directly at a specialized product for handling identity use cases. The app takes on much more responsibility since it will have knowledge of the user's password.

We only mention it here because it is useful to be aware of it even if it does not come recommended.

OAuth Authorization Code grant

The recommended way to do authentication in a native app is a flow called the Authorization Code flow. It might come off as slightly complicated the first time you run into it, but there is a logic behind it. We need the user to enter their credentials manually, but the app should not be aware of them. At the same time, we want the application to be an entity as well when calling into APIs. A diagram would look like *Figure 8.6*:

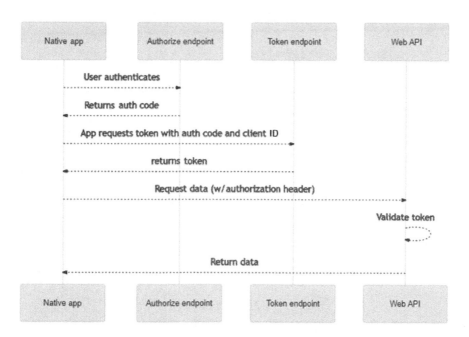

Figure 8.6 – OAuth Authorization Code flow

Both the authorize and token endpoints are located on the identity provider.

This diagram does not cover the low-level details, but a possible attack vector in this scenario is that, for instance, on a mobile device, a malicious app might be able to intercept the auth code and use it for its own non-approved purposes. You are recommended to implement an extension to the flow called **Proof Key for Code Exchange** (**PKCE** – pronounced *pixie*), which ensures only the right app can use a specific auth code.

OAuth Implicit Grant flow

It is mostly clear what a classic web app is and what a classic native app means, but where does something such as a JavaScript-based **Single-Page Application** (**SPA**) fit in? It is sort of a hybrid in the sense that you have code supplied by the browser that is executed locally. This means that you cannot consider it a trusted client. You will see many guides referring to using the Implicit Grant flow for these purposes. It looks like *Figure 8.7*:

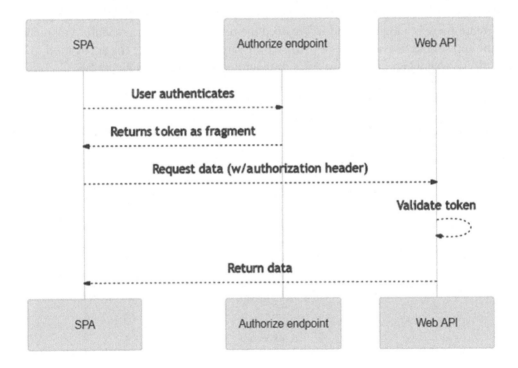

Figure 8.7 – OAuth Implicit Grant flow

The meaning of *fragment* here is that the token will be part of a URL when redirecting back to the SPA instead of returning it in the body of the HTTP response. This is due to how most SPAs don't "jump between pages" like non-SPA web apps and need to consume data through the URL.

While there are use cases where an implicit grant is suitable, and it is being used in a lot of places, the current recommendation is that auth code with PKCE is more suited for most SPAs. Implicit Grant is less secure, so while it is functionally acceptable, it has other drawbacks.

Note that if you are using libraries to provide this functionality, you should try to find out which of the two flows it uses behind the scenes.

OpenID Connect

All of the previous flows focused on acquiring tokens that said "you're allowed to access this API." This is, of course, a very important scenario to solve, but if you try logging in to a web app without touching an API, you often just want to know "who signed in." For this, we have the OIDC flow, or more correctly, a separate protocol building on top of OAuth as seen in *Figure 8.8*:

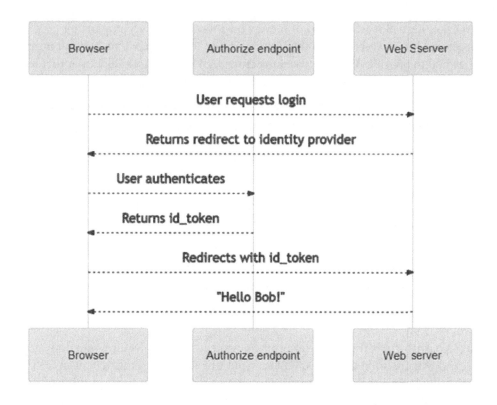

Figure 8.8 – OIDC

The OIDC protocol has some other things included as well that make signing in easier as a developer, which we will get back to in our code samples.

There are other OAuth flows as well, and it can be more elaborate than what we have shown here, but it is out of the scope of this book to cover all the nuances of AuthN and AuthZ.

These flows are no good without an identity provider, so in the next section, we will put everything into context by using a popular provider.

Integrating with Azure Active Directory

Chances are that if you have logged in to a corporate computer the past 20 years, you have used Active Directory, whether you are aware of it or not. AD was introduced with Windows Server 2000 and extended the domain concept introduced in Windows NT 4.0 to provide a complete implementation of centralized identities. When you logged in to your Windows desktop, it provided fairly pain-free access to file shares and servers in an organization as long as you were seated in the office.

With AD, you need at least a couple of servers on-premises and accompanying infrastructure. This isn't feasible in the cloud world of today, but Microsoft built upon what they had to provide **Azure Active Directory** (**AAD**) as a cloud identity provider, breaking free from the constraints of physical locations at the same time.

AD is based on older identity protocols, so the OAuth flows and OIDC are not natively supported, but require the use of **Active Directory Federation Services** (**ADFS**) as an additional service to support what we just described. This does not carry an extra cost over a Windows Server license, but it is recommended to have dedicated servers for this service.

Conversely, AAD was built with the newer protocols in mind, so it does not support the older protocols without additional components.

This means that it is likely that if you want to migrate an existing on-premises app with AD support to AAD, you need to do some rewriting of the identity stack. We will not cover this, but rather go straight to the newer protocols. AAD is based on open standards, and you can fairly easily replace it with other identity providers that comply with the standards, so this isn't a Microsoft lock-in either.

AAD in its basic form is free. There are some advanced security features you don't get for free, and you are limited to 50,000 objects, but this should be sufficient even for many production deployments. Per the technical requirements listed at the beginning of the chapter, we assume you have an AAD tenant for these samples, so you should sign up now if you haven't done so already.

Using AAD unlocks a range of options in the Azure portal. You can, for instance, control whether all the flows we described should be available or whether only a subset is used. In addition, you can specify which users have access, what other data sources the application can access, and more.

If you have an existing web application, it is possible to add support for AAD to this, but to simplify matters, we will be creating a Blazor app from scratch with the wizard in Visual Studio doing the backend configuration in Azure for us:

1. Start Visual Studio 2019 and select **Create a new project**.

2. Select **Blazor App** and click **Next**.

3. Name the solution `Chapter_08_AADAuth`.

4. Click **Change** under **Authentication**.

5. Select **Work or School Accounts** and select **Cloud - Single Organization** as shown in *Figure 8.9*:

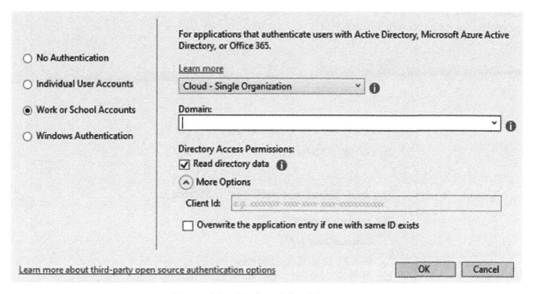

Figure 8.9 – Work or School Accounts

6. Type in the domain name of the AAD tenant you will be using. You will be prompted to sign in if you haven't done so before.

7. Make sure you select **Blazor Server App** and that you have checked **Configure for HTTPS** before clicking **Create**.

If you try running the app, the first thing that will hit you is a sign-in form provided by Microsoft as seen in *Figure 8.10*:

Figure 8.10 – AAD sign in

After typing your username followed by the password, the next thing is a request for permissions as shown in *Figure 8.11*:

Figure 8.11 – Consent notification

Provided you click the **Accept** button, the app will open and in the upper-right corner, you will be greeted with your name. Seems easy enough, but let's take a look at what's going on in the code before adding some more functionality.

If you open `Startup.cs`, you might notice some code you haven't seen so far:

```
public void ConfigureServices(IServiceCollection services)
{
  services.AddMicrosoftIdentityWebAppAuthentication(
    Configuration, ''AzureAd'');
  services.AddControllersWithViews()
    .AddMicrosoftIdentityUI();
  services.AddAuthorization(options =>
  {
    // By default, all incoming requests will be authorized
    // according to the default policy
    options.FallbackPolicy = options.DefaultPolicy;
  });
  services.AddRazorPages();
  services.AddServerSideBlazor()
    .AddMicrosoftIdentityConsentHandler();
}
```

In a previous section, we mentioned how easy it is to swap out identity middleware and we can see here how the startup pipeline has seen the addition of middleware both for handling identity and the related UI.

If we take a look at `appsettings.json`, we can see where our specific configuration is stored:

```
{
  ''AzureAd'': {
    ''Instance'': ''https://login.microsoftonline.com/'',
    ''Domain'': ''contoso.com'',
    ''TenantId'': ''tenant-guid'',
    ''ClientId'': ''client-guid'',
    ''CallbackPath'': ''/signin-oidc''
  },
```

You might find it slightly unfriendly that you are hit with a login prompt before even seeing the web page. There are a lot of pages that offer a default experience when you're not logged in where functionality is unlocked when signing in.

This is controlled by a couple of lines of code in `Startup.cs`:

```
//Comment out the line below like this
//services.AddRazorPages();
//And replace with this
services.AddRazorPages(options =>
{
    options.Conventions.AllowAnonymousToPage(''/_Host'');
});
```

Be aware that this effectively shuts off authorization for all pages in the Blazor app, so you need to enable it for the pages where you need it. (The details of how you change the default behavior varies between the different view engines – MVC, Razor Pages, and Blazor.)

You can replace the contents of `Index.razor` with the following code:

```
@page ''/''
<AuthorizeView>
  <Authorized>
    Hello, @context.User.Identity.Name!
    <table class=''table''>
      <thead>
        <tr>
          <th scope=''col''>Claim Type</th>
          <th scope=''col''>Claim Value</th>
        </tr>
      </thead>
      <tbody>
        @foreach (var claim in context.User.Claims)
        {
          <tr>
            <td>@claim.Type</td>
            <td>@claim.Value</td>
          </tr>
```

```
            }
        </tbody>
      </table>
    </Authorized>
    <NotAuthorized>
      <p>For full functionality please log in</p>
      <a href=''MicrosoftIdentity/Account/SignIn''>Log in</a>
    </NotAuthorized>
</AuthorizeView>
```

This will print all the claims in your token, which only makes sense when logged in, and provide a link for logging in when you have not authenticated yet. This approach is suitable for when you need a page to be available both for logged-in and anonymous users.

If you want to block all the content of a page, you can do this (in `Counter.razor`) by adding the `[Authorize]` attribute:

```
@page ''/counter''
@attribute [Authorize]
<h1>Counter</h1>
```

Users who are not logged in will simply see a message that they are not authorized.

There are a multitude of ways to configure this. You can create policies that require specific claims to be present, you can create roles that control access to a view, and more. We don't recommend making it more complex than necessary though, especially when starting out. It can be cumbersome to troubleshoot, so get the basics right first.

Understanding single tenancy versus multi-tenancy

In the wizard, we chose **Cloud - Single Organization**, but if you checked the dropdown, you probably noticed **Cloud - Multiple Organizations** as well. We should probably explain those.

An organization here is an AAD tenant. This means that if your company structure has multiple tenants, this is considered to be multiple organizations even though it may be only one legal organization. It is a purely technical definition.

When you create a single organization application, that means that only users of one specific AAD tenant will be able to log in, and the data consumed is primarily data constrained to this tenant. If you build an app that is only ever to be consumed by you and your co-workers, this is a good choice as there will be a logical boundary and you don't end up spilling data into other organizations.

For multi-org apps, there are a couple of reasons behind why you would want to change the configuration. Let's say we have a web shop selling computer supplies to businesses. We make the assumption that most of our customers have AAD already – instead of implementing our own user database, we offer sign in with AAD from customers' tenants. Even though we have a shared database of our sales, we can enforce that, for example, only users signing in from `contoso.com` can access the orders tagged with `Contoso` as the company name.

A slightly different setup would be that we are an ISV that sells a piece of software to businesses. If a company is already using AAD, single sign-on would usually be high on their wish list. The app can be architected to create the illusion of being for one organization, but it can reuse a common set of user administration across different companies.

The default setting in a multi-tenant app is that all tenants in AAD are allowed to authenticate. It is possible to restrict this if you want to by editing the token validation parameters, but the most important part of this is that you need to figure out the authorization setup as well.

Understanding consent and permissions

You were asked to grant permissions when running the app, but we didn't really explain this part. The basic concept should be easy to grasp – your AAD account potentially unlocks access to a lot of data if you use other Microsoft services, such as Office 365. We don't want an app to grab whatever it desires, so as a safeguard, the app has to request access and it has to be granted.

There are two types of permissions:

- **Delegated permissions** are permissions that are valid in a user context. For instance, if an app wants to read your calendar, you as the user has to grant this. Your consent is only applicable to you – it does not enable the app to read other users' calendars.

- **Application permissions** are permissions that are valid in the broader app context – often in a backend. Say, for instance, the app needs to be able to list all users in the organization – this is not data that is specific to you. This permission needs to be granted by a global admin. This means that if you are not a global admin, and the app cannot function without these permissions, you cannot use the app before someone in the organization with the appropriate role consents.

As we mentioned previously, the technical term in code for these permissions is *scope*. A default OIDC flow requests the `offline_access` and `User.Read` scopes, and if you want to read the calendar, you would add `Calendars.Read`. This is found in `Startup.cs`:

```
public void ConfigureServices(IServiceCollection services)
{
    services.AddAuthentication
        (OpenIdConnectDefaults.AuthenticationScheme)
    .AddMicrosoftIdentityWebApp(options =>
    {
        Configuration.Bind(''AzureAD'', options);
        options.ResponseType = ''code'';
        options.SaveTokens = true;
        options.Scope.Add(''offline_access'');
        options.Scope.Add(''User.Read'');
        options.Scope.Add(''Calendars.Read'');
    });
    ...
```

Note that while you will not be prompted again to consent to the same set of permissions between separate logins, you will need to re-consent if the app requests more scopes than what you originally consented to.

You might be thinking – how do we figure out what the scopes are named? If you locate the app registration in the Azure portal, you can browse the list dynamically as shown in *Figure 8.12*:

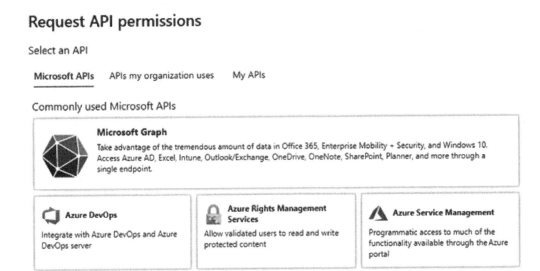

Figure 8.12 – Permissions list in the Azure portal

For Microsoft APIs, it is, of course, also listed in the online documentation, so you don't have to take a guess as to what the permission is called.

Having permission to read the calendar is helpful, but this does not mean that calendar entries start pouring in by themselves. That requires more code. We need to elaborate on a couple of concepts first, though.

Every user in an AAD tenant can authenticate and acquire a token. This is done through the AAD endpoints, and in the code we used, this was done with the `Microsoft.Identity.Web` library. This is intended for backend usage, such as web apps running server side (we used Blazor Server) and protected web APIs.

To acquire tokens on a client, we use a different library, called **Microsoft Authentication Library** (**MSAL**), which can run on native apps in C#, JavaScript-based web apps, and so on. It works with the same endpoints but implements different OAuth flows. When searching the internet, you might also come across a library called **ADAL**, which is the older and deprecated library; you should not be using it any longer.

Calendar data is dependent on having an Office 365 license. This data is exposed through Microsoft Graph, which is a gateway for a number of Microsoft services providing a coherent API surface. To interact with the Microsoft Graph, you can use the Microsoft Graph NuGet package after using one of the aforementioned libraries to acquire a token.

With that covered, we can circle back to the question of how to read the calendar entries.

The client has already acquired a token, so the first approach would probably be to think that this can be leveraged fairly easily. The token is not directly accessible to the app though, as it is stored in the browser session, so you would need to retrieve it with some extra steps. Microsoft has fortunately made these steps much easier with the `Microsoft.Identity.Web` library.

Behind the scenes, the library invokes an OAuth flow called **On-Behalf-Of (OBO)**. We're not painting the full picture of the flow here, but the high-level view is that the app first lets the user authenticate before using the token to perform a second call to the identity provider authenticating as itself as well. This enables the app to build out more complex scenarios when you have a lot of backend APIs.

To make this work, we have to do a couple of things:

1. Go to the Azure portal and locate the app registration in AAD.

2. Go to the **API Permissions** blade and click **Add a permission**.

3. Select **Microsoft Graph**, the **Delegated permissions** permission type, and locate `Calendars.Read` and `Calendars.ReadWrite` in the list.

4. Click **Add permission**.

5. Go to the **Certificates and secrets** blade and click **New client secret**. Give it a name such as `MySecret` and select when it expires, before clicking **Add**.

6. Make a copy of the secret immediately as it will not be retrievable after navigating away from the page.

7. Add new configurations to `appsettings.json`:

```
''AzureAd'': {
    ...
    ''ClientSecret'': ''copied from the portal'',
    ''CallbackPath'': ''/signin-oidc''
},
''Graph'': {
    ''BaseUrl'': ''https://graph.microsoft.com/v1.0'',
    ''Scopes'': ''user.read calendars.read calendars.
        readwrite''
},
''Logging'': {
```

8. Go back to `Startup.cs` and change the code we added previously to look like this:

```
string[] initialScopes = Configuration.GetValue<string>(
  ''Graph:Scopes'')?.Split(' ');
services.AddAuthentication(OpenIdConnectDefaults.
  AuthenticationScheme)
  .AddMicrosoftIdentityWebApp(
    Configuration.GetSection(''AzureAd''))
  .EnableTokenAcquisitionToCallDownstreamApi(
    initialScopes)
  .AddInMemoryTokenCaches()
  .AddMicrosoftGraph(Configuration.GetSection(
    ''Graph''));
```

9. Since this is a Blazor app, we will add a page called `Calendar` to show the calendar entries. The first part is adding the following at the top:

```
@page ''/Calendar''
@using Microsoft.Graph
@inject Microsoft.Graph.GraphServiceClient GraphClient
```

The injected `GraphClient` takes care of passing along the token you need to call Microsoft Graph.

10. You need a code section to actually call the graph:

```
@code{
  private List<Event> eventList = new List<Event>();
  protected override async Task OnInitializedAsync()
  {
    try
    {
      var events = await GraphClient.Me.Events
      .Request()
      .Select(''subject,body,organizer,
        start,end,location'')
      .GetAsync();
      eventList = events.CurrentPage.ToList();
    }
    catch (Exception ex)
```

```
        {
          var error = ex.Message;
        }
      }
    }
```

11. Then, you need to print it all out, as shown in the following code block:

```
<AuthorizeView>
  <Authorized>
    <table class=''table''>
      <thead>
        <tr>
          <th scope=''col''>Subject</th>
          <th scope=''col''>Start</th>
          <th scope=''col''>Entry</th>
        </tr>
      </thead>
      <tbody>
        @foreach (var entry in eventList)
        {
          <tr>
            <td>@entry.Subject</td>
            <td>@entry.Start.DateTime.ToString()</td>
            <td>@entry.End.DateTime.ToString()</td>
          </tr>
        }
      </tbody>
    </table>
  </Authorized>
  <NotAuthorized>
    <p>For full functionality please log in</p>
    <a href=''MicrosoftIdentity/Account/SignIn''>Log in
    </a>
  </NotAuthorized>
</AuthorizeView>
```

We wrap it inside `AuthorizeView` to avoid any errors arising from not being logged in – if you don't log in, you're not getting any data, so it's not risky in that sense to skip it, but we like messages making sense for the user instead of things not working.

12. Running the app and manually appending `/Calendar` to the URL, you should see a list of entries as shown in *Figure 8.13*:

Calendar

Subject	**Start**
.NET Conf 2020	2020-09-10T06:00:00.0000000

Figure 8.13 – Calendar entries

Note that it is common when running in debug mode that you may have to log out and back in again for things to work properly when working with tokens. This can be caused by the browser storing a session while the token cache is emptied between runs (when using the in-memory cache).

We've come a long way, but there are still a few things to look at, such as expanding beyond your current AAD tenant.

Working with federated identity

Since you integrated with a specific AAD tenant assigned to you, it's easy to perceive it as your identity provider. Microsoft operates on a larger scale though, and on a technical level, you are federating with an external identity provider.

So, what does this actually mean?

Going back to our initial example from the real world, you could say that a passport is an example of federated identity. Even if you are not the entity issuing passports, you trust that there is a good procedure in place by the issuing authority and you accept it as proof of identity. You could choose to not trust this identity and build your own system for verifying that people are who they say they are, but it would most likely be time-consuming and expensive if you even managed to provide the same level of authenticity. How much of a hassle it is to order a passport in different countries probably varies, but just imagine how unfriendly it would be as a traveler to acquire multiple passports in the different countries you traveled to.

In the past couple of years, you have most likely seen an option for logging in with Facebook or Google on a website you've visited. Instead of creating a new account, you can click these buttons and as long as you accept that the website is able to read some of your identity attributes, you're good to go. Sure, these providers probably have a lower level of trust than a federal entity in your own country, but odds are they have invested a decent amount of effort into making sure their user account database is secure and not too easily hackable. And for you, as the user, they save you from the effort of coming up with yet another password to remember.

Both passports and Google accounts are examples of federated identity. While your application might have a user database for access and licensing purposes, you only have a reference to their identity since that is provided by someone else that you trust to provide authentication services.

What happens on a high level is that you create an account for the application in a control pane for your chosen identity provider, where you provide a couple of relevant attributes, and correspondingly, you configure metadata as in the previous section, pointing to the identity provider.

.NET 5 and ASP.NET Core 5 provides libraries for assisting you with this, and it's not necessarily hard to do by itself. However, what happens during the life cycle of your app is that you start with Google and Facebook and it's working. Then, someone asks you to add Apple to make it easier for iOS users. And then you add a provider that uses "last name" instead of "surname," breaking your data model. Even if your response is that you love a challenge, it could be that this is causing friction as your login code gets bloated as you start adding increasing logic to handle it that requires new builds and releases.

As you might be able to guess, this leads to the inevitable *There's an Azure service for that*. There is a version of AAD called AAD B2C, which is designed to handle such scenarios. The **B2C** part stands for **business to consumer**, but it's really about external identities in general. The way it works is that you set up a nested federation where your app trusts AAD B2C, and AAD B2C in turn trusts other identity providers. If you need to add a new provider or customize claims, you can do so in Azure without recompiling your app.

There are actually two types of user accounts in AAD B2C: local and social. Social is another term for federated in this context as it doesn't have to be an account on a social network per se. The beauty is that there are several providers pre-created that can be easily added by stepping through a wizard as you can see in *Figure 8.14*:

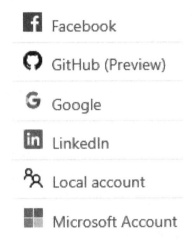

Figure 8.14 – Identity provider selection

If your provider is not on the list, you can add generic OIDC providers. If you want a non-standard configuration, you can even add a non-B2C AAD tenant as an identity provider.

The local account does not federate to other providers but is instead a specialized version of AAD for adding individual accounts with any email address. A regular AD tenant is usually an organization where it's normal that users can look up the details of other users, be part of groups, and so on. In a B2C tenant, each user is an island and cannot see other users. If you remember back to the sample where we created local accounts in the form of a database, you could say that this competes with that, but it's both way more powerful and, in most instances, easier to use than maintaining your own database.

Different types of user journeys (sign up, sign in, password reset) can be configured through wizards, and you can also replace the styling if you so wish.

If you want to go deeper, there's also the option to use custom policies, which entails diving into XML files for a coding-like experience. It offers great flexibility with the option to call into backend APIs during the flows and more. Be warned that this can be quite the opposite of user-friendly, so only use it if the wizard-driven policies don't cover your use case.

While AAD B2C has a different feature set than regular AAD, the endpoints used for acquiring a token are also compliant with standards, so it's a fairly easy job to adapt your code.

In a basic form, you can actually use the same code as we used for authenticating with regular AAD, and change `appsettings.json` to point to a B2C tenant with attributes created in said tenant. This will actually work nicely if you only have one flow defined that handles signing up and signing in. It will not work if you also want to provide options, such as password reset and profile editing.

The recommended way to get started before you have a full overview of the AAD B2C service is having Visual Studio generate things for you, by opting to use B2C as the provider when choosing the authentication configuration during project creation in Visual Studio. The choices can be found under **Individual User Accounts** and **Connect to an existing user store in the cloud** as shown in *Figure 8.15*:

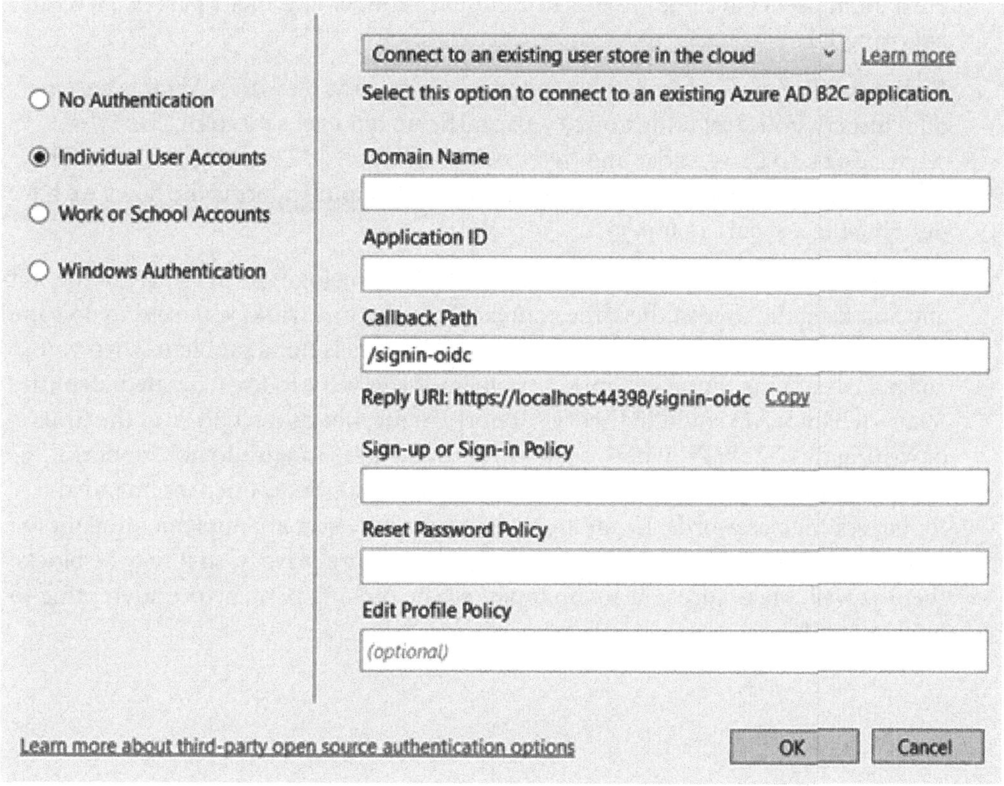

Figure 8.15 – AAD B2C authentication options

At first glance, it might appear like AAD B2C adds complexity for unclear benefits since these things can be achieved directly in the code. To be clear – like so many other things, there are good use cases and there are less-good use cases. The great thing is that it will require very few changes to the code, should you want to use B2C, and most of the work in AAD B2C can be "outsourced" to identity pros.

A note on UIs for identity

Whether you write your own identity implementation from scratch or rely on AAD, you need a UI if the user is to type in a username and password. In general, there are three different approaches to implementing this:

- **Popups**: You can break out a separate smaller window for the user to type in credentials. Once they've been verified, the popups disappear and you're back in the web app. There's nothing wrong with this method from a technical perspective, but a lot of users have popups blocked in their browser and many perceive it as an annoying UI.

- **Redirects**: The method we implemented when integrating with AAD was based on redirects. You start at `https://localhost`, you get sent to `https://microsoftonline.com`, and then back to `https://localhost` again. This is a very common approach. It is easy to implement and supports the flows we have described in a secure manner.

- **Iframe**: The sleekest method is probably to embed the login form as part of the web app and keep the user in the same context. To make this work, you need to do some tricks on the backend with cookies and sessions. This is not a problem when you control everything, but it becomes a problem if you want to use federated identities. Single-tenant AAD could in theory support Iframe, but doesn't do so at the time of writing this book. Providers, such as Facebook and Google, do not support it, due to security implications – for instance, creating login experiences intended for harvesting passwords. In addition, the major browsers are implementing more mechanisms for blocking third-party cookies to ensure privacy, so it may be blocked there as well. Make sure you are on top of all the moving parts before attempting to implement this UI.

Summary

This chapter took us on a journey from basic auth to federated identities. It started with explaining what authentication and authorization are all about. There were details, such as understanding what Base64 encoding and hashing are good for. The sample implementations of AuthN and AuthZ intended to give you a better understanding of what's going on, even though you will probably not implement or use all of these techniques. The walkthrough of OAuth and introducing AAD should put you in a good position to implement production-grade identity in your web apps.

Not every app needs to be super secure, but this should have set you up for web apps that can be more personal than treating all visitors as anonymous users.

With identity covered, the next chapter will dive into another hot topic these days, as we cover the ins and outs of working with containers.

Questions

1. What's the difference between authentication and authorization?

2. Which OAuth flow is the most common and recommended for frontend use cases in web apps?

3. Why would you use AAD B2C?

Further reading

- The Microsoft identity platform documentation, available at `https://aka.ms/aaddev`

- The Microsoft Graph landing page, available at `https://developer.microsoft.com/en-us/graph`

9
Getting Started with Containers

In the previous chapter, we covered identity and how it applies to ASP.NET 5. Identity is core to web application development, so we covered several forms of authentication (*who you are*) and authorization (*what you are allowed to do*). We covered Basic Authentication, OAuth, OIDC, Azure Active Directory, and Federated Identity.

This chapter is about containers and the popular Docker platform. A container is a package of software that includes code and all the dependencies required for it to run. This technique of packaging software came from a need to reliably deploy and run software from a developer's machine in testing and production environments. By using a container, the same package is used in each environment, which greatly reduces the number of things that can go wrong.

We will cover the following topics in this chapter:

- Overview of containerization
- Getting started with Docker
- Running Redis on Docker
- Running ASP.NET Core in a container

By the end of this chapter, you will be familiar with containers, and you will have gained practical experience with creating containers in Docker.

Technical requirements

This chapter includes short code snippets to demonstrate the concepts that are explained. The following software is required:

- **Visual Studio 2019**: Visual Studio can be downloaded from `https://visualstudio.microsoft.com/vs/community/`. The Community edition is free and will work for the purposes of this book.

- **.NET 5**: The .NET framework can be downloaded from `https://dotnet.microsoft.com/download`.

Make sure you download the SDK and not just the runtime. You can verify the installation by opening a command prompt and running the `dotnet --info` cmd as shown in *Figure 9.1*:

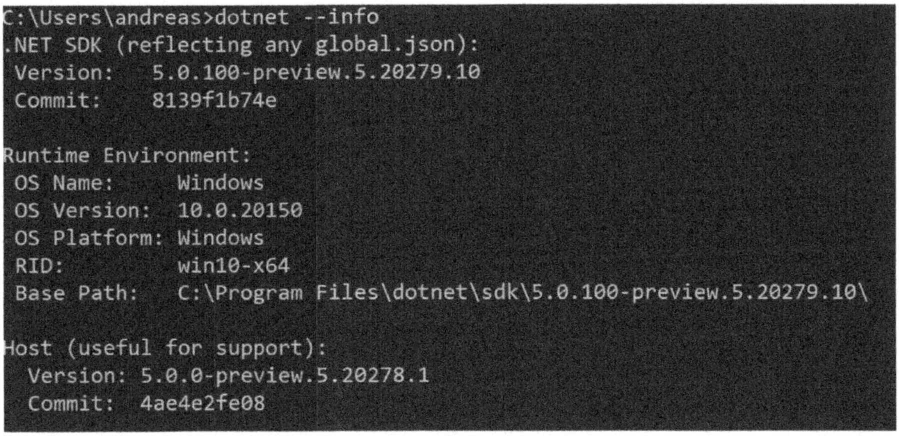

```
C:\Users\andreas>dotnet --info
.NET SDK (reflecting any global.json):
 Version:   5.0.100-preview.5.20279.10
 Commit:    8139f1b74e

Runtime Environment:
 OS Name:     Windows
 OS Version:  10.0.20150
 OS Platform: Windows
 RID:         win10-x64
 Base Path:   C:\Program Files\dotnet\sdk\5.0.100-preview.5.20279.10\

Host (useful for support):
  Version: 5.0.0-preview.5.20278.1
  Commit:  4ae4e2fe08
```

Figure 9.1 – Verifying the installation of .NET

As part of this chapter, we will install Docker. This may require some additional setup depending on whether you are using Windows 10 or Mac. The installation instructions in the *Installing Docker* section are written for Windows 10. In addition to the instructions we provide in the chapter, please use the following resources:

- Docker Desktop on Mac: `https://docs.docker.com/docker-for-mac/install/`

- Docker Desktop on Windows: `https://docs.docker.com/docker-for-windows/install/`

The source code for this chapter is located in the GitHub repository at `https://github.com/PacktPublishing/ASP.NET-Core-5-for-Beginners/tree/master/Chapter%2009`.

Please visit the following link to check the CiA videos: `https://bit.ly/3qDiqYY`

Hardware virtualization

The following instructions and corresponding images are written for a Windows 10 environment. Please see the Docker documentation for instructions for installing on a Mac.

Note

For some steps, administrator privileges may be required.

Before installing any software, let's check whether hardware virtualization is supported. Using Task Manager, view the **Performance** tab. Virtualization support is shown as indicated in *Figure 9.2*:

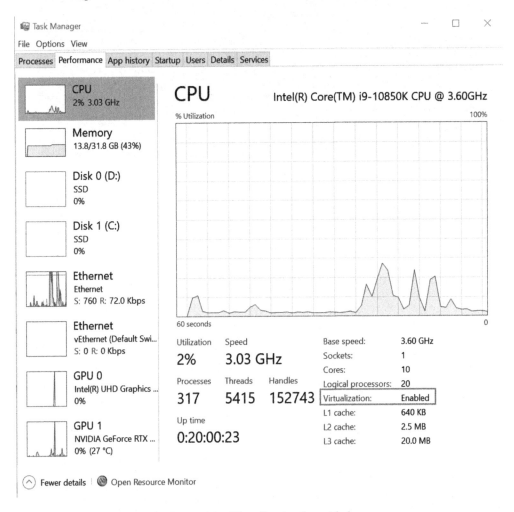

Figure 9.2 – Virtualization is enabled

If hardware virtualization is not enabled, an error message like the following will be shown:

```
Please enable the Virtual Machine Platform Windows feature and
ensure virtualization is enabled in the BIOS.
```

Hardware virtualization is enabled in the desktop BIOS. Please use the documentation supplied by your motherboard manufacturer for instructions.

In addition to hardware virtualization, the **Hyper-V** and **Containers** Windows features must be enabled as shown in *Figure 9.3*:

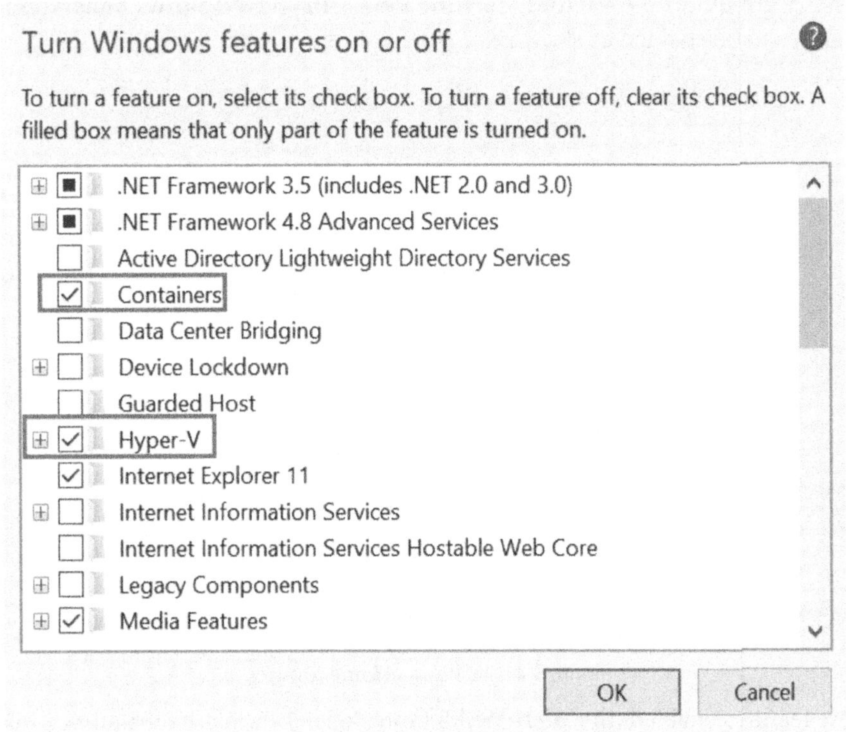

Figure 9.3 – Windows features

That covers the basics of installation. The following two sections are added to help you if you are running on a virtual machine and/or Windows Home.

Virtual machine installation

Installing Docker on a **virtual machine** (**VM**) is very similar to what we just did. The **Container** and **Hyper-V** Windows features must be enabled. Additionally, virtualization does have to be exposed to the virtual machine. This can be done by running the following command (use your own virtual machine name):

```
set-vmprocessor -vmname vmname -exposevirtualizationextensions
$true
```

WSL 2 installation

If you are running Windows Home, you will also need to install WSL 2 to run Linux containers. This requires the **Virtual Machine Platform** and **Windows Subsystem for Linux** features to be enabled as shown in *Figure 9.4*:

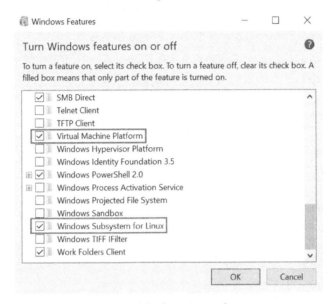

Figure 9.4 – Windows Home features

With those features enabled, the latest WSL2 Linux kernel should be installed. This can be done by downloading and running the package. Please use the link to the *Linux kernel update package for x64 machines* Microsoft documentation: `https://docs.microsoft.com/en-us/windows/wsl/install-win10` for WSL2.

During the installation of Docker Desktop, you will see the following error message if WSL 2 is not installed as shown in *Figure 9.5*:

Figure 9.5 – WSL 2 missing error message

Thankfully, Docker Desktop provides clear instructions on how to install the kernel.

Overview of containerization

The challenge of getting software from a development machine to a production server is harder than it sounds. Differences in the environment can range from hardware to software. Containerization is one approach to addressing this. With containerization, the application and all its dependencies are bundled into a single package or image. This image can then be started, and the running image or instance is called a container.

To explain further, let's look at a traditional application as shown in *Figure 9.6*:

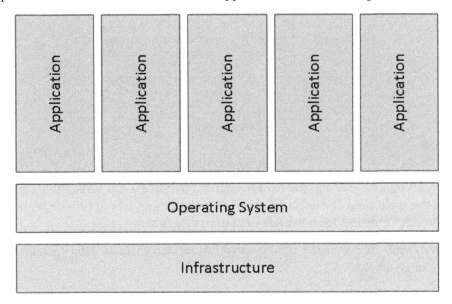

Figure 9.6 – Traditional application

The preceding figure illustrates a traditional application, where applications run on an operating system hosted on infrastructure. An issue might arise with this approach when an application requires different features of the operating system. It is not necessarily that two applications will always require opposing features, but more that it becomes difficult to reliably capture all the requirements of an application. In organizations involving teams of developers and several environments, this becomes unruly without clear documentation or tools to help manage the dependencies of an application.

VMs abstract away the underlying infrastructure to allow multiple VMs to run on a single physical machine as shown in *Figure 9.7*:

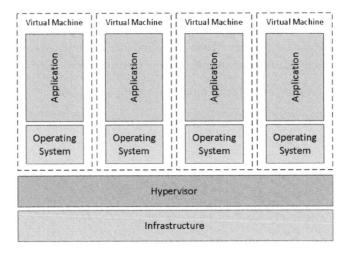

Figure 9.7 – VMs

The previous figure shows a **hypervisor** being used to host several VMs. Each VM contains the application and its own copy of the operating system to run the application. This approach virtualizes the hardware used to run the VMs.

Containerization takes virtualization one step further and virtualizes the operating system as shown in *Figure 9.8*:

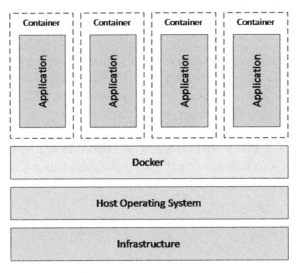

Figure 9.8 – Containers

The preceding figure shows **Docker**, a popular containerization technology, being used to run multiple applications. Notice that with containerization, the application runs on a shared host operating system. One advantage is that the size of a container is much smaller than a VM. The startup of a container is also much faster than that of a VM. One of the most significant advantages of containerization is that the release of software is more predictable, as the application and all of its dependencies are bundled together into a versioned, unchangeable package.

Getting started with Docker

To show a practical example of using containers, we will use the popular container platform Docker. Docker was chosen because of its popularity, ease of use, and its position as an industry leader in containerization. This section of the chapter will provide an overview of Docker and instructions for installing Docker.

What is Docker?

Docker is a platform for operating system-level virtualization for managing and executing packages of software referred to as containers. Each container is a bundle of software and the libraries and configuration required to run the container. The bundle is called an image, and images can be stored locally to the machine running Docker or in registries. A Docker registry is a repository of images. A registry might require authentication; this is called a private registry. Docker registries that don't require authentication are called public repositories, and Docker Hub and Docker Cloud are two popular public Docker registries. Let's look at a common workflow to illustrate what we have discussed so far as shown in *Figure 9.9*:

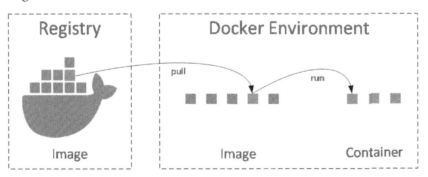

Figure 9.9 – Docker registry

In a Docker registry, a collection of images is stored. In a Docker environment, let's say a development machine, the `pull` command is used to bring a copy of the image into the local environment. Then, the `run` command is used to create an instance of the image called a container. The container can be stopped and started, and its state can be changed. This means that if a container contains a database and the records in the database change, these changes will exist if the container is stopped and started. The image, however, cannot be altered once it is created. Multiple versions of an image can exist, though. This will make more sense when we look at the practical examples.

Let's take this a little bit further and discuss a scenario where containers are developed, tested, and then released to production. Each of these activities will be done in different environments. This is one instance where having a central registry can help us as shown in *Figure 9.10*:

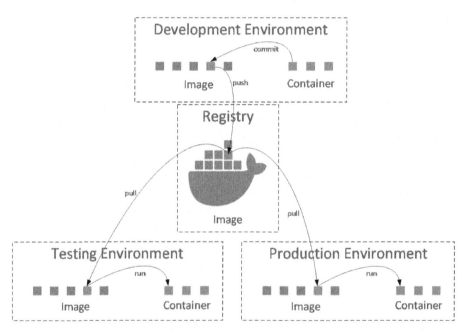

Figure 9.10 – Docker workflow

Images are created in the **Development Environment**. In the previous figure, a **commit** command is used to create an image from a running container. There are several ways to create an image, and we will look at some later in the chapter. The image is then pushed from the **Development Environment** to the **Registry**. From the **Testing Environment**, the image is brought in from the registry using the **pull** command and the container is started using the **run** command. Once the image has been tested and approved, the same image can then be pulled from the registry and **Registry** in the **Production Environment**.

Now that we have a high-level understanding of Docker, let's take a moment to discuss some of its main components.

Image

The first step to understanding Docker is to distinguish between an *image* and a *container*. An image is a versioned file that cannot be altered and really does not do anything. It is a snapshot of our application, and once it is created, it cannot be altered. A container is an instance of an image. A container has a state, for example, running or stopped, and a container has its own state. In some ways, you can think of the relationship between an image and a container in a similar way as the relationship in C# between a *class* and an *object*.

An image can be thought of as being composed of layers. Each layer builds upon the previous layer. For example, the first layer might set up the initial environment. To illustrate, let's use the Ubuntu image, which is an image provided for the popular Linux operating system. A subsequent layer would then be added to include some required components – let's say a database engine such as Microsoft SQL Server. As we mentioned earlier, there are several ways of creating a new image. In the previous section, we mentioned that the `commit` command could be used, but let's talk about using a Dockerfile.

Dockerfile

A Dockerfile is a text file that contains commands used to assemble an image. Using the official Microsoft SQL Server as an example, the Dockerfile used to create the Microsoft SQL Server Linux image (`mssql-server-linux`) comprises four commands.

Take a look at the Dockerfile used to create the image. This is in the public GitHub repository at `https://github.com/microsoft/mssql-docker/blob/master/linux/mssql-server-linux/Dockerfile`:

```
# mssql-server-linux
# Maintainers: Microsoft Corporation (LuisBosquez and twright-msft on GitHub)
# GitRepo: https://github.com/Microsoft/mssql-docker

# Base OS layer: Latest Ubuntu LTS.
FROM ubuntu:16.04

# Default SQL Server TCP/Port.
EXPOSE 1433
```

```
# Copy all SQL Server runtime files from build drop into
# image.
COPY ./install /


# Run SQL Server process.
CMD [ "/opt/mssql/bin/sqlservr" ]
```

The first command, FROM ubuntu:1604, is an example where the first layer is specified as the Ubuntu Docker official image. The next command, EXPOSE 1433, will make port 1433 available to the host operating system. This command is followed by COPY ./install /, which will copy the SQL Server runtime. The last command starts the SQL Server process: CMD ["/opt/mssql/bin/sqlservr"].

When the Dockerfile is executed, a new image will be created, composed of the commands in the file. We will discuss the different commands later in more detail. The purpose of this section is just to introduce the concept of a Dockerfile and how an image is composed of layers.

Container

The running instance of an image, that is, a container, is lightweight, secure, and portable. A container is lightweight because unlike a VM, it has access to resources exposed by the underlying operating system. For example, if the host system can reach the internet, then by default the container has access to the internet. Similarly, by default, a container has full access to available RAM and CPU resources. A container is also isolated from other containers and processes running on the host system. This is why port 1433 was explicitly exposed in the Microsoft SQL Server example in the *Dockerfile* section. A Docker container adheres to an industry standard, meaning it can be run on different platforms and container engines.

Docker Engine

In this chapter, we will be using Docker Engine to run the containers via Docker Desktop. This is important to note because containers follow the **Open Container Initiative (OCI)** standard, meaning that different engines can be used to run the same images. For local development, we might use Docker Desktop, but our testing environment might be hosted in a cloud provider. In the next chapter, we will look at running containers in Azure using Azure Container Instances.

Docker Engine and Azure Container Instances are examples of powerful engines for managing isolated containers. For more advanced scenarios, an orchestration engine is required. Docker Swarm and Kubernetes are examples of orchestration engines that support additional features such as scaling and load balancing, as well as features for authentication and more advanced monitoring.

Now that we have an overview of Docker, let's install it.

Installing Docker

The installation for Docker Desktop can be found on the Docker website. Just download the latest version and install it. Docker does provide comprehensive installation instructions for Mac, Windows, and Linux at `https://docs.docker.com/get-docker/`, so we will not repeat the instructions and requirements here.

In this chapter, we will be using Linux containers for a couple of reasons. The first is that they tend to be smaller so they are quicker to download and start. The second is to illustrate the power of .NET to be able to compile the same source to either Linux or Windows containers.

Once Docker Desktop has been installed and has started, let's run some commands to make sure things are working as expected. You can use command, Bash, or PowerShell to run the Docker CLI commands in this chapter. First, let make sure Docker is up and running by running `docker version`.

There are two parts to the response. The first shows the client as shown in *Figure 9.11*:

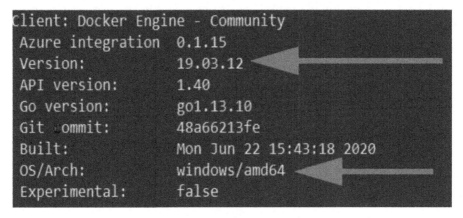

Figure 9.11 – Docker version client

Here you can see the version of Docker Desktop at the time of writing as well as the operating system, Windows, that the client is running.

The second part is the server as shown in *Figure 9.12*:

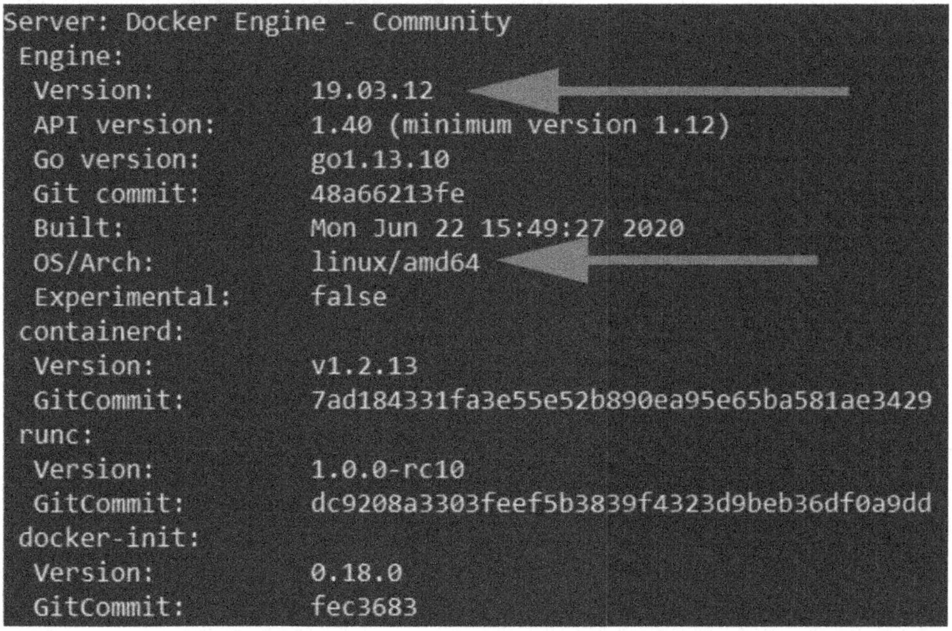

```
Server: Docker Engine - Community
 Engine:
  Version:          19.03.12
  API version:      1.40 (minimum version 1.12)
  Go version:       go1.13.10
  Git commit:       48a66213fe
  Built:            Mon Jun 22 15:49:27 2020
  OS/Arch:          linux/amd64
  Experimental:     false
 containerd:
  Version:          v1.2.13
  GitCommit:        7ad184331fa3e55e52b890ea95e65ba581ae3429
 runc:
  Version:          1.0.0-rc10
  GitCommit:        dc9208a3303feef5b3839f4323d9beb36df0a9dd
 docker-init:
  Version:          0.18.0
  GitCommit:        fec3683
```

Figure 9.12 – Docker version server

Notice the version of Docker Engine as well as the running architecture, `linux`, which indicates that Linux containers can be run.

Another simple test to make sure that all is working is the `docker hello-world` command. Give this a go and if everything looks okay and there are no errors, let's try something a bit more interesting in the next section.

Windows Security Alert

Depending on your particular desktop configuration, you might get an alert asking whether the Docker backend has access to the network as shown in *Figure 9.13*:

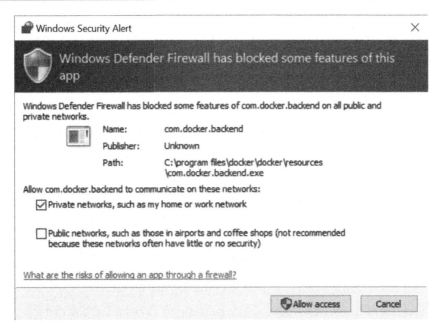

Figure 9.13 – Windows Security Alert

To complete the instructions in this chapter, Docker will need to be able to access Docker Hub to retrieve images.

Running Redis on Docker

In this section, we will run the popular open source in-memory cache **Redis**. Redis is a data structure store, meaning it stores things such as strings, lists, sets, sorted sets, and hashes and supports queries against stored data. Redis has been developed for over a decade, has a large community, and is worth checking out if you have not done so already.

Running Redis as a container for local development makes a lot of sense. By using a container, we don't have to install Redis onto the machine or worry about security permissions. With a container, the setup and security are already done. The limitation, though, is that we only have access to some Redis options. If there is an option that is not supported by the base Redis image, then I recommend you to create custom Redis images using the **Redis image** as a base.

Starting Redis

Start a Redis container using the `run` command:

```
docker run --name myRedis -p 6379:6379 -d redis
```

With this command, we are naming our container `myRedis` and specifying the `redis` image to be pulled. This will pull from Docker Hub and we can see the image being downloaded. Because we will be accessing this from an application in the next section, we need to make sure the default Redis port `6379` is exposed using the `-p` option as shown in *Figure 9.14*:

```
PS C:\Users\jeff> docker run --name myRedis -p 6379:6379 -d redis
Unable to find image 'redis:latest' locally
latest: Pulling from library/redis
d121f8d1c412: Pull complete
2f9874741855: Pull complete
d92da09ebfd4: Pull complete
bdfa64b72752: Pull complete
e748e6f663b9: Pull complete
eb1c8b66e2a1: Pull complete
Digest: sha256:1cfb205a988a9dae5f025c57b92e9643ec0e7ccff6e66bc639d8a5f95bba928c
Status: Downloaded newer image for redis:latest
2d7c56673558afa850c88c98161327a303edcbf0675d928670383de71126a716
```

Figure 9.14 – Our docker run command for Redis

Once the command completes, Redis will be running in a container. You can see the running container by using the `docker container ps` command as shown in *Figure 9.15*:

```
PS C:\Users\jeff> docker ps
CONTAINER ID   IMAGE   COMMAND                 CREATED      STATUS          PORTS                    NAMES
2d7c56673558   redis   "docker-entrypoint.s…"  5 days ago   Up 22 seconds   0.0.0.0:6379->6379/tcp   myRedis
```

Figure 9.15 – The docker ps command

Another useful command is `docker images`, which shows the local images as shown in *Figure 9.16*:

```
PS C:\Users\jeff> docker images
REPOSITORY    TAG      IMAGE ID       CREATED        SIZE
redis         latest   84c5f6e03bf0   12 days ago    104MB
hello-world   latest   bf756fb1ae65   8 months ago   13.3kB
```

Figure 9.16 – docker images

The preceding figure shows the `redis` image with the `latest` tag.

In the next section, we will access Redis from a .NET application, but for now, let's connect to the container and have a look around. We can connect to the container using the `docker exec -it myRedis sh` command. Once we are in the container, we need to enter in a Redis command mode by using the `redis-cli` command. The Redis CLI will allow us to run commands against the cache.

Once we are in the Redis CLI, we will issue some commands to check that Redis is working as expected. The first command, `hset messageFromRedis "absexp"` `"-1" "sldexp" "-1" "data" "Hello from Redis!"`, will create a string in Redis in a format that will allow the .NET application to retrieve it. The good news is setting and retrieving using the Redis SDK is much simpler. The second command, `set key1 value1`, will add a string identified with `key1` and a value of `value1`. The final command, `get key1`, shows that the value of `key1` can be retrieved as shown in *Figure 9.17*:

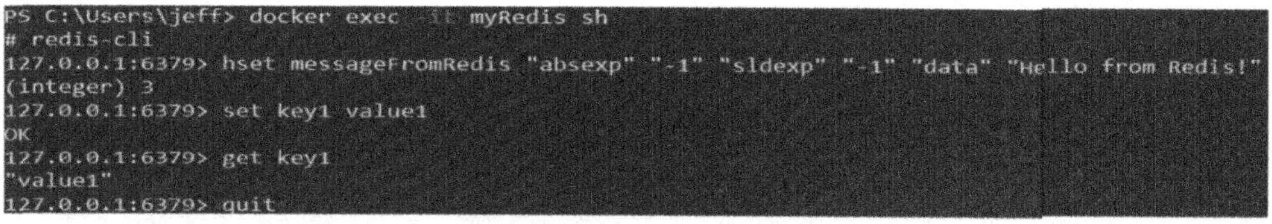

```
PS C:\Users\jeff> docker exec  it myRedis sh
# redis-cli
127.0.0.1:6379> hset messageFromRedis "absexp" "-1" "sldexp" "-1" "data" "Hello from Redis!"
(integer) 3
127.0.0.1:6379> set key1 value1
OK
127.0.0.1:6379> get key1
"value1"
127.0.0.1:6379> quit
```

Figure 9.17 – Redis CLI

You can then exit Redis and the container.

In this section, we started up a Redis container and checked that it was running as expected. In the next section, we will access Redis from another application. To be able to do this, we need to determine the Redis cache address. To determine the IP address, use the `ipconfig` command. If you are not running in a VM, you should see a network belonging to DockerNAT. For example, you should see something like the following:

```
Ethernet adapter vEthernet (DockerNAT):
   Connection-specific DNS Suffix   . :
   IPv4 Address. . . . . . . . . . . : 10.0.73.1
   Subnet Mask . . . . . . . . . . . : 255.255.255.0
   Default Gateway . . . . . . . . . :
```

On a virtual machine, look for a network belonging to `WSL`:

```
Ethernet adapter vEthernet (WSL):
   Connection-specific DNS Suffix   . :
   Link-local IPv6 Address . . . . . :
fe80::8411:e43d:c978:9e70%32
   IPv4 Address. . . . . . . . . . . : 172.23.160.1
   Subnet Mask . . . . . . . . . . . : 255.255.240.0
   Default Gateway . . . . . . . . . :
```

For the next section, record the IPv4 address as we will need it to connect to Docker.

Running ASP.NET Core in a container

In this section, we will create a simple ASP.NET Core application that accesses our Redis container. We will then run the application in a container. The majority of this we will do from the command line, but we will jump into Visual Studio to show some of the great tooling available:

1. The first step is to create a new directory and create a basic .NET web application. In the following *Figure 9.18*, we can see what ASP.NET projects are available by using the `dotnet new ASP.NET -l` command:

```
Templates                                     Short Name      Language        Tags
--------------------------------------------- --------------- --------------- -------------------
ASP.NET Core Empty                            web             [C#], F#        Web/Empty
ASP.NET Core Web App (Model-View-Controller)  mvc             [C#], F#        Web/MVC
ASP.NET Core Web App                          webapp          [C#]            Web/MVC/Razor Pages
ASP.NET Core with Angular                     angular         [C#]            Web/MVC/SPA
ASP.NET Core with React.js                    react           [C#]            Web/MVC/SPA
ASP.NET Core with React.js and Redux          reactredux      [C#]            Web/MVC/SPA
ASP.NET Core Web API                          webapi          [C#], F#        Web/WebAPI
ASP.NET Core gRPC Service                     grpc            [C#]            Web/gRPC

PS C:\Users\jeff> _
```

Figure 9.18 – dotnet new ASP.NET -l

2. Next, we need to create a folder for our solution with the `mkdir Chap9` command and create an empty solution with the `dotnet new sln` command as shown in *Figure 9.19*:

```
PS C:\dev> mkdir Chap9


    Directory: C:\dev


Mode                 LastWriteTime         Length Name
----                 -------------         ------ ----
d-----         1/10/2020   12:03 PM                Chap9


PS C:\dev> cd Chap9
PS C:\dev\Chap9> dotnet new sln
The template "Solution File" was created successfully.
```

Figure 9.19 – dotnet new sln

3. Then we create another folder within the previous one called web with the mkdir web command. Remember to change directory, for example, using cd web, into the created folder. Create a new ASP.NET Core Empty project using the dotnet new web command as shown in *Figure 9.20*:

```
PS C:\dev\Chap9> mkdir web


    Directory: C:\dev\Chap9


Mode                 LastWriteTime         Length Name
----                 -------------         ------ ----
d-----         1/10/2020   12:04 PM                web


PS C:\dev\Chap9> cd web
PS C:\dev\Chap9\web> dotnet new web
The template "ASP.NET Core Empty" was created successfully.

Processing post-creation actions...
Running 'dotnet restore' on C:\dev\Chap9\web\web.csproj...
  Determining projects to restore...
  Restored C:\dev\Chap9\web\web.csproj (in 92 ms).

Restore succeeded.
```

Figure 9.20 – dotnet new web

4. The last step is to add the project to our solution as shown in *Figure 9.21*:

```
PS C:\dev\Chap9\web> cd ..
PS C:\dev\Chap9> dotnet sln add web/web.csproj
Project `web\web.csproj` added to the solution.
```

Figure 9.21 – dotnet sln add

> **Note**
>
> The extra steps to create the web inside the solution folder are to help us in later sections. When adding Container Orchestration Support later, Visual Studio will display our container-related files in a less confusing manner.

Now that we have the solution and project created, go ahead and make sure everything is okay by running the project with the `dotnet run` command. You will need to do this in the web project as shown in *Figure 9.22*:

```
PS C:\dev\Chap9> dotnet run --project web
info: Microsoft.Hosting.Lifetime[0]
      Now listening on: https://localhost:5001
info: Microsoft.Hosting.Lifetime[0]
      Now listening on: http://localhost:5000
info: Microsoft.Hosting.Lifetime[0]
      Application started. Press Ctrl+C to shut down.
info: Microsoft.Hosting.Lifetime[0]
      Hosting environment: Development
info: Microsoft.Hosting.Lifetime[0]
      Content root path: C:\dev\Chap9\web
```

Figure 9.22 – dotnet run

In a browser, go to `http://localhost:5000` and you should be greeted by a familiar message as shown in *Figure 9.23*:

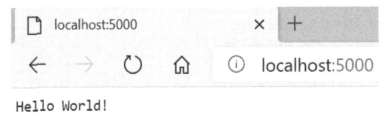

Figure 9.23 – Hello World!

Now that we have our basic web application, we will change the application so it retrieves a custom message from Redis.

Accessing Redis

Let's stop the running application – using *Ctrl + C* is fine to stop the dotnet application – and edit some files. The first file to edit is `web.csproj`; using Notepad is fine. We want to insert the following lines:

```
<ItemGroup>
  <PackageReference Include="Microsoft.Extensions.Caching.
  StackExchangeRedis" Version="3.1.8" />
</ItemGroup>
```

The edited file should look like this as shown in *Figure 9.24*:

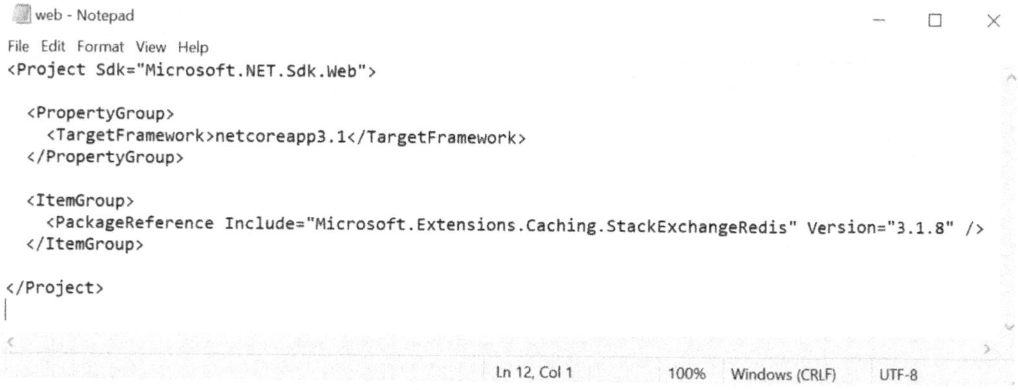

```
web - Notepad                                                          —    □    ×
File Edit Format View Help
<Project Sdk="Microsoft.NET.Sdk.Web">

  <PropertyGroup>
    <TargetFramework>netcoreapp3.1</TargetFramework>
  </PropertyGroup>

  <ItemGroup>
    <PackageReference Include="Microsoft.Extensions.Caching.StackExchangeRedis" Version="3.1.8" />
  </ItemGroup>

</Project>

                              Ln 12, Col 1        100%    Windows (CRLF)    UTF-8
```

Figure 9.24 – web.csproj

The next file to edit is the `Startup.cs` file. I just used Notepad to add a new `using` statement:

```
using Microsoft.Extensions.Caching.Distributed;
```

In the `ConfigureServices` method, we add our link to Redis. It is important to put in your Redis IPv4 address:

```
services.AddStackExchangeRedisCache(option =>
    option.Configuration = "172.23.160.1");
```

The `Configure` method signature needs to be updated to allow the cache to be injected into the method:

```
public void Configure(IApplicationBuilder app,
    IWebHostEnvironment env, IDistributedCache cache)
```

The final step is to replace the static `"Hello World!"` with our message from Redis:

```
await context.Response.WriteAsync(cache.GetString
    ("messageFromRedis"));
```

The following *Figure 9.25* shows the final `Startup.cs` file:

```
Startup.cs - Notepad                                                    —    □    ×
File  Edit  Format  View  Help
using Microsoft.AspNetCore.Builder;
using Microsoft.AspNetCore.Hosting;
using Microsoft.AspNetCore.Http;
using Microsoft.Extensions.Caching.Distributed;
using Microsoft.Extensions.DependencyInjection;
using Microsoft.Extensions.Hosting;

namespace web
{
    public class Startup
    {
        public void ConfigureServices(IServiceCollection services)
        {
            services.AddStackExchangeRedisCache(option => option.Configuration = "172.23.160.1");
        }

        public void Configure(IApplicationBuilder app, IWebHostEnvironment env, IDistributedCache cache)
        {
            if (env.IsDevelopment())
            {
                app.UseDeveloperExceptionPage();
            }

            app.UseRouting();

            app.UseEndpoints(endpoints =>
            {
                endpoints.MapGet("/", async context =>
                {
                    await context.Response.WriteAsync(cache.GetString("messageFromRedis"));
                });
            });
        }
    }
}
                                            Ln 13, Col 10        100%   Windows (CRLF)    UTF-8
```

Figure 9.25 – Startup.cs

Run the application again and refresh the browser to see the updated message as shown in *Figure 9.26*:

Hello from Redis!

Figure 9.26 – Hello from Redis!

In this section, we created a new ASP.NET Core web application using an empty template known as the *Hello World* template. We then added a popular package for connecting to Redis from .NET applications, StackExchange Redis. This is the same client used by large-scale sites such as Stack Overflow. Using this library, we had to add the cache to ASP. NET's dependency injection. Our last step was to use the cache to retrieve a string from our Redis cache running in a Docker container.

Adding container support

We will look at containerizing our ASP.NET Core application in two ways. The first way will create a Dockerfile and commands to create our image and run our container. The second approach will use Visual Studio.

Dockerfile approach

Starting in the root folder of our project, we will publish a release build using the `dotnet publish -c Release` command. This will produce a build of our application so that it is ready to copy to our container as shown in *Figure 9.27*:

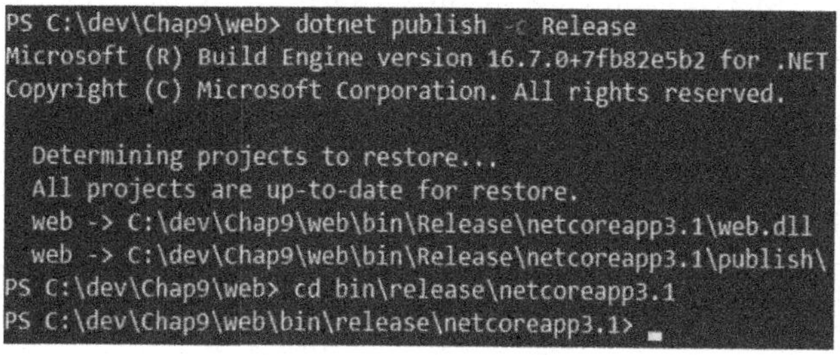

```
PS C:\dev\Chap9\web> dotnet publish -c Release
Microsoft (R) Build Engine version 16.7.0+7fb82e5b2 for .NET
Copyright (C) Microsoft Corporation. All rights reserved.

  Determining projects to restore...
  All projects are up-to-date for restore.
  web -> C:\dev\Chap9\web\bin\Release\netcoreapp3.1\web.dll
  web -> C:\dev\Chap9\web\bin\Release\netcoreapp3.1\publish\
PS C:\dev\Chap9\web> cd bin\release\netcoreapp3.1
PS C:\dev\Chap9\web\bin\release\netcoreapp3.1>
```

Figure 9.27 – dotnet publish

In the `release` folder containing our application, we will create a Dockerfile.

> **Note**
>
> By default, Docker will look in the current folder for a file named `dockerfile` without an extension.

I used Notepad for this and entered the following statements:

```
FROM mcr.microsoft.com/dotnet/core/aspnet:3.1-buster-slim
WORKDIR /app
COPY . .
EXPOSE 80
ENTRYPOINT ["dotnet", "web.dll"]
```

Remember the onion analogy from earlier? The layer that we will start with is one that Microsoft has provided with ASP.NET already loaded. The next command states that we are working in the app folder on the image we are creating. The copy command will copy the contents of our current folder into the app folder of the image. We then make port `80` available outside our image. The final command states that .NET should run `web.dll` when the container starts up. When our containers start, our ASP.NET Core application should be started and listening on port `80`.

After saving the file, let's build our image:

```
docker build . -t myweb
```

If you received an error stating that the file could not be found, then it is likely that you named the file `Dockerfile.txt`. No problem – we can specify the filename using the `-f` parameter:

```
docker build . -f Dockerfile.txt -t myweb
```

If all is well, then you will have a success message stating that the image was built and tagged `myweb:latest`. You can view the images with the `docker images` command as shown in *Figure 9.28*:

```
PS C:\Users\jeff\web1\bin\release\netcoreapp3.1> docker images
REPOSITORY                              TAG              IMAGE ID       CREATED        SIZE
myweb                                   latest           1ec5f8145b46   8 days ago     211MB
web                                     dev              79a7a5d8c9a4   8 days ago     207MB
redis                                   latest           84c5f6e03bf0   2 weeks ago    104MB
mcr.microsoft.com/dotnet/core/sdk       3.1-buster       c4155a9104a8   2 weeks ago    708MB
mcr.microsoft.com/dotnet/core/aspnet    3.1-buster-slim  28de0d96c539   2 weeks ago    207MB
hello-world                             latest           bf756fb1ae65   8 months ago   13.3kB
microsoft/aspnetcore                    latest           db030c19e94b   2 years ago    347MB
```

Figure 9.28 – docker images

And to start our image, we use the `docker run` command, mapping our local port `8080` to the container port `80`:

```
docker run -p 8080:80 myweb
```

In a browser, we can then navigate to the web application and still see our message from Redis as shown in *Figure 9.29*:

localhost:8080   ×   +

←   →   ⟳   ⌂   ⓘ   localhost:8080

Hello from Redis!

Figure 9.29 – ASP.NET Core in a container

We are, of course, just scratching the surface here, but it is a powerful illustration of how easy containers are. So, can Visual Studio make the experience any simpler?

Visual Studio approach

In Visual Studio, open **Solution Explorer**. Go ahead and run the project, and if you are prompted to save a solution file, go ahead and save it in the same folder as the project file. Visual Studio has many features to support Docker container developers. The first feature we will look at is the ability to add a Dockerfile for our project. This is located in the **Solution Explorer** context menu under the **Add** submenu and is called **Docker Support....** This is shown in *Figure 9.30*:

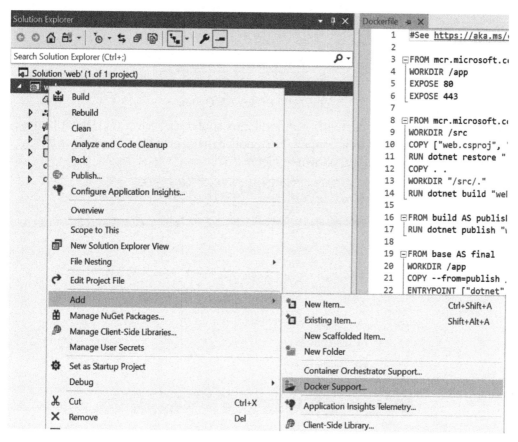

Figure 9.30 – Docker Support…

By selecting this option, Visual Studio will prepare the project to be made into an image. Visual Studio will ask whether the target image should be for a **Linux** or **Windows** operating system as shown in *Figure 9.31*:

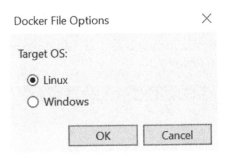

Figure 9.31 – Docker File Options

As our Docker Desktop is currently running Linux containers, select the default **Linux** option. Several things will now happen. First, notice that a new file is created for the project called `Dockerfile` as shown in *Figure 9.32*:

Figure 9.32 – Visual Studio Dockerfile

Go ahead and open the file and notice how there are similarities to the Dockerfile we created in the last section. The main difference is this Dockerfile performs `dotnet build` and `dotnet release` before copying the release to the image.

Also, notice that the run options have changed to show Docker as the run target as shown in *Figure 9.33*:

Figure 9.33 – Visual Studio: Docker run target

If we run the project now, several things will happen. Visual Studio will show a new window called **Containers** as shown in *Figure 9.34*:

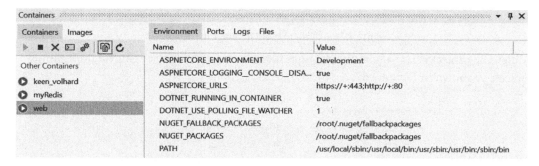

Figure 9.34 – Visual Studio Containers window

This window shows both the running containers and the images on the local machine. In the preceding figure, we can see that there are three containers currently running. The container named web is this project container. You can also see the Redis container named **myRedis** running, as well as a generated name, in this example, **keen_volhard**. Take a moment to explore. For example, if you select the **myRedis** container, then you can see that port 6379 has been mapped as shown in *Figure 9.35*:

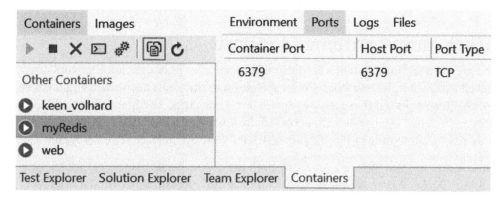

Figure 9.35 – Visual Studio Containers window

Oh, and in case you were wondering, we have full debugging support with the running container. In the `Startup.cs` file, put a breakpoint in the `Configure` method on the line where we retrieve the string from Redis as shown in *Figure 9.36*:

```
32
33    ⊟    app.UseEndpoints(endpoints =>
34          {
35 💡  ⊟          endpoints.MapGet("/", async context =>|
36                  {
37                      await context.Response.WriteAsync(cache.GetString("messageFromRedis"));
38                  });
39          });
40      }
41    }
```

Figure 9.36 – Visual Studio debugging support

When the project is run again, the debug is hit and we are able to investigate the running objects as shown in *Figure 9.37*:

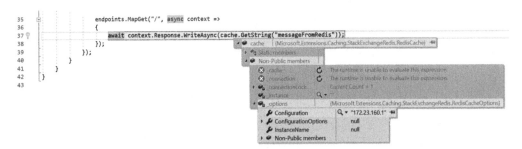

Figure 9.37 – Visual Studio debugging

We will discuss debugging in a later chapter in more detail, but our purpose is to show the tight integration Visual Studio has with Docker and the running containers.

Docker multi-container support

In the previous section, we had a scenario where one container calls another container. We achieved a call from the ASP.NET Core application to the Redis cache by using the host network. This works but there are two significant drawbacks. The first is that the Redis cache can be called by anyone with access to the host network. The second drawback is that there is nothing indicating that our ASP.NET Core application requires Redis.

In this section, we will look at addressing both these drawbacks by using Docker Compose. Docker Compose allows us to combine multiple containers into a single definition. This will allow us to limit access to Redis as well as to indicate that Redis is a requirement for our ASP.NET Core application. We could complete this section without Visual Studio, but we will use Visual Studio to highlight some of the nice features that are available.

Adding Container Orchestration Support

In the Solution Explorer, we have the option to add `Container Orchestrator Support`. This is located in the context menu of a project under the **Add** sub-menu as shown in *Figure 9.38*:

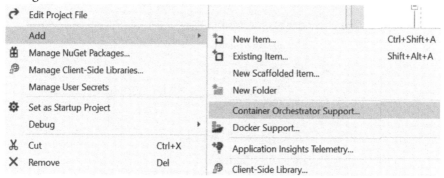

Figure 9.38 – Container Orchestration Support…

You will be prompted for the type of `Container Orchestrator Support` you want. There are two options: **Kubernetes/Helm** and **Docker Compose**. The main difference between the two use cases is whether you require a cluster of engines to host the containers or a single engine. In most circumstances, a cluster would indicate separate VMs or physical machines. In our scenario, we are only interested in hosting on a single Docker Engine instance, so we will select **Docker Compose** as shown in *Figure 9.39*:

Figure 9.39 – Docker Compose

If prompted for the target operating system, select **Linux**. Also, Visual Studio will detect that we have an existing Dockerfile in our project as shown in *Figure 9.40*:

Figure 9.40 – Creating a new Dockerfile

We don't mind overwriting our current Dockerfile, so select **No**.

Looking at the solution now, we will notice some new YAML files as shown in *Figure 9.41*:

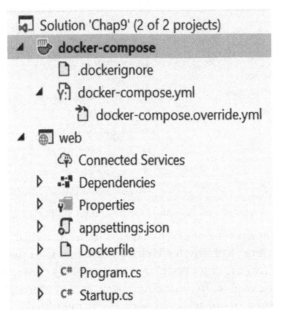

Figure 9.41 – Visual Studio YAML

The `docker-compose.yml` file in the new **docker-compose** section is used to define our orchestration. In this file, we will define the containers, networks, and additional requirements of our orchestration. You will also notice that `docker-compose.override.yml` is collapsed under the file. Don't worry about the details of what is in this file, other than that it provides specifics about running the orchestration in Visual Studio. What we are going to do is delete this file as it will make things simpler if we are only looking at a single `docker-compose.yml` file.

> **Note**
> Be sure to delete the `docker-compose.override.yml` file to avoid confusion later.

The default Docker Compose file specifies that we have one service called web and gives the location of its Dockerfile:

```
version: "3.4"
services:
  web:
```

```
image: ${DOCKER_REGISTRY-}web
build:
  context: .
  dockerfile: web/Dockerfile
```

The version number in the file is significant as it indicates the supported Docker Engine version. For example, 3.4 supports Docker Engine version 17.09.0 and newer. The versions can be found at https://docs.docker.com/compose/compose-file/compose-versioning/. Under services, we have one service named web. The image to be used for the web service is specified as a combination of an environment variable, ${DOCKER_REGISTRY}, and the word web. In new environments, there should not be an environment variable set, so the image will end up being just web. The last thing to point out is that context is a path to a directory and is used with the dockerfile option. In our Docker Compose file, this will result in the Dockerfile being located in the web directory.

Adding Redis to a Docker Compose file

The first thing we need to do is add our redis service to this orchestration. Remember to be careful with indentation as YAML requires indentation rules to be followed. Under the definition of the web service, let's create a new service, redis:

```
version: "3.4"

services:
  web:
    image: ${DOCKER_REGISTRY-}web
    build:
      context: .
      dockerfile: web/Dockerfile

  redis:
    image: redis
    ports:
      - 6379:6379
```

Notice that we are using the default port. When the file is saved, look in the Output window for Container Tools or Build. You should see a Bind for 0.0.0.0:6379 failed: port is already allocated error, as you will still have the previous Redis container running.

Adding an isolated network

What we want to do is run our new orchestration in isolation from the other example. To do this, we need to define a network in the Docker Compose file. This is done simply by adding the network definition to the end of the file and setting this network on the two services:

```
version: "3.4"


services:
  web:
    image: ${DOCKER_REGISTRY-}web
    build:
      context: .
      dockerfile: web/Dockerfile
    networks:
      - chap9

  redis:
    image: redis
    networks:
      - chap9

networks:
  chap9:
```

These changes will define a new network that is isolated from the host machine. This does mean we have to make some additional changes to get our example to work. The first is that we need to expose a port from the chap9 network to the host network so we can browse the site:

```
web:
    image: ${DOCKER_REGISTRY-}web
    build:
```

```
        context: .
        dockerfile: web/Dockerfile
    ports:
      - 80
    networks:
      - chap9
```

In the preceding code block, port 80 is exposed from the chap9 network.

Modifying startup

This also means the port we hardcoded in our Startup.cs file will be incorrect. Let's correct this now by changing from using the IP address to using the name of the service in the new Docker network. This is done in the ConfigureServices method in the startup.cs file:

```
public void ConfigureServices(IServiceCollection services)
{
    services.AddStackExchangeRedisCache(option =>
        option.Configuration = "redis");
}
```

The other thing we will need to do is seed the Redis cache with a default message. This was done previously in a manual step, so we will add some logic to do this if the message has not yet been defined.

For simplicity, this was done in the Configure method by adding the following lines before the app.UserEndpoints command:

```
public void Configure(IApplicationBuilder app,
IWebHostEnvironment env, IDistributedCache cache)
{
...
if(string.IsNullOrEmpty(cache.GetString("messageFromRedis")))
{
cache.SetString("messageFromRedis", "Hello from Redis
    running in an isolated network!");
}
...
}
```

The preceding snippet will set the string with the `messageFromRedis` key only if it is missing. This is a simple example, but hopefully you can see how simple it is to work with a Redis cache.

Potential errors

There are a couple of things you might encounter if things don't go well. The first error to highlight is that if we do not specify a port to expose to the host, we will see the following dialog as shown in *Figure 9.42*:

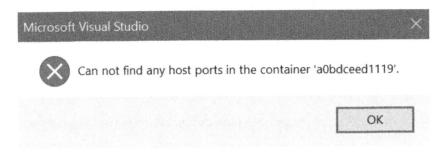

Figure 9.42 – Missing port

This indicates that no ports were specified under the web service in the Docker Compose file.

The second thing is that if the address of the Redis cache does not match, we will get an *unable to connect* error when we try to establish a connection to Redis. Let's illustrate another feature of Docker Compose by passing in the network location as an environment variable. This is done by defining the variable in the Docker Compose file in the web service section.

Adding environment variables

First, in the `startup.cs` file, edit the `ConfigureServices` method to use an environment variable:

```
public void ConfigureServices(IServiceCollection services)
{
    services.AddStackExchangeRedisCache(option =>
        option.Configuration = Environment.
            GetEnvironmentVariable("REDIS_ADDRESS"));
}
```

Then in the Docker Compose file, edit the web service section to include a new environment setting:

```
web:
  image: ${DOCKER_REGISTRY-}web
  build:
    context: .
    dockerfile: web/Dockerfile
  environment:
    - REDIS_ADDRESS=redis
  ports:
    - 80
  networks:
    - chap9
```

Most likely, you will not encounter an error, but an important feature to highlight in an orchestration, is dependent on another container. This can be done in the Docker Compose file by using the depends_on setting:

```
  web:
...
    depends_on:
      - redis
...
```

The following shows our completed docker-compose.yml file:

```
version: "3.4"

services:
  web:
    image: ${DOCKER_REGISTRY-}web
    build:
      context: .
      dockerfile: web/Dockerfile
    depends_on:
      - redis
    environment:
      - REDIS_ADDRESS=redis
```

```
    ports:
       - 80
    networks:
       - chap9

  redis:
    image: redis
    networks:
       - chap9

networks:
  chap9:
```

When running the project, we should see our new updated message as shown in *Figure 9.43*:

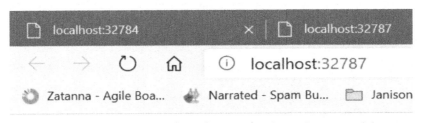

Figure 9.43 – Hello from Redis running in an isolated network!

Let's take a second to look at this a little deeper so that we have more of an understanding of what is going on.

Docker networks

Let's take a look at the currently defined networks by using the docker network ls command as shown in *Figure 9.44*:

```
PS C:\Users\jeff> docker network ls
NETWORK ID          NAME                                          DRIVER    SCOPE
b6318631dc3e        bridge                                        bridge    local
50546522fe41        dockercompose11823690501171496634_chap9       bridge    local
94d2cf293ace        host                                          host      local
e0d28e471a97        none                                          null      local
PS C:\Users\jeff>
```

Figure 9.44 – docker network ls

You should see several networks. The two we will look at in more detail have the `bridge` driver. Using the `docker network inspect bridge` command, let's look at the first network named `bridge`. For now, look at the `Containers` section as shown in *Figure 9.45*:

```
"Containers": {
    "2e96341c3352194ecf128c5e567dd967ee5d0e746e878d8c38f7a0ba0773a366": {
        "Name": "hopeful_snyder",
        "EndpointID": "ddd2261eee0d06737e981840d1133d6648b3ff68a444b2dd9a664f566a139fd1",
        "MacAddress": "02:42:ac:11:00:04",
        "IPv4Address": "172.17.0.4/16",
        "IPv6Address": ""
    },
    "478208fd987b6367f201144f538f6db575861e641c5a2e08ef0fa2c912a75dfe": {
        "Name": "myRedis",
        "EndpointID": "323c645b202eb0d561a799431e7e80a14f5fe748a7045767a85b7be5fe1244e2",
        "MacAddress": "02:42:ac:11:00:03",
        "IPv4Address": "172.17.0.3/16",
        "IPv6Address": ""
    },
    "9f97c8ec6319cf7b64f6ca675d2ff9bb1754e83744f29bcf023486f4393820e2": {
        "Name": "web",
        "EndpointID": "a94527314a3356bef2cba762bafaea8a07cc264382a8bd1989de54c7d8abc49d",
        "MacAddress": "02:42:ac:11:00:02",
        "IPv4Address": "172.17.0.2/16",
        "IPv6Address": ""
    }
},
```

Figure 9.45 – docker network inspect bridge – Containers

By looking at the names of the containers, we can tell that this is the default network, as these are the containers that we created in the first sections of this chapter. This is indicated in the `Options` section as shown in *Figure 9.46*:

```
"Options": {
    "com.docker.network.bridge.default_bridge": "true",
    "com.docker.network.bridge.enable_icc": "true",
    "com.docker.network.bridge.enable_ip_masquerade": "true",
    "com.docker.network.bridge.host_binding_ipv4": "0.0.0.0",
    "com.docker.network.bridge.name": "docker0",
    "com.docker.network.driver.mtu": "1500"
},
```

Figure 9.46 – docker network inspect bridge – Options

Note the default `bridge` option is set to `true`. When we inspect the other bridge network with the `docker network inspect network id` command, we can see that the options indicate this is the `chap9` compose network as shown in *Figure 9.47*:

```
"Labels": {
    "com.docker.compose.network": "chap9",
    "com.docker.compose.project": "dockercompose11823690501171496634",
    "com.docker.compose.version": "1.27.4"
}
```

Figure 9.47 – docker network inspect network id

Take a moment to also inspect the containers in the network as shown in *Figure 9.48*:

```
"Containers": {
    "457d13f60cc337cba85b1e8050aff2b3d8f02d7bdf382a8c57b125e619d62d5f": {
        "Name": "web_1",
        "EndpointID": "8427e507641c0404bc88631f814b232a3803f5d0d60c762a8944580d94a16eb9",
        "MacAddress": "02:42:ac:14:00:03",
        "IPv4Address": "172.20.0.3/16",
        "IPv6Address": ""
    },
    "93660ae53a3426edbe63c0c9bc9f5266cdc00eb53d216e91573f6948a4b121b3": {
        "Name": "dockercompose11823690501171496634_redis_1",
        "EndpointID": "e9f2fe5b29ea95835c206ea50b6cf45549f32e352796d6e8e31e28da3cb4d7bf",
        "MacAddress": "02:42:ac:14:00:02",
        "IPv4Address": "172.20.0.2/16",
        "IPv6Address": ""
    }
},
```

Figure 9.48 – docker network inspect chap9 containers

The ASP.NET Core application and Redis cache containers are shown with their internal addresses.

In this section, we looked at Docker Compose. This allowed us to define a container orchestration involving two containers: an ASP.NET application and a Redis cache. The orchestration was defined to illustrate several features of Docker Compose. The first was the creation of an isolated network for two containers. We also made sure to expose only port 80 on the ASP.NET application. We included a dependency between ASP.NET and the Redis cache using the `depends_on` setting. Additionally, we illustrated how an environment variable can be set and made available to a running container.

Summary

In this chapter, we have covered containers and the popular Docker platform. We provided an overview of containerization and what makes containers different from VMs. We looked at Docker and some of its major components, including images, containers, Docker Engine, and Dockerfiles.

We provided three different examples of running containers. The first was running the popular in-memory cache Redis. This showed how simple it is to start up a new container. Next, we created our own ASP.NET Core container by using just Notepad. The last example used Visual Studio to containerize an existing ASP.NET Core application. This example highlighted some of the nice features that the IDE provides when working with Docker.

Containers and Docker is a big subject. The goal of this chapter is to present some of the highlights and background of this powerful technology. Because of the portability of .NET to both Linux and Windows, it is an ideal framework for building containers.

The next chapter will take ASP.NET to the cloud! We will look at how **Amazon Web Services (AWS)** and Azure can host our ASP.NET solutions.

Questions

1. Would you expect an application to start faster in a container or a VM?

2. Is Redis a relational database?

3. Can you view running containers in Visual Studio?

4. What orchestration type should be used when creating an orchestration involving multiple Docker Engine instances?

5. Was this chapter interesting?

Further reading

- Docker has great documentation and can be found at `https://docs.docker.com/`.

- Microsoft covers Docker and Visual Studio support for containers in their documentation at `https://docs.microsoft.com/en-us/aspnet/core/host-and-deploy/docker`.

- *Learn Docker – Fundamentals of Docker 19.x, Second Edition* by Gabriel N. Schenker, Packt Publishing, `https://subscription.packtpub.com/book/cloud_and_networking/9781838827472`.

- *Docker for Developers* by Richard Bullington-McGuire, Andrew K. Dennis, Michael Schwartz, Packt Publishing,

  `https://subscription.packtpub.com/book/cloud_and_networking/9781789536058`.

Section 3 – Running

Congratulations! You can walk. Now let's learn how to run! In this section, we will explore what it means to build a cloud-native application, and we will also cover federated identity, debugging, unit testing, and integrating with a CI/CD pipeline.

This section includes the following chapters:

- *Chapter 10, Deploying to AWS and Azure*
- *Chapter 11, Browser and Visual Studio Debugging*
- *Chapter 12, Integrating with CI/CD*
- *Chapter 13, Cloud Native*

10
Deploying to AWS and Azure

In the previous chapter, we looked at containers and the Docker platform. Containers are a great way to improve productivity by simplifying the development life cycle and helping to reduce the chances of things going wrong during deployment. We looked at the popular Docker framework and provided some practical examples.

In this chapter, we will provide some examples of hosting your ASP.NET solution on two leading cloud providers, **Amazon Web Services** (**AWS**) and Azure. Both of these providers offer a sophisticated network of servers and infrastructure that is distributed across the globe for hosting your solutions. This is easier than it sounds, as both providers provide tools, **Software Development Kits** (**SDKs**), and extensions to support you.

Our intention is to support those who are not familiar with cloud providers and hosting services on them. But we hope to not just repeat existing tutorials and documentation. Because of this, for some steps, we will direct you to documentation written and made available by the cloud service providers themselves.

We will cover the following topics in this chapter:

- Overview of cloud computing
- Load balancers and website health
- Publishing to AWS using Visual Studio
- Publishing to Azure using Visual Studio

For many users new to AWS and Azure, getting started is challenging. The portals have been designed to help new users and offer supporting documentation and tutorials. We will highlight some of the ones we feel are especially helpful in the *Further reading* section at the end of the chapter.

By the end of the chapter, you will have some familiarity with AWS and Azure. You will have some practical experience in deploying ASP.NET applications using Visual Studio extensions. You will also have experience in reviewing deployed applications in the AWS console and the Azure portal. This chapter introduces cloud providers, and we will look at developing solutions for the cloud in more detail in *Chapter 13, Cloud Native*.

Technical requirements

This chapter includes short code snippets to demonstrate the concepts that are explained. The following software is required to make it work:

- **Visual Studio 2019**: Visual Studio can be downloaded from `https://visualstudio.microsoft.com/vs/community/`. The Community edition is free and will work for the purposes of this book.
- **.NET 5**: The .NET framework can be downloaded from `https://dotnet.microsoft.com/download`.

Make sure you download the SDK and not just the runtime. You can verify the installation by opening a command prompt and running `dotnet --info` as shown in *Figure 10.1*:

```
C:\Users\andreas>dotnet --info
.NET SDK (reflecting any global.json):
 Version:   5.0.100-preview.5.20279.10
 Commit:    8139f1b74e

Runtime Environment:
 OS Name:      Windows
 OS Version:   10.0.20150
 OS Platform:  Windows
 RID:          win10-x64
 Base Path:    C:\Program Files\dotnet\sdk\5.0.100-preview.5.20279.10\

Host (useful for support):
  Version: 5.0.0-preview.5.20278.1
  Commit:  4ae4e2fe08
```

Figure 10.1 – Verifying the installation of .NET

As part of this chapter, we will use extensions in Visual Studio to work with AWS and Azure.

Please visit the following link to check the CiA videos: `https://bit.ly/3qDiqYY`

Working with AWS

An AWS account is required to perform the steps in the *Publishing to AWS* section. The steps in the section have been designed to result in small or no charges for a new AWS account, by using services from the free tier. Charges could be incurred if services other than those specified are used.

To create a new AWS account, use the **Create an AWS Account** button on the AWS portal: `https://aws.amazon.com/`. Additional information on this process is referenced in the *Further reading* section, at the end of the chapter.

We will be using the AWS Toolkit extension, using **Manage Extensions** in Visual Studio, as shown in *Figure 10.2*:

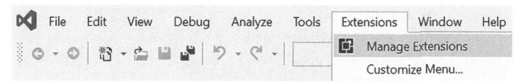

Figure 10.2 – Manage Extensions

The AWS Toolkit can be found by searching for the phrase `AWS Toolkit` and can be seen in *Figure 10.3*:

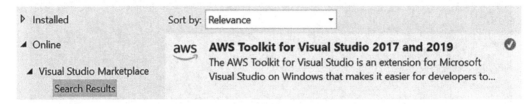

Figure 10.3 – AWS Toolkit extension

Additional information about the installation of the AWS Toolkit for Visual Studio can be found at `https://docs.aws.amazon.com/toolkit-for-visual-studio/latest/user-guide/welcome.html`.

Working with Azure

An Azure account is required to perform the steps in the *Publishing to Azure* section. The steps in the section have been designed to result in no charges for a new Azure account, by ensuring that the usage charges are covered by the $200 USD monthly credit. This credit is applied for all new Azure accounts. Charges may be incurred if services other than those specified are used.

To create a new Azure account, use the **Start free** button on the Azure website: `https://azure.microsoft.com/en-us/free/`. Additional information on this process is referenced in the *Further reading* section at the end of the chapter.

The Azure extension is installed as part of Visual Studio 2019. This can be done using the Visual Studio Installer by selecting the **Modify** option as shown in *Figure 10.4*:

Figure 10.4 – Visual Studio Installer

The **Azure development** package should be selected to add Azure support in Visual Studio as shown in *Figure 10.5*:

Figure 10.5 – Azure development

By selecting the **Azure development** package, Azure-related SDKs, tools, and sample projects are made available.

GitHub source code

The source code for this chapter is in the GitHub repository at `https://github.com/PacktPublishing/ASP.NET-Core-5-for-Beginners/tree/master/Chapter%2010`.

Overview of cloud computing

This section provides only a brief overview of cloud computing, as we will cover both on-premises and cloud computing models in more detail in *Chapter 13*, *Cloud Native*. The purpose of this section is to provide context on cloud computing and some background on the two selected cloud providers. You may want to read both the *Publishing to AWS* and *Publishing to Azure* sections but only perform the steps for one of the providers.

Cloud computing can be thought of as the delivery of computing infrastructure and services over the internet. Before cloud computing gained such popularity, organizations chose to host their services from data centers that they ran themselves. We refer to these data centers as *on-premises*, as they typically are hosted on the premises of the organizations themselves.

In this chapter, we will refer to the required infrastructure and the hosted services as resources. These resources include a wide range of things, including **virtual machines (VMs)**, databases, services for **artificial intelligence (AI)**, and services for processing large amounts of data. The range of resources continues to grow as the market constantly evolves. These resources are available to the public, but they do require a subscription to access them.

Cloud computing models

These resources have been classified into the following broad categories. We are highlighting them here, as you often hear people refer to groups of resources in this way:

- **Infrastructure as a Service (IaaS)**: This category refers to the IT infrastructure that solutions are built upon. Think of this category as the networking, computing, and data storage resources you are renting to your applications. An example of IaaS would be a VM and the disks and networking used by the VM.

- **Platform as a Service (PaaS)**: These resources are often an abstraction over IaaS resources that make it easier to develop and manage applications. These resources remove the need for organizations to manage and provision the underlying resources, which allows organizations to build and maintain applications more easily. An example of such a platform would be a managed database, where the details of the hosting, for example, the VMs and disks required to run the database, are handled by the cloud provider.

- **Software as a Service (SaaS)**: This category contains products and services that are built and managed by the cloud provider or a third party. An example of SaaS would be an email service.

Cloud computing providers

There are many companies that provide cloud computing services, and we will look at the two leading cloud providers: AWS and Azure. We chose them for several reasons:

- They both offer great support for hosting ASP.NET Core solutions.

- Both cloud providers offer IaaS resources, including the provisioning of Linux and Windows VMs, which can be used to host web applications.

- They also both provide several PaaS offerings that simplify the hosting of the ASP.NET Core solutions.

We will be looking at AWS Elastic Beanstalk and Azure App Service later in this chapter. These PaaS offerings are great examples of where underlying infrastructure details have been simplified to allow you to focus on building your solutions.

Amazon Web Services

AWS got its start in 2006 when Amazon, one of the largest retail companies, offered IT infrastructure to be used by organizations. This initial offering has grown into the largest cloud provider, offering hundreds of different resources from data centers across the globe. In July 2020, AWS was estimated to have 31% of the cloud computing market share.

AWS Elastic Beanstalk

In the *Publishing to AWS* section, we will be looking at AWS Elastic Beanstalk. This PaaS offering makes it simple to host ASP.NET Core web applications by simplifying the details of hosting web applications. We chose this offering as it is very commonly used to host web applications, and the deployment to Elastic Beanstalk is integrated into Visual Studio.

One thing we should explain is the difference between an application and an environment. Think of an application as a collection of environments. The environments are related, but they have separate configurations. Think of them as separate versions of the same website. Each environment has its own URL.

A common scenario would be to have a development environment, where new changes are tested by the development team, and a production environment that customers use. The development environment might be configured to use a different database and to only have one instance running. The production environment might use a different database and have multiple instances.

Azure

Azure was released in 2010, and like AWS, it has steadily grown to include hundreds of offerings from data centers around the world. In July 2020, Azure was estimated to have 20% of the cloud computing market share.

Azure App Service

In the *Publishing to Azure* section, we will be using Azure App Service to host the same ASP.NET Core web application that we published to AWS. Like AWS Elastic Beanstalk, this PaaS offering also simplifies the hosting of ASP.NET Core web applications, and the deployment of Azure App Service is integrated with Visual Studio.

Creating a sample ASP.NET Core web application

In this chapter, we will use a simple ASP.NET web application to illustrate some features of AWS and Azure. The sample application has been kept simple, as we want to keep the focus on deploying to the cloud. We will add a new endpoint that returns the health of the application. This will be used by the cloud platform, in order to determine whether the application is healthy.

Our suggestion is that you start with the source code in the GitHub repository, as this chapter is more about the Visual Studio extensions than the ASP.NET Core application. We will describe the steps we took to build the sample example, for those who want to build the application themselves:

1. First, we created the sample application by using the `dotnet new mvc` command in a folder named `Chapter 10 Final`. This is shown in *Figure 10.6*:

```
PS C:\Users\jeff\Source\Repos\ASP.NET-Core-5-for-Beginners\Chapter 10\Chapter 10 Final> dotnet new mvc
The template "ASP.NET Core Web App (Model-View-Controller)" was created successfully.
This template contains technologies from parties other than Microsoft, see https://aka.ms/aspnetcore/3.1-third-party-notices for details.

Processing post-creation actions...
Running 'dotnet restore' on C:\Users\jeff\Source\Repos\ASP.NET-Core-5-for-Beginners\Chapter 10\Chapter 10 Final\Chapter 10 Final.csproj...
  Determining projects to restore...
  Restored C:\Users\jeff\Source\Repos\ASP.NET-Core-5-for-Beginners\Chapter 10\Chapter 10 Final\Chapter 10 Final.csproj (in 102 ms).

Restore succeeded.
```

Figure 10.6 – dotnet new mvc command

2. To make sure the application restored, we used the `dotnet run` command as shown *Figure 10.7*:

```
PS C:\Users\jeff\Source\Repos\ASP.NET-Core-5-for-Beginners\Chapter 10\Chapter 10 Final> dotnet run
info: Microsoft.Hosting.Lifetime[0]
      Now listening on: https://localhost:5001
info: Microsoft.Hosting.Lifetime[0]
      Now listening on: http://localhost:5000
info: Microsoft.Hosting.Lifetime[0]
      Application started. Press Ctrl+C to shut down.
info: Microsoft.Hosting.Lifetime[0]
      Hosting environment: Development
info: Microsoft.Hosting.Lifetime[0]
      Content root path: C:\Users\jeff\Source\Repos\ASP.NET-Core-5-for-Beginners\Chapter 10\Chapter 10 Final
```

Figure 10.7 – dotnet run command

3. We then used a browser to verify that the application returned the home page without an error, as shown in *Figure 10.8*:

Chapter_10_Final   Home   Privacy

Welcome

Learn about building Web apps with ASP.NET Core.

© 2020 - Chapter_10_Final - Privacy

Figure 10.8 – Sample application

This shows that the basic application has been restored without an issue. Now we will add the ability to check the health of the application.

Checking health endpoint

Many applications are designed to support a health endpoint. This endpoint is designed to return a healthy status, when the application instance is functioning as expected. Remember when we talked about one of the benefits of cloud computing being scalability? The health endpoint is useful when an application has multiple instances all working together to handle the requests being sent to a website. With the health endpoint, the instance of the application can report when it is not in a state where it can handle requests successfully.

Let's take a scenario where you have a web application, and at times, the number of messages sent to your application is too great for it to handle. We have two options. We could increase the size of the resource the web application is running on. This is called *scaling up*. We could also add additional resources, known as instances, to handle the messages. This is called *scaling out*. In the cloud, adding additional instances of your application is easy and, in general, is more cost-effective than increasing the size of the resource.

Let's use *Figure 10.9* to discuss this in more detail:

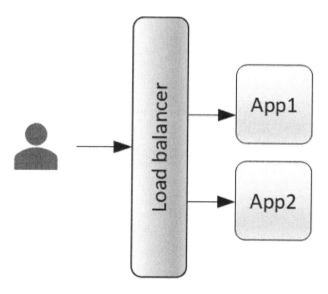

Figure 10.9 – Load balancer with two applications

The preceding figure shows two web applications and a load balancer. In this case, we have a single environment that is composed of two applications. The load balancer is used to distribute the requests to the environment between the two applications. At some point, the number of messages may increase to a point where the two applications cannot handle them. When this happens, it is possible to increase the number of applications as illustrated *Figure 10.10*:

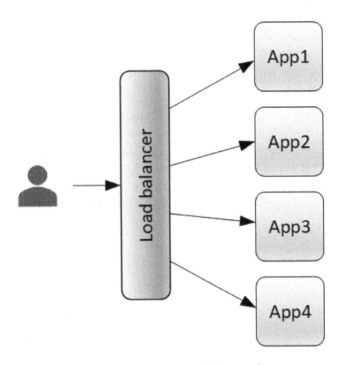

Figure 10.10 – Load balancer with four applications

Now we have four web applications sitting behind the load balancer. Because the load balancer is distributing the requests across all applications, the environment can handle the increased number of requests.

Even after an application is added to an environment, it may take some time for the application to be ready to receive requests. Maybe the application needs to load information into memory first or perform some processing before it is ready. Or, at some point, the application might detect that a required resource is not available. While the application is not able to successfully process requests, it can let the load balancer know by returning an unhealthy response. This will let the load balancer know to not send requests to the application. This is illustrated in *Figure 10.11*:

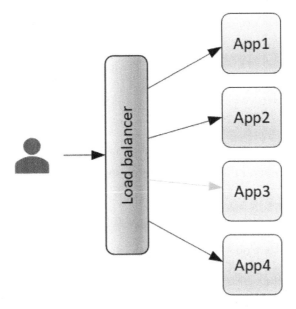

Figure 10.11 – Load balancer with an unhealthy application

In the previous figure, **App3** is returning an unhealthy response to the load balancer. The load balancer will then stop sending requests to the application instance.

So, let's now see how is this done.

Response status codes

The convention is to create an endpoint that is often called "health." This should either indicate that the system is healthy or not healthy. This is done by returning either a response with a status code of 200 (OK) or a response with a status code of 5xx.

> **Note**
>
> 5xx means any status code in the 500-599 range. The convention is to return 503 (Service Unavailable).

For this to make sense, we need to look at what a message looks like in more detail. To do this, let's use our browser's developer tools. I will be using Edge, but the experience in Firefox or Chrome will be similar too. In the browser, press *F12* to launch the developer tools. The developer tools for Edge are shown in *Figure 10.12*:

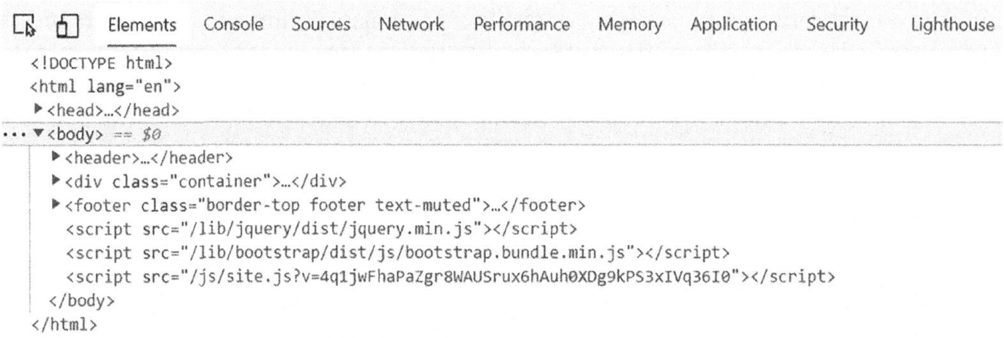

Figure 10.12 – Developer tools for Edge

You will see several tabs, and the one we are interested in is called **Network**. Go ahead and select this tab.

> **Note**
>
> We will discuss developer tools in more detail in *Chapter 11, Debugging and Unit Testing*.

Now that the **Network** tab is open, refresh the home page of our site. You should see something like we see in *Figure 10.13*:

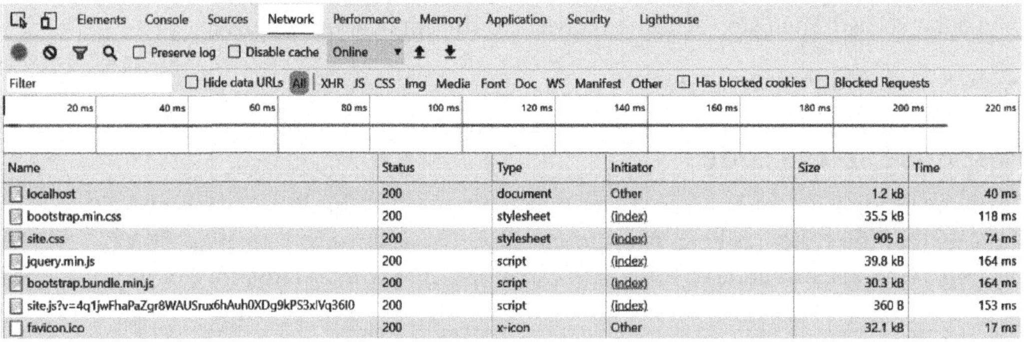

Figure 10.13 – Developer tools Network tab

Each request to the server is listed and includes information such as the type of request, size, and the time it took to receive the response. The column we are interested in is **Status**. In the preceding figure, you can see that each request has a status of 200. This means that each response included a status code of 200, indicating that the response was handled without error.

Now let's try to navigate to an endpoint that does not exist. We can do this by putting / unknown at the end of the URL. Now look at what the response code looks like in *Figure 10.14*:

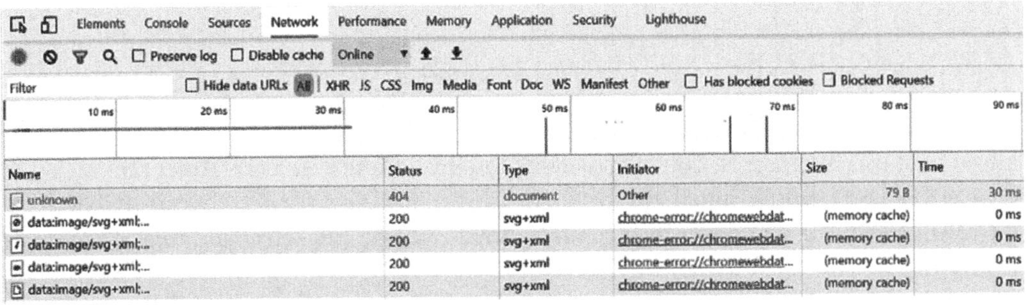

Figure 10.14 – Network log with failed response

The server now responds with a status of 404, which means the page that was requested was not found. In our sample application, we are going to respond with a status code of 503, which means the application is not healthy.

Adding a health endpoint

In this section, we will modify our application to support a health endpoint. This endpoint will either return a healthy or unhealthy response. We will do this randomly; most of the time the response will be healthy but occasionally the endpoint will respond with an unhealthy response.

In ASP.NET Core, there is the Health Checks Middleware to support this in the `Microsoft.Extensions.Diagnostics.HealthChecks` library. Please see the *Further reading* section for more information about this middleware.

First, we need to create a class to implement the IHealthCheck interface. We'll just call it HealthCheck. After you create the class, add : IHealthCheck as shown in *Figure 10.15*:

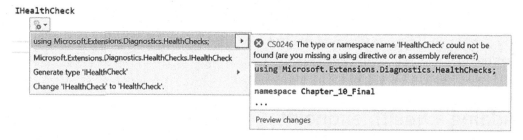

Figure 10.15 – IHealthCheck interface

The reason for the red squiggle under IHealthCheck is that Visual Studio does not know what this interface is. You left Visual Studio by adding a using Health Checks Middleware statement for Microsoft.Extensions.Diagnostics. HealthChecks. If you hover over the IHealthCheck, you can select add this as shown in *Figure 10.16*:

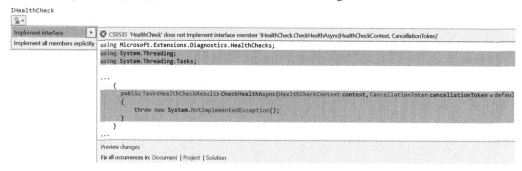

Figure 10.16 – Diagnostics HealthChecks

IHealthCheck will still have a red squiggle because now that Visual Studio knows about the interface, it is telling us we need to implement methods that match. Again, you can add these by selecting **Implement interface** as shown in *Figure 10.17*:

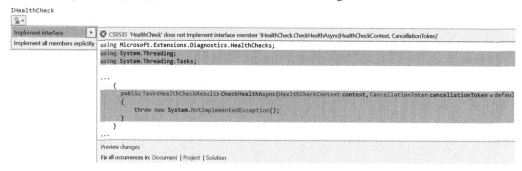

Figure 10.17 – Implementing the IHealthCheck interface

The **Implement interface** option will generate a method for `CheckHealthAsync`. We will replace the `throw` statement with the following lines of code:

```
var random = new Random();

var isHealthy = random.Next(10) != 1;
if (isHealthy)
{
    return Task.FromResult(HealthCheckResult.Healthy());
}
else
{
    return Task.FromResult(HealthCheckResult.Unhealthy());
}
```

The first part of this code snippet uses the `Random` class to generate a random value between 0 and 9. On a 1, we set the Boolean `isHealthy` to `false`; otherwise, it is set to `true`. The second part of the snippet will return either a `HealthCheckResult` status of Healthy when `IsHealthy` is `true` or a status of unhealthy when it is `false`.

> **Note**
>
> We are using `Task.FromResult()` because the interface method is asynchronous, and so it requires a return type of `Task`.

Now that we have our `HealthCheck` implemented, we need to hook up the middleware. To do this, we will update the `Startup` class. In the `ConfigureServices` method of `Status.cs`, add the following line:

```
services.AddHealthChecks().AddCheck<HealthCheck>("web");
```

This adds our `HealthCheck` implementation as a check in the `HealthChecks` middleware. *Figure 10.18* shows the completed `ConfigureServices` method:

```
public void ConfigureServices(IServiceCollection services)
{
    services.AddControllersWithViews();
    services.AddHealthChecks().AddCheck<HealthCheck>("web");
}
```

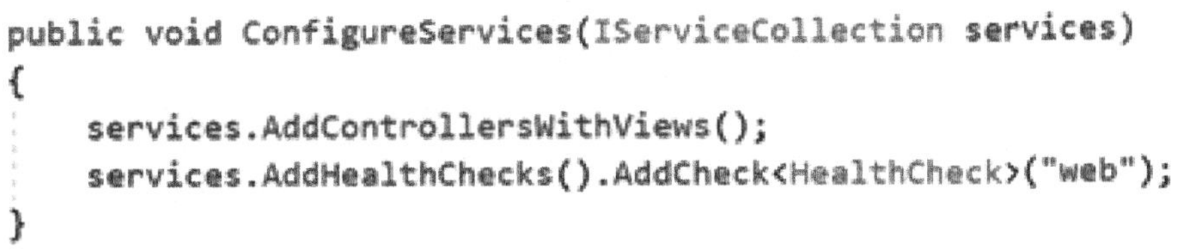

Figure 10.18 – ConfigureServices method

The next step is to add `HealthCheck` as an endpoint. We will put this check at `/health` as this is the convention. To do this, add the following as an endpoint in the `Configure` method:

```
endpoints.MapHealthChecks("health");
```

Figure 10.19 shows the completed method with our inserted line highlighted:

```
public void Configure(IApplicationBuilder app, IWebHostEnvironment env)
{
    if (env.IsDevelopment())
    {
        app.UseDeveloperExceptionPage();
    }
    else
    {
        app.UseExceptionHandler("/Home/Error");
        // The default HSTS value is 30 days. You may want to change this
        // for production scenarios, see https://aka.ms/aspnetcore-hsts.
        app.UseHsts();
    }
    app.UseHttpsRedirection();
    app.UseStaticFiles();

    app.UseRouting();

    app.UseAuthorization();

    app.UseEndpoints(endpoints =>
    {
        endpoints.MapHealthChecks("health");

        endpoints.MapControllerRoute(
            name: "default",
            pattern: "{controller=Home}/{action=Index}/{id?}");
    });
}
```

Figure 10.19 – Configure method

This change simply exposes the health check at `/health`.

Go ahead and run the solution to see this in action. Once the application has started, navigate to the health endpoint by adding `/health` to the URL as shown in *Figure 10.20*:

Figure 10.20 – Health endpoint

Try pressing refresh and you should see the `Unhealthy` response roughly 1 out of 10 times. *Figure 10.21* shows the responses in the developer tools:

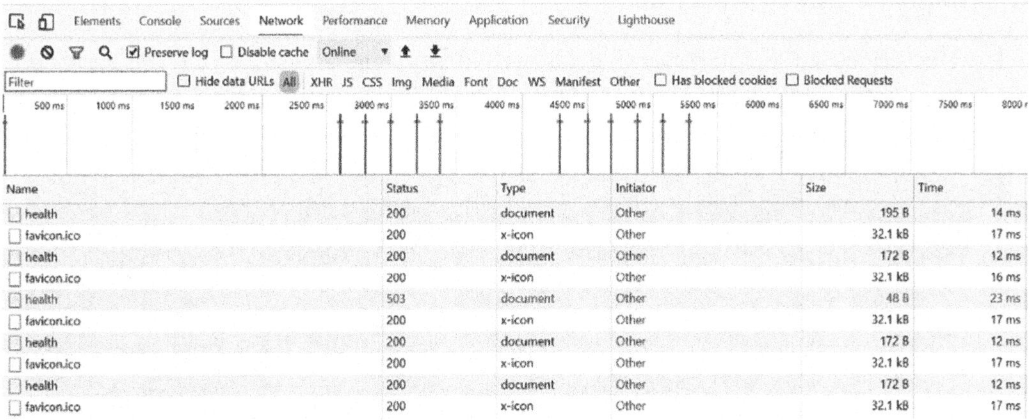

Figure 10.21 – Network log with an unhealthy response

Notice that the third response has a status of `503`. This indicates an `Unhealthy` response.

> **Note**
>
> In the developer tools, use the **Preserve log** option to keep the previous responses in the log.

Now that we have our sample application ready, let's publish this to AWS and Azure!

Publishing to AWS

In this section, we will publish our application to AWS Elastic Beanstalk. At this point, you should have an AWS account created. There are several ways to deploy to AWS Elastic Beanstalk. One way would be in the AWS console directly. Instead, we will use the AWS Toolkit as it simplifies the deployment process. To deploy using the AWS Toolkit, we need to add the required credentials to Visual Studio.

Creating a user for publishing from Visual Studio

In order to get the credentials we need, we will create a user in AWS. This is done in the AWS console. Go ahead and log in:

1. The service we are interested in deals with identity and access. To find this service, use the `Services` dropdown and type `iam` as shown in *Figure 10.22*:

Figure 10.22 – IAM service

2. After selecting this service, select **Users** under **Access management** as shown in *Figure 10.23*:

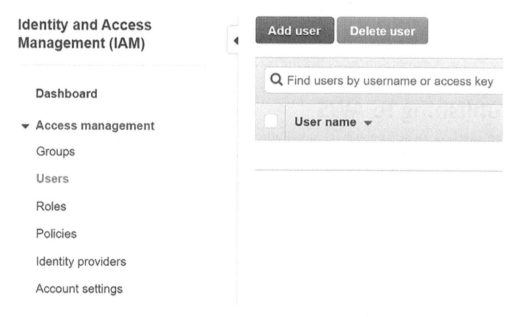

Figure 10.23 – Identity and Access Management (IAM)

3. We want to add a user, so select the **Add user** button. This will start a wizard. The first step sets the user's details. We will add a new user with the name VisualStudioUser. This user will be getting programmatic access as shown here *Figure 10.24*:

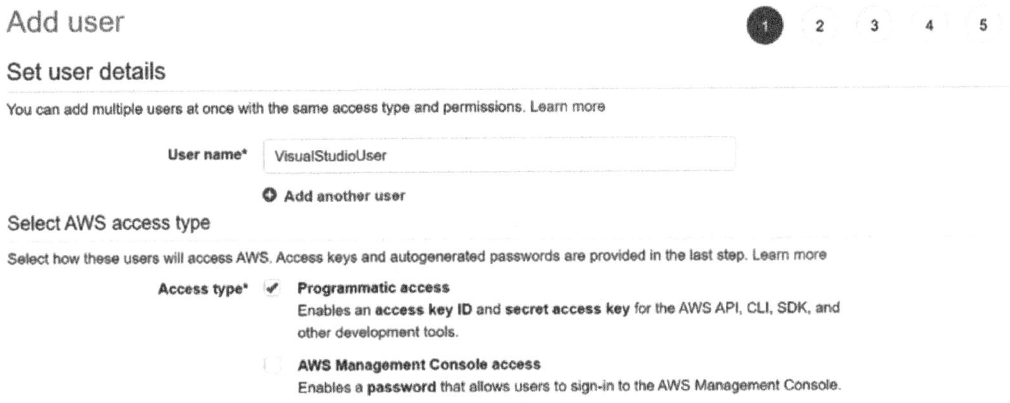

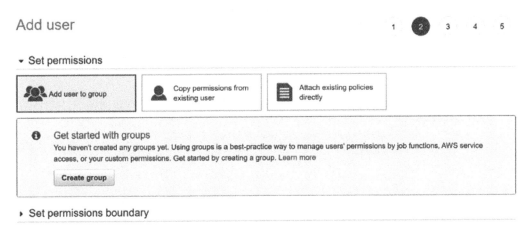

Figure 10.24 – Add user – step 1

4. Next, we want to add some permissions. We'll do this by adding the required permissions to a group and then adding the user to a group. This is a great way of configuring combinations of permissions so that they can be given to multiple users consistently. Select the **Create group** button as shown in *Figure 10.25*:

Figure 10.25 – Add user – step 2

5. We will now create a group named `VisualStudioPublisherGroup`, and we will add two permissions. The first is access to IAM. This can be seen in *Figure 10.26*:

Figure 10.26 – Create group – IAMFullAccess

The second required permission is access to AWS Elastic Beanstalk as you see in *Figure 10.27*:

Figure 10.27 – Create group – AWSElasticBeanstalkFullAccess

6. After you have these permissions selected, proceed to the next step by pressing the **Create Group** button.

> **Note**
> The details of AWS permissions are outside the scope of this chapter. In the *Further reading* section, we will provide resources related to AWS.

Figure 10.28 shows that the user will be added to the new group:

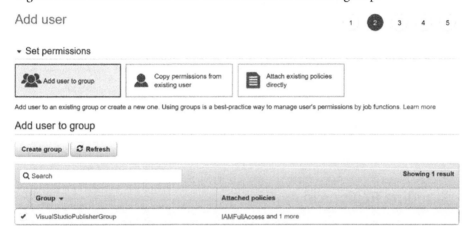

Figure 10.28 – Add user – review

7. For our purposes, we do not need to define any tags, so we can skip the **Tags** step. *Figure 10.29* shows a summary of the user:

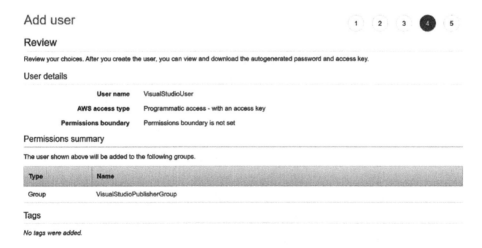

Figure 10.29 – Add user – step 4

8. After clicking the **Create user** button, we are shown a summary of the action as shown in *Figure 10.30*:

Figure 10.30 – Add user – step 5

Go ahead and download the credentials by using the **Download .csv** button. These are the credentials that we will load into Visual Studio.

Understanding Regions in AWS

At this point, we should highlight regions. Cloud providers divide the world into regions. These correspond to a collection of geographically close data centers. AWS resources can either be regional, meaning they are in a specific region, or global. Our user, for example, is global. The web application we are going to deploy will be regional.

A simple way to tell if a resource is global is to look in the top right of the AWS console. When IAM is selected, this is shown in *Figure 10.31*:

Figure 10.31 – AWS global resource

Now, go ahead and find `AWS Elastic Beanstalk` by using the services dropdown as shown in *Figure 10.32*:

Figure 10.32 – AWS Elastic Beanstalk

You will now see the Region *closest* to you has been selected by default. In this example, the Sydney Region has been selected as you can see in *Figure 10.33*:

Figure 10.33 – AWS Elastic Beanstalk Regions

We will deploy our application to a Region. You can either choose the default one or another Region.

Publishing from AWS

In this section, we will publish from Visual Studio to AWS. Let's get started:

1. Back in Visual Studio, right-click on the project and select the **Publish to AWS Elastic Beanstalk...** option as seen in *Figure 10.34*:

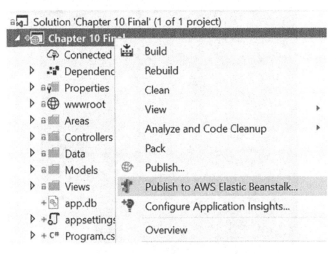

Figure 10.34 – Publish to AWS Elastic Beanstalk...

2. Next, we need to add our credentials. You do this by clicking the image of the person with a plus symbol. This is indicated in *Figure 10.35*:

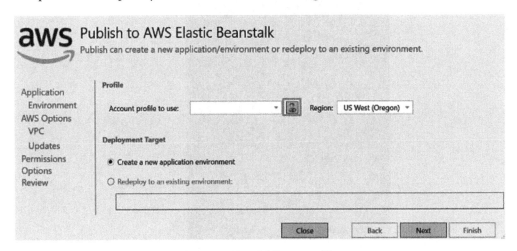

Figure 10.35 – Adding a profile

3. This will present you with a dialog where you can specify the profile name as well as loading the credentials we downloaded *Figure 10.36*:

Profile Name:	VisualStudioPublisher

A profile name of 'default' allows the SDK to find credentials when no explicit profile name is specified in your code or application configuration settings.

Storage Location:	Shared Credentials File

Using the shared credentials file, the profile's AWS credentials will be stored in the <home-directory>\.aws\credentials file. The profile will be accessible to all AWS SDKs and tools.

Access Key ID:	AKIAXUAOG7W64FIRTJHV
Secret Access Key:	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

Import from csv file...

Account Number*:	
Account Type:	Standard AWS Account

Account information can found at: http://aws.amazon.com/developers/access-keys/

* Account Number is an optional field used for constructing amazon resource names

OK   Cancel

Figure 10.36 – Visual Studio AWS profile

In the preceding figure, we supplied a name of VisualStudioPublisher and imported our credentials using the **Import from csv file...** button. We left the default of **Standard AWS Account** and clicked **OK**.

4. Now that we have loaded our credentials, we can specify the Region we want to deploy to as shown in *Figure 10.37*:

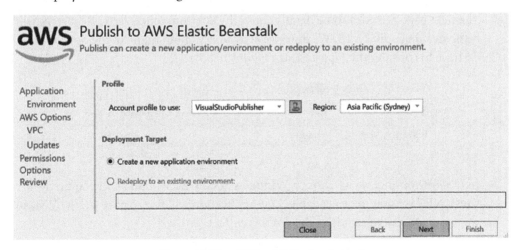

Figure 10.37 – AWS publish wizard step 1

As this is a new application environment, we can only select **Create a new application environment**. Go ahead and click **Next**.

5. In the next step, we specify the name of the application and environment. We also construct the URL of the website we are creating as shown in *Figure 10.38*:

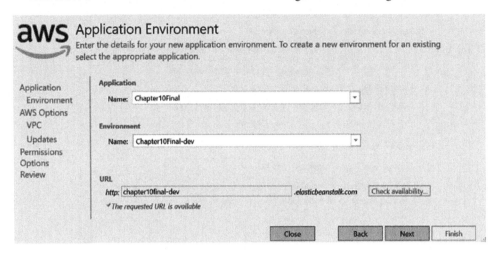

Figure 10.38 – AWS publish wizard step 2

In the preceding figure, we named the application `Chatper10Final` and selected the development environment. You might find that you need to change the URL until you find a free name, and you can use the **Check availability** button to see whether a URL is free. This URL will be global, so it needs to be unique.

Go ahead and press **Next**.

6. The next page provides some details about the environment. Elastic Beanstalk will be hosted on an EC2 VM. We don't have to worry about many of the details, but we do have to consider the type and size *Figure 10.39*:

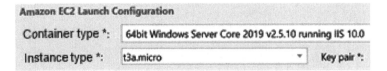

Figure 10.39 – AWS EC2 type and size

In the previous figure, we chose a Windows Server Core build as we required the latest .NET version to be available. Our application will not require a large VM, so we chose **t3a.micro** as it is in the AWS Free Tier.

> **Note**
> Not all AWS Elastic Beanstalk types will support ASP.NET Core 5. To find
> out what environments will support the deployment, please use the AWS
> Elastic Beanstalk release notes: `https://docs.aws.amazon.com/`
> `elasticbeanstalk/latest/relnotes/relnotes.html`.

The other required field is the **key pair** that will allow us access to the environment
after deployment as seen in Figure *10.40*:

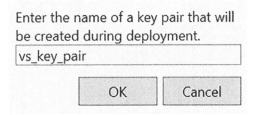

Figure 10.40 – AWS key pair

In the preceding screenshot, we named our key pair `vs_key_pair`.

7. The next parameter to note is **Single instance environment**. When clicked, the
    application can only have one instance. But when unselected, the application will be
    provisioned with a load balancer and will allow more than one instance. It will be
    initially provisioned with one instance.

    To show how to set the health endpoint, deselect **Single instance environment** as
    shown in *Figure 10.41*:

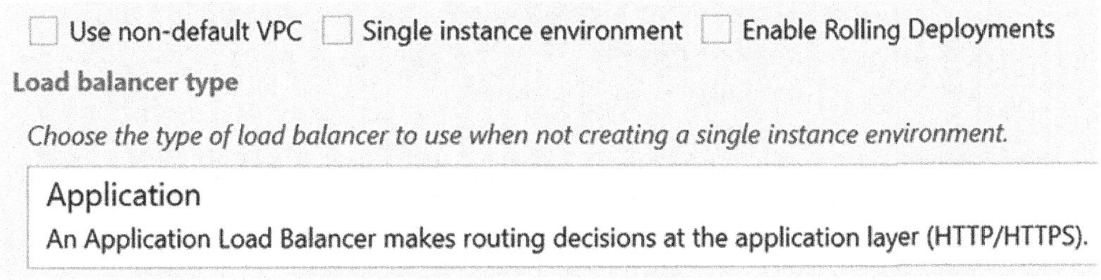

☐ Use non-default VPC ☐ Single instance environment ☐ Enable Rolling Deployments

Load balancer type

Choose the type of load balancer to use when not creating a single instance environment.

Application
An Application Load Balancer makes routing decisions at the application layer (HTTP/HTTPS).

Figure 10.41 – Load balancer type

The default load balancer is what we want. This uses HTTP requests and uses the response status code to determine the health. Continue to the next page as shown in *Figure 10.42*:

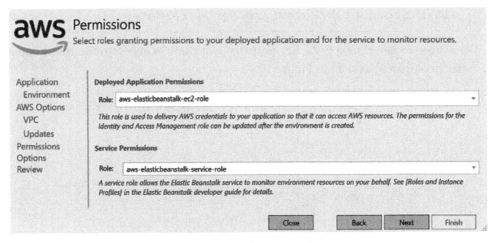

Figure 10.42 – AWS publish wizard permissions step

This page allows you to set the application permissions. For our purposes, the default values are suitable. Continue to the next page as shown in *Figure 10.43*:

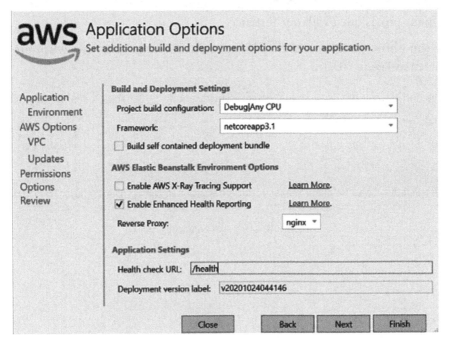

Figure 10.43 – AWS publish wizard options step

8. There are several options listed, but to keep things simple, we will only make two changes to the defaults. The first is to set **Enable Enhanced Health Reporting**. This is a free service and provides additional information about our running service. The second is **Health check URL**. You will only see this if you did not enable **Single instance environment**. We will set this to our health check endpoint, /health.

9. After clicking **Finish**, your options are presented for review as shown in *Figure 10.44*:

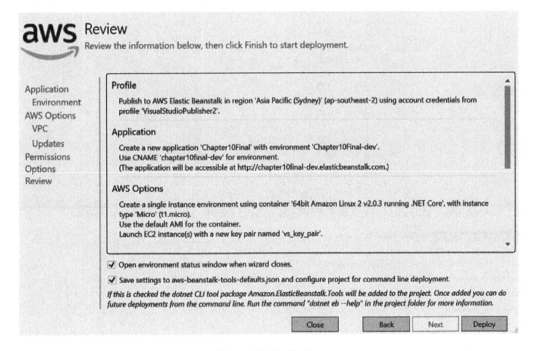

Figure 10.44 – Review

10. When you click **Deploy**, the deployment will begin. This will take time, so be patient.

You can see the status of the deployment in the **Output** window, as shown in *Figure 10.45*:

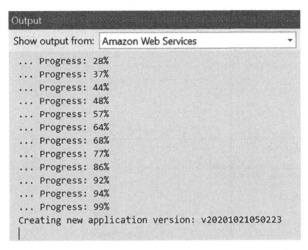

Figure 10.45 – Output

A window showing the AWS application will also be shown in *Figure 10.46*:

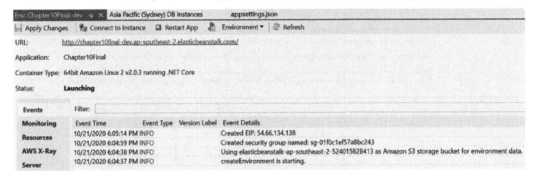

Figure 10.46 – Environment window

This is a great tool to get to know an application. Take a moment to explore some of its features.

As we have enabled our health endpoint, keep an eye on the environment's health:

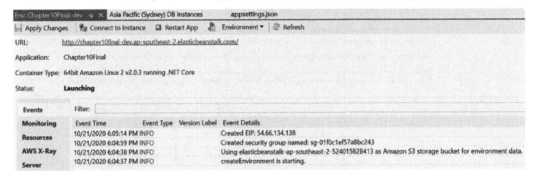

Figure 10.47 – Events

As you can see in the preceding figure, AWS reports when the health endpoint returns an unhealthy response, the 503 status code, as a warning.

Next steps with AWS

AWS Elastic Beanstalk is a great PaaS service for hosting your ASP.NET Core applications, especially when combined with other AWS resources such as databases and storage. We have provided a very simple example to get you started. The next steps will be to explore some of the resources that AWS has made available. These can be found in AWS at the following locations:

- **Working with .NET**: This series of guides is located at https://docs.aws.amazon.com/elasticbeanstalk/latest/dg/create_deploy_NET.html. They include references and guidance for working with .NET in AWS Elastic Beanstalk.

- **Deploying to Elastic Beanstalk**: This series of guides is located at https://docs.aws.amazon.com/toolkit-for-visual-studio/latest/user-guide/deployment-beanstalk.html.

We looked at using the deployment wizard, but there are many other ways of deploying to Elastic Beanstalk. For example in *Chapter 12*, *Integrating with CI/CD*, we will look at deploying solutions directly from GitHub. It is good to explore a technology, in order to find the way that works best for you and your team.

Next, we will see how Azure App Service does things.

Publishing to Azure

In this section, we will publish our application to Azure App Service. At this point, you should have an Azure account created. There are several ways to deploy to an Azure web app, and as with our AWS example, we will use the functionality available in Visual Studio.

Using the Publish wizard in Azure

In our solution, we will use the **Publish** wizard to deploy to Azure App Service.

You start the wizard by right-clicking on the project as indicated in *Figure 10.48*:

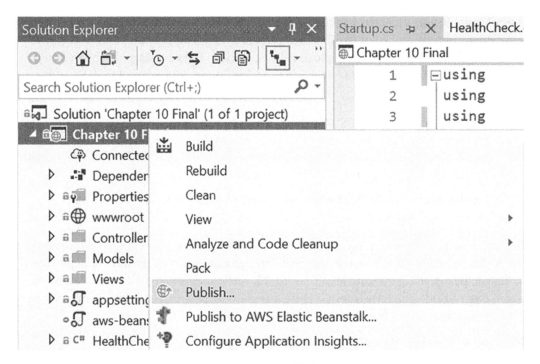

Figure 10.48 – Publish…

This wizard will walk you through a series of steps, and it supports different types of publishing, including Azure, Docker Container Registry, and IIS. We have broken these steps down into specifying what will be deployed, and then specifying where you are deploying to.

Publishing to Azure App Service

We will be publishing to **Azure**, so choose this option as shown in *Figure 10.49*:

Figure 10.49 – Publishing to Azure

The wizard supports publishing to different types of Azure resources. We will be deploying to Azure App Service running on Windows. We could also deploy to App Service running Linux too. We could also deploy the Docker image to Azure Container Registry, with the option to then run the Docker image in Azure App Service. The option to deploy to an Azure VM is also supported.

We will deploy to Azure App Service running on Windows, so select the first option on this page as shown in *Figure 10.50*:

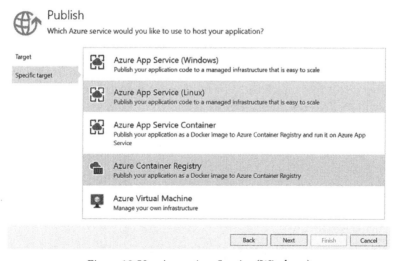

Figure 10.50 – Azure App Service (Windows)

Now that the wizard knows what we are deploying, we are asked to specify where we will be deploying to.

> **Note**
>
> Depending on whether the email associated with your Azure account and the email associated with Visual Studio match, the following pages might be different. The following screenshots are from when the accounts do not match, and/or when you require authenticating with Azure.

Creating a new Azure App Service instance

The next series of steps will create a new Azure App Service instance with the Azure account you created earlier. The first step is to use the **Sign In** link to authenticate to the Azure account. *Figure 10.51* shows the link under **Already have an account?** label:

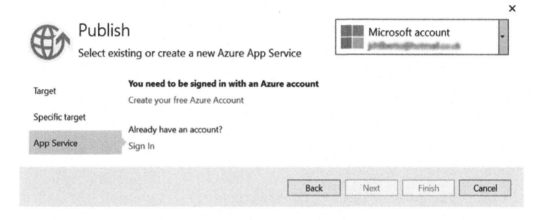

Figure 10.51 – Sign In

After authenticating Visual Studio with your Azure account, you will be shown a list of your existing resources that match the type of resource you are creating. As this is our first resource, you will see (**No resources found**) as shown in *Figure 10.52*:

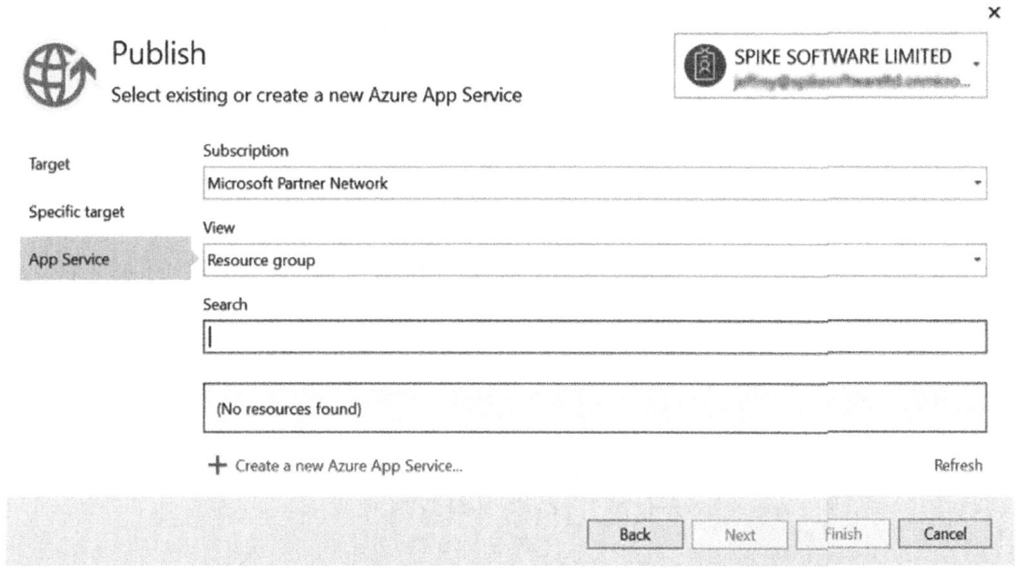

Figure 10.52 – Resource group view

When you're on the page shown in the preceding figure, select the **Create a new Azure App Service** link to define a new resource group with a new hosting plan.

Let's take a moment to define these terms. *Resources* in Azure are grouped into resource groups. This allows logically similar resources to be grouped together, as well as providing a way to manage all the resources in a resource group at the same time. An example of this would be when you are ready to delete a website, you are able to delete the entire resource group and all its resources at the same time.

On this page, we will create a new resource group as shown in *Figure 10.53*:

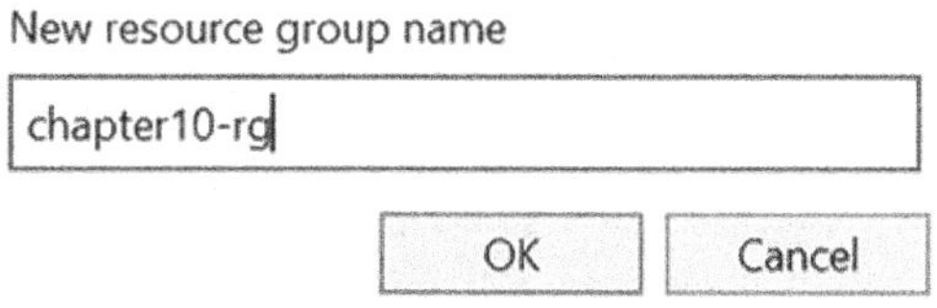

Figure 10.53 – New resource group name

> **Note**
> The names you use do not really matter, but if you want to follow a naming convention, we recommend using the following guide: `https://docs.microsoft.com/en-us/azure/cloud-adoption-framework/ready/azure-best-practices/naming-and-tagging`.

The next step is to create a hosting plan. A hosting plan determines the region, as well as the size of the compute resources used by all instances of the app service. As with AWS Elastic Beanstalk, choose a region near you. The app service size will determine the monthly charge and can range from the Free to Premium pricing tiers. Choose the Free hosting plan if you have it available as shown in *Figure 10.54*:

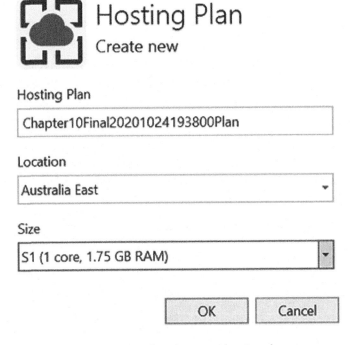

Figure 10.54 – Creating a new hosting plan

In the preceding figure, we kept the default name and chose the Sydney data center. We also chose a size of `Standard 1`. In your situation, you should have access to the free size.

With the region and size defined, we are ready to create the hosting plan. Use the **Create** button to start the creation of the hosting plan as shown in *Figure 10.55*:

Figure 10.55 – Creating a new resource group and hosting plan

Once the hosting plan has been created, you will now see your resource group and app service displayed as shown in *Figure 10.56*:

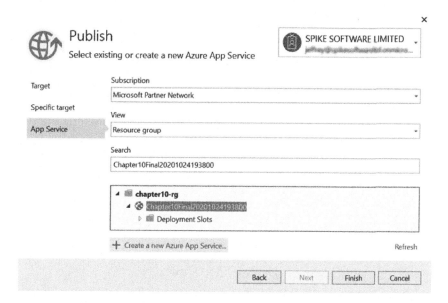

Figure 10.56 – App service defined

Go ahead and click **Finish** to proceed to the next step.

Our publishing profile is now complete. We are now presented with the page as seen in *Figure 10.57*:

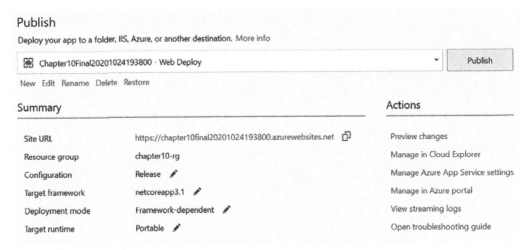

Figure 10.57 – App ready to publish

This shows us the publishing profile that will be used, including the URL that will be generated and the resource group. All the defaults are what we want, so go ahead and press **Publish**.

In the **Output** window, you can view the progress of the build and publish as shown in *Figure 10.59*:

```
Output
Show output from:  Build                                                                    [icons]
    Adding file (Chapter10Final20201024193800\wwwroot\lib\jquery\dist\jquery.min.map).
    Adding file (Chapter10Final20201024193800\wwwroot\lib\jquery\LICENSE.txt).
    Adding file (Chapter10Final20201024193800\wwwroot\lib\jquery-validation\dist\additional-methods.js).
    Adding file (Chapter10Final20201024193800\wwwroot\lib\jquery-validation\dist\additional-methods.min.js).
    Adding file (Chapter10Final20201024193800\wwwroot\lib\jquery-validation\dist\jquery.validate.js).
    Adding file (Chapter10Final20201024193800\wwwroot\lib\jquery-validation\dist\jquery.validate.min.js).
    Adding file (Chapter10Final20201024193800\wwwroot\lib\jquery-validation\LICENSE.md).
    Adding file (Chapter10Final20201024193800\wwwroot\lib\jquery-validation-unobtrusive\jquery.validate.unobtrusive.js).
    Adding file (Chapter10Final20201024193800\wwwroot\lib\jquery-validation-unobtrusive\jquery.validate.unobtrusive.min.js).
    Adding file (Chapter10Final20201024193800\wwwroot\lib\jquery-validation-unobtrusive\LICENSE.txt).
    Publish Succeeded.
    ========== Build: 1 succeeded, 0 failed, 0 up-to-date, 0 skipped ==========
    ========== Publish: 1 succeeded, 0 failed, 0 skipped ==========
```

Figure 10.58 – Output

The other window to note is **Web Publish Activity**. This will provide more detail about the publish activity and is shown in *Figure 10.59*:

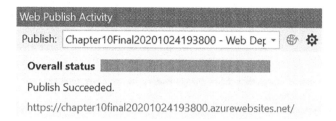

Figure 10.59 – Web Publish Activity

Once the publish has been completed, your default browser will be launched using the site URL. Once the website is loaded in the browser, navigate to the health endpoint as shown in *Figure 10.60*:

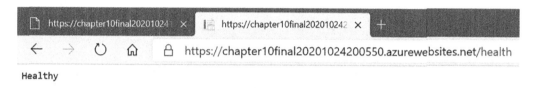

Figure 10.60 – Azure App Service health endpoint

The endpoint shown in the previous figure depicts that our website is healthy. Press the refresh button several times. You should see a mix of mostly healthy responses, but there are a few unhealthy responses. This indicates that our health endpoint is working as expected.

> **Note**
>
> Similar to AWS Elastic Beanstalk, it is not known what the support for ASP.NET will be when you are working through these examples. You might have to target an older version of the framework depending on what is available. This is a handy map that show .NET compatibility with Azure App Service: `https://aspnetcoreon.azurewebsites.NET/#.NET%20Core%20SDK`.

Now that we have our solution deployed, let's see how Azure supports the health endpoint.

Health check

To see our health endpoint in action, we need to view this in the Azure portal. Like AWS, Azure realizes that the first time viewing the portal can be daunting. There is a lot of information to take in. Like AWS, Azure has a feature to help you track down a resource – search.

At the top of the page, there is a search bar. The portal will filter all services, resources, and documentation when you use this feature. We typed in chapter as shown in *Figure 10.61*:

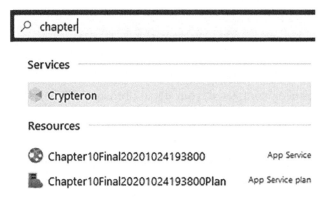

Figure 10.61 – Azure portal search

This shows how app services and app service plans that match the entered value. Select the app service you published.

To the left of the selected app service, you will see **Menu** options. The option we want is in the **Monitoring** section and is called **Health check (Preview)**. You can see this in *Figure 10.62*:

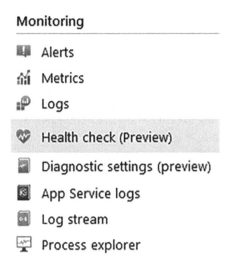

Figure 10.62 – Health check menu

The preceding figure shows this option, and at the time of writing, this feature was in preview as indicated.

When you select the health check option, you are presented with the ability to enable the feature, and you can define the path to the endpoint as shown in *Figure 10.63*:

🖫 Save   ✕ Discard   ⟳ Refresh   ⌐ Metrics   ♡ Send us your feedback

ⓘ Your site has a single instance which will not be removed if it becomes unhealthy. However, you can still set up Azure Monitor Alerts based on the health status.

Health check

ⓘ Health check configuration changes will restart your app. To minimize impact to production apps, we recommend setting it up on a staging slot and swapping it into production.

Health check increases your application's availability by removing unhealthy instances from the load balancer. If your instance remains unhealthy, it will be restarted. Learn more

Health check   ⦿ Enable

                        ○ Disable

Path *   ┌─────────────────────────────┐
                        │ /health   │
                        └─────────────────────────────┘
                        ● This is the path we'll ping to check for unhealthy instances.

Figure 10.63 – Health check path

The preceding figure shows the health check enabled with our /health path defined. Also, note the information displayed at the top making it clear what action Azure will take if the instance is unhealthy. In our case, we are only running a single instance, so Azure will only alert us when the instance is unhealthy. If we have multiple instances running, then the unhealthy resource would be removed and a new resource would be brought online to replace it.

Once the health check has been enabled, navigate to the **Metrics** option. This is also in the **Monitoring** section, as indicated in *Figure 10.64*:

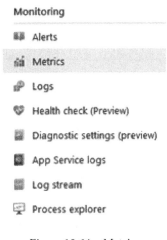

Monitoring

▦ Alerts

▦ Metrics

⌨ Logs

♥ Health check (Preview)

▥ Diagnostic settings (preview)

▦ App Service logs

▦ Log stream

▦ Process explorer

Figure 10.64 – Metrics

The metric we are interested in is **Health check status**. Go ahead and add this metric, as shown in *Figure 10.65*:

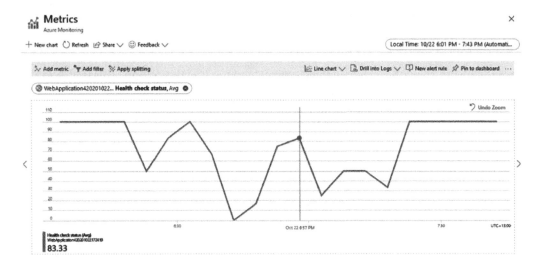

Scope	Metric Namespace	Metric	Aggreg
Chapter10Final202010242...	App Service standard m... ⌄	Select metric ⌄	Select

Gen 2 Garbage Collections
Handle Count
Health check status
Http 101
Http 2xx
Http 3xx
Http 401

Figure 10.65 – Adding Health check status

Leave the metric running for some time in order to see how the health of the application looks over time. You should end up with a graph where the application is mostly healthy. *Figure 10.66* is an example of how our metric appeared:

Figure 10.66 – Metrics

Take a moment to explore the other metrics that are available. These are a simple, yet effective way to monitor your app services.

Azure next steps

Azure App Service is a great PaaS service for hosting your ASP.NET Core applications. Like AWS Elastic Beanstalk, App Service can be integrated with other services hosted in Azure, other cloud providers, and even on-premises. We have provided a very simple example to get you started. The next steps will be to explore some of the resources that Azure has made available. These can be found in Azure, at the following locations:

- **Azure Quickstarts**: These quickstarts provide different languages and deployment options for working with Azure App Service: `https://docs.microsoft.com/en-us/azure/app-service/quickstart-dotnetcore?pivots=platform-linux`.

- **Host and deploy**: This collection of deployment articles provides a great resource for looking at different ways of deploying ASP.NET Core: `https://docs.microsoft.com/en-us/aspnet/core/host-and-deploy/azure-apps/?view=aspnetcore-3.1&tabs=visual-studio`.

Summary

In this chapter, we looked at using AWS and Azure to host our ASP.NET Core applications. We had a brief introduction to cloud computing, including looking at how resources are categorized as IaaS, PaaS, and SaaS. Using these classifications helps when discussing the different products and services offered by AWS and Azure. We also discussed how load balancers can be used to direct traffic to multiple instances of a website. We looked at how a website can use a health endpoint to respond to load balancers about the state of its health.

We then saw two practical examples of deploying a sample ASP.NET Core application to AWS and Azure. For both examples, we used functionality supported in Visual Studio that simplifies the deployment process. We encourage you to look over the next steps for both cloud providers as well as the links in the *Further reading* section. This will provide more context around what these cloud providers offer and the different types of deployment.

The next chapter will cover the essential topic of debugging and unit testing. This will cover looking at some features that ASP.NET Core and Visual Studio have for logging application activity. We will also highlight some of the most useful features of debugging in Visual Studio. The chapter will also cover building unit tests, including coverage of some of the great features provided by Visual Studio.

Questions

1. A virtual network allows you to define paths or routes between devices and other networks. This resource is an example of what cloud computing model?

2. Are health endpoints only available with AWS?

3. Is Azure only supported in Visual Studio?

4. Which cloud provider is better: AWS or Azure?

Further reading

- Information on health checks in ASP.NET Core can be found at `https://docs.microsoft.com/en-us/aspnet/core/host-and-deploy/health-checks`.

- Information on creating a new AWS account can be found at `https://aws.amazon.com/premiumsupport/knowledge-center/create-and-activate-aws-account/`.

- A module for creating a new Azure account and understanding billing: `https://docs.microsoft.com/en-us/learn/modules/create-an-azure-account/`.

- *Hands-On Azure for Developers* by Kamil Mrzygłód, from Packt Publishing, available at `https://www.packtpub.com/product/hands-on-azure-for-developers/9781789340624`.

- *Learning AWS – Second Edition* by Aurobindo Sarkar and Amit Shah, from Packt Publishing, available at `https://www.packtpub.com/product/learning-aws-second-edition/9781787281066`.

11

Browser and Visual Studio Debugging

In the previous chapter, we looked at deploying ASP.NET Core applications to the two leading cloud providers: AWS and Azure. Both cloud providers have excellent support for managing the cloud from within Visual Studio. The chapter serves as an introduction to cloud computing, and we will cover cloud computing in more detail in *Chapter 13, Cloud Native*.

In this chapter, we'll look at how both the browser and Visual Studio help us to understand, as well as support, the development of our ASP.NET Core applications. Building software is complex and knowing how to use the tooling available, is essential for producing high-quality code. Fortunately, all leading browsers have built-in support for analyzing, debugging, and viewing web applications. As Visual Studio is the **integrated development environment (IDE)** that we have been using in most of our chapters, we will explore the capabilities you should be aware of when developing ASP.NET Core applications. We will be using a **Progressive Web Application (PWA)** to illustrate the features built into the browser and Visual Studio.

We will cover the following topics in this chapter:

- PWAs

- Debugging with browser tools

- Debugging with Visual Studio

By the end of the chapter, you will have a good understanding of how to effectively use both a browser and Visual Studio for debugging. By effectively using the tooling available to us, we gain insights into the code we are creating. This will increases your capabilities at building and understanding web applications. This chapter is about coding smartly, using the browser developer tools and Visual Studio support, for debugging and analyzing our ASP.NET Core applications.

Technical requirements

This chapter includes short code snippets to demonstrate the concepts that are explained. The following software is required:

- **Visual Studio 2019**: Visual Studio can be downloaded from `https://visualstudio.microsoft.com/vs/community/`. The Community edition is free and will work for the purposes of this book.

- **.NET 5**: The .NET framework can be downloaded from `https://dotnet.microsoft.com/download`.

Make sure you download the SDK and not just the runtime. You can verify the installation by opening Command Prompt and running the `dotnet --info` command, as shown in *Figure 11.1*:

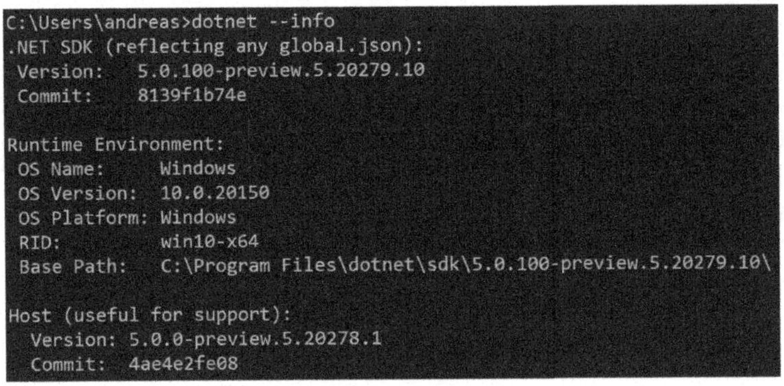

```
C:\Users\andreas>dotnet --info
.NET SDK (reflecting any global.json):
 Version:   5.0.100-preview.5.20279.10
 Commit:    8139f1b74e

Runtime Environment:
 OS Name:     Windows
 OS Version:  10.0.20150
 OS Platform: Windows
 RID:         win10-x64
 Base Path:   C:\Program Files\dotnet\sdk\5.0.100-preview.5.20279.10\

Host (useful for support):
  Version: 5.0.0-preview.5.20278.1
  Commit:  4ae4e2fe08
```

Figure 11.1 – dotnet - -info

The preceding screenshot shows the version at the time of writing this chapter.

Please visit the following link to check the CiA videos: `https://bit.ly/3qDiqYY`

Browser

In this chapter, we will be using Chrome to show how a browser's developer tools can help debug your ASP.NET Core web application. Edge, Safari, Firefox, and other browsers also support developer tools in much the same way. You are encouraged to explore developer tools using, the browser of your choice.

GitHub source

The source code for this chapter is in the GitHub repository at `https://github.com/PacktPublishing/ASP.NET-Core-5-for-Beginners/tree/master/Chapter%2010`.

Setting up the sample application

The application for this chapter will be based on the sample application for the **Blazor WebAssembly (WASM)**. This application was chosen because it provides enough complexity to be interesting, as well as providing a good basis for a real-world application. This example ASP.Net Core web application shows us a good example of a **Single-Page Application (SPA)**. In many ways, the application's behavior is more like a desktop application than a traditional website.

When we built a PWA in *Chapter 6, Exploring Blazor Web Frameworks*, that PWA sent messages to a SignalR Hub, which distributed messages to the server in real time. In *Chapter 6, Exploring Blazor Web Frameworks*, we installed the application to show the application running as a native application while still posting messages to the server.

In this section, we will create a similar SPA, and using the tools available in the browser, we will explore more what a PWS means. By the end of this section, you should have more appreciation, of why this technology is exciting.

Creating a progressive web application

We will start by creating a Blazor application using the Blazor WASM template. I prefer doing this from the command line, but you will get the same results from within Visual Studio:

```
dotnet new blazorwasm
```

Go ahead and run the created application, as shown in the following command:

```
dotnet run
```

After the application has started, navigate to the site to see if it displays correctly.

> **Note**
> We'll be using Chrome in this chapter, but most of these steps will work equally well with another browser.

The page we are going to make the focus of this chapter is **Counter**, as shown in *Figure 11.2*:

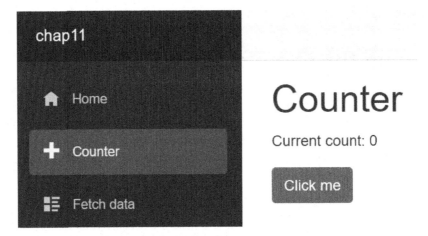

Figure 11.2 – Counter page

The first thing to notice is if you increase the counter by pressing **Click me**, navigate away to another page, and then navigate back to the page, the current count is reset back to 0. This is because the current count is being stored in the page memory. As soon as the page is refreshed, the value of the current count is reset back to 0.

Let's open the project and navigate to the counter page, as indicated in *Figure 11.3*:

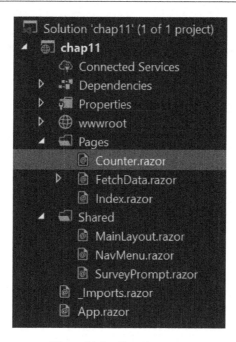

Figure 11.3 – Counter.razor

This page simply uses a variable to maintain a count. On each button click, the count is incremented. The following is the source:

```
@page "/counter"

<h1>Counter</h1>

<p>Current count: @currentCount</p>

<button class="btn btn-primary" @onclick="IncrementCount">
    Click me</button>

@code {
    private int currentCount = 0;

    private void IncrementCount()
    {
        currentCount++;
    }
}
```

The important thing to note is the variable, `currentCount`, is a private member variable. It is not initialized with a variable and its value is not stored anywhere. This means when the page is refreshed, it is reset back to 0.

Saving the state of an application

When an application is being executed, the content and information of the application will change. The state of the application is a collection of information that can be used to describe the application at a point in time. This is important because if we save the state of the application, then we can restore the application back to a point in time.

The counter is an example where the application is storing the state of the counter per page refresh. This means the state of the counter only lasts until the next time the page is loaded.

For a web application, we have several options for storing the state of the application. For the purposes of this discussion, let's just concentrate on the user state – in other words, the state pertaining to a single user.

The following table provides a summary of some common ways to store state:

Storage	Description	Use case
Page	State is not persisted between page refreshes	This state is commonly used when building up form information. The information is then persisted to one of the locations in the rows below.
Session	State is saved in the browser's session	This state is used when information should be recorded related to the current session but not between sessions.
Local	State is saved in the browser's local storage	This state is used when information should be stored between sessions
Cookies	State is saved as a browser cookie	This state is useful when information should be exchanged between the browser and the server in a secure manner.
Server	State is saved on the server	This approach is less common but may fit some scenarios.
Database	State is stored in a database	This is used when information should not be dependent on the machine or browser used to access the application.

There are more than we just listed, but even with just the options in the table, we have some choices. In *Chapter 7, APIs and Data Access*, we looked at storing data in a database. We also touched on using Redis Cache in *Chapter 9, Getting Started with Containers*. That provides us with an example of storing state on the server.

In this chapter, we will look at accessing the browser's session and local storage to store application state. To explain why this fits well with a PWA, let's spend some time discussing these modern web applications.

Understanding PWAs

PWAs are applications developed using common web technologies and are intended to work on standards-compliant browsers including Edge, Chrome, Safari, and Firefox. These applications differ from websites by some key features:

- Installable

- Work offline

- Support for background tasks

- Support for push notifications

> **Note**
> Early in the development of web applications, it was common to store user state on the server. These are referred to as **stateful**. Stateful applications are less common now, as **stateless** applications are more scalable and tend to suit web application scenarios more.

By using the debugger tools, we will be able to get more insight into an ASP.NET Core Blazor WASM application and see how it supports building a PWA. We looked at the installable feature in *Chapter 6, Exploring Blazor Web Frameworks*. In this chapter, we'll use the debugger tools to get more insight into how PWAs differ from other web applications. We will also look at how offline testing is supported in the browser. The use of debugger tools will also provide insights into how to design our PWA applications.

In the *Further reading* section, we will provide more information about PWAs.

With our sample application, we want to store the state of the counter. In a more traditional website, we would store the state of the application in a database each time the counter is increased and retrieve the value when the page is loaded. In our sample PWA, we will use the browser's ability to store information in session and local storage.

Let's add this in the next section.

Accessing browser session and local storage

The ability to access browser session and local storage is supported in JavaScript. This access takes the form of a dictionary of strings. You use a key to retrieve a string and place it into storage. In our case, we will take a C# object and serialize it into JSON and store the result.

storageHandling.js

The following will create a JavaScript file that will be used to access session and local storage:

1. The first step is to add a JavaScript file named `storageHandling.js` in the `wwwroot` folder. *Figure 11.4* screenshot shows the location of the file:

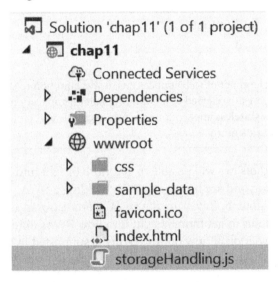

Figure 11.4 – storageHandling.js

2. We will be creating four functions in this file, and the first function is shown in the following code block:

```
function SetLocalStorage(key, value) {
    if (key == null) {
        console.error("SetLocalStorage called without
            supplying a key value.");
    }

    if (localStorage.getItem(key) != null) {
```

```
        console.warn("Replacing local storage value with
            key:" + key);
    }


    localStorage.setItem(key, value);
}
```

The `SetLocalStorage` function will put the given value into local storage using the supplied key. We added a couple of checks that will write to the console using two different levels: error and warning. We did this mostly to show how they are reflected in the browser tools later in the chapter.

3. The following code block retrieves the value stored at a given key:

```
function GetLocalStorage(key) {
    console.debug("GetLocalStorage called for
        key:" + 8key);


    return localStorage.getItem(key);
}
```

Again, we added a write to the console, but this time we are logging at a debug level. The reason for this will make more sense later.

4. The following code block contains two functions for setting and retrieving a value from session storage.

```
function SetSessionStorage(key, value) {
    sessionStorage.setItem(key, value);
}


function GetSessionStorage(key) {
    return sessionStorage.getItem(key);
}
```

These four methods will provide our Blazor code to access local and session storage.

5. For the JavaScript file to be loaded, we will add it to our `Index.html` file located in the `wwwroot` folder:

```
<body>
    <app>Loading...</app>
```

```
<div id="blazor-error-ui">
    An unhandled error has occurred.
    <a href="" class="reload">Reload</a>
    <a class="dismiss"></a>
</div>
<script src="_framework/blazor.webassembly.js">
</script>
<script src="storageHandling.js"></script>
</body>
```

The previous code block shows the reference to the new storageHandling.js file in bold.

6. Next, we will define the information that we want to store. This is done in a C# file called UserState.cs and is shown in the following code block:

```
namespace Chatper11
{
    public class UserState
    {
        public int Counter { get; set; }
    }
}
```

For our purposes, we will just be storing a single integer for the counter value.

7. In order to access session and local storage, we will be creating two classes: SessionStorageProvider and LocalStorageProvider. These will both implement IStorageProvider:

```
using System.Threading.Tasks;

namespace Chapter11
{
    public interface IStorageProvider
    {
        Task Set(string key, string value);
        Task<string> Get(string key);
    }
}
```

In the previous code block, you can see the interface defines two methods: Set()
and Get(). These will make more sense when we look at the classes that implement
the interface.

8. The following code block is the start of the storage provider that will handle session
    storage:

```
using Microsoft.JSInterop;
using System.Threading.Tasks;


namespace Chapter11
{
    public class SessionStorageProvider :
    IStorageProvider
    {
        private readonly IJSRuntime JSRuntime;

        public SessionStorageProvider(IJSRuntime
            jsRuntime)
        {
            jsRuntime = jsRuntime;
        }

        // Get
        // Set
    }
}
```

Notice how we are passing in the IJSRuntime dependency? This is available for
Blazor applications and allows us to call JavaScript functions from C#.

9. The next code block calls the JavaScript GetSessionStorage function that we
    defined in the storageHandling.js file:

```
public async Task<string> Get(string key)
{
    return await jsRuntime.InvokeAsync<string>
        ("GetSessionStorage", key);
}
```

10. The following code block calls the JavaScript `SetSessionStorage` function from the `storageHandling.js` file:

```
async Task IStorageProvider.Set(string key, string value)
{
    await JSRuntime.InvokeVoidAsync("SetSessionStorage",
                                    key,
                                    value);
}
```

11. The following code block is for a storage provider, for accessing local storage:

```
using Microsoft.JSInterop;
using System.Threading.Tasks;

namespace Chatper11
{
    public class LocalStorageProvider : IStorageProvider
    {
        private readonly IJSRuntime jsRuntime;

        public LocalStorageProvider(IJSRuntime jsRuntime)
        {
            JSRuntime = jsRuntime;
        }

        public async Task<string> Get(string key)
        {
            return await _jsRuntime.InvokeAsync<string>
                ("GetLocalStorage", key);
        }

        async Task IStorageProvider.Set(string key,
            string value)
        {
            await JSRuntime.InvokeVoidAsync(
                "SetLocalStorage", key, value);
        }
```

```
        }
    }
```

The preceding `LocalStorageProvider` is very similar to the `SessionStorageProvider`, and it only differs in the JavaScript methods that are called.

ApplicationStorage.cs

The next class we will define will be used to manage our `UserState` with either session or local storage. This provides us with a convenient way of using either type of storage, without requiring us to duplicate the serialization logic:

1. To begin with, let's create the basic structure of our class, as shown in the next code block:

```
using Microsoft.Extensions.Logging;
using System.Text.Json;
using System.Threading.Tasks;


namespace Chapter11
{
    public class ApplicationStorage<TStorageProvider>
    where TStorageProvider : IStorageProvider
    {
        readonly IStorageProvider StorageProvider;
        readonly ILogger<ApplicationStorage
            <TStorageProvider>> Logger;


        public ApplicationStorage(TStorageProvider
            storageProvider, ILogger<ApplicationStorage
            <TStorageProvider>> logger)
        {
            StorageProvider = storageProvider;
            Logger = logger;
        }


        // GetUserState()
        // SetUserState()
}
```

The important thing to note is this generic class requires two dependencies. The first is an instance of a class that implements the IStorageProvider interface. We have two, so this should not be a problem. The other is an instance of ILogger<>. We will talk about this more later, but first, let's finish the two methods.

2. The first method is GetUserState() and is shown in the following code block:

```
public async Task<UserState> GetUserState()
{
    var value = await StorageProvider.Get("UserState");

    if (value == null)
    {
        Logger.LogDebug("UserState initialized.");
        return new UserState();
    }

    return JsonSerializer.Deserialize<UserState>(value);
}
```

The GetUserState() method will use the StorageProvider to retrieve the saved version of UserState. If we do not have any state saved, then this method will create a new UserState. Take note that we deserialize the value we retrieve from storage before returning.

3. The second method is SetUserState() and is shown in the following code block:

```
public async Task SetUserState(UserState value)
{
    await StorageProvider.Set("UserState",
        JsonSerializer.Serialize(value));
}
```

The `SetUserState()` method saves the serialized value of the given `UserState` to the `StorageProvider`.

> **Note**
> If you are not familiar with serialization, think of this as a way of representing an object as a string. This is useful for saving an object to storage, as in our case, or when integrating with other systems.

4. The last bit of setup that we need to do is to add our dependencies to ASP.NET Core dependency injection. This is done in the `Program.cs` file. Insert the following lines before the call to `RunAsync()`, as shown in the following code block:

```
builder.Services.AddScoped<LocalStorageProvider>();
builder.Services.AddScoped<SessionStorageProvider>();

builder.Services.AddScoped<ApplicationStorage
    <LocalStorageProvider>>();
builder.Services.AddScoped<ApplicationStorage
    <SessionStorageProvider>>();
```

These statements set up our created classes, so they will be injected at runtime.

There is one additional registration we will make that will add logging. This is slightly different in Blazor, so we will cover this in the following section.

Logging in Blazor

Web Assemblies (WASMs) are compiled assemblies conforming to an open standard that's supported to run in most browsers. The objective is to provide native application performance while still running in a browser. This does mean that some features in ASP. NET Core will require some different handling. We already saw this with requiring the use of the `Microsoft.JSInterop` library in our Blazor pages, in order to access JavaScript functions. Logging also requires different handling.

Fortunately, our friends in the .NET community have created a set of open source projects to help us. The package we are interested in is called `Blazor.Extensions.Logging`. This can be added to the project, using the following package manager command:

```
Install-Package Blazor.Extensions.Logging -Version 1.1.1
```

With the package installed, we can add the following code block in the `Program.cs` file:

```
builder.Services.AddLogging(builder => builder.
    AddBrowserConsole());
```

This will add a logger for writing to the browser's console. We will see this in action later in the chapter, when we are looking at *Sources* in the *Using debugging tools in the browser* section.

There is one additional step to get the logging to work. In the `Index.html` file, we need to add a reference to a JavaScript file:

```
<script src="_content/Blazor.Extensions.Logging/
    blazor.extensions.logging.js" defer></script>
```

This will load the required JavaScript to log to the console.

> **Note**
>
> Additional information on `Blazor.Extensions.Logging` can be found in the GitHub repository at `https://github.com/BlazorExtensions/Logging`.

Now that we have our dependencies defined, we can modify the **Counter** page.

Modifying the Counter page to track the count

In this example, we will be using page, session, and local storage to illustrate the differences between them. Of course, you would normally just pick the best one for the scenario, but we felt this made an interesting illustration to really show the differences well:

1. The first thing we will do is inject our dependencies into the page. At the top of the page, insert the following code block:

    ```
    @using Microsoft.Extensions.Logging;
    @inject ApplicationStorage<LocalStorageProvider>
    LocalState
    @inject ApplicationStorage<SessionStorageProvider>
        SessionState
    @inject ILogger<Counter> Logger
    ```

This lets ASP.NET Core know we want instances of the two
ApplicationStorage classes, as well as an instance of the logger.

2. Next, remove the existing markup, as shown next:

```
<p>Current count: @currentCount</p>
```

3. And replace the removed markup with the following:

```
<table class="table">
    <thead>
        <tr><td></td><td>Count</td></tr>
    </thead>
    <tbody>
        <tr><td>Page    </td><td>@currentCount</td></tr>
        <tr><td>Session</td><td>@currentSessionCount
        </td></tr>
        <tr><td>Local   </td><td>@currentLocalCount</td>
        </tr>
    </tbody>
</table>
```

The previous code block creates a table to show our three counters.

4. In the code section, add two more private variables to hold our displayed counts,
    as shown here:

```
private int currentCount = 0;
private int currentLocalCount = 0;
private int currentSessionCount = 0;
```

5. Let's create a method for retrieving the count from storage:

```
private async Task<int> GetCountFromStorage<T>(
    ApplicationStorage<T> provider) where T :
    IStorageProvider
{
    var state = await provider.GetUserState();
    return state.Counter;
}
```

The previous code block uses a given `ApplicationStorage` provider to retrieve the `UserState` from storage. The count is then returned.

6. Next, we will create a method to save the count, as follows:

```
private async Task<int> IncrementCountInStorage<T>(
    ApplicationStorage<T> provider) where T :
    IStorageProvider
{
    var state = await provider.GetUserState();
    state.Counter++;
    await provider.SetUserState(state);
    return state.Counter;
}
```

The previous code block will retrieve the `UserState` from the given provider. The count will then be incremented on the `UserState`, saved back to the provider, and then the updated count will be returned.

7. The next step is to retrieve the current values of the count when the page first loads, as shown in the following code snippet:

```
protected override async Task OnInitializedAsync()
{
    currentLocalCount = await GetCountFromStorage(
        LocalState);
    currentSessionCount = await GetCountFromStorage(
        SessionState);
}
```

The previous code block launches when the page is initializing. It will retrieve the latest counts from the local storage and session storage. The retrieved values are then saved to the page's member variables.

8. The last step is to update what happens when the button is pressed. Replace the current `IncrementCount()` method with the following:

```
private async void IncrementCount()
{
    currentCount++;

    currentSessionCount = await IncrementCountInStorage(
        SessionState);
    currentLocalCount = await IncrementCountInStorage(
        LocalState);

    StateHasChanged();
}
```

This method updates the page, session, and local storage counts, using the methods we created earlier. The last step is to alert Blazor that the state of the page has changed. This is important, as if this is not done, the page will always show the previous count and not the latest count.

With all the changes in place, go ahead and start the website. After navigating to the site and pressing the button a couple of times, you should see something like *Figure 11.5* depicts:

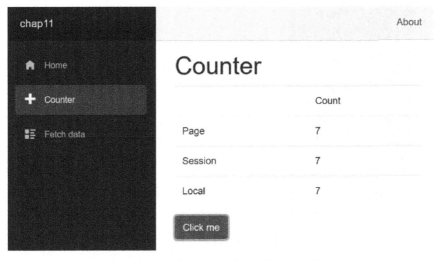

Figure 11.5 – Counter page after 7 clicks on Click me

The previous image shows the counters in sync. Great! Now let's see what happens when the page is refreshed. You will see something similar to *Figure 11.6*:

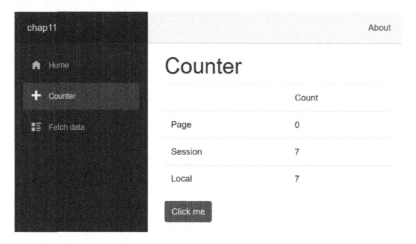

Figure 11.6 – Counter page after refresh

This is interesting, because it shows the page count resetting, as we expected from the original behavior. But now the counts stored in session and local storage are not lost.

Let's see what happens when we open a new tab and navigate to the **Counter** page You will see something similar to *Figure 11.7*:

Figure 11.7 – Counter page new session

This shows us that each tab will have its own session, but local storage is persisted between sessions. Go ahead and close the browser and start it again. After navigating to the **Counter** page again, you will see local storage is still shown.

This little exercise gives us a good understanding of these three types of storage: page, session, and local storage. With this knowledge, we can more effectively plan how we want to store information in the browser. Page-level storage makes sense for forms and information that we don't want to retain between page refreshes. Session storage should be used for information that we don't want to share with other sessions. The information collected in a multiple-page wizard might be a good candidate. And local storage would be good for information that we want to share with all instances of the browser on the individual's machine.

Oh, and what about between different browsers? See *Figure 11.8*

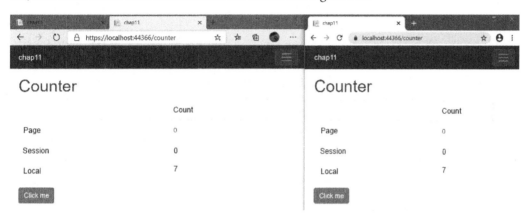

Figure 11.8 – Counter page new browser

The previous screenshot is the same website open on Edge and Chrome. You can see that the local storage is not shared between the browsers.

Now that we have a working application with some interesting components, let's look at how the debugging tools in the browser can help us gain more of an understanding of our applications, and help us to write better applications.

Using debugging tools in the browser

We will use the application we wrote in the last section to explore major features of the browser's debugging tools. Fortunately, the major browsers have all taken a very similar approach to this, so a lot of what we will cover will be applicable to Edge, Chrome, Safari, and Firefox. For example, on a Windows machine, pressing *F12* will access the browser tools in each browser.

Let's look at the tabs shown in the browser tools. We are going to have a look at **Elements**, **Console**, **Sources**, **Network**, and **Application**, as indicated in *Figure 11.9*:

Figure 11.9 – Developer tools tabs

In the following sections, we will look at the tabs indicated in more detail. For additional information, including information on the tabs we are not covering, please see the *Further reading* section at the end of the chapter.

The Elements tab

The **Elements** tab provides insights into the **document object model (DOM)** including CSS. This allows us to get an insight into the markup of the page and how it is presented. On the **Counter** page, let's have a look at this in more detail. See *Figure 11.10*:

```html
Elements   Console   Sources   Network   Performance   Memory   Application   Security
<!DOCTYPE html>
<html>
▼<head>
    <meta charset="utf-8">
    <meta name="viewport" content="width=device-width, initial-scale=1.0, maximum-scale=1.0, user-
    scalable=no">
    <title>Chapter11</title>
    <base href="/">
    <link href="css/bootstrap/bootstrap.min.css" rel="stylesheet">
    <link href="css/app.css" rel="stylesheet">
  </head>
▼<body>
  ▶<app>…</app>
  ▶<div id="blazor-error-ui">…</div> == $0
    <script src="_framework/blazor.webassembly.js"></script>
    <script src="_content/Blazor.Extensions.Logging/blazor.extensions.logging.js" defer></script>
    <script src="storageHandling.js"></script>
  ▶<script type="text/javascript">…</script>
    <script src="_framework/wasm/dotnet.3.2.0.js" defer integrity="sha256-
    mPoqx7XczFHBWk3gRNn0hc9ekG1OvkKY4XiKRY5Mj5U=" crossorigin="anonymous"></script>
  </body>
</html>
```

Figure 11.10 – Elements tab

In the previous screenshot, we are shown the DOM that makes up our counter page. This allows us to see what CSS and JavaScript files have been referenced. Notice our `storageHandling.js` and `blazor.extensions.logging.js` files are referenced. Take a moment to drill into the `<app>` node to see the DOM making up our table. Refer to *Figure 11.11*:

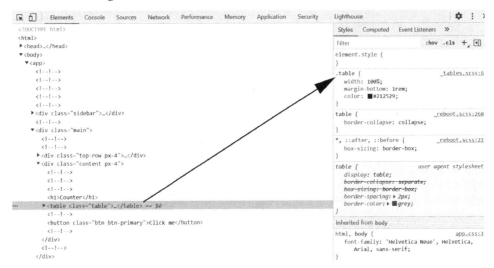

Figure 11.11 – Elements tab CSS

In the previous screenshot, notice how we have drilled into the DOM to the `<table>` element. With the element selected, we are shown the styles being applied. In the screenshot, we can see the `<table>` element has the class `.table` being applied. Take a moment to explore the **Elements** tab.

A nice feature is **Inspect**. Go ahead and right-click on the **Click me** button and select **Inspect**, as shown in *Figure 11.12*:

Figure 11.12 – Inspect element

This will navigate you immediately to the button in the DOM. Now, in the **Styles** panel, change the background color of the button, as shown in *Figure 11.13*:

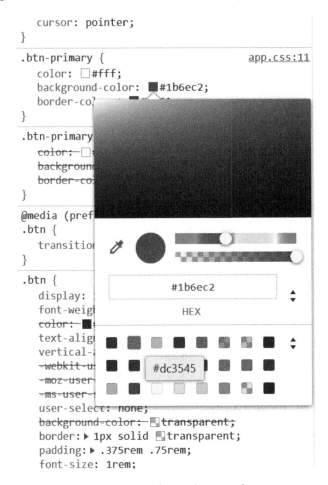

Figure 11.13 – Altering button color

This is a great way to quickly see how changes to CSS will affect your pages. Take a moment to explore this feature. Don't worry about breaking anything, as you can always refresh the page to remove any of your changes.

Before we move to the **Console** section, look at this handy feature, as indicated in *Figure 11.14*:

Figure 11.14 – Mobile view

This provides us with the ability to quickly check the responsiveness of our page. For example, this is providing us a view of how the **Counter** page looks on a mobile device when it is rotated. See *Figure 11.15*:

Figure 11.15 – Counter as viewed in mobile

After you have done some exploring, let's move on to the **Console** tab.

The Console tab

The **Console** tab provides access to logged messages, as well as the ability to run JavaScript commands. After selecting the tab, go ahead and refresh the page. You should then see something like *Figure 11.16* depicts:

Figure 11.16 – Console

The first three messages are about Blazor and the loading of the WASM. This gives us some insight immediately into the technology of WASM. Go ahead and drill into the second line, as shown in *Figure 11.17*:

```
▼ blazor Loaded 6.16 MB resources                                                    blazor.webassembly.js:1
  This application was built with linking (tree shaking) disabled. Published applications will be significantly smaller.
  ▼ Loaded 6.16 MB resources from cache                                              blazor.webassembly.js:1
    ▼ Object 🔲                                                                      blazor.webassembly.js:1
      ▶ Blazor.Extensions.Logging.dll: {responseBytes: 6020}
      ▶ Chapter11.dll: {responseBytes: 11929}
      ▶ Chapter11.pdb: {responseBytes: 8337}
      ▶ Microsoft.AspNetCore.Components.Forms.dll: {responseBytes: 15132}
      ▶ Microsoft.AspNetCore.Components.Web.dll: {responseBytes: 24344}
      ▶ Microsoft.AspNetCore.Components.WebAssembly.dll: {responseBytes: 25976}
```

Figure 11.17 – Blazor messages in the Console tab

This shows us that the logic of our application, as well as the references, are being sent to the browser as libraries.

Take a moment to run the following two JavaScript commands:

```
localStorage.
setItem("Cats",'{"Bengal":4,"Siamese":2,"Calico":3}')
localStorage.setItem("Languages",'{"Java":2,"TSQL":3,"C#":5}')
```

The commands illustrate how we have access to JavaScript functions. In this example, we are adding two additional keys to `localStorage`. This will also help make the **Sources** section more interesting.

Go ahead and change the logging level to **Verbose**, as shown in *Figure 11.18*, by using the **All levels** dropdown in the menu:

Figure 11. 18 – Logging levels

By adjusting the logging level to **Verbose**, we will be sure to see all the log messages. We can reduce the number of visible messages by deselecting levels that we are not interested in viewing.

After increasing the count by clicking the **Click me** button, you will see some log messages, as shown in *Figure 11.19*:

Figure 11. 19 – storageHandling.js link

These are related to the JavaScript messages we wrote in the `storageHandling.cs` file. Go ahead and click on the link to the JavaScript, as shown in the previous screenshot.

This will take you to our next section to discuss, **Sources**.

The Sources tab

The **Sources** tab will provide us with insight into the different files that make up our page. As we navigate from the **Console** tab, you should see something similar to *Figure 11.20*:

Figure 11.20 – storageHandling.js on the Sources tab

Go ahead and put a breakpoint by clicking on row number 7. After using the **Click me** button again, the browser will pause in the debugger on line 7, as shown in *Figure 11.21*:

```
app.css    _tables.scss    service-worker.js    00755c3a    storageHandling.js ✕

 1 function SetLocalStorage(key, value) {  key = "UserState", value = "{"Counter":17}"
 2     if (key == null) {
 3         console.error("SetLocalStorage called without supplying a key value.");
 4     }
 5
 6     if (localStorage.getItem(key) != null) {   key = "UserState"
 7         ▶console.▶warn("Replacing local storage value with key:" + key); ⚠
 8     }
 9
10     localStorage.setItem(key, value);
11 }
```

Figure 11. 21 – Console breakpoint

This will provide us with insight into what is happening. First, we can see the values that have been sent into the method for key and for value. Notice how the value is a JSON string holding the current count value.

Another feature to highlight is being able to view the state of variables by hovering over them. See *Figure 11.22*:

```
 5
 6         if (localStorage.getItem(key) != null) {  key = "
 7            ▶con  le ▶warn("Replacing local storage valu
 8         }            Storage
 9
10         lo     BestCats: "{"Bengal":4,"Siamese":2,"Calicc
11 }           Languages: "{"Java":2,"TSQL":3,"C#":5}"
12            UserState: "{"Counter":17}"
13 functi     length: 3
14    co    ▶ __proto__: Storage                        +
```

Figure 11.22 – Debugging hover over

In the preceding screenshot, we are able to see that localStorage has three keys and also their values. This shows the current UserState having a value of 17 for Counter. We can also see the two entries we added to local storage by running commands in the **Console** tab.

Let's move onto the **Network** tab.

The Network tab

The **Network** tab provides you with a way to monitor and influence network activity. We looked at the **Network** tab previously, in *Chapter 10, Taking ASP.NET to the Cloud*. In that chapter, we saw how we could review the messages being sent, including viewing the status code. In this section, we will point out another useful feature that allows you to control the network connection.

In the menu bar, find the dropdown that says **Online** and click on it. This is shown in *Figure 11.23*:

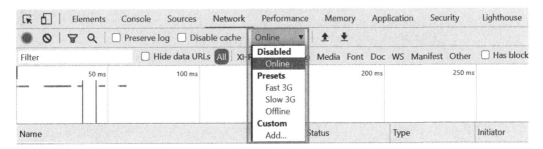

Figure 11.23 – Network

This allows you to affect the network, from slowing it down to disabling it altogether. Go ahead and set the network to **Offline**. After doing so, navigate the website to different pages. You should not see any change in its behavior. This is because the application has been loaded into the browser and is now running without any connection to the server. As an exercise, go ahead and try this with another project from a previous chapter, for example, *Chapter 7, APIs and Data Access*.

From the *Chapter 7, APIs and Data Access*, project, we have the WeatherForecast endpoint, as shown in *Figure 11.24*:

```
[{"date":"2020-11-24T10:22:10.2154382+13:00","temperatureC":27,"temperatureF":80,"summary":"Chilly"},
{"date":"2020-11-25T10:22:10.2175576+13:00","temperatureC":-17,"temperatureF":2,"summary":"Balmy"},
{"date":"2020-11-26T10:22:10.2175608+13:00","temperatureC":27,"temperatureF":80,"summary":"Mild"},
{"date":"2020-11-27T10:22:10.2175612+13:00","temperatureC":22,"temperatureF":71,"summary":"Freezing"},
{"date":"2020-11-28T10:22:10.2175615+13:00","temperatureC":5,"temperatureF":40,"summary":"Sweltering"}]
```

Figure 11.24 – WeatherForecast endpoint

The endpoint simply returns a JSON result containing weather information. When we disable the network, you can see the response is no longer returned from the server as shown in *Figure 11.25*:

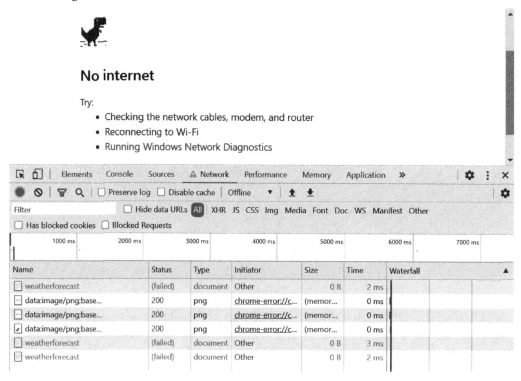

Figure 11.25 – No internet

The preceding example is extreme, as we are testing with the network available and without the network available. It is also possible to test when the network is slow or fast. This allows us to see how our application behaves in different circumstances.

When you are ready, go ahead and set the network back to **Online**, as we don't want this to interfere with steps in later sections.

Let's proceed to the last tab that we will cover in this section, **Application**.

The Application tab

The **Application** tab allows you to inspect and manipulate the resources that have been loaded for the web application. In this section, we will look at how we can view and update local and session storage.

To view the local storage, expand the **Local Storage** section, as shown in *Figure 11.26*:

Figure 11.26 – Local Storage

This will provide us with a view of the entries in local storage, as well as a way to add new entries. Go ahead and double-click the next empty row, as shown in *Figure 11.27*:

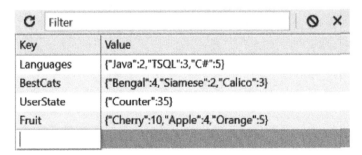

Figure 11.27 – Editing Local Storage

This will allow you to enter new values into local storage. You are also able to do the same with session storage.

Next, select **Clear storage**, as shown in *Figure 11.28*:

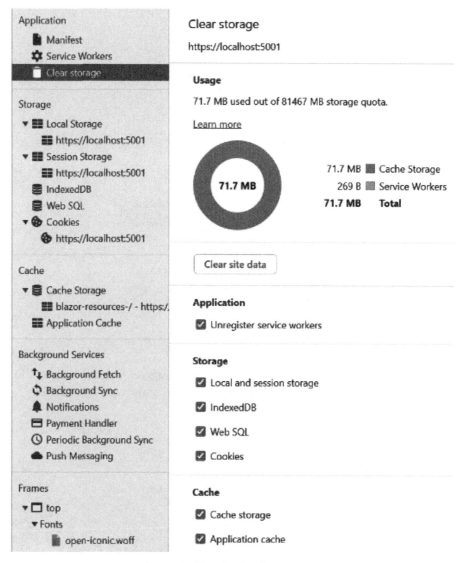

Figure 11.28 – Application storage

The **Clear storage** section provides us with a summary of the storage the current application is using. We can also clear the storage, with control over what aspects of the storage we should clear. If you want to clear the application from storage, including resetting the counts, go ahead and click **Clear site data**.

When you are ready, let's go back to Visual Studio and view some of its features for debugging.

Debugging in Visual Studio

As we have seen with browser developer tools, the capabilities of Visual Studio for debugging cannot be covered in a single chapter. Our objective will be to highlight some of the features so you have a good understanding of the fundamentals.

Controlling the application launch and target

The first thing in Visual Studio we will look at is controlling how the application is launched. Below the menu, there is a toolbar that shows the launch settings. *Figure 11.29* shows this menu bar expanded:

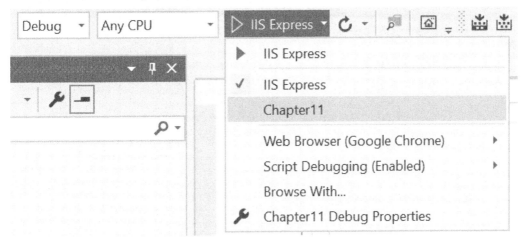

Figure 11.29 – Launch settings

This allows us to control how the application is launched, and in the preceding screenshot, we have two options: **IIS Express** and **Chapter11**. These values tie into the launch settings, and the file controlling these options is in the **Properties** folder as shown in *Figure 11.30*:

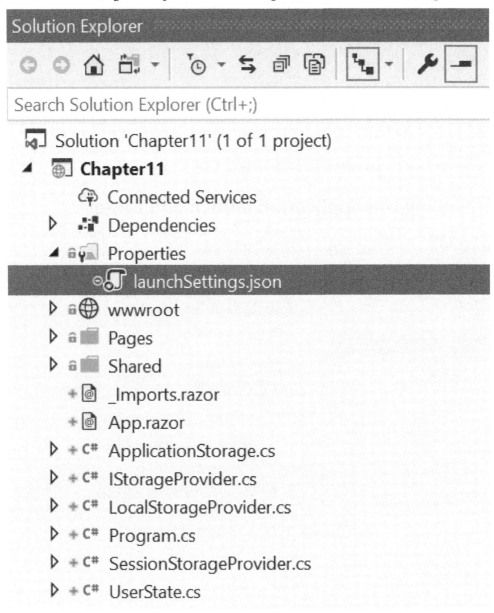

Figure 11.30 – Launch Settings JSON

In the launchSettings.json file, we can see two entries in the profiles section that correspond to the two launch options. Our preference is to not launch in IIS Express, but instead run the dotnet project directly. To limit the option to just the project, we will remove the IIS settings and the IIS Express profile as shown in the following code snippet:

```
{
  "profiles": {
    "Chapter11": {
      "commandName": "Project",
      "launchBrowser": true,
      "inspectUri": "{wsProtocol}://{url.hostname}:{url.port}
        /_framework/debug/ws-
        proxy?browser={browserInspectUri}",
      "applicationUrl":"https://localhost:5001;
        http://localhost:5000",
      "environmentVariables": {
        "ASPNETCORE_ENVIRONMENT": "Development"
      }
    }
  }
}
```

In the JSON discussed before, we limited the launch options to just our project. This will alter our launch window to just our project as shown in *Figure 11.31*:

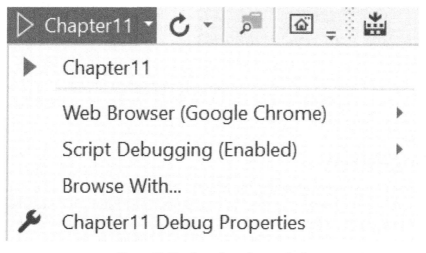

Figure 11.31 – Launch settings revised

Another common feature to use is to change the browser used during debugging. Visual Studio will provide a list of the browsers installed. See *Figure 11.32*:

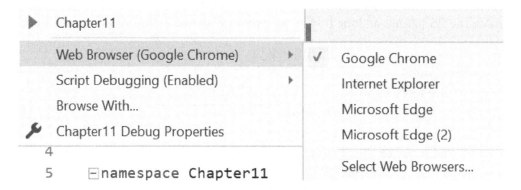

Figure 11.32 – Setting the web browser

In the preceding screenshot, we selected **Google Chrome** to be launched. Now when we start the project by either clicking the **Debug** button or pressing *F5*, we should see both a console window starting as well as Chrome. See *Figure 11.33*:

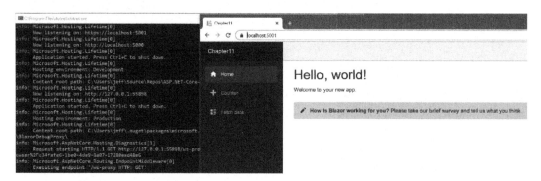

Figure 11.33 – Console and web browser starting

In the previous screenshot, we can see the console running our project, as well as our application running in Chrome. We like the view of the logging messages in the console and we will cover this in the next section.

Logging activity

In this section, we will look at setting the logging level of your application. An important thing to note is all the libraries involved in your project are emitting messages but only a few of them are being displayed. For this to make sense, go ahead and create an appsettings.json file for your project as shown in *Figure 11.34*:

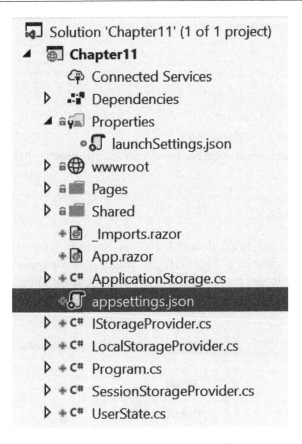

Figure 11.34 – appSettings.json file

In the file, first set it to the following JSON:

```json
{
    "Logging": {
        "LogLevel": {
            "Default": "Debug"
        }
    }
}
```

After creating the `appsettings.json` file and setting the contents, go ahead and launch the project. You should now see a large amount of logging in the console. There is a lot of useful information here, especially when things are not quite working as expected. In most cases though, it is too much information, so we want to filter out some of the messages.

To do this, modify the existing JSON to the following code:

```
{
  "Logging": {
    "LogLevel": {
      "Default": "Debug",
      "Microsoft": "Warning",
      "Microsoft.AspNetCore.Hosting.Lifetime": "Information"
    }
  }
}
```

The preceding JSON is setting the default log level to Debug. This is the lowest level of logging, which means show us all log messages. The next line is applied on top of this. This line says we only want to see warning messages from Microsoft libraries. The final line says the for the messages relating to hosting, we want to see Information messages or more severe.

Figure 11.35 shows the levels of severity:

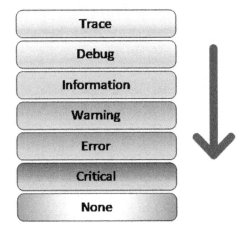

Figure 11.35 – Logging levels

In the preceding diagram, the increasing log level indicates that only messages at and below a specific level will be shown. For example, if the log level was set to **Error**, then only messages with a level of **Error** or **Critical** would be shown. **None** indicates that no messages will be shown.

This is particularly useful when diagnosing issues that are not directly tied to your code. In the next section, we will look at debugging issues in your code.

Setting a breakpoint

In this section, we will look at debugging in Visual Studio. The debugging experience with the Blazor WASM application is a little bit different than other projects as we are dealing with client code that has been compiled. In other words, this is code that is running in the browser, but it is not JavaScript. As we saw earlier in the chapter, the browser developer tools do have a powerful debugger for JavaScript, but this debugger will not allow us to debug compiled assemblies. To do this, we need Visual Studio.

Let's start by adding two breakpoints. A breakpoint is just a spot in our code where we want Visual Studio to stop the execution, or break, so that we can inspect what is happening. In this example, we will be adding a breakpoint in a C# class as well as a JavaScript function to show the versatility of Visual Studio.

First, in the `ApplicationStorage` file, set a breakpoint in the `GetUserState()` method by clicking to the right of the line number as shown in *Figure 11.36*:

```
                        0 references | 0 changes | 0 authors, 0 changes | 0 exceptions
18                      public async Task<UserState> GetUserState()
19                      {
20                          var value = await StorageProvider.Get("UserState");
21
22                          if (value == null)
23                          {
24                              Logger.LogDebug("UserState initialized.");
25                              return new UserState();
26                          }
27
28                          return JsonSerializer.Deserialize<UserState>(value);
29                      }
30
```

Figure 11.36 – GetUserState() breakpoint

Next, in the `storageHandling.js` file, place a breakpoint in the `SetLocalStorage()` method as shown in *Figure 11.37*:

```
Chapter11 JavaScript Content Files                                      ▼  GetSessionStorage
1    function SetLocalStorage(key, value) {
2        if (key == null) {
3            console.error("SetLocalStorage called without supplying a key value.");
4        }
5
6        if (localStorage.getItem(key) != null) {
7            console.warn("Replacing local storage value with key:" + key);
8        }
9
10       localStorage.setItem(key, value);
11   }
```

Figure 11.37 – SetLocalStorage() breakpoint

This breakpoint will stop the execution when we are replacing the value in local storage.

To see these in action, start the application by pressing the *F5* key and then navigate to the **Counter** page. The execution should pause, and you should be directed back to Visual Studio. See *Figure 11.38*:

```
        2 references | 0 changes | 0 authors, 0 changes | 0 exceptions
18   ⊟  public async Task<UserState> GetUserState()
19      {
20          var value = await StorageProvider.Get("UserState");
21
22   ⊟      if (value == null)
23          {
24              Logger.LogDebug("UserState initialized.");
25              return new UserState();
26          }
27
28          return JsonSerializer.Deserialize<UserState>(value);
29      }
```

Figure 11.38 – Triggered breakpoint

The first question is are we dealing with local storage or session storage? It is not obvious as we are dealing with a generic class. The good news is this can be found in the **Locals** debug window. Most likely, this will be located at the bottom of Visual Studio, but if not, you can add the window under the **Debug** menu as shown in *Figure 11.39*:

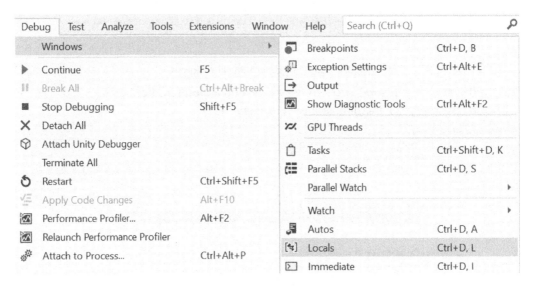

Figure 11.39 – Locals window

Looking at our **Locals** window, we can see we are dealing with the
`SessionStorageProvider`:

Figure 11.40 – Locals window view

Go ahead and press *F5* to continue. Then increase the count. The same breakpoint will
trigger again but go and skip ahead by pressing *F5*. You should then stop in the JavaScript
file as shown in *Figure 11.41*:

```javascript
Chapter11 JavaScript Content Files

1    function SetLocalStorage(key, value) {
2        if (key == null) {
3            console.error("SetLocalStorage called without supplying a key value.");
4        }
5
6        if (localStorage.getItem(key) != null) {
7            console.warn("Replacing local storage value with key:" + key);
8        }
9
10       localStorage.setItem(key, value);
11   }
```

Figure 11.41 – JavaScript triggered breakpoint

Like the previous breakpoint, the **Locals** window provides us with details about the state
of the current variables. This is shown in *Figure 11.42*:

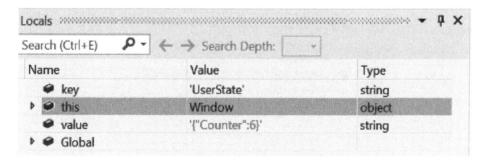

Figure 11.42 – Locals window values

The Visual Studio debugger does show the values, but you can also change the values. For example, if I want to change the count, I can double-click the value and edit it, as you can see in *Figure 11.43*:

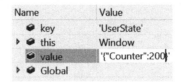

Figure 11.43 – Editing a local variable

In the preceding screenshot, I am editing the value to 200. Once the value is saved, continue processing by pressing *F5*.

Go ahead and delete the breakpoints you have set. An easy way to do this is by using the command in the **Debug** menu:

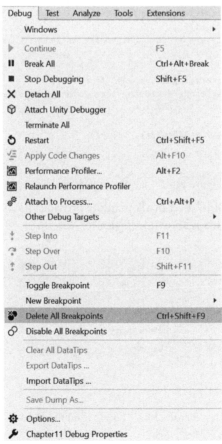

Figure 11. 44 – Delete All Breakpoints

As it says, this command will delete all the breakpoints in the project. You can also disable all breakpoints. This is handy if you want to just temporarily stop breaking, but you also want to retain the breakpoints in case you want to enable them later.

In the next section, we will look at adding conditions to our breakpoints.

Using conditional breakpoints

As we said earlier, there are so many features of debugging, that we are not able to cover them all in a chapter, but we will cover one more: conditional breakpoints. This feature is very useful, as you often only want to break when a certain condition happens.

Let's say we only want to break when the value of our count reaches 10. We can do this by setting a condition on our breakpoint. In the `SetUserState()` method of the `ApplicationStorage` class, set a breakpoint. Then right-click on the breakpoint and select the **Conditions…** option, as shown in *Figure 11.45*:

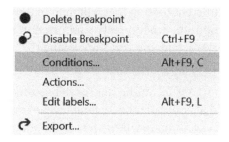

Figure 11.45 – Conditions

The condition could be when a value changes or when a condition becomes true. In *Figure 11.45*, we are setting the condition to `10`:

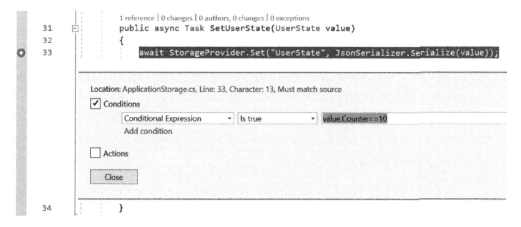

Figure 11.46 – Condition logic

Now when we start debugging, the breakpoint will only be hit when the value of the counter becomes 10. In *Figure 11.47*, we have stopped, and we have expanded the value of the UserState value:

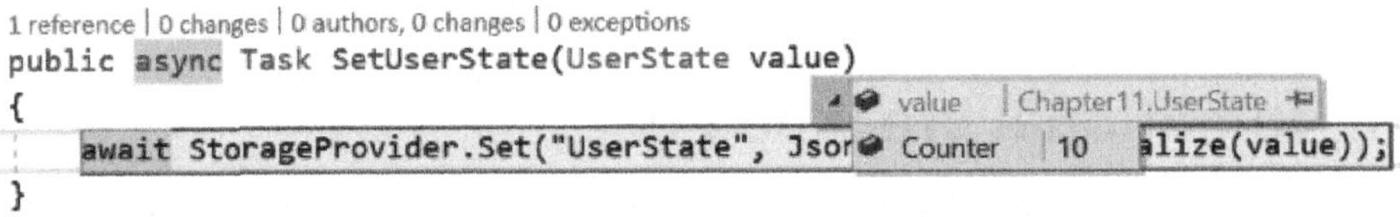

Figure 11.47 – Conditionally triggered breakpoint

This is just a taste of what Visual Studio can do to help you debug your ASP.NET Core applications. We will include some links for further reading.

Summary

In this chapter, we covered different tooling that will help in developing ASP.NET Core applications. We looked at common functionality supported in all major browsers. This included viewing log messages, debugging code, reviewing the network, and looking at the files and storage of our application.

We also looked at what support Visual Studio has for debugging and running ASP.NET Core applications. We looked at adjusting the logging level of our application. We also used breakpoints to stop the execution for us to view and update variables.

The next chapter will cover automating our deployments using GitHub Actions. This will provide us with a better way of getting our ASP.NET Core projects delivered in a more efficient and consistent way than manually deploying them.

Questions

1. Are PWAs run in the browser or on a server?

2. In a system that maintains stock levels for a company, if I wanted to save the details of a product so that others can view them, should I use session storage, local storage, or a database?

3. Is Chrome the only browser that supports developer tools?

4. Can Visual Studio debug JavaScript?

Further reading

- Information about PWAs by Mozilla Developer Network: `https://developer.mozilla.org/en-US/docs/Web/Progressive_web_apps`

- Information about PWAs by Google Developers: `https://developers.google.com/web/ilt/pwa`

- Information about PWAs by Microsoft Docs: `https://docs.microsoft.com/en-us/microsoft-edge/progressive-web-apps-chromium/`

- *Progressive Web Application Development by Example* by Chris Love, from Packt Publishing, available at `https://subscription.packtpub.com/book/application_development/9781787125421`

- Information about JavaScript interoperability by Microsoft Docs: `https://docs.microsoft.com/en-us/aspnet/core/blazor/call-javascript-from-dotnet`

- Information about Chrome DevTools: `https://developers.google.com/web/tools/chrome-devtools`

- Information about Edge Developer Tools: `https://docs.microsoft.com/en-us/microsoft-edge/devtools-guide`

- Visual Studio Debugging tour at Microsoft Docs: `https://docs.microsoft.com/en-us/visualstudio/debugger/debugger-feature-tour?view=vs-2019`

- Visual Studio Debugging documentation: `https://docs.microsoft.com/en-us/visualstudio/debugger/?view=vs-2019`

12
Integrating
with CI/CD

In the previous chapter, we looked at how both the browser and Visual Studio assist us in developing our ASP.NET Core applications. As we saw, great tools and IDEs help us to build high-quality software.

In this chapter, we will look at how best practices in software development also contribute to building better software. Our example of best practices will be **continuous integration (CI)** and **continuous delivery (CD)**.

We will cover the following topics in this chapter:

- An overview of CI/CD
- Introducing GitHub
- Building CI/CD using GitHub Actions

By the end of the chapter, you will have a good understanding of how CI/CD fits into the **software delivery lifecycle (SDLC)**. You will learn the benefits of CI/CD, as well as what challenges are addressed by applying CI/CD. You will understand how GitHub provides support for building CI/CD workflows. You will also have a practical example of deploying an ASP.NET Core project using CI/CD.

Technical requirements

In this chapter, we will only use GitHub to complete the practical example of deploying an ASP.NET Core project, using GitHub Actions. This means you will only need a modern browser, such as Chrome, Edge, Firefox, or Safari, and a GitHub account. GitHub offers a free account that is suitable for all steps covered in this chapter.

You will need a GitHub account to complete the steps. The page `https://github.com/join` can be used to create an account.

GitHub source

The source code for this chapter is in the GitHub repository at `https://github.com/PacktPublishing/ASP.NET-Core-5-for-Beginners/tree/master/Chapter%2012`.

Please visit the following link to check the CiA videos: `https://bit.ly/3qDiqYY`

An overview of CI/CD

CI and CD are modern approaches to software delivery, where automation is used to improve quality and reduce delay. In this section, we will define CI/CD and explore the issues addressed by this best practice.

First, let's provide some background.

Understanding why CI/CD

In order to appreciate CI/CD, let's describe a typical development process *Figure 12.1* shows the development process:

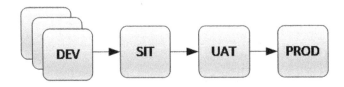

Figure 12.1 – Development process

In the previous diagram, we are showing how we might have a team of developers all developing software on their own devices. The developer changes are then promoted to a **systems integration** (**SIT**) environment for initial testing. Once these have been verified, the changes then progress to a **user acceptance testing** (**UAT**) environment. Again, after a round of testing, these changes are progressed into **production** (**PROD**) with a reasonable amount of confidence.

At some point, the team wants its latest changes to be deployed to the SIT environment. It might be the responsibility of one of the developers to get the latest changes on to their development machine and build and produce a package for the SIT environment. One issue with this is as the changes are being made on different development machines, there is the potential for one change to impact another change. This might not be discovered until the build for SIT is created.

Another issue with this approach is because the build is being performed on a development machine, required build dependencies might not be discovered until a build is performed on another machine. Imagine a scenario where the developer who usually performs the builds is having a well-deserved break. Of course, instructions were left on how to perform the build and create a package of the latest changes, but a dependency was missed. It could be a costly exercise to find the missing dependency.

These issues are addressed with CI.

Continuous integration

CI increases the confidence we have in the code we are producing by using automation. The steps for the building of a package varies, but the following are the key points about CI:

- The source is maintained in a version-controlled repository.
- The source is built in a known environment.
- The building of the source is automated.

By having the source in a version-controlled repository, like GitHub, for example, we have confidence that only what we want to have changed has changed. This ensures our development team all merge to the same location, and we can review the merges to make sure they are complete and accurate.

By building the source in a known environment, we ensure that all required dependencies are available. In most situations, a known environment would be a dedicated build machine or VM. In the *Building CI/CD using GitHub Actions* section, we will be using Linux VMs that have been provided by GitHub. This means we have a consistent platform to use for our build, and if there are any required dependencies, we are responsible for ensuring they are made available. For example, we require .NET 5.0 to be available to build our sample application, and this will be added to the Linux VM as a separate step.

The building of the source will be automated. This both improves efficiency and reliability. It is more efficient for an automated series of steps to be run as it frees individuals up so they can concentrate on other activities. This is more reliable as we remove the possibility of a human forgetting to perform a step.

> **Note**
>
> A common step in CI is to run unit tests. Unit tests are tests designed to verify functionality. These tests can be manually run, or they can be run as part of the build process.

By automating the build process and performing the packaging of the solution in a known environment, we have been able to increase efficiency and improve our confidence in the changes our development team is making. As we know from studies of the SDLC, the sooner an issue is detected, the less costly it is to fix. By identifying any build failures or breaks in functionality before the change has been deployed, we have greatly reduced the cost of fixing these issues. Before CI, broken builds might have only be detected before a release was required, so it might have been days since the original change was made. In the *Creating a CI/CD workflow* section, we will set our CI to be performed with each check-in to the repository.

Next, we will look at how CD can be used to improve the delivery process.

Continuous delivery

Now, imagine if each environment was made up of several servers. As an example, let's take a load-balanced example, as shown in *Figure 12.2*:

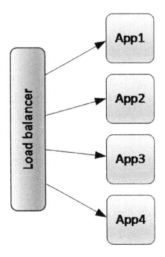

Figure 12.2 – Load-balanced application

It is possible that each environment has a different number of servers. For example, SIT might only require two servers, while PROD, being more heavily used, might require 10 or more servers. The important point here is that different environments might vary, and for a single release, multiple servers may need to be updated.

Additionally, each release of the software might require multiple steps. For example, imagine we are releasing an ASP.NET Core application. For each release, we may need to remove the previous version, add the new version of the application, and then perform some custom configuration. The details are not important. What is important is that we have a series of steps that must be followed accurately, otherwise the released software might not run correctly. Before automation, the process would have been done manually. Manual steps introduce the potential for mistakes and missed steps.

Like CI, CD uses automation to greatly improve the efficiency and confidence of the delivery process. As each environment might require multiple servers to be updated, and for each server, multiple steps, avoiding a manual process makes sense to save time as well as to reduce the chance of mistakes when a step is not followed correctly or is missed.

> **Note**
> Continuous deployment refers to when every change progresses all the way into the final environment, after passing all required checks. In short, the entire process is automated, and only the changes failing an automated test are prevented from being released.

In short, CI/CD uses automation to greatly improve the SDLC by making the release of new software changes more efficient and more predictable. Through the addition of automated tests, we can improve the confidence that changes are not incorrectly altering the behavior in unexpected ways. By detecting issues as early as possible, we greatly reduce the cost of fixing them. Automation helps our teams to work more effectively as they are not performing the build and deployment steps manually. And automation helps reduce the mistakes that arise from manual tasks due to human error.

Now that we have a good understanding of CI/CD, let's look at what support GitHub has for CI/CD in the next section.

Introducing GitHub

In this section, we'll look at GitHub and its support for CI/CD. GitHub is a provider of hosted tools enabling many capabilities required for software development. The backbone of GitHub is Git, a reliable source code version control system. But GitHub is more than just Git and offers online utilities that meet many requirements of distributed software development.

> **Note**
>
> Azure DevOps is another Microsoft service for building CI/CD. In many ways, the experience of building CI/CD is the same, and we encourage you to take the time to investigate Azure DevOps, as it may provide a better CI/CD platform for your requirements. We will discuss Azure DevOps in *Chapter 13, Cloud Native*.

In the next section, we will look at the different plans supported by GitHub.

Is GitHub free?

Yes, the base services provided are free. For many community projects and/or projects involving smaller teams, the free subscription works well. Let's briefly look at how the different plans compare, as shown in the following table.

Free	Team	Enterprise (includes all of the Team plan)
Unlimited public and private repos	Unlimited public and private repos	Unlimited public and private repos
Unlimited collaborators	Code owners and required reviewers	SAML single sign-on
2,000 Actions minutes per month	3,000 Actions minutes per month	50,000 Actions minutes per month
500 MB of GitHub Packages storage	2 GB of GitHub Packages storage	50 GB of GitHub Packages storage

Note that there is also a GitHub One plan, which provides everything in the Enterprise plan while adding more features for larger enterprises, such as 24/7 support, more metrics, and access to Learning Lab courses.

The great thing is you can join under a free subscription, and when your situation changes so that you require more storage or actions per month, you can upgrade your plan to the appropriate plan.

In the next sections, we will review some of the features of GitHub before we proceed to our CI/CD example.

Some Git terminology

As we have been using GitHub in the previous chapters, we assume some familiarity with Git. So far, it could have been possible to complete all chapters without creating your own *fork* of the code. A fork is a copy of a repository, often called a repo for short, that will sit in your account. This means you can do anything you want with it, including making changes. You might find an issue when upgrading some packages to later versions, for example. This would then allow you to fix the change, verify it worked, and post the changes back to the original repo, called a *master*.

There are several other terms you should be familiar with for this chapter, so we've listed them in the following table:

Repository, repo	A collection of version-controlled files
Fork	Copy of a repo
Master	Original copy of a repo
Branch	A copy of the repo pointing to a version of the repo
Commit	A version of the repo files
Merge	The joining of two or more versions of the repo. Think of this as blending the two histories together
Pull	Retrieves the commits from the source branch that do not exist in the target branch
Push	Sends the commits from the source branch to the target branch
Pull Request	A way of notifying others about changes in a source branch that should be merged into a target branch

The preceding table simplifies the terms to a degree, but it is enough for us to provide our example for CI/CD. We'll include some references in the *Further reading* section at the end of the chapter.

In the next section, we will perform a fork of the Packt library.

Making a copy of the repo

If you have not already created a fork, you do this by using the **Fork** button on the Packt source page at `https://github.com/PacktPublishing/ASP.NET-Core-5-for-Beginners` as shown in *Figure 12.3*:

Figure 12.3 – Fork

This will create your own copy in your GitHub account. From here, we will be able to complete setting up CI/CD in the CI/CD using GitHub Actions.

Before we do, let's cover some of the other features of GitHub besides providing Git.

GitHub support for CI/CD

GitHub Actions is available with all free subscriptions and provides support for automating the build and deployment of applications. These don't have to be web-based applications or even applications at all. For example, some organizations use GitHub for document management and GitHub Actions for distributing the documentation within an organization. But we are interested in using GitHub Actions to implement CI/CD, and this section will provide an overview of what GitHub Actions can do.

GitHub Actions allows us to define a series of steps, called a workflow, that can be triggered by a specified event. The event can be based on another event, scheduled, or manually triggered. For example, in the Building *CI/CD using GitHub Actions* section, we will use the Git push event to trigger our workflow.

Each workflow can consist of one or more jobs. A job is a series of sequential steps designed to run on a specified type of runner. Think of a runner as a class of VM. For example, you might have a requirement to build a Windows package or to use a specific type of hardware. The runner defines what type of machine is required. The runner can be GitHub-hosted or self-hosted. In our CI/CD example, we will be using a GitHub-hosted Linux VM to build our ASP.NET Core application. This is because the target environment that we will be hosting our application in is Linux.

Within a single workflow, it is possible to use a combination of runners. For example, you might have a single workflow that performs two jobs. The first is to build a Windows image, and the second builds a Linux image. One workflow will run on a Windows runner while the second will run on a Linux runner. By default, each job will run in parallel. In our CI/CD example, we will show how a dependency can be created between two jobs. When a dependency is created, the jobs are not run in parallel but in dependency order.

As we said earlier, a job is a series of steps. Each step can be either an action or a command. An action is a combination of commands. These are made public by GitHub or members of the community. You can also author your own actions. For example, your organization might have a proprietary signing process that you want to use in several workflows. You can then author a private action and reference it in your workflows. We will use both action and command steps in the CI/CD example in the following section.

The workflow is defined in a YAML file. If you remember from *Chapter 9, Containers*, YAML is a file format that has been designed to be human-readable with minimum syntax. This does mean that whitespace, for example, tabs and space characters, is significant. Fortunately, GitHub has a YAML editor that both provides IntelliSense and visible hints to help the authoring process. We'll use the editor in the next section when we create our CI/CD workflow.

Now that we have a background in CI/CD and GitHub Actions, let's proceed to the next section and create our CI/CD workflow to deliver our ASP.NET Core application.

Building CI/CD using GitHub Actions

Now that we have discussed CI/CD and had a look at some of the capabilities provided by GitHub, let's have a look at using GitHub Actions to deploy an ASP.NET Core application. As we have forked the Packt master into our own repo in the previous section, *Making a copy of the repo*, we are ready to begin.

Our plan is to deploy an ASP.NET Core WASM application to GitHub Pages. We covered the sample WASM application in the previous chapter. The next section gives an overview of GitHub Pages.

What is GitHub Pages?

GitHub Pages is a convenient and powerful way to host a static website using all the power of GitHub, including global distribution, without worrying about hosting. In many cases, it is a convenient way to host a website with information about the repository it is associated with. But there is no reason why it cannot be used in other circumstances. For example, in Google or Bing, search `build a blog in GitHub Pages` as an example. And, as the static website is sourced in GitHub, the site content is stored in a private or public version-controlled repository.

The source of the static website can either be a special folder in your main branch called /docs, or it can be a separate branch. In our example, we are going to publish the content of the project to a separate branch. GitHub Pages is normally powered by Jekyll, a static website generator. In our case, we don't need static to power our website, so we need to disable Jekyll.

This is done by simply creating a file called .nojekyll. In GitHub, navigate to the wwwroot folder inside of the Chapter 12 sample project. Remember to do this in the forked copy we made previously as shown in *Figure 12.4*:

Figure 12.4 – Create a new file

In the previous screenshot, we can see both the location of the wwwroot folder and the dropdown to create a new file. Once selected, simply enter the name, .nojekyll, and save by committing the change as shown in *Figure 12.5*:

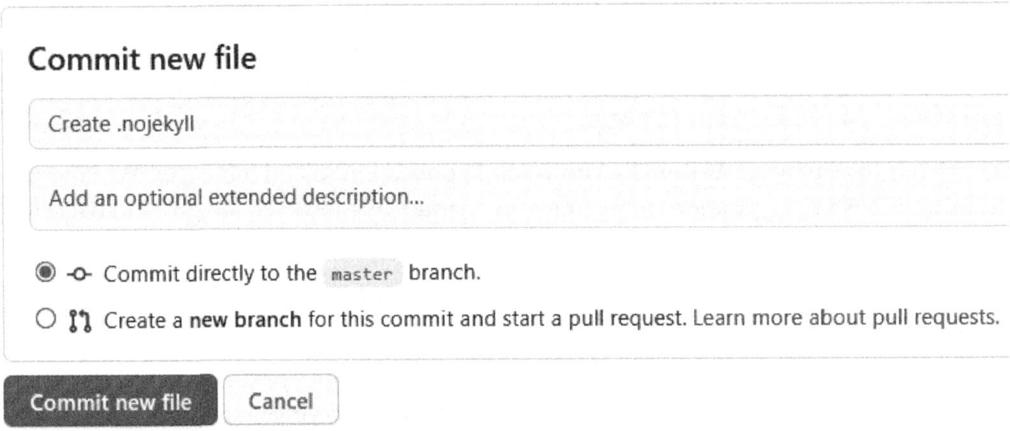

Commit new file

Create .nojekyll

Add an optional extended description...

⦿ ⎓ Commit directly to the `master` branch.

◯ ⌥ Create a **new branch** for this commit and start a pull request. Learn more about pull requests.

[Commit new file]   [Cancel]

Figure 12.5 – Commit new file

By placing the file in the wwwroot folder, the file will be included when we publish the website later. Now that will let GitHub know we don't need Jekyll, let's get started with GitHub Actions.

Creating a CI/CD workflow

GitHub Actions allows us to build a CI/CD workflow. In other tools for managing CI/CD, such as Azure DevOps, which we will talk about in *Chapter 13, Cloud Native*, you see this referred to as a pipeline. The term CI/CD pipeline, or workflow, basically refers to a sequence of automated actions. In our example, we will have two main jobs in this sequence: building the project and deploying the project.

These actions are contained in a YAML file. Let's go ahead and create one. In GitHub, click on **Actions** in the menu bar as shown in *Figure 12.6*:

Figure 12.6 – Actions menu

As our repository does not have any existing actions, we are greeted with several options, including several templates to help us get started. Have a read through them to get an idea of the different supported scenarios, and when ready, select the option to **set up a workflow yourself** as shown in *Figure 12.7*:

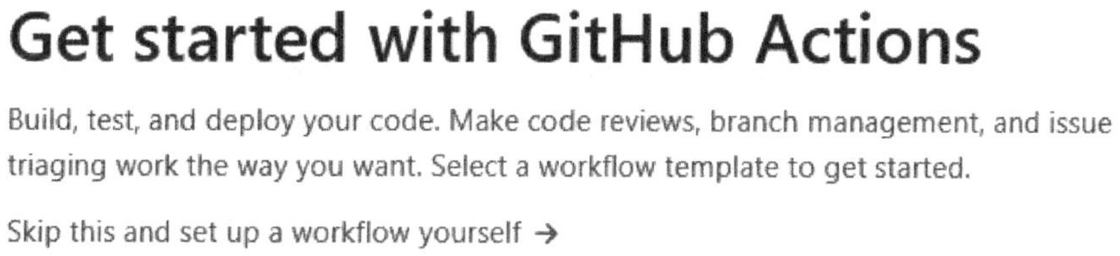

Get started with GitHub Actions

Build, test, and deploy your code. Make code reviews, branch management, and issue triaging work the way you want. Select a workflow template to get started.

Skip this and set up a workflow yourself →

Figure 12. 7 – Set up a workflow yourself

This will create a starting YAML file, but let's replace the generated file with the following content so we can explain the different parts as we complete them:

```yaml
name: Build and Deploy ASP .NET Core Chapter 12 to GitHub Pages

on:
  # trigger the workflow only when a push happens in Chapter 12

jobs:
  build:
    steps:
      # steps to build the application

  deploy:
```

```
steps:
    # steps to deploy the application
```

The name is useful to describe the workflow. A good name is useful in identifying the purpose of the workflow. Imagine you have one workflow for deploying to a development environment or a production environment. This should be reflected in the name to avoid confusion.

Next, we define what triggers our workflow. This can range from a manual trigger to pulls or pulls to the repository, or on a schedule. The different capabilities can be found in the *Further reading* section at the end of the chapter.

Go ahead and replace the existing comment as follows:

```
on:
  push:
    branches: [ master ]
    paths:
    - 'Chapter 12/Chapter_12_GitHubActions_Examples/**'
```

The previous code snippet will cause the workflow to trigger when a push is performed on the master branch in the `Chapter 12` folder. This means whenever a change is committed to the repository in any folder under `Chapter 12`, this workflow will be run.

Now that we have the trigger defined, let's complete the build job in the next section.

Creating a continuous integration job

In this section, we will define our CI or build job. This job will comprise the following steps:

1. Retrieve the source code from the repository.

2. Set up the .NET environment.

3. Publish the ASP.NET Core application.

4. Save the published application as an artifact.

After you read the list, you might wonder why we have the first couple of steps?

The answer brings us to the first part of setting up our job. Each job runs on build runners. These are pre-configured Windows or Linux VMs. You can use your own runners, known as self-hosted runners. For our purposes, we will use a Linux VM by adding the following code snippet shown in bold:

```
jobs:
  build:
    runs-on: ubuntu-latest
    steps:
```

Now that we have specified that our build job should be run on a Linux VM, let's add our first step:

1. After the `steps:` line, add the following code snippet:

    ```
    - uses: actions/checkout@v2
    ```

    There are two main types of steps: `run` and `uses`. The `run` step is used to execute commands on the runner. The `uses` command will execute a community action. Think of a community action as a repository containing a group of `run` statements created to accomplish a task. In the previous code snippet, we are executing version 2 of the checkout community action. The checkout action will check out the repository so the workflow can access it.

    > **Note**
    >
    > You can read the details on the checkout repository at `https://github.com/actions/checkout`.

2. The next step sets up .NET on the runner. Unless we set up the .NET environment, the runner will not be able to run any required `dotnet` commands:

    ```
    - uses: actions/setup-dotnet@v1
          with:
            dotnet-version: '5.0'
    ```

    In the previous code snippet, we will be using the community `setup-dotnet@v1` action, and we need to specify the version of .NET we require.

3. The next step is to run the `publish` command. This is shown in the following code block:

```
- name: Publish app
      run: dotnet publish -c Release './Chapter 12/
  Chapter_12_GitHubActions_Examples/Chapter12.csproj'
```

The previous command illustrates how a name can be associated with a step, and this is supported for `uses` steps also. The command to publish has the `Release` configuration specified as well as the project file that we are publishing.

4. In order to be able to reference the published application in the next job, we are going to publish or save the published application as an artifact. You have 500 MB of storage, so we are going to use some of that to store our published application:

```
- name: Save artifacts
      uses: actions/upload-artifact@v2
      with:
        name: myWASM
        path: './Chapter 12/Chapter_12_GitHubActions_
  Examples/bin/Release/net5.0/publish/wwwroot'
```

The previous snippet will upload the content specified in the `path` parameter as an artifact called myWASM.

This completes the first job called `build`. This workflow will run whenever a check-in is published to `Chapter 12`. The source will be downloaded to a Linux runner, it will be built, and the output will be saved as an artifact. The completed job is shown in the next code snippet:

```
  steps:
  - uses: actions/checkout@v2
  - uses: actions/setup-dotnet@v1
    with:
      dotnet-version: '5.0'
  - name: Publish app
    run: dotnet publish -c Release './Chapter 12/
        Chapter_12_GitHubActions_Examples/Chapter12.csproj'
  - name: Save artifacts
    uses: actions/upload-artifact@v2
    with:
      name: myWASM
```

```
path: './Chapter 12/Chapter_12_GitHubActions_Examples/
       bin/Release/net5.0/publish/wwwroot'
```

Now that the CI part of our workflow has been defined, let's proceed to the CD part.

Creating a continuous deployment job

In this section, we will define a CD job to deploy the published artifact to a new repository called `pages`. To do this, we need to set up the `pages` repository, download our artifact, and then save the changes.

> **Note**
>
> The CD job has been created using basic Git commands. We suggest exploring community actions instead of always writing your own. One of the benefits of GitHub is you are part of a large community of developers. GitHub Marketplace is a great place to start.

Like our CI job, we also must specify the build runner to use to run our job. We will also use a Linux VM as indicated in the following snippet:

```
deploy:
  needs: build
  runs-on: ubuntu-latest
  steps:
```

Also, notice the difference shown in the preceding code snippet, when compared to the CI job. We have specified that the `build` job needs to have completed without error before the `deploy` job will run. If we had not done this, then both the `build` and the `deploy` jobs would be run in parallel. In our case, this would not work, because we need the artifact published in the `build` job in order to deploy to GitHub Pages:

1. Like the first step in the `build` job, we will first perform a checkout to set up our GitHub workspace on our VM:

    ```
    - uses: actions/checkout@v2
    ```

2. Next, we will create a new branch to contain our GitHub Pages WASM application:

    ```
    - name: Create pages branch
      continue-on-error: true
      run: |
        git config --global user.name "GitHub Actions"
    ```

```
git config --global user.email "your@email.com"
git checkout -B pages
```

The preceding series of commands first sets up information about the current user. This provides GitHub with context and will be used when the check-ins are performed. The next step issues a command to switch to the pages branch. The -B flag will create a new branch, if one does not already exist.

3. The next step in our job is to clear the branch of the existing files:

```
- name: Clear pages branch
    continue-on-error: true
  run: |
      git rm -rf .
      git commit --allow-empty -m "root commit"
      git push -f origin pages
```

The preceding code will remove any existing files, commit the change to the repository, and then push this back to the repository. This step is required, in case we already have files in the repository from a previous deployment.

4. Now that we have cleaned the folder, we want to download the output that we created in the build job:

```
- name: Download build artifact
    uses: actions/download-artifact@v2
    with:
    name: myWASM
```

The preceding command uses a community action to download the artifact called myWASM.

5. The final step will commit the changes back to the pages branch:

```
- name: Commit changes
  run: |
      git add .
      git commit -m "publishing WASM"
      git push --set-upstream origin pages
```

In the previous command, the files from the downloaded artifact are added back to the repository, committed, and then pushed back to the repository.

This completes our workflow. Go ahead and save the file and proceed to the next section.

Monitoring actions

Now that our CI/CD workflow has been defined, it is time for us to trigger the workflow. As we have used the path filter on changes made to the `Chapter 12` folder, let's edit one of the files.

In the `Code` tab, navigate to the `wwwroot` folder as shown in *Figure 12.8*:

Figure 12.8 – wwwroot folder

In that folder, select the `index.html` file and use the pencil icon to edit the file as shown in *Figure 12.9*:

Figure 12.9 – Pencil icon

Go ahead and change the text in the title element as shown in *Figure 12.10*:

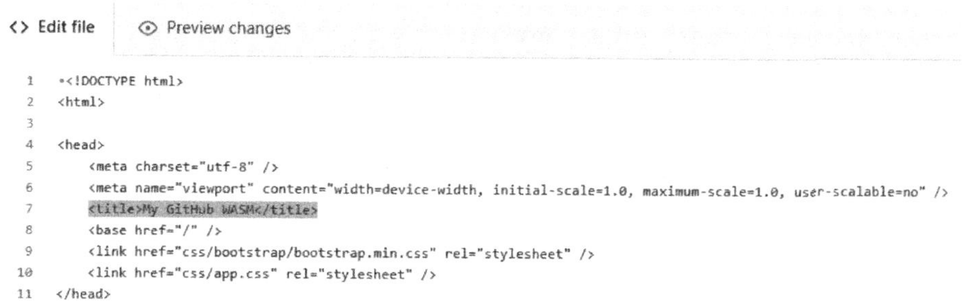

```
1   *<!DOCTYPE html>
2   <html>
3
4   <head>
5       <meta charset="utf-8" />
6       <meta name="viewport" content="width=device-width, initial-scale=1.0, maximum-scale=1.0, user-scalable=no" />
7       <title>My GitHub WASM</title>
8       <base href="/" />
9       <link href="css/bootstrap/bootstrap.min.css" rel="stylesheet" />
10      <link href="css/app.css" rel="stylesheet" />
11  </head>
```

Figure 12.10 – Editing the title

After committing the change, navigate to the **Actions** tab. You should see something similar to *Figure 12.11*:

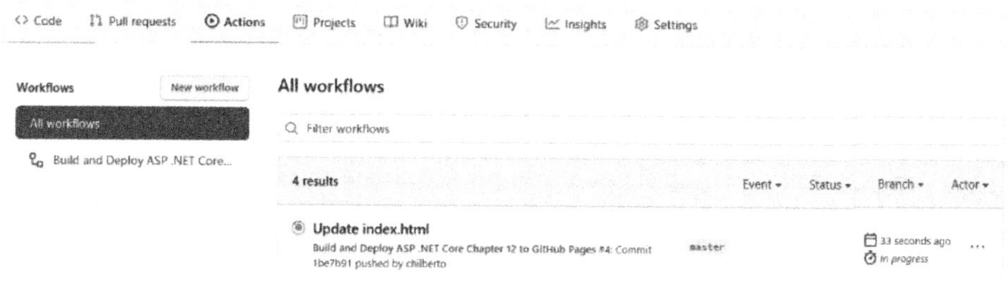

Workflows | New workflow | **All workflows**

All workflows

Q Filter workflows

Build and Deploy ASP .NET Core...

4 results | | | | Event ▾ | Status ▾ | Branch ▾ | Actor ▾

Update index.html
Build and Deploy ASP .NET Core Chapter 12 to GitHub Pages #4: Commit 1be7b91 pushed by chilberto | master | 33 seconds ago | In progress

Figure 12.11 – All workflows

This shows that a workflow has been triggered and is currently running. The history of previous runs will be available. Let's click on the running workflow to see the details of what is happening.

This will change the view to show the jobs that are running in the workflow. In the *Figure 12.12*, the **Build and Deploy ASP.NET Core Chapter 12 to GitHub Pages** workflow includes two jobs, **build** and **deploy**, and has completed the workflow without error:

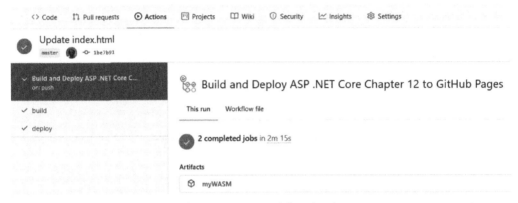

Figure 12.12 – Workflow detail

Also, notice how the produced artifact, **myWASM**, is shown. The artifact is a ZIP file, which allows you to download the file in case you need to troubleshoot any issues.

There is one last step we need to do before we can view our GitHub Pages.

Configuring GitHub Pages

In this section, we will set up GitHub Pages. We will be hosting the output of our CI/CD workflow using GitHub Pages, and fortunately, GitHub Pages provides a flexible way to select where in the repository the content is located:

1. GitHub Pages can be configured under the **Settings** tab:

Figure 12.13 – Settings

2. In **Settings**, scroll down until you find the section about **GitHub Pages**, as shown in *Figure 12.13*:

GitHub Pages

GitHub Pages is designed to host your personal, organization, or project pages from a GitHub repository.

Figure 12.14 – GitHub Pages

The previous figure shows that GitHub Pages is currently disabled.

3. To enable it, we select the **pages** branch as shown in *Figure 12.15*:

Figure 12.15 – The pages branch

4. After saving, the URL of your GitHub Pages site will be shown. It should be similar to *Figure 12.16*:

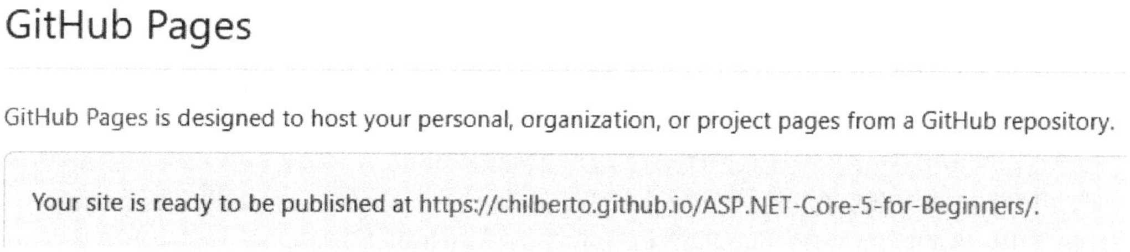

GitHub Pages

GitHub Pages is designed to host your personal, organization, or project pages from a GitHub repository.

Your site is ready to be published at https://chilberto.github.io/ASP.NET-Core-5-for-Beginners/.

Figure 12.16 – GitHub Pages published URL

5.   After clicking on the URL, we will encounter an issue as seen in *Figure 12.17*:

Loading...
An unhandled error has occurred. Reload ✕

Figure 12.17 – Loading issue

6.   If you review the errors in the browser's developer tools (press *F12* to access them), you will see several of the files are not able to be loaded as shown in *Figure 12.18*:

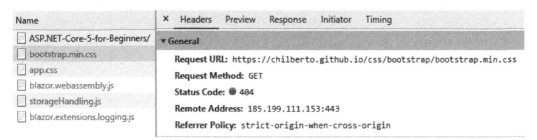

Figure 12.18 – 404 errors

7.   Go ahead and navigate to the **Network** tab and press refresh to load the page again. You should see the same network errors, but this time if you click one of the failed requests, you will get some additional information as shown in *Figure 12.19*:

Name	×	Headers	Preview	Response	Initiator	Timing
ASP.NET-Core-5-for-Beginners/	▾ General					
bootstrap.min.css						
app.css		**Request URL:** https://chilberto.github.io/css/bootstrap/bootstrap.min.css				
blazor.webassembly.js		**Request Method:** GET				
storageHandling.js		**Status Code:** ● 404				
blazor.extensions.logging.js		**Remote Address:** 185.199.111.153:443				
		Referrer Policy: strict-origin-when-cross-origin				

Figure 12.19 – Request URL

In the preceding figure, notice the URL is not constructed correctly. The correct URL should have the name of our repository included. In the example, this would be `https://chilberto.github.io/ASP.NET-Core-5-for-Beginners/css/bootstrap/bootstrap.min.css`.

Fortunately, the fix is simple.

Fixing the base reference

In this section, we will set the base reference for our website. We need to do this as GitHub is not hosting the pages at the root of the website but under the repository name. This means we need to insert the repository name into the URL:

1. Back in the **Code** tab, navigate to the wwwroot folder and select the index.html file. In the file, locate the base element as shown in *Figure 12.20*:

```
26 lines (22 sloc)  781 Bytes

1    <!DOCTYPE html>
2    <html>
3
4    <head>
5        <meta charset="utf-8" />
6        <meta name="viewport" content="width=device-width, initial-scale=1.0, maximum-scale=1.0, user-scalable=no" />
7        <title>My GitHub WASM</title>
8        <base href="/" />
9        <link href="css/bootstrap/bootstrap.min.css" rel="stylesheet" />
10       <link href="css/app.css" rel="stylesheet" />
11   </head>
```

Figure 12.20 – Updating the base element

2. Update this line to be the following:

```
<base href="/ASP.NET-Core-5-for-Beginners/" />
```

3. After committing the change, the workflow will be triggered again. Wait until this has completed.

4. Once done, refresh the GitHub Pages, and you should see the ASP.NET Core WASM application as shown in *Figure 12.21*:

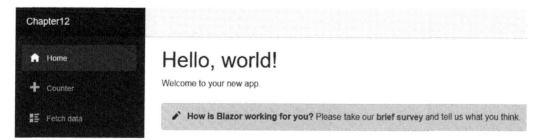

Figure 12.21 – Hello, world!

Depending on your browser and the speed of GitHub refreshing the change, you might need to wait an additional minute before you notice the change. If the change still is not reflected, try clearing or disabling your browser's cache.

You can do this on the **Network** tab by selecting **Disable cache** as shown in *Figure 12.22*:

Figure 12.22 – Disable cache

After we have disabled the cache on the **Network** tab, and now that we have a basic CI/CD workflow running, let's look a bit more into what is happening.

Logging the CI/CD workflow

Unfortunately, sometimes things don't work. One of the reasons to automate the build and deployment of applications is to prevent human error, but how do we investigate when there is something not working with our CI/CD workflow? This section will break our CI/CD workflow to illustrate how to investigate when there are issues in a build step:

1. To do this, let's cause a syntax error in our code. In the code branch, navigate to the project file as shown in *Figure 12.23*:

Figure 12.23 – Breaking the project

2. Inside the project file, find the section that specifies the target framework as shown in *Figure 12.24*:

```
<PropertyGroup>
    <TargetFramework>net5.0</TargetFramework>
</PropertyGroup>
```

Figure 12.24 – Target framework

The previous screenshot shows the project file is specifying .NET 5.0 as the target framework.

3. Go ahead and change this value to `netcoreapp3.1`, as shown in the next code snippet:

```
<TargetFramework>netcoreapp3.1</TargetFramework>
```

After committing the file, the workflow will start automatically, but then it will fail when the ASP.NET Core project is published.

4. Click on **Actions** and then running workflow and monitor the workflow until it fails as depicted in *Figure 12.25*:

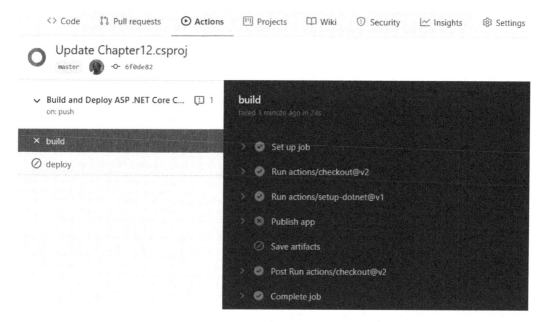

Figure 12.25 – Failure publishing app

The preceding screenshot shows the status of the workflow after the failure. Notice how the **build** step indicates the **Publish app** step failed. Also notice that the following step, **Save artifacts**, did not run. And, the following job, **deploy**, also did not run as we had specified that it had a dependency on the **build** job completing without error.

5. We can expand the **Publish app** step to view additional details. Have a look through the log to find where the error is reported. An example of this is given in *Figure 12.26*:

```
33    /home/runner/work/ASP.NET-Core-5-for-Beginne
      Microsoft.AspNetCore.Components.WebAssembly
      supports: net5.0 (.NETCoreApp,Version=v5.0)
34      Failed to restore /home/runner/work/ASP.NE
35    Error: Process completed with exit code 1.
```

Figure 12.26 – Error reported

6. Take a moment to find the cause of the failure. You should find the text *5.0.0 is not compatible with netcoreapp3.1*, which indicates that the packages we are trying to use are not compatible with the .NET Core 3.1 framework.

There is one nice feature we would like to highlight. You will notice that each line in the log is numbered. If you click on the number, then you will notice the URL changes. For example, we clicked on the first failure on line 32 and our URL changed to `https://github.com/chilberto/ASP.NET-Core-5-for-Beginners/runs/1409342784?check_suite_focus=true#step:4:32`. The URL can then be shared with other teammates, and instead of saying *the build is broken, please investigate*, the URL can be sent to teammates to direct them immediately to the reported issue.

We will include more information about GitHub Actions in *Further reading* as we have only highlighted some of the basic functionality and features.

Next steps with GitHub Actions

There are many features in GitHub Actions that are worth mentioning, especially when we consider enterprise scenarios. In the example we used in the previous sections, we are deploying to a single environment, and in many enterprise scenarios, there will be multiple environments. Each environment might require a different configuration, for example, connection strings. One way of solving this requirement is by using **secrets**.

A repository secret is an encrypted variable that can be used in a GitHub Action. In both public and private repositories, only users with the appropriate access can view and maintain secrets. A secret is defined in the **Settings** sub-menu as indicated in *Figure 12.27*:

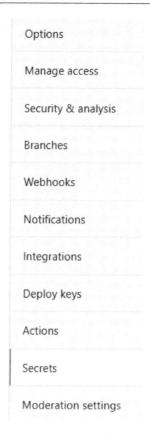

Figure 12.27 – GitHub Secrets

Once the secret has been defined, it can be accessed in a GitHub action. As an example, let's say we have three secrets defined for each environment's database access as shown in *Figure 12.27*:

Secrets

New repository secret

Secrets are environment variables that are **encrypted**. Anyone with **collaborator** access to this repository can use these secrets for Actions.

Secrets are not passed to workflows that are triggered by a pull request from a fork. Learn more.

🔒	PROD_DATABASE_KEY	Updated 2 minutes ago	Update	Remove
🔒	QA_DATABASE_KEY	Updated 1 minute ago	Update	Remove
🔒	SIT_DATABASE_KEY	Updated 1 minute ago	Update	Remove

Figure 12.28 – Defining secrets

In a GitHub Action, the value can be accessed by using the following syntax:

```
${{ secrets.QA_DATABASE_KEY }}
```

In the preceding code, the value held in the QA_DATABASE_KEY secret will be substituted into the action. This is both more secure than storing in our YAML file, and it provides a convenient way to reuse the same script for multiple environments.

To see why it is more secure, we need to look at our workflow. In the repository, navigate back to the root of the repository as shown in *Figure 12.29*:

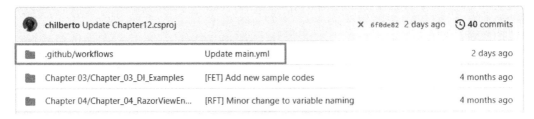

Figure 12.29 – .github/workflows folder

In the previous screenshot, we can see a folder, `.github/workflows`, has been created. This location is where GitHub stores the workflows in the repository. If you look inside the folder, you will see the workflow we created earlier:

Figure 12.30 – main.yml

Another feature to highlight is the GitHub API. The GitHub API provides a programmatic way to access GitHub. This can be combined with GitHub Actions by setting the workflow to be triggered, based on a GitHub API event. For example, imagine a scenario where a release to production only happens when the testing lead approves the release. This might be done in another system designed to manage test cases called **SystemX**. When the approval is done, SystemX uses a webhook to notify GitHub by creating a tag. A tag is a common way of marking a release.

> **Note**
>
> A webhook is a lightweight web service. See `https://docs.github.com/en/free-pro-team@latest/rest` for more information.

We then create a workflow that is triggered when a tag is created, by using the following:

```
on:
  create
```

This is one example of how different features can be used together to build a CI/CD process that fits your requirements.

Another important aspect to mention is the CI/CD process does not have to be combined into a single workflow. We did this in our example, but we could have had a separate CI and CD workflow. The CI workflow would still publish a package, and the CD workflow would be triggered when a package is added to the registry. The following code snippet provides the required trigger:

```
on:
  registry_package:
    types: [published]
```

We will include additional links in the *Further reading* section.

Summary

In this chapter, we discussed CI/CD and provided a practical example using GitHub Actions. CI/CD provides a better way of getting our ASP.NET Core projects delivered. It is more efficient than manual deployment and less error-prone. Even the simple sample application we provided has multiple deployment steps. For larger projects, the number of steps could become great enough to make deployment to large environments impractical.

GitHub has great support for CI/CD, using GitHub Actions. We automated both the build and deployment of an ASP.NET Core WASM application. The workflow used both commands and community actions. Our sample workflow was triggered by a Git push to the repository, and in the *Next steps with GitHub Actions* section, we highlighted how the GitHub API could be used to trigger workflows by other GitHub events.

In the next chapter, we will look at building cloud-native applications. This is more than just picking a great technology, for example, ASP.NET Core, for building your applications. We will look at different categories of cloud services. We will look at the design decisions that you need to make when building for the cloud, compared to more traditional applications.

Questions

1. Does GitHub Actions require a paid plan?

2. Can you only use GitHub for web applications?

3. Does GitHub Actions require both CI and CD to be in the same workflow?

4. Can you use CI/CD when deploying to cloud providers?

Further reading

- Git overview provided by Git at: `https://git-scm.com/`

- GitHub overview provided by the GitHub team at: `https://guides.github.com/activities/hello-world/`

- GitHub Actions provided by the GitHub team at: `https://docs.github.com/en/free-pro-team@latest/actions`

- Information about triggering workflows by the GitHub team at: `https://docs.github.com/en/free-pro-team@latest/actions/reference/events-that-trigger-workflows`

- *Progressive Web Application Development by Example* by Chris Love, from Packt Publishing, available at: `https://subscription.packtpub.com/book/application_development/9781787125421`

- *GitHub Essentials: Unleash the power of collaborative development workflows using GitHub, Second Edition* by Achilleas Pipinellis, from Packt Publishing at: `https://subscription.packtpub.com/book/web-development/9781789138337`

- *Implementing Azure DevOps Solutions* by Henry Been, Maik van der Gaag, from Packt Publishing at: `https://subscription.packtpub.com/book/cloud_and_networking/9781789619690`

13
Developing Cloud-Native Apps

No buzzword has been more prominent over the past couple of years than *cloud*, and for developers, this has been extended to the term *cloud-native apps*. Looking at the lower-level details in the C# language, you would expect these to work pretty much the same wherever the code is executed, so you are left wondering whether there is anything to it or whether it is just hype.

Chapter 10, *Deploying to AWS and Azure*, demonstrated a number of cloud deployments. In this chapter, we will dive deeper and go through things you need to understand and consider when building cloud-native applications, as well as reviewing concepts that are central to cloud computing.

We will cover the following areas in this chapter:

- What makes an application cloud-native?
- Understanding the role of DevOps
- Understanding cost in the cloud
- Cloud storage versus local disk
- Introducing Infrastructure as Code
- Learning about monitoring and health

This chapter covers both practical code examples to bolster the cloud developer role and theory that would be more in the realm of a cloud architect. The aim is not that you will be a fully fledged architect at the end of this chapter, but rather that you understand how some of the cloud paradigms affect you as a .NET developer.

Technical requirements

This chapter includes short code snippets to demonstrate the concepts that are explained. The following software is required to make these work:

- Visual Studio 2019: Visual Studio can be downloaded from `https://visualstudio.microsoft.com/vs/community/`. The Community edition is free and will work for the purposes of this book.

- Some of the samples require you to have an Azure subscription. If you don't have one already, you can create one by going to the Azure portal (`https://portal.azure.com`) and signing up for a free account.

- The DevOps examples refer to Azure DevOps. A single developer can sign up for a free account at `https://dev.azure.com`.

For lab purposes, all of the samples in this chapter are possible to test free of charge, but regional-specific requirements might require the use of a credit card for verification purposes.

The source code for this chapter is in the GitHub repository at `https://github.com/PacktPublishing/ASP.NET-Core-5-for-Beginners/tree/master/Chapter%2013`.

Please visit the following link to check the CiA videos: `https://bit.ly/3qDiqYY`

What makes an application cloud-native?

Before diving into how cloud applications are implemented, and what you need to consider, we need to look into what cloud apps are. This includes both definitions of cloud operating models in general, what makes the cloud different to on-premises, and an investigation of these differences in more detail. There is no standardized text book answer for the term *cloud-native*, or a list of checkboxes to tick, but this chapter attempts to shed some light on common practices associated with the term.

With cloud computing, you will hear all kinds of *as a Service* suffixes, with some making more sense than others. As explained in *Chapter 10, Deploying to AWS and Azure*, the pillars here are the following three acronyms:

- **IaaS – Infrastructure as a Service**
- **PaaS – Platform as a Service**
- **SaaS – Software as a Service**

A classic analogy for explaining these is *pizza as a service*. At one end of the spectrum, you have the scenario where you start in your kitchen with flour, tomatoes, and all the other ingredients needed. You have full control of everything and can customize things to your liking. At the other end of the spectrum, you are going to a restaurant where you point to an entry in a menu, wait a couple of minutes, and have it delivered to your table. In between, you have options where, for example, you buy pre-made dough and sauces to make it more of a LEGO-building experience at home.

If you are a good cook, you can probably get good results by making everything from scratch. However, even if you happen to enjoy this task, there is no denying that it is more work than dining out. If you happen to be a terrible cook, it is probably better to just place an order at your local pizza take-away.

To not drift too far from the technical themes, the responsibilities you have versus what the cloud provider is responsible for, can be illustrated as shown in *Figure 13.1*:

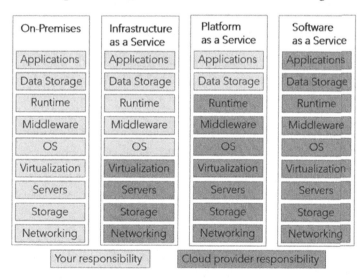

Figure 13.1 – XaaS responsibility

As you can see, more control means more responsibility.

We all love having the full range of options available to us that on-premises hardware gives us, but in practice, the restaurant experience can be pretty nice as well. Early cloud services were often too narrow to be used outside tightly defined boundaries, but these days there are usually a lot of ways to tweak the services to your liking, so this is less of an issue.

IaaS has advantages over the on-premises model, but most of these will be of less interest to developers than to individuals concerned with infrastructure. Having virtualized hardware is great, but most developers have already abstracted themselves away from figuring out which cable goes where in the back of a server rack. Going more or less directly from on-premises to IaaS is possible, due to the fact that the top five layers can be bundled into a **virtual machine** (**VM**).

If you're already running VMs on-premises, this move can be fairly easy, as it can be uploaded as it is with just a few operating system settings reconfigured. If you're not using virtualization and running directly on the server, or *bare metal* as it's often called, there are tools for migrating the workload to VMs that you can subsequently migrate to the cloud. This type of cloud migration is called **lift and shift**. While this is a possible, and sometimes recommended, re-hosting model, it is not considered *cloud-native*. A VM running in the cloud still means attending *Patch Tuesday*. (Microsoft releases patches every second Tuesday of the month, hence the nickname.)

SaaS is great for end users – some of these services can be purchased with very little technical insight and they *just work*. Of course, if you want to learn how to make a good pizza, it's of little help buying the finished product, so even though you may enjoy the services, it might not help you build new applications for your purpose.

As a developer, PaaS will usually be the sweet spot for building new services. Instead of building every piece of the stack yourself, you can pick the best pre-made components and build on top of these. For instance, you will need a web server of some sort, and you want to make sure it can run your programming language and associated frameworks, but you don't really care about the low-level details of how that is provided. And a web server itself is just an empty shell with no value before apps are installed.

Arguably you could say that a service such as Office 365 is both a SaaS and a PaaS, since it offers a rich API layer for integration with your own services, but such observations don't change the basic models.

This will serve as useful background information, when we delve into the next topic, where we compare classic on-premises characteristics to the cloud equivalents.

Comparing characteristics of on-premises versus the cloud

The first thing many say when they hear about cloud computing is that's it's just another data center, and that it's really no different than putting up a couple of racks on your own, as long as you install the right software. And in one sense, that is correct. While most companies cannot afford the scale of Azure and Amazon, you have options for installing various cloud solutions on-premises, thereby replicating the experience.

There are still a couple of differences, though, and you can talk about there being different mindsets. In *Figure 13.2*, you can see a comparison of the traits of classic on-premises software versus the cloud-native models:

On-premises	Cloud
Monolithic, centralized	Microservices, decentralized
Designed for predictable scalability	Designed for elastic / dynamic scalability
Relational Databases	Polyglot data/storage technologies
High data integrity/consistency (ACID)	Low data integrity / eventual consistency
Serial and synchronous processing	Parallel and asynchronous processing
Designed to avoid failure. Important metric: Mean Time Between Failure (MTBF)	Designed to expect failure. Important metric: Mean Time To Resolve (MTTR)
Few and large updates	Frequent but small updates
Manual administration	Automated administration
"Snowflake" servers (Pets)	Idempotent infrastructure (Cattle)

Figure 13.2 – On-premises characteristics versus cloud characteristics

It is possible to be at various stages in between the extremes, and these are just the general traits. It is entirely possible to do *cloud things* even if you're not using a public cloud provider.

Let's elaborate on these traits in the following sections.

Monolithic versus microservices architecture

Software architecture is a large topic, and once you move from *simple apps* to building *systems*, there are many design-time decisions that can trip you up. When the boundary for compute was buying new servers in a rack, you often ended up with a monolith by default. If you told the operations department that you wanted separate servers for the backend and the frontend, they would laugh before rejecting your request. Separation of the two would be okay, only if the load generated required more computers.

In the cloud, this should no longer be a worry. If you design a container-based solution with microservices for different tasks, you are paying for the total compute. The monolithic server is no longer a boundary, and you should not be constrained by it. This is not to say that every piece of software built should be broken into microservices, but usually you will want to look into it when planning the architecture.

Planning for scalability

Knowing how much computing power you need is hard. Yes, you can make educated guesses, but there's still some randomness you are not in control of. Should you over-provision and buy more hardware than you need? What if you don't have enough hardware when the load hits you – how quickly can you get more servers into the rack?

One of the reasons why Amazon got into the cloud provider business was the scalability problem. Like many online retailers, Amazon sells way more items in the last part of the year leading up to Christmas than they do the rest of the year, and they needed a lot of horsepower to handle this, so they built multiple data centers to handle the load. The problem is – after the clear-out sales in January, the compute power sat there idle just costing them money. The business opportunity was that this excess capacity could surely be provided to other companies, and billions of dollars of revenue later, we can say that this was a good idea.

If you have a cloud-native application, you can design for this type of scale. It does not take weeks to order a server and have it delivered. You can reduce it to mere minutes for creating VMs and, depending on your workloads, it may even be a matter of seconds.

Do take note that the cloud also has some limits, so if you know Black Friday is coming up, you should not plan on allocating hundreds of servers the night before – you may not be able to do so without a heads up to the cloud provider.

There are two types of scaling mechanisms – scale up and scale out.

Scaling up versus scaling out

Scaling up is when you add more units of compute. Instead of having two servers handling the load, you add another one, meaning you have three.

Scaling out is adding more resources to your compute units. Adding more memory and more storage would be good examples of this. The number of servers stays the same.

To decide which one is the right model for you, it's necessary to figure out what is driving your resource consumption. If the CPU is sitting between 20 to 30% load, but the memory is in the 90+ range, add more memory (scale up). If the CPU is hitting its maximum load, add more server instances (scale out).

The exact details, in terms of how you do this, depends on which service you are using, but most of the available services will have options for setting up some kind of autoscaling mechanism that will let you add more power when you need it. For full dynamic handling, you can usually also scale down automatically, and you can also schedule things to be turned off when you know there will be little load.

Working with different database types

When you think of a database on-premises, very often they are some implementation of SQL. (This could be MS SQL, Oracle, MySQL, or others.) These are relational databases and rely on a database model of tables with relations between them.

For instance, a table for a `Person` entity could look like *Figure 13.3* in the Visual Studio designer:

	Name	Data Type	Allow Nulls	Default
⚷	Id	int	☐	
	FirstName	varchar(50)	☑	
	LastName	varchar(50)	☑	
	Address	varchar(50)	☑	
	ZipCode	varchar(10)	☑	
	State	nchar(2)	☑	

Figure 13.3 – Person table

The corresponding SQL code would be something like this:

```
CREATE TABLE [dbo].[Person]
(
    [Id] INT NOT NULL PRIMARY KEY,
    [FirstName] VARCHAR(50) NULL,
    [LastName] VARCHAR(50) NULL,
    [Address] VARCHAR(50) NULL,
    [ZipCode] VARCHAR(10) NULL,
    [State] NCHAR(2) NULL
)
```

In C# code, you are more likely to use a syntax, such as Linq, as that is more developer-friendly, but the principles are the same in both cases.

This is an example of the data being adopted to **schema on write**. When you write to the database, the SQL engine will verify that your data is correct – if you try to write a string into an integer field, it will not work.

There is usually also some locking mechanism to ensure that application A and application B cannot write to the same attribute at the same time. Given good throughput on the database server, this might not be noticeable, but it's not to be ignored for multi-user scenarios.

This is great for many use cases, as it ensures high integrity and consistency. For use cases such as a bank account, this is what you want. Having sloppy mechanisms, for how money goes in and out of the account, is bad for everyone.

The drawback is that it requires the code for writing to the database to be more complex, and even with beefy hardware, it will be inherently less capable of ingesting larger amounts of data in a short time frame.

As an option, a more cloud-like offering would be document databases (such as Azure Cosmos DB and MongoDB).

If you have thousands of IoT sensors capturing data, your focus is getting the data into the database. If one temperature reading is off by one degree, it's probably not a major issue. You want throughput, so instead of enforcing the schema on write, you just insert a JSON document with the contents you like.

When you need to extract the data and present it, you probably need to have some rules for the data type – this is called **schema on read**. This gives you the option of handling a datetime value, such as a string representation when it's just for display purposes and as an actual datetime type when you need to handle it as such.

A JSON instance of a person could look like this:

```json
{
  "FirstName": "John",
  "LastName" : "Doe",
  "Address" : "One Microsoft Way",
  "ZipCode" : "98052",
  "State" : "WA"
}
```

In this instance, we see that we don't adhere to the schema constraints defined for a SQL record. We just treat the attributes as plain text.

Inserting this into a Cosmos DB database, using an SDK, would look something like this:

```
ItemResponse<Person> personResponse = await
   this.container.CreateItemAsync<Person>(johndoe, new
   PartitionKey(person.LastName));
Console.WriteLine("Created item in database with id: {0} ",
   personResponse.Resource.Id);
```

Note that this code omits the class definition and connection to the database, but it illustrates how you just supply a JSON document to create a new item.

When you have a globally distributed document database, this pattern makes it harder to always be in sync, which is why we often refer to **eventual consistency**. Going back to the bank account example, this is probably not what you want, but if someone watching a stats dashboard in Europe has a delay of a couple of seconds compared to the US, that's probably not a problem.

Delays in storing data isn't just about the database technology; it is also about getting synchronization and multi-processing right.

Synchronicity and multi-processing tasks

Parallel processing and asynchronous requests are not exclusive to the cloud. On the hardware side, there have been many abstractions over the years, since true parallelism is hard to achieve, but as an end user, you always want the experience of things happening at the same time, with no dependency on other things going on in the background.

The cloud was built with this in mind. When you have services that need to handle billions of requests daily, it's just not possible to handle this by neatly and orderly processing one request at a time. As a user of the cloud, you might not have to deal with that volume of requests, but you should still look at it as a default.

Asynchronous behavior is important when creating web apps, because most likely you want to have a snappy experience for the user. When you block the UI for seconds while waiting for an API call backend to time out, you will have unhappy users.

Fortunately, the .NET templates help you in this regard by generating async code where applicable.

As an example, you could have the following in a controller in a web app, as synchronous code:

```
[HttpGet]
public string HelloWorld()
{
    return "Hello World";
}
```

If you were to rewrite it to asynchronous code, it might look like this instead:

```
[HttpGet]
public async Task<string> HelloWorld()
{
    return "Hello World";
}
```

It is important to be aware that you open yourself to bugs that are harder to troubleshoot. For instance, if you instantiate an HTTP client call and dispose of the connection, before actually receiving the response, it can be interesting stepping through the debugger to figure out.

As always, you need to understand what you are trying to do, but in general, this is the preferred method for cloud-native.

Avoiding failure versus expecting failure

One of the hardest things we do in code is handling the unexpected, and this applies whether you run in the cloud or in locally installed hardware. The way it is handled might differ between these two hosting options.

If you have 10 enterprise-grade servers on-premises, the odds are that unless they fail in the first couple of weeks, they are going to work for a long time. If one fails, you call the hardware supplier and have a technician come on site to repair it.

You can build redundancy in your code, of course, but it may be limited to assuming two servers are available and needing a manual switchover between them if one fails.

If you have 100,000 servers, the odds are that more than one is going to fail in the course of a year, just by doing the probability math. The cloud providers have abstracted this problem away from you as a developer. They buy servers by the container, and the scale of the operations means it is not guaranteed a technician will be able to replace failed hardware in a short enough time frame for it to not have an impact, which is why the cloud is designed to keep operating, even when individual pieces start to fail.

Even when the hardware is not failing, there's the risk that the operating system requires updates. If an important security update is rolled out, the cloud provider will not wait until it is convenient for you to apply it – they will do it as soon as possible.

Many of us have experienced software that makes assumptions that you will always be able to shut it down in an expected and correct manner. It could be that it expects to lock resources when running that are to be released on shutdown, or other things where the assumption is made that the system is stable and available. When things go wrong and you start it up again, you're greeted with a message that the previous shutdown failed, so you're asked to jump through these hoops to get back up and running.

This is not the way to do it in the cloud. You should expect that the processes can be killed in unplanned manners, and the important thing is to make sure that new instances are able to spin up as quickly as possible, without manual intervention.

Note that backup is a separate consideration. You should always make sure you have a strategy for backing up and restoring vital data, regardless of how and when the system goes down.

Understanding cloud update schedules

With limited scaling options and the need to plan the availability of resources, the on-premises world usually practices planned downtime. Many companies still have maintenance windows that you must hit for updating your software. This often involves developers having to be available either to perform updates or be on call if something bad happens during the night or at weekends.

With good cloud-native code and tooling, this should be a thing of the past. The cloud provides mechanisms for deploying to a staging site, where you can do basic testing and do a one-click switch to turn it into the production version if the testing passes. Or, you can have two versions deployed to production and configure so-called A/B testing, where only some of the users are exposed to the new version to see how they respond.

It all boils down to business needs. If you operate on the scale of Google, Facebook, or Netflix, there is never a *good time* to go offline. The services are accessed around the clock on all days of the year. It is also not an option to only do big-bang updates once a quarter – if you have an improvement for the site ready, it should go live as soon as possible.

With source control tooling, we've learned to check in early and check in often. Cloud native also means to release early and release often.

Administration of servers and services

As a developer, it's not unlikely that you think of administration as something reserved for the administrator. For some things, this is very much true – if someone maintains a Windows server on-premises or in the cloud for you, it's not a concern for you how it's administered.

Unfortunately, in real life, the developer doesn't always get to avoid all admin tasks. To minimize the risk, you should create your applications to require as little administration as possible. If, upon a reboot, there is a page of instructions to follow to get your services up and running in the right order, how are you going to handle things when the cloud automatically scales and creates 10 new instances? (Hint: you better learn a scripting language.)

Pets versus cattle

An often-used analogy concerning resources in the cloud versus resources on-premises is *pets versus cattle*. With on-premises hardware, it's something physical and relatable. A frequent administrator activity is figuring out a naming scheme for the servers – this could be Greek gods, mountains, superheroes, or the names of Ford car manufacturing plants. (All of these have been observed in actual server environments.) Certain peculiarities might be observed as well – *that server has a slightly different hard drive/ power supply/network card…* In other words – the servers are pets.

In the cloud, you don't get to name hardware resources, and frankly you probably don't want to figure out how to name a million servers with individual names either. You don't care which brand the hard drives or memory sticks are either. You expect that when you order 100 GB of storage and 8 GB of RAM, that will be pretty much the same thing each time you order. This is treating resources as cattle. When you buy milk from the grocery store, you really don't care if *cow number 143* or *cow number 517* was responsible for producing it.

The mentality of this is only one part of it though. You need tooling for this as well.

When you have pets, you can handle things on a one-by-one basis. For instance, if we were to provide instructions for you to create a web app in Azure for running code in this book, the instructions might read like this:

1. Log in to the Azure portal.

2. Click **Create a resource**.

3. Choose **Web App** from the list.

4. Create a new resource group in the dropdown.

5. Select a name and the region closest to where you are.

6. Select **.NET Core 5** as the runtime stack and **Windows** as the operating system.

7. Skip **Monitoring** and **Tags** and go to **Review + create**.

8. If there are no errors, click **Create**.

You'll see something similar to *Figure 13.4*:

Basics	Monitoring	Tags	**Review + create**

Summary

Web App
by Microsoft

Details

Subscription	
Resource Group	foo
Name	foobook
Publish	Code
Runtime stack	.NET Core 3.1 (LTS)

App Service Plan (New)

Name	ASP-foo-9baf
Operating System	Windows
Region	Central US
SKU	Standard
Size	Small
ACU	100 total ACU
Memory	1.75 GB memory

Monitoring (New)

Application Insights	Enabled
Name	foobook
Region	Central US

Figure 13.4 – Example of the Web App creation wizard in the Azure portal (.NET 5 not available at the time of writing)

How do you handle this when you're told to create 20 web apps? How do you make sure you're consistent each time and always get it right? If you want cattle, you need a standardized procedure that is repeatable.

You can start with the manual approach and still produce applications that are cloud native, but if you want to go all in, you will probably want to investigate **Infrastructure as Code** (**IaC**). (There will be more on this in the *Introducing Infrastructure as Code (IaC)* section.)

As previously stated, these are all common traits, and you can put your own touch on your environment, whether it's in a public cloud or your own data center. When treated as individual checklist items, you can *fix it*, but it more or less leads to a wider reaching term called **DevOps**.

Understanding the role of DevOps

DevOps is often used without further distinction in terms of exactly what is meant by it, other than it being something that you require in order to be more agile. Most people will agree that it is about delivering continuous value by using a combination of products, the right people, and processes to enable this.

We will not be exploring the people and process parts of DevOps in depth as this is, after all, a technical book. The important takeaway here is that if you want to increase agility, you need to have processes that reflect this. For instance, you can have tooling in place for rolling out new updates multiple times a day. If you have a procedure that says every release has to be approved manually by different QA and testing teams, that simply will not work. It fits in well with few and large updates, but not with frequent but small updates.

On the technical side, the term for what you want is **Continuous Integration** (**CI**) and **Continuous Deployment/Delivery** (**CD**). In *Chapter 10*, *Taking ASP.NET to the Cloud*, we showed how to get your code from Visual Studio into Azure and AWS. There's a frequently used one-liner when it comes to Visual Studio though – *friends don't let friends right-click publish*. *Chapter 12*, *Integrating with CI/CD*, took note of this and showed how to get this working with *GitHub Actions*.

GitHub has been one of the most popular services for developers for many years now, but the addition of GitHub Actions is a fairly recent development that happened after GitHub was acquired by Microsoft. The *tried-and-tested* solution in the Microsoft ecosystem would be Azure DevOps. Both services are being worked on and improved, but at the time of writing, Azure DevOps has a slightly more mature offering for enterprise scenarios, as well as a broader feature set.

Azure DevOps is not exclusive to cloud-native applications. It can be used for on-premises as well, and there's even a demo of it being used for building software for the Commodore 64 (for those of you old enough to have heard of that computer) to illustrate that it is in no way locked down to Microsoft languages or frameworks.

Azure DevOps has multiple features available to help you build a software development life cycle in the cloud:

Figure 13.5 – Azure DevOps features

Here are the use cases of the features:

- **Azure Boards** is for managing work items and the general flow of development tasks.

- **Azure Repos** is for storing your code and the versioning history.

- **Azure Pipelines** is for setting up build and release (CI/CD).

- **Azure Test Plans** is for setting up the testing and QA of your code.

- **Azure Artifacts** is for managing libraries and modules. This can be used for setting up your own NuGet feeds.

Under **Azure Pipelines,** you have **Pipelines** for setting up builds (the naming convention is confusing at best). You have what is called the classic wizard that enables you to set up a build for a range of solutions in a user-friendly way. This wizard lets you pick from a list of templates as shown in *Figure 13.6*:

.NET Desktop
Build and test a .NET or Windows classic desktop solution.

Android
Build, test, sign, and align an Android APK.

ASP.NET
Build and test an ASP.NET web application.

Azure Web App for ASP.NET
Build, package, test, and deploy an ASP.NET Azure Web App.

Docker container
Build a Docker image and push it to a container registry.

Maven
Build and test a Java project with Apache Maven.

Python package
Create and test a Python package on multiple Python versions.

Xcode
Build, test, archive, or package an Xcode workspace on macOS.

Figure 13.6 – Azure Pipelines classic wizard

This gets you going quickly and is great for exploratory work, but it is not the recommended approach for the long term. The recommended approach is defining your pipeline using YAML files, which are text-based files. YAML is how GitHub Actions does it as well, but the two implementations are currently not equal, so you cannot copy the content of the files back and forth. If you choose YAML instead of classic, you will be thrown into a textual definition like *Figure 13.7*:

```
◆ Infrastructure / azure-pipelines.yml * ⬟

1    # Starter pipeline
2    # Start with a minimal pipeline that you can customize to build and deploy your code.
3    # Add steps that build, run tests, deploy, and more:
4    # https://aka.ms/yaml
5
6    trigger:
7    - master
8
9    pool:
10     vmImage: 'ubuntu-latest'
11
12   steps:
13   - script: echo Hello, world!
14     displayName: 'Run a one-line script'
15
16   - script: |
17       echo Add other tasks to build, test, and deploy your project.
18       echo See https://aka.ms/yaml
19     displayName: 'Run a multi-line script'
20
```

Figure 13.7 – Azure Pipelines YAML definition

YAML is a markup language used for things such as Kubernetes configuration files and many other services as well, so this isn't specific to Microsoft either. It is generally more user friendly to write than XML and JSON, but, on the other hand, it's picky on things such as white spaces and indentation, so there are things you need to take in here as well before mastering the format. (Indentation is two characters: three will break.)

With this approach, you can treat your build definitions as part of the code (you can check it into the same repository as the application's code).

Also, under **Azure Pipelines**, you will find **Releases**, which are tightly linked to builds. This is about taking the output of a pipeline and deploying it. Let's look at the Azure Pipelines wizard.

Similar to the build wizard, you have multiple options for where you want the code to live:

 Azure App Service deployment

Deploy your application to Azure App Service. Choose from Web App on Windows, Linux, containers, Function Apps, or WebJobs.

 Deploy a Java app to Azure App Service

Deploy a Java application to an Azure Web App.

 Deploy a Node.js app to Azure App Service

Deploy a Node.js application to an Azure Web App.

 Deploy a PHP app to Azure App Service and Azure Database for MySQL

Deploy a PHP application to an Azure Web App and database to Azure Database for MySQL.

 Deploy a Python app to Azure App Service and Azure database for MySQL

Deploy a Python Django, Bottle, or Flask application to an Azure Web App and database to Azure Database for MySQL.

 Deploy to a Kubernetes cluster

Deploy, configure, update your containerized applications to a Kubernetes cluster.

Figure 13.8 – Azure Pipelines release classic wizard

There are more options than we could capture in these screenshots, so do take a look if you need something else. Building and releasing container-based apps is different to a non-containerized C# web app. Java, Python, and PHP all have their specifics as well, whether it's how to produce the executables or pushing them to a server.

Release definitions can also be defined as YAML files and checked into the repository.

Compared to the manual steps often involved in deploying software, this represents a nice improvement. It is not unheard of in legacy setups that the process for releasing new builds involves the developer building on their local machine, and then copying the result to a file share, before logging in to a different computer where the files are copied from the share and deployed. Trying to do full DevOps in such a regime is hard, but the examples presented in this section demonstrate that it should not be necessary to do so any longer. Code can be built, deployed, and run in the cloud without the legacy approach.

So, lots of good stuff, but there's no such thing as a free lunch in the cloud either; everything has a cost.

Understanding cost in the cloud

Computing brings more value for your money than it ever has, but there will always be costs associated with computers, and in business, costs usually need a justification. Many people have a misconception about services being cheaper by default in the cloud than running on-premises, but the picture is more complex than you would think at first sight, so we should explain parts of this picture.

Creating estimates for large solutions and becoming an Excel ninja is beyond the scope of this book, but in the cloud, developers are often the first line when someone asks where the money is going.

Most companies can afford to go and buy servers that you can install in your office with specs that will run either a few web apps or a couple of virtual machines. When compared with virtual machines in the cloud, you may very well think that it's just another way of paying for these servers.

In the cloud, there are two primary mechanisms for billing customers – fixed pricing and consumption-based pricing:

- **Fixed pricing** is where something has a cost per time unit, be it hours/days/months; for instance, a VM that is billed based on how many hours it's on per month. If the CPU is loaded to the max or barely doing anything, the cost stays the same. To save money, you turn it off or scale down the hardware of it. A simple act such as turning off a test environment during nights and weekends can reduce your bill by 50%.

- **Consumption-based pricing** is where you pay for how much you use of a resource. This could be storage, where you pay per gigabyte, or a messaging system, where you pay for events occurring. These resources can be left on 24/7 without any extra cost – if you don't use it during the night, it doesn't cost anything.

When building solutions, you often need to combine these. In Azure, for instance, you could have an Azure app service that is billed by time and left on around the clock, whereas you have a Cosmos DB instance for storing data where you pay based on the throughput capacity.

The cost of a service on-premises is usually more complex than the cost of the physical server alone as well. You have the basics, such as the electricity bill and an internet connection, but there is a lot more to it. You need networking gear. You need storage. You need duplicates of everything for high availability and redundancy. You need the knowledge to configure said redundancy. If you are a small business, you might not even be able to build comparable infrastructure to what the big players can do. So, make sure you're comparing apples with apples, instead of complaining that a banana looks different.

If you do things right, you will save money in the cloud, and if you get it wrong, it may cost more than on-premises.

The cost of storage is one consideration, but storage also works differently in the cloud.

Cloud storage versus local disk

Storage on your developer computer is an easy thing to understand. Even a budget laptop has an SSD these days, and while it might not compare with the premium options out there, it's usually sufficient for a simple web app. You store your stuff in `C:\foo` and there are no major worries unless Windows crashes or something similar.

Moving your code to production changes a few things. Your code can still remain in `C:\foo` on your virtual machine, but the hard drives underneath are possibly configured differently. This is still not a problem, however.

Storage is cheap these days, at least until you factor in other things. One SSD in a laptop might not cost that much, but if you want to deploy a web app running locally, you can bring out the calculator to add on extra costs. Since a hard drive can fail, you need to double up and put two drives in a mirror. But since that only handles redundancy, you need two more drives for handling backup (which must also tolerate a drive failure). Ideally, you need them in different computers with high-speed networking in between, not to mention that the building might burn down, so you need more physical locations. It's the gift that keeps on giving.

There's an old joke that goes: *How many programmers do you need to change a light bulb? None, it's a hardware issue.*

It's a good thing that we can say the same thing about storage.

If you are the hardware guy, you'll love cloud storage, since you can change the answer to *None – it's someone else's problem.*

The powerful thing about cloud storage is that cloud providers already have thousands of disks, high-speed networking, and multiple locations.

We will not delve into the details here, but you need to take a look at the available options for your provider to make the right choice. At the cheap end of the range, you have archival storage where the price is low, but it's only intended for files that are not in active use (hence the name *archival*), which cannot be used for a running web app. At the pricier end, you have high-speed NVMe drives automatically replicated across multiple regions of the world.

Letting hardware be hardware, you, as a developer, also need to understand that things are changing slightly on your end as well.

Ephemeral versus persistent storage

Usually, in cloud setups, you cannot treat the local drive as persistent. If you run a web app on a Windows-based host, you will usually have a local drive, so writing a temporary file to the `c:\foo` folder will work. When the host is rebooted, you can expect it to be gone, which is great if it really was temporary, and bad if you expected it to be present after rebooting. (Remember – you might not have control of when the host reboots in the cloud.)

The same applies if you run your app in containers. Each container will have some local space to store the app itself, but a container can be killed off at any point in time, so you need to handle this fact accordingly.

To get around this phenomenon, one of the basic services in cloud services is *storage*. In Azure, the most frequently used service for this purpose is **Azure Blob storage**.

Storing and reading files in Azure Blob storage

If you skip all the complexities in terms of avoiding overwriting existing files, checking the current folder, and everything else, you can get away with the following code snippet to output a string to a file and read it back with output to the console:

```
Using System;
using System.IO;
namespace Chapter_13_FileStorage
{
  class Program
  {
    static void Main(string[] args)
    {
      File.WriteAllText("foo.txt", "Hello World");
```

```
        Console.WriteLine(File.ReadAllText("foo.txt"));
    }
  }
}
```

This code will also run in the cloud, but with the caveats mentioned that it might disappear at any time.

If we were to do the same with Azure Blob storage, the steps would be slightly different:

1. Use the Azure portal to create a new storage account. To do so, you need to provide the desired configuration for what kind of storage you want, whether to replicate the data geographically, and the location you want it in:

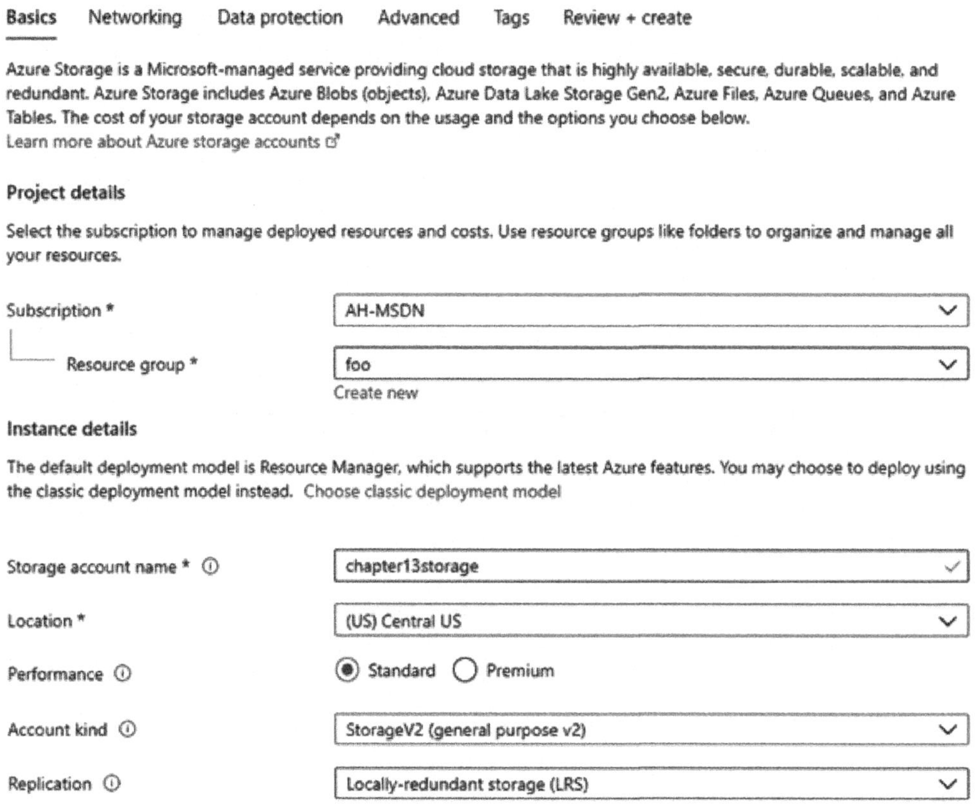

Basics   Networking   Data protection   Advanced   Tags   Review + create

Azure Storage is a Microsoft-managed service providing cloud storage that is highly available, secure, durable, scalable, and redundant. Azure Storage includes Azure Blobs (objects), Azure Data Lake Storage Gen2, Azure Files, Azure Queues, and Azure Tables. The cost of your storage account depends on the usage and the options you choose below.
Learn more about Azure storage accounts ⬨

Project details

Select the subscription to manage deployed resources and costs. Use resource groups like folders to organize and manage all your resources.

Subscription * | AH-MSDN   ⌄ |

└─── Resource group * | foo   ⌄ |
                                     Create new

Instance details

The default deployment model is Resource Manager, which supports the latest Azure features. You may choose to deploy using the classic deployment model instead. Choose classic deployment model

Storage account name * ⓘ | chapter13storage   ✓ |

Location * | (US) Central US   ⌄ |

Performance ⓘ   ◉ Standard ○ Premium

Account kind ⓘ | StorageV2 (general purpose v2)   ⌄ |

Replication ⓘ | Locally-redundant storage (LRS)   ⌄ |

Figure 13.9 – Azure storage account creation

2. There are many settings you can review, but for the purposes of this exercise, just skip straight to **Create**.

3. Go to the resource you just created and step into the **Storage Explorer** option as shown in *Figure 13.9*:

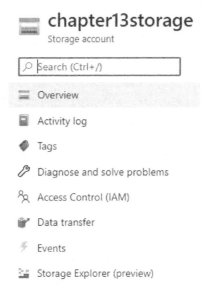

Figure 13.10 – Storage account blade in the Azure portal

4. Right-click on **Blob Containers** and choose **Create blob container**. Name it foo and make sure the access level is set to private.

5. Go to the **Access Keys** blade and copy the connection string for **key1**, as you will need it for your code.

6. Open up a command-line window, go to the root directory of your solution, and type the following command:

```
dotnet add package Azure.Storage.Blobs
```

7. Modify and add the existing code, like this:

```
using System;
using System.IO;
using Azure.Storage.Blobs;
using Azure.Storage.Blobs.Models;
namespace Chapter_13_FileStorage
{
    class Program
    {
```

```
static async System.Threading.Tasks.Task
Main(string[] args)
{
    File.WriteAllText("foo.txt", "Hello World");
    Console.WriteLine(File.ReadAllText("foo.txt"));


    //Set up the connection and a blob reference
    string connString = "copied-from-Azure-Portal";
    BlobServiceClient blobServiceClient = new
      BlobServiceClient(connString);
    BlobContainerClient blobContainerClient =
      BlobServiceClient.GetBlobContainerClient("foo");
    BlobClient blobClient =
      BlobContainerClient.GetBlobClient("foo.txt");
    //Upload to Blob Storage
    using FileStream uploadFileStream = File.OpenRead
      ("foo.txt");
    await blobClient.UploadAsync(uploadFileStream,
      true); uploadFileStream.Close();
    //Download from Blob Storage
    BlobDownloadInfo dl = await blobClient.
      DownloadAsync();
    using (FileStream dlfs = File.OpenWrite(
      "fooBlob.txt"))
    {
        await dl.Content.CopyToAsync(dlfs);
        dlfs.Close();
    }
    Console.WriteLine(File.ReadAllText("fooBlob.txt"));
    }
  }
}
```

8. The console should print the same string value, Hello World, twice, if everything worked.

At first glance, this might seem complicated – it will become easier once you've gotten used to it. It is not apparent from a small example like this, but you will appreciate the benefits of this once you start scaling out the number of components that need to access the files.

Be aware that it does have implications in terms of performance, since things need to go over the wire.

Dealing with storage latency

Whether you run code on the computer on your desk or in the cloud, transferring data to and from storage is not instantaneous. With small amounts of data, you're not likely to notice, but a millisecond here and there adds up.

If your application requires a cache layer, you should look into solutions such as *Azure Cache for Redis*, which stores data in-memory, and which reduces the need for involving a disk. In *Chapter 9*, *Containers*, we took a look at using a pre-built image with Redis, and this would be a good way to get going with such a solution.

We will not create the next web app or storage account in the portal, but rather we will look at how we could use the cattle approach instead, when we take a look at IaC next.

Introducing Infrastructure as Code (IaC)

When referring to creating web apps through the Azure portal, we mentioned that the better solution at scale is to look into IaC, but we didn't explain this further. So, what does IaC actually mean?

Creating web apps through the Azure portal isn't so bad. You get a wizard that guides you through it, and it will catch some errors as you go along; if you try to create a web app with characters not valid for DNS, it will say so.

If you've ever worked with on-premises software installations or, for that matter, created software to be installed by others, you might have run into less-friendly procedures. There might be installation guides that need to be followed to the letter, and since you didn't study the list of prerequisites, you find on page three of the wizard that you need to cancel out to install a SQL server, before you can return to the installation.

Common to both of these approaches is the fact that they are prone to inconsistent and incorrect deployments, and the fact that it simply does not scale if you want to create larger numbers of installations and instances.

This is the main problem that IaC aims to solve. As we saw with build and release definitions that you can check into your code, the same applies to IaC definitions.

There are two basic forms of IaC – imperative and declarative.

Imperative IaC

With this approach, you specify exactly what you want and in what order. It is great for automation, but you need to handle the dependencies yourself. If you try to create a web app without creating the resource group first, it will fail. Examples of imperative IaC include Azure PowerShell and the Azure CLI. Going with the example of creating a web app, it would look like this in PowerShell:

```
$location = "North Europe"
# Creating Resource group
New-AzResourceGroup -Name rg-webapp -Location $location
# Creating App Service Plan
New-AzAppServicePlan -Name webapp -Location $location
-ResourceGroupName rg-webapp -Tier Free
# Creating web app
New-AzWebApp -Name webapp -Location $location -AppServicePlan
webapp -ResourceGroupName rg-webapp
```

In the Azure CLI, it will look as follows:

```
# Creating Resource group
az group create -l northeurope -n rg-webapp
# Creating App Service Plan
az appservice plan create -g rg-webapp-n webapp
# Creating web app
az webapp create -g rg-webapp -p webapp -n webapp
```

There isn't a clear answer to which of these is best, and you will see that the syntax has similarities, but for both you can see how it follows a recipe-looking approach.

Declarative IaC

With declarative IaC, you focus less on the *how* and more on the *what*. Instead of the step-by-step approach, you define that you want a web app with a given set of attributes, specify dependencies, and let the provisioning engine handle the rest. This means that in the case of Azure being the cloud, you let the tooling figure out that the app service plan is in place before creating the web app.

The Azure native version of declarative IaC is ARM templates. The syntax is too verbose to include a complete example, but it is JSON-based, and this would be the code needed for the app service part of a deployment:

```
"resources": [
  {
    "type": "Microsoft.Web/serverfarms",
    "apiVersion": "2020-06-01",
    "name": "[variables('appServicePlanPortalName')]",
    "location": "[parameters('location')]",
    "sku": {
      "name": "[parameters('sku')]"
    },
    "kind": "linux",
    "properties": {
      "reserved": true
    }
  },
```

Since ARM can become quite complex, there are mixed feelings about it, but it has two major things going for it:

- Since it's native to Azure, you will usually be provided with an example in the portal, when creating a resource manually, so it's possible to use the wizard as a helper for generating custom code.

- Being integrated with Azure, it automatically keeps track of the state of resources. If you deploy a template building on a previous template, the engine will, for instance, know that the resource group already exists and will not try to create it once more.

Another popular tool supporting both Azure and Amazon (and a couple of other providers) is *Terraform*, by HashiCorp.

Once again, looking at creating a web app, a basic example could look like this:

```
provider "azurerm" {
  version = "~>2.0"
  features {}
}
resource "azurerm_resource_group" "rg" {
  name     = "rg-webapp"
  location = "northeurope"
}
resource "azurerm_app_service_plan" "appserviceplan" {
  name                = "webapp"
  location            = azurerm_resource_group.rg.location
  resource_group_name = azurerm_resource_group.rg.name
  sku {
    tier = "free"
  }
}
resource "azurerm_app_service" "webapp" {
  name                = "webapp"
  location            = azurerm_resource_group.rg.location
  resource_group_name = azurerm_resource_group.rg.name
  app_service_plan_id = azurerm_app_service_plan.
    appserviceplan.id
}
```

If you are not familiar with ARM templates, this looks more user friendly on the face of it, but it is a new format to learn nonetheless. It also has the drawback of having to track the state handling manually by storing the state in separate files. It is still a useful tool, and Microsoft also provides Terraform examples for parts of the Azure documentation.

Taking it to the next level, there's also *IaC as Code* (not an official term, mind you). A tool called *Pulumi* provides a coding layer on top of Terraform, enabling you to write C# code for creating infrastructure with everything you're already familiar with from regular programming.

This topic is large, and learning all the nuances of it may be too much for a programmer focusing on building the apps and not the surrounding infrastructure. In smaller organizations and one-man bands, you may be assigned responsibility for this part of the cloud as well, so if you are that person, it could be valuable to dig further into this.

Rounding off the chapter, we will take a quick look at monitoring and health.

Learning about monitoring and health

A misconception of how things work in the cloud is that the cloud provider handles the health of your app. We saw in the first part of this chapter the division of responsibility going from IaaS to SaaS, where the provider takes greater responsibility as you move to the right. If you go all the way to SaaS, it is true that the provider has to handle pretty much everything that isn't a user error, but as stated earlier, the sweet spot for developers is usually PaaS, where there is still some responsibility on your part.

This means that if the response time of a web app as experienced by the user is not acceptable, you need to be aware of this and figure out how to handle it. If storage in the cloud goes down, you need to understand how to remediate this. The *you* part here could be handled differently, depending on your organization, but in most instances, it is not the cloud provider that will be responsible, even if they have mechanisms for helping you along the way.

Web apps in Azure have some built-in tools at your disposal as shown in *Figure 13.11*:

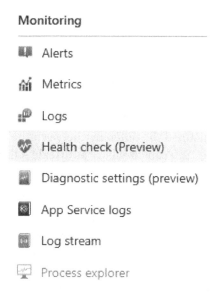

Figure 13.11 – Azure web app Monitoring blade

The ones with *log* in the name are different ways to track down error conditions and are useful for debugging purposes. **Log stream** will let you see the logs in real time, so if you output errors to the console in your app and you are able to replicate the problem in the user interface, this is very useful.

Metrics can be used both for planning and real-time decisions. You can see the number of requests, the response time, how many HTTP-based errors are thrown, and so on:

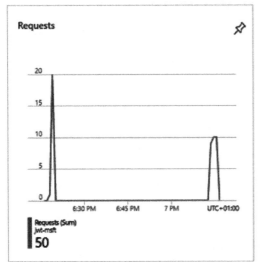 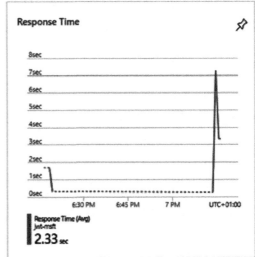

Figure 13.12 – Azure Metrics for an Azure web app

Alerts also have multiple purposes. For instance, if the count of errors is too high, it can send a text message and/or email that someone needs to take a look at the logs. It is also possible to send details to other Azure services to invoke actions, based on a list of conditions.

Related to monitoring, but not in the same menu section, you can find **Scale up** and **Scale out** (under **Settings**). We explained the difference between the two in a previous section, and this is natively supported. You can configure **autoscale** – this means that when a metric is above a specified threshold for a time range (to avoid triggering on short spikes), Azure will automatically add more resources to your web app.

To keep track of the health of your app, it helps if you use mechanisms in your code that make it easier to set up things correctly in the cloud. We showed in *Chapter 10, Taking ASP.NET to the Cloud,* how you could add a health endpoint to your app. This endpoint should be added to the monitoring you set up in Azure (or AWS) and corresponding alert mechanisms. To be fair, adding an endpoint such as this should be considered on-premises as well, but the mechanism used for monitoring will possibly be different.

Remember what we said earlier – build things with the expectation that they will fail and construct a health and monitoring strategy that helps you handle this.

Summary

Building cloud-native apps covers more than a simple relocation of bits from one data center to another.

We did not dive deep into everything here, but we covered a broad range of topics, starting with understanding what cloud native is all about and the general traits of on-premises versus cloud. We covered the technical differences between databases and storage options, a short DevOps intro, and, going outside the developer role, we briefly delved into topics such as IaC, before rounding off with a few pointers regarding monitoring and health.

You should now have an understanding of why you would want to consider cloud application models and what are the things that you need to consider, before using the cloud. You have also learned the differences, compared to on-premises, with regard to the mindset for the cloud and acquired an understanding of DevOps tools and services. Also, you have understood why IaC might make life easier for building the services you need in the cloud.

Even if you don't go all in on the cloud yet, there should be things here that can be applied to your *old-school* software as well.

Questions

1. What are the three basic models for cloud computing?

2. What's the difference between schema on write and schema on read?

3. Why would you look into IaC?

Further reading

- AZ-900 Learning Path, by Microsoft, available at `https://docs.microsoft.com/en-us/learn/paths/az-900-describe-cloud-concepts/`

- Introduction to the Microsoft Azure Well-Architected Framework, by Microsoft, available at `https://docs.microsoft.com/nb-no/learn/modules/azure-well-architected-introduction/`

Assessments

This section contains the answers to the questions from all the chapters.

Chapter 1 – Introduction to ASP.NET Core 5

1. .NET Classic was tightly coupled with the Windows operating system. This prevented any cross-platform ambitions, and it was less than ideal for cloud usage and microservices. .NET Core removed some of these barriers; it provides a cleaner API surface and a leaner footprint.

2. Yearly releases are in November. Every 2 years, the release is Long-Term Support.

3. Web apps, based on the MVC pattern, are primarily made up of three components: M (as in *Model*) is the data structure for the application; V (as in *View*) is for the user interface; and C (as in *Controller*) represents the components that sit between the model and view and shuffles the data between them.

4. These are properties that are only intended to be set at the time of object creation, and they cannot be changed subsequently.

5. Yes, technically it is possible, but it is difficult and highly discouraged. Consider implementing RESTful APIs or gRPC instead.

Chapter 2 – Cross-Platform Setup

1. Windows, Linux, MacOS, iOS, and Android.

2. This is a component of Windows that lets you run Linux within Windows, but it's run natively, instead of as an emulation layer.

3. A self-contained .NET app includes everything it needs to run, so it does not require a separate installation of the .NET framework. This means it can also run on a system that either does not have .NET installed, or one that has a different version of the framework installed.

4. Compiling a cross-platform app makes the app run on a different platform, but it does not ensure that all the code is correct for the platform it was compiled for. This means that you, as a developer, must make the code itself compatible with the platform, and not just the executable.

Chapter 3 – Dependency Injection

1. There are four types of dependency injections (DIs): constructor, method, property, and view injections. The constructor injection is the most commonly used approach for building ASP.NET Core applications.

2. There are three types of DI lifetimes: transient, scoped, and singleton.

    Use a transient lifetime when you are unsure about how you should register the service. This is the safest option to use, and it's probably the most commonly used because services are created each time they are requested. This lifetime works best for lightweight and stateless services because they are disposed at the end of the request. Be aware, though, that a transient lifetime can potentially impact the performance of your application, especially if you are working on a huge monolith application, where the dependency reference is massive and complex.

    Use a scoped lifetime when you want an object to be created once per client web request. This is to ensure that related calls (to process dependent operations) will be contained in the same object instance for each request. A good example (of using a scoped lifetime) is registering a database service or context, such as Entity Framework Core.

    Use a singleton lifetime for services that are expensive to instantiate, because objects will be stored in memory (and can be reused for all the injections within your application). Services that are registered as a singleton will only be created once, and all the dependencies will share the same instance of the same object, during the entire lifetime of the application. A good example of using a singleton is registering a logger or application configuration.

3.   The Add() method is the most commonly used approach to register services in the DI container. The Add() method creates a registration for the service, and it can potentially create duplicate registrations, which can impact the behavior of your application. The TryAdd() method will only register services when there is no implementation already defined for a given service type. This prevents you from accidentally replacing previously registered services. So, if you want to safely register your services, then consider using the TryAdd() method instead.

Chapter 5 – Getting Started with Blazor

1.   You can create web applications using either Blazor Server or Blazor WebAssembly. Blazor also provides support for building native and hybrid mobile applications, which are called Blazor Mobile Bindings.

2.   The big selling point for Blazor is not having to learn hardcore JavaScript in order to build SPA web applications. Learning the framework itself is easy, as long as you know basic HTML and CSS. It was designed to help C# developers take advantage of their skills, to easily transition to the web paradigm when they are building SPA-based web applications.

Chapter 8 – Working with Identity in ASP.NET

1.   Authentication is about who you are, and authorization is about what you can do.

2.   The recommended flow for most of these use cases is the authorization code flow (with PKCE).

3.   Azure AD B2C makes it easier to integrate with external identity providers, both because it abstracts the implementation away from your code, and how it allows fine-grained control of the sign-up and sign-in experience.

Chapter 9 – Getting Started with Containers

1.   Containers are much smaller to store and faster to start than virtual machines. This is because the abstraction of a container is at the operating system level, whereas the abstraction of a virtual machine is at the hardware level.

2.   Though Redis can support persistent volumes, it is not intended as a replacement for a RDBMS.

3. Yes! You can view images and containers, as well as easily view logs, ports, and other settings.

4. Hopefully, you enjoyed this chapter as much as we enjoyed writing it.

Chapter 10 – Deploying to AWS and Azure

1. Virtual networks (VNETs) make up an Infrastructure as a Service offering that allows you to define routing. This enables connections (between devices and networks) to be granted or denied. For example, a VNET might have a rule that allows only a specific IP address or port to receive requests from the internet.

2. Defining health endpoints is a common practice, and is supported by most on-premises and cloud load balancers. Both AWS Elastic Beanstalk and Azure App Services support health endpoint monitoring.

3. Both AWS and Azure have excellent tooling available in Visual Studio. We thought it was important to show how ASP.NET Core and Visual Studio are widely supported on more than just Azure.

4. We intentionally left any judgement out about which cloud provider is better. Both cloud providers offer great support for hosting ASP.NET Core applications, ranging from small organizations to large enterprises.

Chapter 11 – Browser and Visual Studio Debugging

1. PWAs are delivered from a server, but they are only run in the browser.

2. Session and local storage are only visible to the running browser. In most circumstances, the best choice would be a database to share information to a large group of users.

3. No, all the major browsers support the developer tools.

4. Yes, Visual Studio can debug JavaScript and C# running in the same project.

Chapter 12 – Integrating with CI/CD

1. No, GitHub Actions is available in the Free plan. However, there is a limit to how much you can store and how many times you can run your workflows.

2. GitHub can be used to store source code, documents, or any collection of files.

3. GitHub Actions provides several types of triggers that allow for the CI/CD process to be split into multiple files.

4. CI/CD makes a lot of sense when deploying to cloud providers such as Azure and AWS. In many ways, the cloud is ideal for CI/CD, and we'll cover this more in the next chapter.

Chapter 13 – Developing Cloud-Native Apps

1. IaaS – Infrastructure as a Service, PaaS – Platform as a Service, and SaaS – Software as a Service.

2. Schema on write is the classic SQL model where you need to adhere to rules when inputting new data. Schema on write is the more flexible way to input dynamic data and to define the structure when you use the data.

3. Infrastructure as code helps you to automate the creation of resources in a repeatable and consistent way, at scale.

Other Books You May Enjoy

If you enjoyed this book, you may be interested in these other books by Packt:

Modern Web Development with ASP.NET Core 3 - Second Edition

Ricardo Peres

ISBN: 9781789619768

- Understand the new capabilities of ASP.NET Core 3.1
- Become well versed in how to configure ASP.NET Core to use it to its full potential
- Create controllers and action methods, and understand how to maintain state
- Implement and validate forms and retrieve information from them
- Improve productivity by enforcing reuse, process forms, and effective security measures
- Delve into the new Blazor development model
- Deploy ASP.NET Core applications to new environments, such as Microsoft Azure, AWS, and Docker

Practical Microservices with Dapr and .NET

Davide Bedin

ISBN: 9781800568372

- Use Dapr to create services, invoking them directly and via pub/sub

- Discover best practices for working with microservice architectures

- Leverage the actor model to orchestrate data and behavior

- Use Azure Kubernetes Service to deploy a sample application

- Monitor Dapr applications using Zipkin, Prometheus, and Grafana

- Scale and load test Dapr applications on Kubernetes

Leave a review - let other readers know what you think

Please share your thoughts on this book with others by leaving a review on the site that you bought it from. If you purchased the book from Amazon, please leave us an honest review on this book's Amazon page. This is vital so that other potential readers can see and use your unbiased opinion to make purchasing decisions, we can understand what our customers think about our products, and our authors can see your feedback on the title that they have worked with Packt to create. It will only take a few minutes of your time, but is valuable to other potential customers, our authors, and Packt. Thank you!

Index

Made in the USA
Middletown, DE
14 July 2021